Kaurna Warrapiipa

KAURNA DICTIONARY

Kaurna Warrapiipa

KAURNA DICTIONARY
Kaurna to English, English to Kaurna

PRODUCED AND WRITTEN FOR
Kaurna Warra Pintyanthi and Kaurna Warra Karrpanthi
by Rob Amery, Susie Greenwood and Jasmin Morley

Wakefield Press

Published by Kaurna Warra Pintyanthi
Discipline of Linguistics, School of Humanities
The University of Adelaide
South Australia 5005

in association with

Wakefield Press
16 Rose Street
Mile End
South Australia 5031
www.wakefieldpress.com.au

First published 2021
Reprinted 2022, 2023, 2024

Copyright © Kaurna Warra Pintyanthi, 2021
Copyright and ownership of the Kaurna language remains with the Kaurna people

All rights reserved. This book is copyright. Apart from any fair dealing for the
purposes of private study, research, criticism or review, as permitted under
the Copyright Act, no part may be reproduced without written permission.
Enquiries should be addressed to the publisher.

Front cover painting by Katrina Karlapina Power
Illustrations by James Tylor
Cover designed by Stacey Zass
Text designed and typeset by Michael Deves, Wakefield Press

ISBN 978 1 74305 921 0

 A catalogue record for this book is available from the National Library of Australia

   Wakefield Press thanks Coriole Vineyards for continued support

Contents

Acknowledgements —————————————————————————— vi

Foreword – Taylor Tipu Power-Smith ————————————————— vii

Other Kaurna Learning Resources ———————————————————— viii

The Kaurna Language and People ———————————————————— 1

    Kaurna Sounds and Spelling ————————————————————— 4

    Kaurna Words ——————————————————————————— 7

    Kaurna Grammar —————————————————————————— 11

    Translating into Kaurna ——————————————————————— 14

        List of abbreviations used for parts of speech ————————————— 15

        List of abbreviations used for sources ——————————————— 16

DICTIONARY

KAURNA – ENGLISH ——————————————————————————— 17

ENGLISH – KAURNA: WORD FINDER ————————————————————— 96

Acknowledgements

Many people contributed to the development and production of this Kaurna Dictionary. It would be impossible to acknowledge all of them, but some general acknowledgements are in order.

Jane Simpson and her students at the University of Sydney provided the original electronic files; Jasmin Morley transferred them into Toolbox; and Howard Amery refined the Toolbox files.

James McElvenny produced the 2014 pilot Kaurna Dictionary.

Rosey Billington transferred the dictionary files into the FLEx databas; Nick Thieberger provided IT advice; and Susie Greenwood ensured consistency within FLEx and in the exporting of the FLEx files.

Jack Kanya Buckskin supplied vocabulary related to football, golf, playing cards and alcohol.

Members of KWP/KWK developed new terms in the context of KWP and KWK meetings and
some new terms were developed in the context of Kaurna language classes. Several Kaurna individuals are acknowledged as the source of certain words within the dictionary.

Rob Amery was responsible for overall management of the project, checking source materials and was consultant linguist.

Susie Greenwood served as assistant linguist, undertaking the marathon task of checking and re-checking drafts until completion.

Funding was provided by AIATSIS and Indigenous Languages and the Arts (ILA).

Foreword

Taylor Tipu Power-Smith

As the daughter, and granddaughter of strong and passionate Kaurna women, I am immensely proud and honoured to be writing the foreword for such a symbolic resource. My heart is bursting with happiness for my Ancestors and for the Elders that didn't live to see the result of their hard work. This dictionary brings us a step closer to fluency and right now in this moment, I am more hopeful than ever, that one day Kaurna babies will be speaking in their mother's tongue.

As the main point of reference for Kaurna words and spellings, it was necessary to explore all avenues to best maintain language integrity. This thoughtful and magnificent resource is a result of years and years of thorough research and as a Kaurna person, I am grateful and happy to know the due diligence that was taken to ensure my Ancestors and Kaurna language were honoured accordingly.

A wealth of knowledge, it brings together the old and new, highlighting the depth and genius of traditional words and phrases whilst showcasing the incredible evolution of a sleeping language. It speaks volumes of the resilience and determination of those that have worked tirelessly to make this dream come to life.

As a teacher of Kaurna, I truly appreciate how the dictionary can be used in a contemporary way whilst remaining respectful to its ancient origins. It gives a license to create meaningful dialogue and magnifies our respect for those that walked and talked here before us. For those wanting to begin their journey, it is a warm and authentic invitation to curiosity, and deeper knowing.

As a comprehensible and readily available resource the dictionary is an invaluable tool that strengthens Kaurna language and community, by providing insight into the past and offering a world view of the present.

For Kaurna people, this is not only a reclamation of our language, but a reclamation of our space; helping us secure the future for the generations yet to come and honouring those that paved the way for us.

Kaurna is the future for the Adelaide Plains and the future belongs to us.

The Kaurna Language and People

Kaurna is the name used to refer to the language of the Aboriginal people who occupied the Adelaide Plains and surrounding districts prior to European colonisation. Although the name 'Kaurna' was not used at that time, it is the name which most Kaurna people use to identify themselves today.

The arrival of Europeans had devastating consequences for Kaurna people. They suffered from population decline due to introduced diseases and the kidnapping of women, loss of access to their homelands, depletion of game animals for food and the contamination of important water sources like Karrawirra Pari (the Torrens River). Eventually the new colonial government began removing Kaurna children from their families and sending them to residential schools far away.

By the 1860s, most Kaurna people were living outside of their traditional homelands, and were no longer using their language. It was not until the 1980s, as Kaurna people who had moved back into the Adelaide area began to reassert their unique identity that the language started to be learned and used again.

Today Kaurna is spoken and studied at various skill levels by both Kaurna and non-Kaurna people throughout Kaurna country, and is used in many public settings such as dance performances and Welcome to Country speeches. Many organisations, programs, buildings, rooms, parks and so on now have Kaurna names and the language has been incorporated into a number of prominent public artworks. More and more Kaurna signage is appearing. We hope that this dictionary will be a useful contribution to the ongoing revival of this beautiful and precious language.

The sources

This dictionary has been compiled from all the known primary sources of Kaurna language and incorporates new words that have been created through the Kaurna language program which started around 1990.

Kaurna language was studied and written down by many Europeans during the early years of colonisation (between 1836 and around 1850). None of these people were trained linguists and most of them had never learnt an Australian language before. As a result, some of what they recorded was incomplete or only semi-accurate. Also, each person spelled Kaurna words in their own way, so there is lots of variation in the historical sources we worked from.

This is an outline of how we compiled the dictionary:

1. We located all known records of Kaurna language and combined them in a single database.
2. We identified where different people had recorded the same word but spelled or defined it differently and unified these entries so all the information about each word is in one place.
3. We studied the sound system of the Kaurna language in order to find a regular and user-friendly way to spell Kaurna words. When we were not sure about how a word originally sounded we looked at related languages to see if they have the same word. Languages like Adnyamathanha, Nukunu and Kuyani that have been studied by modern linguists share some words with Kaurna, which can give us a hint about the correct pronunciation of words.
4. Sometimes we were not sure about how the word originally sounded. In those cases we made an educated guess.
5. For each head-word we wrote a clear definition in modern English (the sources use very old-fashioned language), giving example sentences where possible, and listed the sources where the word or sentence was recorded.
6. We also made an English-Kaurna finder list, to help users locate Kaurna words.

As an example of how one word looked in the sources, compare the words for *karla/kardla* 'fire; firewood':

Abbreviation	Author/Researcher	Year	Entry	Translation
TS	Teichelmann & Schürmann	1840	gadla	fire, fuel, wood
TM	Teichelmann Ms	1857	garla	fuel (seems to denote fire when issuing from the fuel, the fuel belonging to the whole idea of the word)
WY	William Wyatt	1837–39	kerla	firewood
WS	William Williams	1840	cur-la	fire
ST	Edward Stephens	1889	coorla	fire
RO	George Augustus & son Charles Robinson	1837	cull.lar	fire
GA	Joseph Paul Gaimard	1826	kalla	bois 'wood'
GA	Joseph Paul Gaimard	1826	kalla	brûler 'to burn'
GA	Joseph Paul Gaimard	1826	alla	feu 'fire'
KO	Hermann Koeler	1836–37	kálla	Feuer 'fire'
BL	John McConnell Black	1920	ka*l*a	fire

Note that when Gaimard gives the word *alla* 'fire' he misses the first consonant which he does hear in *kalla* 'wood' and *kalla* 'to burn'. When he records *kalla* 'wood' his gloss is too general, as *kardla/karla* specifically refers to 'firewood'. His recording of *kalla* 'to burn' indicates that Gaimard is not aware of the difference between nouns and verbs in Kaurna, and this meaning is recorded in error, though it is a plausible error in circumstances where neither party had an understanding of each other's language. Like Koeler and Robinson, he misses the retroflex 'rl' sound. Either these observers simply did not hear the retroflexion, as it does not occur in their mother tongues, or if they did hear it, they did not know how to represent it in writing.

The entry for *kardla* or *karla* looks like this in the dictionary.

kardla (var. **karla**) *n* (1) fire, flame, burning embers *Kardlarlu ngai ngadli.* 'The fire has burnt me.' *Kardlarlu payanthi.* 'The fire burns (you).' *Kardlapulyu wantith'ai.* 'I will sleep without a fire.' *kardla parranthi* 'to light a fire' *karlarlu panthi* 'to set on fire' $_{TS,TM,WI,RO,GA,KO,ST}$ (2) firewood, kindling, fuel *Kardla katintu'rna!* 'Fetch firewood!' *Kardla piti kurntantu, yalakant'ina mai'athu yungkutha.* 'Cut the wood first, then I will give you some food.' *Kardla wapi-urti, pardi turtu-trrukarringu ngu.* 'Don't touch the wood. The rice will be easily upset.' *Kardlarna katintu'rna, ngu niina wantinki, yuritina niina, kardlangka kumarnila.* 'Fetch the wood you disobedient fellow, or you shall lie near another fire.' $_{TS,TM,WY,GA,KO}$ (3) heat, hot *Kardla purruna.* 'It is hot.' $_{TM}$ (4) light *tirntu kardlarlu* 'when the sun is shining' $_{TM}$

    kardla parranthi [kardla parra-nthi] *v-tr* light a fire, kindle a fire
    kardla parrinthi [kardla par-ri-nthi] *v-intr* warm (oneself) $_{TS}$
    kardla purtultu *n* firestick $_{TM}$
    kardla tadlanyi *n* flame $_{TM}$
    kardla-kardlantu [kardla-kardla-ntu] *adj* very hot, heated $_{TS,TM}$
    kardlapanthi [kardla-pa-nthi] (var. **karlapanthi**) *v-tr* warm (something) $_{TS}$
    kardlaparti [kardla-parti] *n* native bee $_{TS}$
    kardlapinti [kardla-pinti] *n* hell $_{TS}$
    kardlapurruna [kardla-purruna] *adj* still burning $_{TS}$
    kardlarlu parrinthi [kardla-rlu pa-rri-nthi] *v-tr* warm (something) $_{TM}$
    kardlayapa [kardla-yapa] *n* (1) firepit $_{TS}$ (2) hell $_{TS}$ (3) oven (wood-fired) $_{NEW}$
    kardlayirdi [kardla-yirdli] (var. **kardlayiri**; **karlayiri**) *n* light source $_{TS}$

The structure of Dictionary entries

Each dictionary entry begins with the headword, which in the case of *kardla* above, has a variant form *karla*. In fact, *kardla* is the careful pronunciation or citation form, but this word is mostly pronounced *karla* in casual speech. Following the headword and variants, if any, its part of speech is identified. *Kardla* is a noun, so is identified as *n*. Sometimes a word may have several senses. In the case of *kardla*, four different senses are identified (fire, firewood, heat and light) and a number of example sentences from the historical sources are provided to illustrate these different senses. The main entry is followed by compounds and derivations which include or depend on the headword. These are indented to show that they are subentries. Some of the compounds have interesting etymologies. For instance, *kardla tadlanyi* 'flame' is literally 'fire tongue'. You can trace the etymology of compounds and derivations by looking up the individual words. The material in square brackets shows the meaningful parts of the word (or morphological breakdown). So *kardlarlu parrinthi* has five morphemes or meaningful parts, each of which should appear as a separate entry in the dictionary. The source of each word, expression or sentence example is shown with subscript initials. Subscript $_{NEW}$ indicates that the word or expression has been developed (or its meaning extended) since 1990 as a result of Kaurna language revival efforts. Lists of abbreviations used in the dictionary are found at the end of this introduction.

KAURNA SOUNDS AND SPELLING

In 2010, a revised Kaurna spelling system was adopted. Prior to 2010, Teichelmann & Schürmann (1840) spelling was used. Revised spelling is systematic and consistent and is based on the principle that each sound is associated with a unique symbol. There are just a few exceptions to this principle and a few simple spelling rules to learn as explained below.

The following letters and letter combinations make up the Kaurna Alphabet:

a aa ai au dl dlh dly dn dnh dny i ii k l lh ly m n ng nh ny p r rd rdn rdl rl rn rr rt t th ty u ui uu w y

These letters represent the distinctive sounds of the Kaurna language. There are many digraphs (two letters used to represent one sound) and trigraphs (three letters to represent one sound) in the Kaurna alphabet. Just as **sh** in wishing is not simply an **s** followed by an **h** (we don't say wis-hing as separate syllables), in the same way **dl** is not simply a **d** followed by an **l**. The two letters **dl** represent a single sound described further below

Vowels

There are actually just three short vowels in Kaurna: **a i u** and their long forms **aa ii uu** plus the vowel blends (diphthongs) **ai au ui**.

a	as in the English words: m**a**ma, p**a**pa, vis**a** or Maori h**a**k**a**
i	as in the English words: b**i**t, p**i**t, s**i**t
u	as in the English words: p**u**t, b**u**tcher
aa	as in the English words: f**a**ther, B**a**rt,
ii	as in the English words: t**ea**, k**ey**, sk**i**
uu	similar to the vowel in the English words: c**oo**ler, fl**u**, S**ue**
ai	as in the English words: p**ie**, sp**y**, H**ai**nan
au	as in the English words: p**ow**er, t**ow**n, M**au**i
ui	similar to the vowel in the English word: b**oy**

Consonants

The Kaurna consonant sounds **l m n w y** are pronounced much the same as the same English letters.

Voicing

The Kaurna spelling system uses **p t k** (as opposed to **b d g** in Ngadjuri and Narungga). The pronunciation of **p** is sometimes 'p' and at other times closer to 'b'. Similarly the pronunciation of **t** often sounds like 'd' and **k** often sounds like 'g', especially if they follow a nasal or l-sound.

Interdentals

Kaurna has sounds made with the tongue in between the teeth (interdental). You will notice that the digraphs for these three sounds all contain an **h** which indicates that the tongue is between the teeth. The 'h' here is not pronounced as it is in English.

th	is like the **d** in the English word: wi**d**th, but *unlike* the **th** in **th**ink, **th**is, wi**th** or la**th**e
nh	is like the **n** in the English word: te**n**th
lh	is like the **l** in the English word: fi**l**th

The **d**, **n** and **l** in wi**d**th, te**n**th and fi**l**th are interdental because they anticipate the following interdental fricative 'th' sound, but the sound written **th** in English is not the same as the Kaurna **th**. No air passes through the mouth with Kaurna **th**.

Retroflex sounds

The Kaurna retroflex sounds do not occur in Australian English and are pronounced with the tongue tip curled slightly back from where it occurs when saying the English sounds 't' 'n' 'l'. These same sounds are common in Indian-English and many other Aboriginal languages. These three digraphs all contain an **r** which indicates that the tongue tip is retroflexed (curled back). The letter **r** is not a true 'r' sound.

- **rl** is similar to **l** and occurs in *pu**rl**a* 'they (2)'
- **rn** is similar to **n** and occurs in *ma**rn**i* 'good; fat'
- **rt** is similar to **t** and occurs in *wa**rt**u* 'wombat' (cf *watu* 'branch')

Alveopalatal sounds

These sounds are produced with the blade of the tongue placed behind the bottom and top teeth. **ty** is similar to the 'ch' in church or the 'j' and 'dg' in judge, but the tongue is further towards the front of the mouth.

- **ty** is similar to the sound in the English words: bu**tch**er, go**t-ch**a, **j**u**dg**e
- **ny** as in the middle of the English words: Bu**ny**an, o**ni**on
- **ly** is similar to the sound in the English words: mi**lli**on, wi**ll-y**ou

Prestopping

'L' sounds and 'n' sounds in Kaurna may be pre-stopped (preceded by a 'd' sound). These pre-stopped sounds then pattern as single consonants. The pre-stopped and non-pre-stopped versions can be intermixed and both mean the same. For instance the word for 'house' is both *warli* and *wardli*. 'Fire' is both *karla* and *kardla*. Notice that the **rd** here is part of the trigraph **rdl** and is totally different to the **rd** 'r' sound discussed below. Whilst **dnh** and **dny** are part of the Kaurna sound system, no words containing these sounds are known. The pre-stopped sounds occurring in Kaurna are:

- **dlh** this sound occurs in *mu**dlh**a* 'nose'
- **dl** this sound occurs in *mi**dl**a* 'woomera'
- **rdl** this sound occurs in *wa**rdl**i* 'house; home'
- **dly** this sound occurs in *ku**dly**u* 'black swan'
- **dn** this sound occurs in *wa**dn**a* 'boomerang'
- **rdn** this sound occurs in *wa**rdn**inthi* 'to fall; to drop; to be born'

The Velar Nasal, ng

The 'ng' sound in Kaurna occurs at the beginning of words and syllables (as in ***ng**u**ng**ana* 'kookaburra'), but is exactly the same sound as the 'ng' in English.

- **ng** as in the middle/end of the English words: ri**ng**ing, si**ng**er,

Rhotics or 'r' sounds

There are three 'r' sounds in Kaurna: **r rd** and **rr**.

- **r** is exactly the same as in Australian English: **r**oa**r**ing
- **rd** is a quick flap or tap (similar to the **tt** when said quickly in English bu**tt**er it).
- **rr** is 'rolled' or 'trilled' like the 'r' sound in Scottish English, Italian or Indonesian

Syllable structure

Most Kaurna words consist of just two syllables, though there are a fair number of three-syllable words and a small number of words consisting of just one syllable. With compounding, reduplication and the addition of suffixes, Kaurna words can be much longer. Consider *panpapanpalyarninthi* 'conferencing', *turathuranti-apiti* 'photocopier' and *ngathaityarnungku* 'from me; by me'.

Most syllables are open and consist of a consonant followed by a vowel (CV). Closed syllables CVC are relatively common and just a few CVCC syllables are found in the middle of words. The handful of words beginning with the **trr** cluster contain CCV and CCVC syllables. By contrast with English which allows a wide range of syllable types, the number of syllable types allowed in Kaurna words is very small.

Stress

The first syllable in Kaurna words is always stressed. In longer words, the 3rd syllable receives secondary stress (e.g. the bold syllables in **Ngang**ki**pa**ring**ga**). As stress is regular and predictable, there is no need to mark it.

Sounds at the beginning and end of words

Kaurna words can only commence with **i**, **k**, **m**, **n** [nh], **ng**, **p**, **t** [th] **w**, **y** and very occasionally **a**. Note that when Kaurna words commence with the letters **n** and **t**, these sounds are actually interdental **nh** and **th**. In the word *t*u*th*a 'grass' and in reduplicated words like *t*adli*th*adli 'frypan' the **t** at the beginning and **th** in the middle are exactly the same sound pronounced in exactly the same way. The majority of Kaurna words begin with a single consonant. However, a handful of words begin with the **trr** cluster (e.g. *trr*uku 'centre', *trr*ukanthi 'dribbling'). All Kaurna words end in a vowel.

Pronunciation

To learn how to pronounce Kaurna words, you can follow the written guidelines above. But you can also listen to the audio and video resources that KWP has produced. The *Kaurna Alphabet Book* (2nd edition) is a good place to start. It has an accompanying CD of a PowerPoint with embedded sound resources. If you click on the words that illustrate a particular sound/spelling, you will be able to hear how those words are pronounced.

The *Tirkanthi 'Learning' Kaurna* CD with Jack Kanya Buckskin has a series of introductory lessons. You can listen to them in the car as you are driving to work.

There are also many video and audio clips on YouTube on the web. The KWP Kaurna Language Learning Hub (https://www.youtube.com/channel/UChOOYOnJuEeydJK0OjN_Fpw) has a number of playlists, including *Kaurna for Kids*. There you will find the many episodes of the Pirltawardli Puppet Show as well as Kaurna songs ('We are Australian'; 'Heads Shoulders, Knees and Toes', and so on), language lessons and conversations. You can also find Kaurna videos on Facebook and Instagram, and more links and information on the new Kaurna Warra website (www.kaurnawarra.org.au).

Spelling conventions

Hyphenation
When Kaurna words take a vowel-initial suffix, a hyphen is inserted before the suffix as in *pari-arra* 'along the river' or *warri-apinthi* 'seeking'. A hyphen is also inserted in compound words where two vowels come together as a result of the loss of a consonant as in *ngutu-atpanthi* 'teach' [ngutu-(ng)atpanthi]. As with English, there is no clear pattern for compounds. Sometimes they are written as two separate words (e.g. *miitu kuu* 'bedroom'), sometimes hyphenated (e.g. *taa-partu* 'thick-lipped') and sometimes written as one word (e.g. *tipukardla* 'gunpowder; matches').

Spelling of bound pronouns
Kaurna has short-form bound pronouns that are attached to other words, in addition to independent pronouns. *Ngai* 'I' is reduced to -'*ai* when attached to another word. Some, like -'*rla* 'they 2' and -'*rna* 'they plural' have the same form as other noun suffixes (-*rla* 'dual' and -*rna* 'plural'). In order to make it clear that these are pronouns, they are always preceded by an apostrophe. Bound pronouns include -'*ai*, -'*athu*, -'*iina*, -'*intu*, -'*adli*, -'*adlu*, -'*rla* and -'*rna*.

Spelling of placenames
Kaurna placenames often end in the locative suffixes -*ngka* or -*ila* 'in, at, on'. When these suffixes occur on common nouns they are spelt -*ngka* and -*ila*. However, when they occur on a proper noun (an actual name) they are spelt -*ngga* and -*illa*. So the two words *nurlungka* 'on the curve' and Nurlungga 'at Nurlu = Noarlunga' are pronounced exactly the same but spelt slightly different.

You will see placenames spelt in many different ways, but increasingly councils are adopting the revised spelling illustrated in this book.

Spelling of personal names
Some Kaurna people prefer to use their own spelling or keep the old T&S spelling in their own names. Others have adopted the revised spellings used here. Kaurna people are free to choose the spelling of their own names.

KAURNA WORDS

Shared words
Kaurna is part of a language family, and it shares some words with related languages, just as English, a Germanic language, shares words with other Germanic languages. For instance, German has *Hand* 'hand', *Knie* 'knee', *Schulter* 'shoulder' and many other words that share a common origin with English.

There are several reasons why the same word can exist in different languages.

- It can be because the languages are descended from a common source language, just like cousins might inherit the same features from their common grandparents. English shares some words with Persian and Indian languages for this reason.
- It can be because people have been interacting for a long time and pick up words they like from each other's language. English borrowed lots of words from their French neighbours in the past, including: 'face', 'bronze', 'fatal', 'saint', and 'tradition'.
- It can be because people need a word for a new idea or invention and borrow its name from the language it is associated with. English got the word 'tsunami' from Japanese and 'banana' from a language in West Africa.

For Australian Aboriginal languages there is an extra reason why languages might share the same words. In many Aboriginal cultures it is customary to avoid using the name of a person who has recently died and other words that sound similar to it. That means people often had to find alternative words to use. Since most Aboriginal people could speak several other languages besides their own, they could use a word from another language during the mourning period.

For example, in the 1830s there was a boy living at Pirltawardli called *Kadli* which means 'dog'). If he had died, then Kaurna people could have started using either the word *putyita* or *wirka* which also mean 'dog'. Because Aboriginal cultures and languages are so much older than European languages, it is impossible for us to tell which language these words originally came from using linguistics.

Apart from the new words that Kaurna people have created in recent years, all the words in this dictionary were recorded in the first few years of colonisation of South Australia. Some people have expressed concern about local language programs taking words from other languages. Because the words in this dictionary were written down very early on, when Kaurna people were still living in their own homelands and practising their own culture, you can be confident that all these words were authentic parts of the Kaurna language spoken at that time. Of course, some of these words are also part of other languages, and it is interesting to see what these connections show us about the relationships between Aboriginal groups that existed before Europeans arrived.

New words

All living languages change. If the Kaurna language continues to be spoken and used then it will also continue to evolve. One contemporary change is the creation of new words by Kaurna people, to enable them to talk about modern ideas, objects and activities that are important in their lives.

Examples of some areas where new words have been created include: household items, electrical goods, sports, fishing, playing cards and school activities; foods that didn't exist in the 1840s; concepts like reconciliation, culture, Easter, a base-10 number system, months of the year, etc.

Of course all Kaurna people can use their language as they see fit, but vocabulary and resource creation activities associated with Kaurna Warra Pintyanthi (including this dictionary) always aim to use the processes and patterns inherent in the historical Kaurna language spoken at the time of colonisation.

Strategies for forming new words in Kaurna

The historical Kaurna sources reveal a wide range of strategies for forming new words in Kaurna. These strategies include:

1. Semantic Extension

Very often an existing word in the language was used to refer to new items or concepts that resembled the old word in some way in the minds of Kaurna speakers. For instance, Kaurna people used *maki* 'ice' for 'glass', *nantu* 'male grey kangaroo' for 'horse', *wauwi* 'female grey kangaroo' for 'sheep'. Sometimes the meaning was extended because the concepts were related. For instance, *tirntu* 'sun; time' was extended to 'clock'. Semantic extension has been used in recent times in *warri* 'air conditioner' from *warri* 'wind', *karntu* 'electricity' from *karntu* 'lightning', *yarta* 'floor' from *yarta* 'earth; ground', *tura* 'picture; image, photo' from *tura* 'shade, shadow' and *puntuntu* 'helicopter' from *puntuntu* 'dragonfly'.

2. Compounding
There are many examples where two words have been joined together to form a compound to refer to new things. Some historical examples include *kudnawardli* 'toilet' (from *kudna* 'faeces' + *wardli* 'house'), *tipukardla* 'gunpowder; matches' (from *tipu* 'spark' + *kardla* 'fire'), *makithau* 'window' (from *maki* 'ice; glass' + *tau* 'hole') and *makithura* 'mirror' (from *maki* 'ice; glass' + *tura* 'shade; shadow; picture; image'). There are many compounds with *pinti* 'pit; grave' for animals and items introduced from Europe, such as *pinti miyu* 'white person', *pintimai* 'European food', *pinti pitha* 'European goose', *pinti kudlu* 'European flea' and so on. Some recent compounds include *kudlikuru* 'sink' (from *kudli-* 'wash' + *kuru* 'container'), *tadlipurdi* 'soap' (from *tadli* 'spit; foam' + *purdi* 'stone') and *mukarntu* 'computer' (from *mukamuka* 'brain' + *karntu* 'lightning; electricity').

3. Reduplication
Reduplication or doubling of the word is sometimes used to form new words for new things. Some historical examples include *murdumurdu* 'flour; bread' (from *murdu* 'dust; ashes'), *pirrkipirrki* 'peas' (from *pirrki* 'bit; piece') and *tadlithadli* 'frypan' (from *tadli* 'spit'). Recent examples include *wardliwardli* 'township' (from *wardli* 'house'), *wayiwayi* 'motor' (from *wayi-* 'move') and *murlamurla* 'towel' (from *murla* 'dry').

4. The Suffix *-ti*
The addition of the suffix *-ti* to a verb root produces the thing that performs the action of the verb. For example, *nurlinthi* means 'turn, twist'. If we take *nurli-*, the root of this word, and add *-ti* to form *nurliti*, this is the Kaurna word for 'key', quite literally, 'the twister' or 'turning thing'. Other words formed in a similar fashion include *piltiti* 'scissors' (from *piltinthi* 'cut off, through'), *warkiti* 'pincers' (from *warkinthi* 'pinch'), *karnkati* 'any instrument by which something is raised; a string; handle; spade; spoon' (from *karnkanthi* 'lift, raise, dig, draw out') and *kurliti* 'brush' (from *kurlinthi* 'rub, clean, erase'). Some modern examples include *markati* 'pencil' (from *markanthi* 'trace, imitate'), *yuwati* 'plug' (from *yuwanthi* 'stop'), *tarnparriti* 'anchor' (from *tarnparrinthi* 'adhere, stick to') and *ngatparriti* 'sinker' (from *ngatparrinthi* 'sink').

5. Reduplication plus Suffix *-ti*
When the suffix *-ti* is combined with reduplication of the root, the result is the thing habitually used for the action of the verb. Historical examples include *tikathikati* 'chair' (from *tikanthi* 'sit'), *pakipakiti* 'knife' (from *pakinthi* 'cut') and *karnkarnkati* 'spoon' (from *karnkanthi* 'raise'). *Padnipadniti* 'car' (the thing for habitually travelling in) and *karrikarriti* 'aeroplane' (the thing for habitually flying in) have been formed by analogy.

6. The Suffix *-la* plus Reduplication
A more complicated pattern of reduplication occurs with the suffix *-la* to form the person who does the action. Let's take the verb root, *kampa-* 'cook'. If we add the suffix *-la* to give *kampala* and then reduplicate it leaving off the first consonant of the second component and the last vowel of the first component [*kampal(a) + (k)ampala*] we get *kampalampala* 'cook; baker' (the person who cooks/bakes). Historical examples of new terms formed in this way include *pintyalintyala* 'Creator' and *mankulankula* 'Angel' (the helper). Some modern examples include *tayilayila* 'builder' (from *tayinthi* 'build'); *tirkalirkala* 'student' (from *tirkanthi* 'learn'), *karrilarrila* 'pilot' (from *karrinthi* 'fly') and *pardu pakilakila* 'butcher' (lit. meat cutter-uperer).

7. Reduplication plus the Suffix -*nya*

When the verb root is reduplicated and the suffix -*nya* is added, this turns the verb into a noun denoting the action of the verb. For instance, *padminthi* is the verb 'jump', but *padmipadminya* is the event 'jumping' (a noun). So if we need words for the various sporting events in the Olympic Games, then this is the way to do it.

8. The Suffixes -*paltha* 'covering' and -*ana* 'towards' for items of clothing

In the mid-nineteenth century, Kaurna people formed the words *tidnapaltha* 'shoes' (lit. 'foot covering' and *yarkupaltha* 'stockings' (lit. 'leg covering'). These days Kaurna uses *warnupaltha* 'nappy' (lit. 'bum covering') and *ngamipaltha* 'bra' (lit. 'breast covering'). Teichelmann & Schürmann (1840) document *tiki-ana* 'waistcoat' (lit. 'to the ribs'), *kanthi-ana* 'trousers' (lit. 'to the thigh'), *nuki-ana* 'handkerchief' (lit. 'to the snot') and *mukarti-ana* 'hat' (lit. 'to the head'). These days we use *warltu-ana* 'scarf' (lit. 'to the neck'). These suffixes are a useful resource for forming new words for other items of clothing.

9. The Suffixes -*tidli* 'having', -*tina* 'without' and -*purtu* 'full of'

These three suffixes are useful for forming new descriptive words for new things that pick up on the presence of absence of a particular feature. *Kanyatidli* (lit. 'money having') is used for 'rich; moneybags' whilst *kanyatina* (lit. 'money without') means 'broke'. *Warpulayitina* (lit. 'without work') means 'unemployed' and *wardlitina* (lit. 'house without') means 'homeless' of course, while *kudnapurtu* is a useful insult. These suffixes are very useful for forming new expressions on the spot as they can be attached to a wide range of words.

10. The Suffixes -*rli* 'resembling', -*pira* 'on account of, about, for' and -*pina* 'inclined to; crazy over'

The suffixes -*rli*, -*pira* and -*pina* could potentially be used to form new words. The suffix -*rli* could be added to a wide range of words. The suffix -*pina* is especially useful for forming nicknames. *Yartapira* 'landform' (lit. 'on account of or about the land') was used in the *Kaurna Learner's Guide*.

11. Backformation

In the nineteenth century, Kaurna people used the word *kapi* 'tobacco'. *Kapi* is derived from the verb *kapinthi* 'vomit', the effect that tobacco was said to have had on people when they first tried tobacco. Some recent backformations are *ngutu* 'knowledge' from the verb *ngutu-atpanthi* 'teach, instruct' (lit. 'putting *ngutu* in') and *yailtya* 'belief' from *yailtyanthi* 'believe; think, suppose'.

12. Onomatopoeia

In the mid-nineteenth century Kaurna people used the word *pakapakanthi* 'trot', and applied the term to horses. *Pakapakanthi* is most likely at onomatopoeic word based on the sound of the horse trotting. *Pithapitha-apinthi* 'iron (clothes)' was another nineteenth century onomatopoeic word. In recent times, Jack Kanya Buckskin used the word *niinyi* 'motorbike'. He was aware of the Yolŋu Matha onomatopoeic word *dayndayn* 'motorbike' that is used in northeast Arnhemland.

13. Borrowing

A language like English borrows many words freely from other languages. However, very few borrowings are documented in Kaurna historical sources, and these days, Kaurna people are rather reluctant to borrow too many words from English or from other Aboriginal languages. Some historical borrowings from English include *Yiuwa* 'Jehovah', *tulya* 'soldier; police', *piipa* 'book; letter; paper' and *mani* 'money' (though these days *kanya* 'rock; money' is much preferred over *mani*). Some recent borrowings from English include *kiwiti* 'squid', *wumi* 'worm' and *Yiitya*

'Easter'. *Naalha* 'echidna' has also been borrowed from the neighbouring Nukunu language as surprisingly, no word for 'echidna' was ever recorded in Kaurna wordlists. But Nukunu and Kaurna share many words, so there is a reasonable chance that *naalha* may well have been a Kaurna word anyway. *Kuula* 'koala' has been borrowed from Dharuk, the original source language spoken in Sydney, rather than 'koala', the changed or corrupted form of the word resulting from a mis-reading of handwriting that is used in English.

14. Loan Translation or Calquing

An historical example of a loan translation in Kaurna is *kardlapinti* 'hell' (lit. 'fire pit'). Some modern examples include *tukuwingkura* 'microwave' (lit. 'small wave') and *mukarntu* 'computer' (lit. 'electric brain' being a direct translation of the Maori term). Kaurna is more willing to adopt loan translations rather than direct borrowings. A beautiful example is *maityuwampi* 'bicycle' (lit. 'bat wing') inspired by the Adnyamathanha word *mikawiri* which has the same meanings. *Marawiti* 'octopus' (lit. 'many hands') is another loan translation of the corresponding Narungga term. *Puntuntu* 'helicopter', mentioned under semantic extension, is a loan translation of the Tiwi term.

KAURNA GRAMMAR

Grammar consists of two main parts: syntax, which concerns the rules for stringing words together, and morphology, the rules that govern the internal structure of words. The way in which Kaurna grammar works is typical of Aboriginal languages.

Unlike in English, Kaurna word order is free and every possible combination of Subject, Verb and Object has been recorded. However, the most frequent word order was the Subject followed by the Object and with the Verb last. This freedom of word order is made possible because of suffixes or endings on the nouns.

Kaurna does not use prepositions, such as in, on, at, to, from, for, with, by etc. It uses suffixes instead. So any given noun may have many different endings. Consider these on the words *wardli* 'house' and *miyu* 'man; person':

Wardli 'house; home'
- wardlidla 'two houses'
- wardlirna 'houses' (more than two)
- wardlingka 'in the house'; 'on the house', 'at the house'
- wardli-ana 'to the house'; '(to) home'
- wardlinangku 'from the house'; 'from home'
- wardli-arra 'through the house'
- wardlityangka 'in the vicinity of the house'
- wardlidla-ityangka 'in the vicinity of the two houses'
- wardlirna-ityangka 'in the vicinity of the houses' (more than two)
- wardlitidli 'having a house'
- wardlitina 'without a house' (i.e. 'homeless')
- wardlitya 'for a house' (e.g. 'househunting')
- wardlidli 'resembling a house'
- wardlidlaku wartingka 'between the houses'
- wardlipina 'homebody'

Miyu 'man; person'
- miyu 'man; person' e.g. *Miyu padni.* 'The man went.'
- miyurlu 'man; person' (affected someone or something) (e.g. *Miyurlu ngangki martinthi* 'The man is hugging the woman.')
- miyuku 'man's' (e.g. *miyuku mutyarta* 'the man's clothes')
- miyurla 'two men; two people'
- miyurna 'men; people' (more than 2)
- miyu-itya 'to the man; for the man'
- miyu-ityanungku 'from the man; from the person'
- miyu-ityangka 'with the man; with the person
- miyuni 'to the man' (e.g. *Ngathu kardla miyuni yungki* 'I gave the firewood to the man')
- miyutina 'without a man' (i.e. single)
- miyutidli 'having a man' (i.e. married)
- miyurli 'resembling a man'
- miyupina 'crazy about men'
- miyupurtu 'full of men'

Let's look at the suffixes taken by adjectives. *Marni* 'good' is a typical adjective. But this word is also a noun meaning 'fat' or 'grease'.

Marni 'good' (a typical Adjective)
- marnintyarla 'better; best'
- marnirninthi 'getting better; becoming fat'
- marnirni 'got better; became fat'
- marnirningutha 'will get better; will get fat'
- marninthi 'to be fat; to grease or anoint'
- marnirrinthi 'to grease or anoint each other'
- marniti 'boy greased and painted with red ochre (as part of an initiation ceremony)'

Pronouns are words like 'I', 'me', 'my', 'you', 'they', 'them', 'we', 'us', 'he', 'she', 'him', 'hers', etc. There are many more pronouns in Kaurna than in English as Kaurna pronouns are differentiated for singular (one), dual (two) and plural (more than two) as well as according to their role or function in the sentence. For instance, *niina, nintu, niwa, niwarlu, naa* and *naarlu* all translate as 'you'. And there are many additional forms like *nintaityanungku, niwadlityanungku* and *naalityanungku* which all translate as 'from you' or 'by you' and *nintaityangka, niwalityangka* and *naalityangka* which all translate as 'with you' but their use depends on how many people are spoken to.

Kaurna verbs also have many more suffixes or endings than English verbs. By way of example, consider some of the endings on *paki-* 'cut' and *tika-* 'sit':

Paki- 'cut' (a typical Transitive Verb)
- pakinthi 'cutting'
- paki 'cut' (over and done with)
- pakithi 'cut' (indefinite)
- pakitha 'will cut'
- pakirti 'don't cut'
- pakinana 'having cut'

- pakima 'if (it were) cut'; 'when (it was) cut'
- pakititya 'in order to cut'
- pakintu! 'cut!' or 'Cut it!' (talking to just one person)
- pakingwa! 'cut!' or 'Cut it!' (talking to two people)
- pakinga! 'cut!' or 'Cut it!' (talking to more than two people)
- pakitina 'without cutting'
- pakirna 'let it be cut!'
- pakituwayi 'lest it be cut'; 'so it doesn't get cut'
- pakiti 'cutter' (the thing used to cut with)
- pakilakila 'cutter' (the person doing the cutting)
- pak'adlu 'let's cut' (more than two of us)
- pak'adli 'let's cut' (the two of us)
- pak'athu 'I'll cut'

Tika- 'sit' (a typical Intransitive Verb)
- tikanthi 'sitting'
- tiki 'sat'
- tikathi 'sat' (indefinite)
- tikatha 'will sit'
- tikarti 'don't sit'
- tikanana 'having sat'
- tikama 'if (he had) sat'; 'when (she) sat'
- tikatitya 'in order to sit'
- tika! 'sit!' (talking to just one person)
- tikaingwa! 'sit!' (talking to two people)
- tikainga! 'sit!' (talking to more than two people)
- tikatina 'without sitting'
- tikarna 'let them sit!'
- tikati 'sitter' (the thing which sits)
- tikatikanya 'sitting' (the activity)
- tikapinthi 'sitting (someone or something) down'
- tikapi 'sat (someone or something) down'
- tikapingutha 'will sit (someone or something) down'
- tik'ai 'I'll sit'
- tik'adli 'let's us 2 sit'
- tik'adlu 'let's sit'

It is very important to know the difference between transitive verbs like 'cut' and intransitive verbs like 'sit'. Transitive verbs have an object. You cut something, whether it be grass, meat, bread and so on. Intransitive verbs do not have an object. Some of the suffixes only appear on transitive verbs. The singular command *pakintu!* 'cut' takes the suffix *-ntu*, whereas the singular command *tika* 'sit!' does not and the subject differs in form (*miyurlu* 'the man' is the subject of *pakinthi* 'cutting' whilst *miyu* 'the man' is the subject of *tikanthi* 'sitting').

TRANSLATING INTO KAURNA

Translating from one language into another is seldom a straightforward task. English and Kaurna words very often have a different range of meanings. The subject of the English word 'run', for instance, can refer to people, animals (but not snakes), rivers, ink, fences, vines, pipes, taps, engines, meetings, arguments and so on. The subject of the Kaurna word *yakanthi* probably only referred to humans and animals. *Yakanthi* also means 'chase, hunt, pursue', which are different verbs in English. English expressions are often not able to be translated directly or literally. When looking for a Kaurna equivalent of an English word in the finder list, always make sure that you look up the Kaurna word itself. Then you will be able to see the range of meanings that this word has and perhaps some example sentences illustrating how the word is used.

The Word Finder section on page 96 is not an English-Kaurna dictionary, but a tool to find an approximate equivalent of the English word in the Kaurna language. By referring to the Kaurna word you have found in the Kaurna-English dictionary, you can find a more accurate Kaurna expression.

On many occasions, you will not be able to find a Kaurna equivalent for many English words you try to look up. When this happens, try to think of another word with a similar meaning. Perhaps the word you are looking for is a technical term which has not yet been encoded into Kaurna. Or perhaps it is a gap in the record where we would have expected there to be a Kaurna word, but no-one bothered to record it. We are slowly filling the gaps and developing technical terms.

When translating from English into Kaurna, always use the dictionary in conjunction with the learner's guide. To translate an English sentence into Kaurna, we need to have some understanding of Kaurna grammar. Let's take a simple example 'I went to the shops with my mother'. Now there are eight words in this English sentence, but the equivalent Kaurna sentence has just four words. First look for the content words in the English to Kaurna Word Finder list. We find 'shop' is *titawardli*. 'Mother' is *ngangkita*, but if we keep looking we see that there is a single word *ngaityai* meaning 'my mother'. There are two words meaning 'I', *ngai* and *ngathu*. But which one should we use? And there is no entry for 'went'. Well, 'went' is the past tense inflection of the verb 'go' (*padninthi* in Kaurna), so we need to consult the grammar to find the word for 'went'. It is in fact *padni* in Kaurna. We can simply ignore the English word 'the'. It has no counterpart in Kaurna. But suffixes *-ana* and *-ityangka* are used in Kaurna instead of the prepositions 'to' and 'with'. So in Kaurna we end up with *Ngai titwardliana padni ngaityai-ityangka*. (lit. 'I shops-to went my mother-with'). Remember that English has SVO (Subject + Verb + Object) word order, whereas Kaurna prefers SOV (Subject + Object + Verb) word order, though word order is actually fairly free in Kaurna.

Now let's see what happens when we translate the English sentence 'I saw my neighbour at the shops'. This time we use *ngathu* 'I' because 'see' has an object. In the previous sentence, 'go' has no object, but with 'see', I see something/somebody. Unlike 'my mother' which is one word in Kaurna, 'my neighbour' is two words *ngaityu niipu*, just like in English. The Kaurna translation of 'I saw my neighbour at the shops' is *Ngathu ngaityu niipu naki titwardlingka*. (lit. 'I my neighbour saw shops-at'). This time, the English sentence has seven words and the Kaurna sentence has five. In the previous sentence, I went 'to' the shops, so *titawardli* took the Allative suffix *-ana* 'to; towards'. This time, I am 'at' the shops, so *titawardli* takes the Locative suffix *-ngka* 'in, at, on'.

Idiomatic expressions are notoriously difficult to translate and it would be extremely unlikely that we could translate them literally. Some examples of Kaurna idioms include *Tadli pudna-pudnai*. 'It's boiled' (Lit. 'the spit has arrived') and *Ngai tiya wartangka warrapantu* 'Repeat after me' (Lit. 'say behind-at I tooth'). The literal translations of these expressions sound rather weird in English. In the same way, if we translate English idioms, such as 'let's get the ball rolling', into Kaurna literally then these literal Kaurna translations are also going to sound quite weird in Kaurna.

List of abbreviations used for parts of speech

adj	Adjective
adv	Adverb
cli	Clitic
dem	Demonstrative
inter	Interrogative or Question Word
intj	Interjection
loc	Locative or Locational
n	Noun
num	Number or Numeral
pro	Pronoun
suff	Suffix
temp	Temporal or Time Word
v-imp	Imperative Verb or Command
v-intr	Intransitive Verb
v-tr	Transitive Verb

List of abbreviations used for sources

AN	George French Angas (1846; 1847)
BA	Daisy Bates (1919) (vocabulary sourced from Ivarrityi)
BL	John McConnell Black (1920)
CA	William Cawthorne (1842–1846)
CH	J. Chittleborough (1906)
CO	Herbert Thomas Condon (1962; 1968; 1975)
EA	G. Windsor Earl (1838) in J. Lhotsky (1839)
EY	Edward John Eyre (1845)
GA	Joseph Paul Gaimard (collected in 1826; published in 1833)
GR	George Grey (1840s)
KL	Samuel Klose (1840s) – hymns (as translated by Teichelmann & Schürmann)
KO	Hermann Koeler (1836–37)
NEW	Developed since 1980
PI	Louis Piesse (1839; 1840)
RO	George Augustus Robinson and son Charles Robinson (1837)
ST	Edward Stephens (1889)
TI	Norman Barnett Tindale (20th Century)
TM	Teichelmann Manuscript, 1857
TS	Teichelmann & Schürmann, 1840
TRAD	Traditional - still used by the Kaurna community in 1980
WI	William Williams (1840)
WY	William Wyatt (collected between 1837 and 1839; published in 1879)

To find out more about how Kaurna grammar works, consult *Kulurdu Marni Ngathaitya! 'Sounds Good to Me'*, the Kaurna Learner's Guide (also published by Wakefield Press). If you understand the suffixes that go on nouns and verbs, you can form many more words yourself than those that appear in this dictionary.

Another book, *Kaurna for Smarties*, is under development. *Kaurna for Smarties* will further complement the *Kaurna Alphabet Book*, Kaurna Learner's Guide, Kaurna Dictionary, songbooks, funeral book and on-line resources to complete a comprehensive set of resources to assist the Kaurna language learner. Look out for *Kaurna for Smarties*, also to be published by Wakefield Press.

A set of distinctive Kaurna playing cards is also available and other teaching resources are under development.

KAURNA – ENGLISH

A a

'adli => **ngadli** *pro*

'adlu => **ngadlu** *pro*

'ai => **ngai** *pro*

'akurti => **wakurti** *adv*

alya *cli, intj* (1) expresses surprise, concern or uncertainty *Waa-alya pia pa?* 'Where (on earth) is he?' ᴛꜱ,ᴛᴍ (2) attaches to nouns to show affection or endearment for the one named. *Warrityalya!* 'Look, (there is) Warritya!' *Ngaityu yungantalya!* 'My dear brother!' ᴛᴍ,ᴛꜱ (3) attaches to nouns to form an expression of thanks. *Ngaityalya.* 'Thanks!' *Wangka'dlu: Mathanyantalya!* 'Let's say: Our dear Lord!' ɴᴇᴡ (4) emphatic marker, attaches to other words to add emphasis or emotional focus *Yakalya!* 'Oh dear!' *Naa-alyama pa kurnta?* 'Have you perhaps killed him?' ᴛꜱ,ᴛᴍ

-alya *suff (on verbs)* continuous action marker *Nganaityantalyama pa kurnta?* 'Why have you then beaten him?' *pamalyarninthi* 'to continue, persevere in spearing' ᴛᴍ

-ama => **-ma**

-amu => **namu**

-ana (var. **-kana**; **-tana**₂) *suff (on nouns)* (1) to, towards (somewhere/something) (allative) *Wardli-ana'ai muringutha.* 'I will go home.' *Kardla tawarrikana'ai padnitha.* 'I shall go to the large fire.' *Warru-ana parltintu!* 'Throw it outside!' ᴛꜱ,ᴛᴍ (2) attaches to a body part to derive an article of clothing *mukarta-ana* 'hat' *nuki-ana* 'handkerchief' *tiki-ana* 'waistcoat' *turti-ana* 'coat, jacket' *yarku-ana* 'trousers' ᴛꜱ,ᴛᴍ

-anangku => **-nungku**

-anta₁ (var. **-nta**₁; **-nti**) (1) *suff (on nouns)* exclusively belonging to *Ninku-anta* 'Your own' ᴛꜱ,ᴛᴍ (2) *suff (on nouns)* indicates exclusivity of the agent *ngathunta* 'I myself (and no one else)' *nintu-anta* 'You alone' ᴛᴍ (3) *suff* entirely-, at all- *yaku-anta* 'not at all' *nurnti-anta* 'entirely away' ᴛꜱ,ᴛᴍ

-anta₂ (var. **-nta**₂) *suff (on nouns)* attaches to words for bodyparts to denote something of the same shape ᴛᴍ

-api [(w)api-(nthi)] (var. **-kapi**; **-pi**) *suff (on verbs)* make (someone/something happen/do something) (causative) *warninthi – warni-apinthi* 'to fall, to be born – to cause (someone) to fall, to give birth to (someone)' *manta-apinthi* 'to tell a lie – to cause (someone) to lie, to misrepresent (someone)' ᴛꜱ,ᴛᴍ

-arra (var. **-tarra**) *suff (on nouns)* (1) along, alongside, parallel with (perlative) *pari-arra* 'alongside the river' *mukurtarra* 'along the range of hills' *Papaltu-arra tarralyi wantitha.* 'The fence will run alongside the stump.' *Tapa-arra padninga!* 'Go along, follow the road' *pulthu-arrapinthi* 'to make alongside of' ᴛꜱ,ᴛᴍ (2) across *wadlatarra* 'tree lying across a river to walk over' ᴛꜱ,ᴛᴍ (3) through *mudlhatarra* 'through the nostrils' ᴛꜱ,ᴛᴍ (4) denotes location (relative to someone/thing) *munatarra* 'going ahead, taking the lead' *munarra padninthi* 'going ahead, taking the lead' *kurtarra padninthi* 'passing close by someone' ᴛᴍ

arratina *n* deceased mother *ngaityu arratina, niina* 'my deceased mother, you are' ᴛᴍ

'athu => **ngathu** *pro*

D d

-dla => **-rla**

'dli => **ngadli** *pro*

-dlu => **-rlu**

'dlu => **ngadlu** *pro*

-dna => **-rna**

I i

idla *n* (1) joey; young male kangaroo ᴛᴍ (2) puppy, young one ᴛꜱ (3) pubic area (male) ᴛᴍ

-idla => **-tidla**

-idli => **-tidli**

idlu [iya-rlu] (var. **irdlu**) (1) *dem* this one (ergative) *Idluntya pikidlu pudnatha pa.* 'In the present moon (cycle) he will come.' ᴛꜱ (2) *temp* this time *Yalakanta, ngai kumpathi idlu.* 'Just now, when I left.' *Yalaka, niina parni murithi idlu, ngathu pardu ngarki.* 'Yesterday, when you came, I ate meat.' ᴛᴍ

idlu-urla [idlu-(p)urla] *dem* these two (dual) ᴛꜱ,ᴛᴍ

idlu-urlaku [idlu-(p)urla-ku] *dem* of these two (genitive dual) ᴛꜱ

idlu-urlani [idlu-(p)urla-ni] *dem* to these two (dative dual)

idluntya [idlu-ntya] *dem* this one (ergative, emphatic) *Nata ngai padninthi, ngai kuntu pungkurrinthi idluntya yartarlu.* 'I'm going now, I feel uneasy in this place.' TM

idluntyanta [idlu-ntya-nta] he himself/she herself alone (is the agent) TM

ika *n* piece; bit TM

   ika-payanthi [ika-paya-nthi] *v-tr* take large bites, devour TM, TS

-ila (var. **-illa**) *suff (on nouns)* in, at, on (locative) *mutyartila* 'in (the pocket of) the clothes' *mukartila tikanthi* 'to live in the hills' *kartakila* 'on the shoulder' *tarralyila* 'in the box; on the table' TS (*NB Use '-illa' on proper nouns (i.e. names of people and places) and '-ila' for common nouns*)

-illa => **-ila**

ilya *n* snake – red-bellied black snake TM, TS

ilyala (var. **kilyala**) *n* waves at the shore; surf TM

'ina => **niina** *pro*

ingkarninthi [ingka-rni-nthi] *v-tr* (1) enquire, ask about (someone) TS (2) look out for, wait for (someone) who you know is coming *Ninku ngai ingkarnitha* 'I will wait for you.' TM, TS

inha (1) *dem* this one (thing or person) TS (2) *loc* here *Inhaintya ngai katpirrirni-utha.* 'I will wait here.' *Nintu inhaintya kardla parra?* 'Did you light a fire here previously?' TM

   inha tirntu when the sun is at this point TM
   inhaintya [inha-intya] *loc* here TM
   inhaintyanta [inha-intya-nta] *loc* right here TM
   inhangku [inha-ngku] from this place TM
   inhangkuntya [inha-ngku-ntya] proceeding from this place TM
   inhanungku [inha-nungku] from this person TS

inhaku [inha-ku] *dem* his; her; its (possessive) TM, TS

   inhaku-angki [inha-ku-(ng)angki] his/her mother TM
   inhakuntya [inha-ku-ntya] his, hers, its TM
   inhakuyarli [inha-ku-yarli] his/her father TM

inpanthi [inpa-nthi] *v-tr* (1) meet, fall in with *Ngulthingka ngadlu nanturna inpa.* 'We met the horses at night.' *Nintu ngai nganaitya yaku warra-inpa?* 'Why don't you answer me?' TM, TS (2) border (something, e.g. a person, river, district), be bounded by TM

   inparrinthi [inpa-rri-nthi] *v-intr* meet each other TM, TS

-intya (see also: **-ntya**) *suff* having

-intyarla [-ntya-rla] (var. **-nyarla**) *suff* -er, more (comparative/superlative) *karra-intyarla* 'higher' *yakintyarla* 'deeper' TS

-intyidla *suff (on verbs)* *kurnta-intyidla* 'after he has beaten' TM

-inyana *suff* on account of having, because (one) has (already/previously) TM

ipila *n* sounds made during ceremonies TS, TM

ipilayinthi [ipi-ayi-nthi] *v-intr* put (oneself) somewhere; position (oneself) somewhere TM

ipinthi [ipi-nthi] *v-tr* pour; sprinkle *kauwi-urlu ipinthi* 'throwing water (on someone)' TS, TM

   ipidlipidla [ipi-l(a)-ipi-la] *n* pourer, sprinkler (person) TS, TM
   ipiti$_1$ [ipi-ti] *n* shower; sprinkler NEW

ipiti$_2$ => **yipiti**

irdi (see also: **yaitya**) (1) *adj* native, vernacular, proper, own, belonging to the country *irdi miyu* 'a native person' TM, TS (2) *adj* fresh TS (3) *adv* voluntarily, gratuitously TS

irdlu => **idlu**

irra *n* fight; battle *irra karrinthi* 'to rise, stand, go out for a fight' *irra murinthi* 'to go to fight' *irra padninthi* 'to go out to fight' TS, TM

   irrapina [irra-pina] (var. **pirrapina**) (1) *n* warrior TS (2) *adj, n* quarrelsome, antagonistic, belligerent person; someone who likes to fight TS, TM
   Irrapina Tirntu *n* ANZAC Day NEW

irrka *n* pile; heap *irrka pungkunthi* 'to put in a heap, to accumulate' TS, TM

   irrkantinthi [irrka-nti-nthi] *v-intr* accumulate TM
   irrkapanthi [irrka-pa-nthi] *v-tr* heap up; accumulate; pile up TM
   irrkuta *n* sore; ulcer; swelling; abscess TS, TM
   irrkutantinthi [irrkuta-nti-nthi] *v-intr* swell; become sore TS, TM

itharti *n* something to lie or sleep on (e.g. dry grass, a skin), mattress, bed TM, TS

'iti => **piti** *adv*

itirra *adv* (1) carelessly, without observing TM, TS (2) unintentionally, without being noticed TS, TM

   itirrantinthi [itirra-nti-nthi] *v-intr* be oblivious, unaware TM

-itpina [(y)itpi-na] *suff (on nouns)* father of- *Kadlitpina* 'father of Kadli' *Pitpauwitpina* 'father of Pitpauwi' TM

itu *dem* these *Ituntya, nganarna?* 'These things here, what are they?' *Itu, ngangkurna mairna? Ngangkurna* *pia?* 'Whose provisions are these? Whose indeed?' TS, TM

ituku [itu-ku] of these ones, genitive plural demonstrative pronoun

ituntya [itu-ntya] these (emphatic) TM

itya *n* flesh; lean meat *itya yarthurrinthi/itya murta warninthi* 'to grow lean, the flesh falls away' TS, TM, GA

itya kata fleshy, corpulent TM

itya tauata fleshy, corpulent TM

ityatina [itya-tina] *adj* thin, lean, TS, TM

ityatina warputina [itya-tina warpu-tina] *adj* having neither flesh nor bone, incorporeal TS

-itya (var. **-litya**; **-titya**) **(1)** *suff* for-, in order to-, it attaches to a noun or verb to indicate that this was the purpose or goal of an action (purposive) *Niina nganaitya pudni? – Mardla nakutitya.* 'Why did you come? – Just to look.' *kauwitya padninthi* 'to go for water' TS
(2) *suff (on nouns)* towards- (someone), for motion towards people. It always attaches to the ergative form of pronouns (allative) *Nintaitya'ai padnitha.* 'I will come to you.' *kadli-adli patinthi miyu-itya* 'to let the bier run against a man' i.e. to accuse him of causing the death' *turlarninthi miyu-itya* 'be angry with someone' *marnkarrinthi miyu-itya* 'to beg, beseech someone' TS

ityangka [itya-ngka] (var. **yityangka**) *loc* close by; nearby TS, TM, WI, ST, WY, BL

-ityangka [-itya-ngka] (var. **-lityangka**) *suff (on nouns)* **(1)** with (someone). Always attaches to the ergative form of pronouns (comitative) *Ngathaityangka tika-tika.* 'Live with me.' TS, TM **(2)** at-, to- (someone), *Niina nganaityangka maingki-maingki?* 'Who are you laughing at?' *Yaku ngai nata parnalityangka pudna-utha.* 'I will not go to them now.' *Ngathu-ityangka pa pudlurrithi.* 'He told me.' *mutyarta miyu-ityangka ngatpanthi.* 'to dress someone' *Turnki ngatha-ityangka parltarrinthi.* 'The coat will throw itself from me. (i.e. it will wear off my body)' TS, TM

-ityarnungku (var. **-lityarnungku**) *n* **(1)** motion from a person *Miyu-ityarnungku* 'from the man' TM, TS **(2)** origin *Taayaparnalityarnungku warra pudni* 'Out of (his) mouth, from (his) lips, the word came' *Naalityarnungku parna yarnki* 'They are infected from you. or They caught the infection from you.' TM, TS

ityarrinthi [itya-rri-nthi] *v-tr* approach; come near to TM

Ivaritji *n* misty rain BL, BA (*ipinthi*)

iya **(1)** *dem* this (thing or person) here TM, TS **(2)** *loc* this place here *Iya ngai warnitha, iyaintya wakinha.* 'I will very likely fall here, here it's dangerous' *Waa? – Iya!* 'Where? – Here!' TM, TS

iyalya! *intj* here it is (I have found it)! TM

iyamu *loc* along here TM

iyangka in this here TM

iyani *dem* to this one (dative) TM

iyarnti 'here along on -'. TM

iya! *intj* hey! TM

iyaitya => **yaitya**

K k

kaaru *n* **(1)** blood *kaaru marrarrinthi* 'to bleed profusely' TS, TM, WY **(2)** pulse WY **(3)** wine TM **(4)** grape juice TM **(5)** grapes NEW

kaaru-kaaru *n, adj* red TS

kaaru-marrarninthi [kaaru-marra-rni-nthi] *v-intr* rejoice; be glad TS

kaaru-wayinthi [kaaru-wayi-nthi] *v-intr* bleed TM

kaarurninthi [kaaru-rni-nthi] *v-intr* recover; get over *Kudlampi kaarurningku.* 'Leave (him) alone (he's) recovering.' TM

kaaruwardli [kaaru-wardli] *n* blood vessel TS

kaaruyarta [kaaru-yarta] *n* vineyard NEW

kadla *n* gap; opening; joint; space *kadla pungkunthi* 'to make an opening in the battle line.' *Nintu pa kadla-kadlanthi.* 'You are taller than him.' TM

kadli *n* dog, dingo *kadli-irla* 'two dogs' *kadlirna* 'dogs' TS, TM, WY, WI, BL, GA, KO, CH

kadli mathanya [kadli matha-nya] *n* dog owner TS

Kadlitipari [kadli-ti(ya)-pari] *n* Para River WI, WY

Kadlitiya [kadli-tiya] *n* Gawler WY

kadliyuri [kadli-yuri] *n* corner of a page in a book folded over like a dog's ear NEW

kadliyuri-apinthi [kadli-yuri-(w)api-nthi] *v-tr* fold the corner of the page over NEW

kadliyurinthi [kadli-yuri-nthi] *adj* dog-eared NEW

kadli-adli [kadli-(k)adli] (var. **kadli-kadli**) *n* corpse; dead person *kadli-adli wangkanthi* 'to question the deceased' TS, TM

kadli-adli patinthi [kadli-(k)adli pati-nthi] accuse someone of causing another person's death TM

kadlunthi [kadlu-nthi] *v-tr* **(1)** stride, tread upon, press with the foot *Namu kadluninyana purrutyi kalyawayitha.* 'Treading on it like that it will all get spoilt.' TS, TM **(2)** press down hard; to compact something; to ram (earth) *Waadlu'athu kadlutha?* 'What shall I ram it with?' ᴛꜱ **(3)** incubate eggs by sitting on them ᴛᴍ **(4)** inquire of the dead (during an inquest) ᴛᴍ

kadlurrinthi [kadlu-rri-nthi] *v-intr* **(1)** lean (on something) *Kadlurringurti!* 'Don't lean (on it)!' ᴛꜱ **(2)** be heavy, weigh down, press heavily ᴛᴍ **(3)** be downcast, look sad, sulky ᴛꜱ **(4)** hang downward ᴛᴍ

kadngi *n* white ant; termite ᴛꜱ,ᴡʏ

kadnginguya *n* cricket species ᴡʏ

kadnu (var. **kanu**) *n* Jew lizard, bearded dragon ᴛꜱ,ᴛᴍ,ᴡʏ

kadnumarnguta [kadnu-marngu-ta] (var. **kanumarnguta**) *n* bullroarer ᴛꜱ

kaiku *n* pus ᴛꜱ,ᴛᴍ

kaikurninthi [kaiku-rni-nthi] *v-intr* get infected; fester *Kaaru kaikurninthi* 'The blood is becoming inflamed' ᴛᴍ

kailya => **kalya**

kailyu => **kalyu**

Kainka Wirra *n* name of the lake in the Botanic Gardens ɢʀ

kaintyirrinthi [kaintyi-rri-nthi] *v-tr* get infected by; suffer from; be affected by *Kawarta miyu yaku nurrutidlu kaintyirrinthi.* 'The northern men are not affected by the enchantment.' ᴛᴍ

kaityanthi [kaitya-nthi] *v-tr* **(1)** put down ᴛᴍ **(2)** send (e.g. on an errand) *Ngu'athu muiyu mankunthi, parni kaityantu.* 'I like that (woman), send (her) here.' ᴛᴍ,ᴛꜱ **(3)** set in place (as in setting quartz teeth in a spear) ᴛᴍ,ᴛꜱ **(4)** lay an egg ᴛᴍ,ᴛꜱ

kaityita *n* goanna ᴘɪ

-kaiyinthi => **wayinthi**

kaka *n* head ᴛᴍ

kaka-aka [kaka-(k)aka] (var. **kaka kaka**) *n* lover; spouse ᴛᴍ

kaka-kartarla [kaka-kart(u)-(t)a-rla] *n* couple, husband and wife ᴛᴍ

kaka-mankunthi [kaka-manku-nthi] *v-tr* put under foot ᴛᴍ

kaka-ngatpanthi [kaka-ngatpa-nthi] *v-intr* dive (into or under) ᴛꜱ,ᴛᴍ,ᴡʏ

kaka-papanthi [kaka-pa-pa-nthi] *v-tr* **(1)** date, flirt with, court (someone) ᴛꜱ,ᴛᴍ **(2)** make love (to someone) ᴛꜱ,ᴛᴍ

kaka-wardninthi [kaka-wardni-nthi] (var. **kaka-warninthi**) *v-intr* **(1)** fall down ᴛꜱ,ᴛᴍ **(2)** nod when sleeping ᴛꜱ

kakapiti [kaka-piti] *n* pillow; mattress ᴛᴍ

kakirra₁ *n* moon *Kakirra tarnanthi.* 'The moon is rising.' *Kakirra mirimirilyainthi.* 'The moon is shining.' ᴛꜱ,ᴛᴍ,ᴡʏ,ɢᴀ,ʀᴏ,ꜱᴛ

kakirra munthu full moon ᴛᴍ

kakirra warntaingki [kakirra warnta-ingki] waning moon ᴛᴍ

kakirra₂ *n* mussel (shellfish) ᴛᴍ,ɢᴀ,ᴡʏ

kalta *n* sleepy lizard ᴛꜱ,ᴡʏ,ᴘɪ

kaltinthi [kalti-nthi] *v-tr* command; demand; request; ask; beg ᴛꜱ,ᴛᴍ

kalti-apinthi [kalti-(w)api-nthi] *v-tr* order; command *Muinmu ngai parna kalti-apinina.* 'They often used to order me.' ᴛꜱ,ᴛᴍ

kaltikaltinya [kalti-kalti-nya] *adj* domineering person; demanding person; constantly asking ᴛꜱ,ᴛᴍ

kaltirrinthi [kalti-rri-nthi] *v-intr* ask for oneself ᴛꜱ

kalya (var. **kailya**) **(1)** *n* small piece, bit, fragment ᴛᴍ **(2)** *adj* active, lively, sprightly ᴛᴍ

kalya-kadlunthi [kalya-kadlu-nthi] *v-tr* tread to pieces ᴛᴍ

kalya-pungkunthi [kalya-pungku-nthi] *v-tr* break up; pound (to powder) ᴛᴍ

kalyarni-apinthi [kalya-rni-(w)api-nthi] *v-tr* break up ᴛᴍ

kalyarninthi [kalya-rni-nthi] *v-intr* dissolve; melt ᴛꜱ,ᴛᴍ

kalyamarru [kalya-marru] *adj* lively; active; cheerful; gay ᴛꜱ

kalyu (var. **kailyu**) *n* myrtle ᴡʏ

kamami *n* maternal grandmother (mother's mother) ᴛꜱ,ᴛᴍ,ᴡʏ

kamilya *n* grandchild of kamami (of mother's mother) ᴛꜱ,ᴛᴍ

kamilyata *n* relative with the same 'kamami' ᴛᴍ

kampanthi [kampa-nthi] *v-tr* **(1)** cook; bake; roast; burn *Kardlangka kampanana, yaku pika-pikarnitha?* 'After it's been roasted in the fire, it will become soft won't it?' ᴛꜱ,ᴛᴍ,ᴡɪ,ꜱᴛ **(2)** boil *Waa'adli kauwi kampatha? – Yaku'athu naki.* 'Where will we boil the water? – I don't know.' ᴛꜱ,ᴛᴍ

kampa-tharralyi *n* cooking bench ɴᴇᴡ

kampakuru [kampa-kuru] *n* saucepan ɴᴇᴡ

kampalampala [kampa-l(a)-(k)ampa-la] *n* cook; baker ᴛꜱ

kamparrinthi [kampa-rri-nthi] *v-intr* be hot; be oppressive *Tirntu kamparrinthi.* 'The sun is burning.' ᴛꜱ

kamparriti [kam-pa-rri-ti] *n* kitchen; bakery ᴛꜱ,ᴛᴍ

kamparriti wardli *n* oven ᴛᴍ
kamparriti warta cook, baker ᴛᴍ
kampati [kampa-ti] *n* stove ɴᴇᴡ
-kana => **-ana** *suff* (on nouns)
kangata *n* berry species ᴛꜱ
kangkanthi [kangka-nthi] *v-tr* (1) bear a child *Ngaityu yangarrarlu wakwaku kangki.* 'My wife has had a baby.' ᴛꜱ,ᴛᴍ,ᴡʏ (2) accompany, lead (someone) *Wanti kangka'ntu* 'Where are you accompanying (him) to?' *Ngauwarna mai kangkantu!* 'Take the ngauwa with you and give (them) food.' *Padluni kangki wartaitya.* 'He will lead you around (as his wife).' *Ngana miyu nintu kangkanthi?* 'Who will you go with?' ᴛᴍ (3) draw, pull, drag (something) out *warru-ana kangkanthi* 'to pull, drag (outside)' ᴛᴍ
   kangkalangkala [kangka-l(a)-(k)angka-la] *n* parent, care-giver *shiipi kangkalangkala* 'one who tends or raises sheep (shepherd)' ᴛꜱ
   kangkarri-purka [kangka-rri-purka] *n* woman with many children; mother of many children ᴛꜱ,ᴛᴍ
   kangkarrinthi [kangka-rri-nthi] *v-intr* give birth *Puki kangkarrinana* 'She had been having young.' *Kangkarringkutha pa.* 'She (the dog) is going to have pups.' ᴛꜱ,ᴛᴍ
kangkarlta *n* totemic name; totem generally derived from some animal or natural phenomenon ᴛꜱ,ᴛᴍ
kangkulya *n* seedpod from red gum ᴛꜱ
kantapi *n* (1) tool used for preparing skins ᴛᴍ,ᴄᴀ (2) the preparation of a kangaroo or other skin, which is done by scraping and smoothing the inside ᴛꜱ
   kantapinthi [kantapi-nthi] *v-tr* (1) use a 'kantapi' ᴛꜱ,ᴛᴍ (2) prepare animal skins by scraping ᴛꜱ,ᴛᴍ

kantapi

kantarda *n* (1) vegetable resembling a radish ᴛꜱ,ᴛᴍ (2) radish ɴᴇᴡ
kantarla *n* sweat; perspiration ᴛꜱ,ᴛᴍ,ᴡʏ,ᴘɪ,ᴡɪ,ꜱᴛ
   kantarlangkanthi [kantarla-ngka-nthi] *v-intr* be sweaty, in a sweat ᴛꜱ,ᴛᴍ
   kantarlantinthi [kantarla-nti-nthi] *v-intr* sweat; perspire ᴛᴍ
kantarra *n* basket – for carrying a baby ʙʟ
kanthi *n* (1) thigh ᴛꜱ,ᴡʏ,ᴡɪ,ᴇᴀ,ꜱᴛ,ᴋᴏ (2) leg of lamb ᴛꜱ,ᴡʏ
   kanthi-ana (var. **kanthi-anurla**) *n* pants; trousers ᴛꜱ
   kanthi-apa [kanthi-(y)apa] *n* underpants; underwear; undies ɴᴇᴡ

kanthiuta *n* owl (undefined) ᴘɪ
kantu *n* bullfrog ᴛꜱ
kanu => **kadnu**
kanuitya [kanu-itya] *n* grasshopper (undefined) ᴡʏ
kanumarnguta => **kadnumarnguta**
kanunta *n* mallow plant ᴡʏ
kanya *n* (1) stone, rock ᴛꜱ,ᴛᴍ (2) money ɴᴇᴡ
   kanyanthi [kanya-nthi] *v-tr* stew (in an earth oven); bake (in an earth oven); steam (in an earth oven) ᴛꜱ,ᴛᴍ,ᴡɪ,ꜱᴛ
   kanyawardli [kanya-wardli] *n* bank (financial institution) ɴᴇᴡ
   kanyayapa [kanya-yapa] *n* cooking pit or earth oven ᴛꜱ
kanyanya *n* (1) crowd, big group of people *kanyanya tikanthi* 'to sit in a crowd' ᴛꜱ,ᴛᴍ (2) heap ᴛꜱ
kapa *n* marrow (bone marrow) (bodypart) ᴛꜱ
kapa-apata *n* quail ᴛꜱ,ᴡʏ,ᴄᴏ
kapanthi [kapa-nthi] *v-tr* (1) cast out, send away (someone) ᴛꜱ (2) press (as little stones when lying on them) ᴛꜱ (3) repel, fend off (an attack) ᴛᴍ (4) force off, split (something, as in a wedge splitting wood) ᴛᴍ
   kapakapanthi [kapa-kapa-nthi] *v-tr* be harsh to; be unkind to; treat unkindly; send (someone) away ᴛꜱ,ᴛᴍ
kapi *n* (1) vomit ᴛᴍ,ɢᴀ (2) tobacco ᴛꜱ,ᴡʏ,ʙʟ,ᴘɪ
   kapi marranthi [kapi marra-nthi] vomit ᴛᴍ
   kapinthi [kapi-nthi] *v-intr* vomit; be sick; spit ᴛꜱ,ᴛᴍ,ɢᴀ,ᴘɪ,ᴡʏ
-kapi => **-api**
kararrinthi [kara-rri-nthi] *v-intr* (1) be proud and haughty ᴛꜱ,ᴛᴍ (2) rise over, pass over (something) ᴛᴍ
   kararri-purka [kara-rri-purka] *n* proud person; haughty person ᴛꜱ,ᴛᴍ
Kararru *n* moiety name ᴛɴ
kardalta *adj* blue/green; green/blue ᴛꜱ
kardi *n* emu ᴛꜱ,ᴄᴏ,ᴡʏ,ᴡɪ,ꜱᴛ
   kardiwapa [kardi-wapa] *n* emu feathers in a tuft ᴛꜱ,ᴄᴀ

kardiwarpa

karditpi *n* wart ᴛꜱ
kardla (var. **karla**) *n* (1) fire, flame, burning embers *Kardlarlu ngai ngadli.* 'The fire has burnt me.' *Kardlarlu payanthi.* 'The fire burns (you).' *Kardlapulyu wantith'ai.* 'I will sleep without a fire.' *kardla parranthi* 'to light a fire' *karlarlu panthi* 'to set on fire' ᴛꜱ,ᴛᴍ,ᴡɪ,ʀᴏ,ɢᴀ,ᴋᴏ,ꜱᴛ (2) firewood, kindling, fuel *Kardla katintu'rna!* 'Fetch firewood!' *Kardla piti kurntantu, yalakant'ina mai'athu yungkutha.*

'Cut the wood first, then I will give you some food.' *Kardla wapi-urti, pardi turtu-trrukarringu ngu.* 'Don't touch the wood. The rice will be easily upset.' *Kardlarna katintu'rna, ngu niina wantinki, yuritina niina, kardlangka kumarnila.* 'Fetch the wood you disobedient fellow, or you shall lie near another fire.' TS, TM, WY, GA, KO **(3)** heat, hot *Kardla purruna.* 'It is hot.' TM **(4)** light *tirntu kardlarlu* 'when the sun is shining' TM

   kardla parranthi [kardla parra-nthi] *v-tr* light a fire, kindle a fire

   kardla parrinthi [kardla par-ri-nthi] *v-intr* warm (oneself) TS

   kardla purtultu *n* firestick TM

   kardla tadlanyi *n* flame TM

   kardla-kardlantu [kardla-kardla-ntu] *adj* very hot, heated TS, TM

   kardlapanthi [kardla-pa-nthi] (var. **karlapanthi**) *v-tr* warm (something) TS

   kardlaparti [kardla-parti] *n* native bee TS

   kardlapinti [kardla-pinti] *n* hell TS

   kardlapurruna [kardla-purruna] *adj* still burning TS

   kardlarlu parrinthi [kardla-rlu pa-rri-nthi] *v-tr* warm (something) TM

   kardlayapa [kardla-yapa] *n* **(1)** firepit TS **(2)** hell TS **(3)** oven (wood-fired) NEW

   kardlayirdi [kardla-yirdli] (var. **kardlayiri**; **karlayiri**) *n* light source TS

kardlu-ardlu [kardlu-(k)ardlu] *n* buttocks; upper thighs TS, TM

   kardlumuka [kardlu-muka] *n* testicles TS, TM

   kardluti [kardlu-ti] *n* girdle made of hair or fur TS, TM, CA, WY

karku *n* **(1)** sheoak *(Casuarina)* TS, TM, WY **(2)** small spade or scoop made from sheoak wood TS, TM, EY

   karku-marngu *n* seedpod from sheoak tree TS, WY

karla => **kardla**

karlta *n* shout; call; cry TS, TM, WY

   karlta pathinthi [karlta pathi-nthi] *v-intr* produce a shout TM

   karlta-karltanya [karlta-karlta-nya] *n* **(1)** calling, crying TS **(2)** cryer, bawler TM

   karlta-manthi *v-tr* sing – like Europeans do TS, TM

   karlta-yakarrinthi [karlta-yaka-rri-nthi] *v-intr* run around shouting TM

   karltanthi [karlta-nthi] *v-tr* call; shout; cry *Karltarti!* 'Don't shout!' TS, TM

karlta-thukutya [karlta-thukutya] *n* kneecap; patella TS

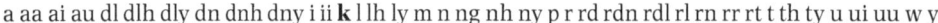
karku

karltapinti [karlta-pinti] *n* inside of the elbow TS, WY

karltathakarra [karlta-thakarra] *n* corpse; dead person *Karltathakarra; padlu warruwarruthi.* 'The corpse; he summoned (it).' *Yaintya ninku karlta-thakarra, yaintya wirntaitpa.* 'Here (is) your corpse, here (is) the spear tip.' TS, TM

karltu *n* **(1)** heart TS, WY, WI, ST **(2)** pit of the stomach TS **(3)** lungs TM

   karltu tartanthi 'shut up' the lungs when dying TM

   karltu turtpurninthi become weak and die of Tuberculosis TM

karltu *n* ant (inch) WY, PI

   karltu-arltuku [karltu-(k)arltu-ku] *n* red-tipped pardalote (bird) CO

   karltukarltunyi [karltu-karltu-nyi] (var. **karltu-arltunyi**) *n* ant (small) TS, PI

karnkanthi [karnka-nthi] *v-tr* **(1)** lift, raise, dig out, draw out *Tinyarrarna parni kawainga! Yalarra ngadlu karnka.* 'Boys come here! We have lifted (the food) out already!' TS, TM, PI **(2)** fend off a spear, block an attack, ward off TM

   karnkati [karnka-ti] *n* **(1)** spoon TS, WI **(2)** handle, spade, string, anything which is used to lift something up TS

karnkinthi *v-intr* laugh TS, GA, RO, WY

karntu *n* **(1)** thunder, lightning TS, TM, GA, WI, WY, ST **(2)** large bird TM **(3)** electricity NEW

   karntiipa [karnt(u)-(p)iipa] *n* email NEW

   karntu nguyuti [karntu nguyu-ti] *n* electric heater NEW

   karntungari [karntu-ngari] *n* electric wire; electric cord NEW

   karntuwarti [karntu-warti] *n* scorpion TS

   karntuyapa [karntu-yapa] *n* electric oven NEW

karnu *n* hill; mountain *karnungka* 'in the hills' TS, TM

   karnu mipurli *n* mountain galaxias (fish) *(Galaxias olidus)* NEW

   Karnu warra *n* a northern dialect TS

karra₁ *n* red gum tree TS, TM, GA, WI, WY, ST

   karra-warnka [karra-warnka] *n* person who has fallen from a gum tree TS

   karrapiri [karra-piri] *n* bedstead TM

   karrawadlu [karra-wadlu] *n* bush, scrub (vegetation) TS

   karrawirra [karra-wirra] *n* forest of red gum trees TS

karra₂ (var. **karta**₂) *loc* high, up, on top, above *Pinti miyurlu nantu kartanangku pirkupi.* 'The white man was shooting from on horseback.' *rapiti wardli karralti* 'over the rabbit's hut' TS,TM,WY

karra mankunthi [karra manku-nthi] *v-tr* pick up; hand up TS

karra manthi [karra ma-nthi] *v-tr* pick up; take; hand over TS

karra nuunthi [karra nhu-(nh)u-nthi] (var. karra nununthi) *v-tr* (1) point upwards TS (2) flourish or brandish weapons at, threaten (someone) TS (3) irritate; challenge; stir up *Kartamirurlu ngurlu, Kadlitpirdlu ngurlu tulyarna karranuunu.* 'That Kartamiru and that Kadlitpi have stirred up the soldiers (caused them to come).' TM

karra-intyarla [karra-intya-rla] *adj* higher, highest TS

karra-karra very high TM

karralika [karra-lika] (1) *loc* on high TM (2) *n* heaven TM (3) *n* spirit world NEW

karrapaka [karra-paka] *adj* shallow; superficial TM

karrawintha [karra-wintha] *n* brown-breasted honeyeater (bird) (*Meliphaga*) WY

karradla (var. **karradlu**; **karraidla**) *loc* far away; distant *karradlunungku* 'from a distance' TS,TM,RO,WI,WY

karraki *n* person whose younger brother has died TS

karrampu mankunthi [karrampu manku-nthi] *v-tr* catch (in your hand) TS,TM

karrampu ngarkunthi [karrampu ngarku-nthi] *v-tr* eat while you walk along TM

Karrauntungga [karra-(k)untu-ngka] *n* Hindmarsh WI,WY,TS

karrinthi [karri-nthi] *v-intr* (1) fly GA,WY,TS (2) stand up TS,TM,WY (3) get out of the way, make room, go off TM,TS

karrikarri! [karri-karri] *intj* get up! get out of the way! *Miiturti! Karrikarringwa!* 'Stop sleeping! Get up! (you two)' WY,RO

karrikarrinya [karri-karri-nya] *adj* flying *pardu karrikarrinya* 'bird (flying meat)' TS

karrikarriti [karri-karri-ti] *n* aeroplane NEW

karriparti [karri-parti] *n* beetle (longicorn/longhorn) WY

karrka₁ *n* dusk; sunset; twilight; sundown *karrkadlu* 'at dusk, during the evening' TS,TM,WY

karrkarlu [karrka-rlu] *temp* tonight (early in the evening) TS

karrkawarri [karrka-warri] *n* evening breeze TS

karrka₂ *n* bream (fish) (*Acanthopagrus butcheri*) WI,WY,ST

karrkala *n* pigface; mesembryanthemum TS,WY

karrkala

karrkanya *n* hawk species TS,WI,WY,CO,ST

karrku (1) *n* red ochre TS,TM,PI,WY,KO (2) *adj* red colour NEW

karrku purdita smooth oval stone used for preparing red ochre TS

karrpa *n* (1) prop, pillar, support (for something) TS,TM (2) pause in a song TM (3) full sentence TM

karrpanthi [karrpa-nthi] *v-tr* support, prop up *Kaurna Warra Karrpanthi* 'KWK – Supporting Kaurna Language' NEW

karta₁ *n* lap TS,TM

karta₂ => **karra₂**

karta₃ *n* scrub; bush; undergrowth WY,PI

karta₄ *n* island; Kangaroo Island *Waatha Karta?* 'Where is Kangaroo Island' TM

karta pakinthi [karta paki-nthi] twist (something) off, work (something) off by turning it TM

karta-arta [karta-(k)arta] *adj* separate; scattered; one after another TM

karta-artarninthi [karta-(k)arta-rni-nthi] *v-intr* separate; scatter *yara karta-artarninthi* 'to scatter or separate from each other' TM

kartaityarri [karta-itya-rri] *adj* compressed TM

kartaka *n* shoulder *kartakidla* '(two) shoulders' *kartakila* 'on the shoulder' TS,TM,KO

Kartamiru [karta-miyu] *n* birth-order name: first born (male) TS,TM,EY,WI,WY,ST

kartantu *n* skin; hide (of large animals) TS,TM

Kartanya (var. **Kartani**) *n* birth-order name: first born (female) TS,TM,EY,WY,WI,KO,ST,CH

karti *n* human blood TM

kartinya [karti-nya] *n* menstruation *kartinya wayinthi* 'to be menstruating, to have your period' TS,TM

kartu *n* wife (wife) TS,TM

kartu-tidli [kartu-tidli] *adj* married (man) TS

kartu-tina [kartu-tina] *adj* unmarried, single (man) TS

kartutangkurla [kartu-tangk(a)-(p)urla] (var. **kartarla**; **kartutarla**) couple, pair, husband and wife TS,TM

katha *n* (1) digging stick TS,CA,WY,AN,KO,CH (2) two-edged fighting stick, club TS,EY,WI,GA,KO (3) mast WI

katha

katha wirri *n* two-edged fighting stick (decorated with streaks like the wirri) CA, EY

kathi *n* (1) exhaustion, weakness, fatigue *Yitpi parltarrinthi kathi-urlu* 'My soul is wearing out from fatigue.' TS, TM (2) hiccup TS

   kathi mintamintarrinthi [kathi minta-minta-rri-nthi] feel fatigued TM

   kathi pudnanthi [kathi pudna-nthi] breathe heavily, becoming exhausted TM

   kathi pudnapudnanthi [kathi pudna-pudna-nthi] breathe heavily, be exhausted TS

   kathinthi [kathi-nthi] *v-intr* (1) breathe heavily due to exhaustion TM (2) hiccup TS

kati *n* crab species PI

katinthi [kati-nthi] *v-tr* (1) fetch, bring *Parni katintu!* 'Bring it here!' *Itu ngaityu yunga-itya katinga!* 'Bring these to my elder brother!' TS, TM, WY (2) carry (somewhere) *Angkilirna katithi Apramirna karta-ana* 'The angels carried him to Abraham's bosom.' TS, TM, WY

   katirrinthi [kati-rri-nthi] *v-intr* fetch TS

katpa *n* facial hair WY

katpa-atpa [katpa-(k)atpa] *n* parakeet; parrot species (small) TS, PI, WY

katpamartu [katpa-martu] *n* wattlebird PI

katparntu (var. **katparnta**) *n* temples TS, TM, KO

katparti *n* pillow *Purdi katpartila wanti mukarta.* 'the head has a stone for its pillow.' TS, TM

katpikama *n* capsicum NEW (from English 'capsicum')

katpinthi [katpi-nthi] *v-intr* (1) look sad, dejected, sullen, morose TS (2) be sad, dejected, sullen, morose TS

   katpirrinthi [katpi-rri-nthi] (var. **katpi-katpirrinthi**) *v-intr* (1) wait for (someone) *Ninku warrarna ngai katpirr-utha.* 'I will await your commands.' TM (2) be in a serious frame of mind, meditate, sit in deep thought TM

katungki *n* large shrike (bird) WY

Kaurna *n* Adelaide Plains people, language of the Adelaide Plains WY (from Ngarrindjeri *kornar* 'men, people')

kauwa (1) *n* cliff face; precipice *kauwangka wankurrinthi* 'to climb up a precipice' TS, TM (2) *adj* steep TS

   kauwamarlta [kauwa-marlta] *n* cliff edge TM

kauwani *n* father-in-law (of a man) TM

   kauwanata [kauwana-ta] *n* father-in-law relationship TM

kauwanu *n* maternal uncle (i.e. mother's brother) WY

kauwawa *n* cousin (mother's brother's/father's sister's child) TS, TM, BA, WY

kauwi *n* water TS, TM, BL, GA, RO, WI, WY, ST, KO, CH

   kauwi nguyuti *n* water heater NEW

   kauwi tartanthi [kauwi tarta-nthi] occupy the water TM

   kauwiku [kauwi-ku] *n* steam TS

   kauwimiila [kauwi-miila] *n* (1) drizzling rain TS (2) small drops of water, e.g. spray from a whale TS

   kauwirlta [kauw(i)-(p)irlta] *n* platypus NEW

   kauwirninthi [kauwi-rni-nthi] *v-intr* get wet *kauwirnituwayi yarta* 'lest the floor get wet' TM

   kauwirrka [kauw(i)-irrka] (var. **kawirrka**) (1) *n* broth, gravy TS, TM (2) *adj* wet, full of water, soaked TS (3) *n* sauce NEW

   kauwiyapa [kauwi-yapa] *n* indentation above the collarbone TS

kawai! *intj* come! *kawai wangka'dli* 'let us come and talk' *parni kawai!* 'come hither! come here!' *miyu kawai* 'someone is coming' TS, TM, WY, BL, RO, WI, KO, CH

   kawainga! *v-imp* come here! (you plural) TM

   kawaingwa! *v-imp* come here! (you dual) TM

kawana *n* bald coot; swamp hen ST, TS

kawanta *n* north *Cowandilla (kawantila)* 'in the north' *kawantukana, kawantuana* 'to the north' TM, WY

   kawarta *dir* northerly TM

kawapupa *n* mountain parrot ST

kawu *n* topknot pigeon TS

kaya *n* spear which is thrown with the midla TS, TM, WY, CA, GA, WI, ST

   kayamunthu [kaya-munthu] *n* (1) stem of yakka TS (2) shaft of spear TS

   kayarrka [kaya-rrka] *adj* tall and thin; slender TM

   kayawari [kaya-wari] *n* spearpoint KO

kidlala *adj* (1) loose; shaky TS, TM (2) wavering or tottering; unstable TS, TM

kilyala => **ilyala**

kirrki *n* tree sap or resin TS

kitikitinthi [kiti-kiti-nthi] *v-tr* tickle TS

   kitilitila [kiti-l(a)-(k)iti-la] *n* a person who tickles TS

kitya *adj* salty; bitter (taste) TS, TM

kiwiti *n* squid NEW (from English 'squid')

kiyakawukutu *n* kookaburra ST

ku *n* steam ᴛᴍ

ku! *intj* okay; alright ᴛᴍ

ku(k)arrinthi => **kurrinthi**

kudla *adv* (1) alone, separate, by one's self / itself *Kudla'athu wapi-utha.* 'I will do it myself.' *Kudla wantinku.* 'It shall lie by itself.' *Kudla wantantu!* 'Let it be!' *Kudla ngadli miyurti tikanthi* 'We are alone, without a man.' ᴛꜱ,ᴛᴍ (2) in vain, for no reason, pointlessly ᴛꜱ

    kudlaityapinthi [kudla-itya-pi-nthi] *v-tr* reserve; keep aside *Maiyarta ngadluku padlu-unungku kudlaityapi.* 'He has reserved farm land for us.' ᴛᴍ

    kudlayurlu [kudla-yurlu] *adj* (1) quiet, peaceable ᴛꜱ (2) moping, sitting by one's self ᴛᴍ

kudlila *n* winter ᴛꜱ,ᴛᴍ,ᴡɪ,ꜱᴛ

    kudlilurlu [kudlil(a)-urlu] *temp* during the winter ᴛᴍ

kudlinthi [kudli-nthi] *v-tr* wash; clean ᴛꜱ,ᴛᴍ

    kudli kuu *n* bathroom ɴᴇᴡ

    kudlikuru [kudli-kuru] *n* sink; wash basin; bath ɴᴇᴡ

    kudlinyangkanthi [kudli-nya-ngka-nthi] *v-tr* do the dishes, wash the dishes ᴛᴍ

    kudlirrinthi [kudli-rri-nthi] *v-intr* wash (oneself) ᴛꜱ,ᴛᴍ

    kudlithirntu [kudli-thirntu] *n* bathtime ɴᴇᴡ

    kudliti [kudli-ti] *n* washing machine ɴᴇᴡ

kudlu *n* native louse ᴛꜱ,ᴛᴍ,ᴡʏ,ᴋᴏ

kudlyu *n* black swan (*Cygnus atratus*) ᴛꜱ,ɢᴀ,ᴄᴏ,ᴘɪ,ᴡʏ

kudmu *n* dew; fog ᴛꜱ,ᴛᴍ

kudna *n* (1) faeces, excrement, poo (of humans), shit, dung ᴛꜱ,ᴛᴍ (2) small intestines; bowels *Matumidla tarnparrinthi kudnangka.* 'The spleen is attached to the guts' ᴛᴍ

kudnanthi [kudna-nthi] *v-tr* disembowel; eviscerate; gut ᴛꜱ

    kudnapanthi [kudna-pa(a)-nthi] *v-tr* smear (something) with faeces ᴛꜱ

    kudnapurtu [kudna-purtu] *adj* (1) dirty, full of faeces, shitty, daggy (sheep) ᴛꜱ (2) full of shit, talking rubbish, bullshit (nonsense) ɴᴇᴡ

    kudnatinthi [kudna-ti-nthi] *v-intr* defecate; poo; shit; evacuate the bowels ᴛꜱ,ᴛᴍ

    kudnawardli [kudna-wardli] *n* toilet ᴛꜱ

-kudna *suff* (on nouns) stingy with *maikudna* 'someone who won't share food' ᴛꜱ,ᴛᴍ

Kudnartu [kudnu-(k)artu] *n* birth-order name: third born (female) ᴛꜱ,ᴇʏ,ᴡʏ

kudnu (1) *adj* innocent, guiltless ᴛꜱ (2) *adv* without reason ᴛꜱ

    kudnuna [kudnu-na] *adj* ignorant; innocent ᴛꜱ

Kudnuitya [kudnu-itya] *n* birth-order name: third born (male) ᴛꜱ,ᴇʏ,ᴡɪ,ᴡʏ,ꜱᴛ

kuikuru *loc* in the rain ᴛᴍ

kuinga *n* heron ɢᴀ

kuingkukuingkula [kuingku-kuingku-la] *n* nasal bone ᴛꜱ

kuinpinthi [kuinpi-nthi] *v-tr* (1) chew (something) ᴛᴍ (2) think (something) over, consider ᴛᴍ

    kuinpi kangkanthi [kuinpi kangka-nthi] *v-tr* remember (after trying to recall something) ᴛᴍ

kuinyu *n* (1) dead person, skeleton ᴛꜱ,ᴛᴍ,ᴡʏ (2) death personified, devil, evil monster *kuinyurlu katinthi* 'to be taken away by death' ᴛꜱ,ᴛᴍ,ᴄᴀ,ᴇʏ,ɢᴀ,ᴡʏ (3) European, white person ᴛʀᴀᴅ

    kuinyu murrkanthi [kuinyu murrka-nthi] *v-intr* lament for a dead person ᴛꜱ,ᴛᴍ

    kuinyu purtpurrinthi [kuinyu purtpu-rri-nthi] *v-tr* speak of the dead ᴛꜱ,ᴛᴍ

    kuinyunta [kuinyu-nta] *adj* (1) sacred, forbidden *kuinyunta mai* 'food that is forbidden to eat' ᴛꜱ,ᴛᴍ,ᴡɪ,ᴡʏ,ꜱᴛ (2) dangerous, lethal, bringing death ᴛꜱ

    kuinyuntapinthi [kuinyu-nta-(wa)pi-nthi] *v-tr* revere; consider sacred or forbidden ᴛꜱ,ᴛᴍ

    kuinyurninthi [kuinyu-rni-nthi] *v-intr* die ᴛᴍ

kuiyu (1) *adj* ill, sick, painful ᴛꜱ,ᴛᴍ (2) *n* pain, illness, sickness ᴛᴍ

    kuiyurninthi [kuiyu-rni-nthi] *v-intr* get sick ᴛᴍ

kukanthi [kuka-nthi] *v-tr* (1) scrape, scratch (something) *Pirri-urlu'athu tidna kukanthi* 'I scratch the foot with the nail' ᴛꜱ,ᴛᴍ,ᴡʏ (2) dig (with the hand in loose soil) (not deeply) *tudnu wari kukanthi* 'to always dig in a zig zag' ᴛꜱ,ᴛᴍ,ᴡʏ

    kukalukala [kuka-l(a)-(k)uka-la] *n* person who digs or scrapes, labourer, miner ᴛꜱ

    kukarrinthi [kuka-rri-nthi] *v-intr* (1) cry; scream; weep ᴛꜱ,ᴡʏ (2) scratch oneself ᴛᴍ

    kukarriti [kuka-rri-ti] *n* itch; scratching ᴛꜱ,ᴛᴍ,ᴡʏ

kukanyi *n* prop; support ᴛᴍ

kukatka *n* kookaburra ᴛᴍ,ᴡʏ

kuku (1) *adj* sore, sick, painful, ill, wounded ᴛꜱ,ᴛᴍ,ᴡʏ (2) *n* disease, sickness, wound, sore *kuku ngarntanthi* 'to have or be suffering from a sore or illness' ᴛꜱ,ᴛᴍ,ᴡɪ,ꜱᴛ

    kukurninthi [kuku-rni-nthi] *v-intr* become sore, ill or diseased ᴛᴍ,ᴛꜱ

    kukutina [kuku-tina] *adj* healthy, free from disease ᴛꜱ

kukuwardli [kuku-wardli] *n* hospital_NEW

kulturnta *n* snoring_TS, TM

kulurdu *n* noise_TS

kulurdu tirntu *n* alarm clock_NEW

kuma (1) *num* one_TS, TM, WY, WI, ST, KO, CH (2) *adv* also, too *Niina kuma.* 'You too.'_TS (3) *pro* another (indefinite, ergative) *kumanurlu* 'another'_TS

kuma mamaityarri [kuma (ku)ma(ku) ma-itya-rri] *adv* gradually; one after another_TM

kuma marnkutyila [kuma marnkuty(a)-ila] *num* third (fraction)_NEW

kuma miyu a stranger_TS

kuma paintya [kuma paintya] *loc* on the other side; opposite_TM

kuma partirrka [kuma part(u)-irrka] *num* one hundred_NEW

kuma partirrka kuma [kuma part(u)-irrka kuma] *num* one hundred and one_NEW

kuma pukilyarlu [kuma puki-lya-rlu] the day before yesterday_TS, TM

kuma purlaityila [kuma purlaity(a)-ila] *num* half_NEW

kuma yarapurlangka *num* quarter_NEW

kumangka [kuma-ngka] *adj* together_TM

kuma-kumangka [kuma-kuma-ngka] one after another_TM

kumangka malturri-apinthi [kuma-ngka maltu-rri-(w)api-nthi] *v-tr* assemble; collect; gather_TS

kumangka malturrinthi [kuma-ngka maltu-rri-nthi] *v-intr* stay together; remain in a group_TS

kumanti [kuma-nti] only one_TM, WI, ST

kumanti wapiwarra karrpa *n* simple sentence_NEW

kumanu *pro* another_NEW

kumanukana [kumanu-kana] to another (allative)_TM

kumanurlu *pro* another; someone (ergative)_TS, TM

kumapurtu *adv* all together; all at once; simultaneously_TS, TM

kumarluku [kuma-rluku] *adv* once_TS, TM

kumarlukunti [kuma-rluku-nti] only once_TS, TM

kumarru [kumarru] *adv* individually_TM

kumarta [kuma-rta] *adj* (1) different, distinct, separate *Wardlingka kumartila wanti ngai.* 'I will sleep in a different house.'_TS (2) own, belonging to one's self *Pintiwityu ngai yungkuntu kumarta-tangka! Yangadlinti mukantarrituwayi.* 'Give me a needle of my own! Later on you might forget (it).'_TM

kumartapinthi [kuma-rt(a)-(w)api-nthi] *v-tr* (1) separate, divide (people, things)_TS (2) keep, retain, reserve (for oneself)_TM

kumauwata [kum(a)-(th)awata] *num* one thousand_NEW

Kumiki [kum(a)-(p)iki] *n* January_NEW

Kumirntu [kum(a)-(th)irntu] *n* Monday_NEW

kumirrka [kum(a)-irrka] *num* ten_NEW

kumirrka kuma [kum(a)-irrka kuma] *num* eleven_NEW

kumirrka kumiwurra [kum(a)-irrka kum(a)-(w)iwurra] *num* eleven million_NEW

kumirrka marnkutyi [kum(a)-irrka marnkutyi] *num* thirteen_NEW

kumirrka marru [kum(a)-irrka marru] *num* sixteen_NEW

kumirrka mila [kum(a)-irrka mila] *num* fifteen_NEW

kumirrka ngarla [kum(a)-irrka ngarla] *num* eighteen_NEW

kumirrka pauwa [kum(a)-irrka pauwa] *num* nineteen_NEW

kumirrka purlaityi [kum(a)-irrka purlaityi] *num* twelve_NEW

kumirrka purliwurra [kum(a)-irrka purl(aityi)-(w)iwurra] *num* twelve million_NEW

kumirrka wangu [kum(a)-irrka wangu] *num* seventeen_NEW

kumirrka yarapurla [kum(a)-irrka yarapurla] *num* fourteen_NEW

Kumirrkaiki [kum(a)-irrka-(p)iki] *n* October_NEW

kumirrkawata [kum(a)-irrk(a)-(th)awata] *num* ten thousand_NEW

kumirrkiwurra [kum(a)-irrk(a)-(w)iwurra] *num* ten million_NEW

kumiwurra [kum(a)-(w)iwurra] *num* one million_NEW

kumaranki *n* fungus species_PI

kumarru *n* name for a relative (undefined)_TS

kumatpi *adv* quickly; fast_TS, TM

kuma-kumatpi very quickly_TM

kumpanthi [kumpa-nthi] *v-intr* leave; disappear *Warti takanila warra kumpanthi.* 'The (sound of the) speech disappears in the large space.' *Kumpaninyana, padlu kunta.* 'Because (she) had gone away, he beat (her).' *Kumpanina ngathu yailtya.* 'I thought (the rain) had gone.' *Pa inuntya kumpi.* 'He's left this place.' *Parna kumpanintyidla, niinanti parni padningki.* 'After they have gone, you alone come here.'_TS, TM, WI, ST

kumpa-kumpanthi [kumpa-kumpa-nthi] go away forever, leave for good and not return ᴛᴍ

kumpapinthi [kumpa-(wa)pi-nthi] *v-tr* remove; make someone leave ᴛᴍ

kumpapiti [kumpa-(wa)pi-ti] *n* eraser ɴᴇᴡ

kumpu (var. **kumpurra**) *n* (1) urine, pee ᴛs,ᴛᴍ,ᴡʏ (2) rainbow *miyu kumpu* 'the male or outer rainbow' *ngamaitya kumpu* 'the female or inner rainbow' ᴡʏ

kumputinthi [kumpu-ti-nthi] *v-intr* urinate; pee; piss *Kumputinth'ai (or) Kumputi'ngai* 'I am urinating' ᴛs,ᴛᴍ

kumpulya *n* ant species ᴛs

kumpurru *n* pubic bone ᴛs

kumumardi *n* constellation name ᴛs

kunadna *n* female wallaby ᴡɪ,sᴛ

Kunakaya Marrutya *n* personal name (male) ᴡʏ

kunga *n* son ᴛɪ

kungarrinthi [kunga-rri-nthi] *v-intr* (1) smell *Ngarrpa pia kungarrinina nakuthi.* 'Perhaps (the cat) has perceived the smell of a mouse.' ᴛs,ᴛᴍ (2) cause a smell, stink, smell bad ᴛᴍ,ᴡʏ

kungkurla *n* yabby, freshwater crayfish *(Cherax destructor)* ᴛs,ᴛᴍ,ᴡɪ,ᴡʏ,ᴋᴏ,sᴛ

kungkurra *n* breakers; surf; foam of the ocean ᴛs

kungkurri *n* edible gum; edible sap ᴛs,ᴡʏ

kuntanyi *n* (1) flower of the banksia, native honeysuckle tree ᴛᴍ (2) sweet water that has had tarnma soaked in it ᴛs (3) cordial, soft drink ɴᴇᴡ

kuntanyimai [kuntanyi-mai] *n* orange (fruit) ɴᴇᴡ

kuntaru *n* spear adorned with feathers (ceremonial) ᴘɪ

Kunthi *n* Chinese or Asian person ᴛʀᴀᴅ (from Ngarrindjeri 'bald')

kunthikuru [kunthi-kuru] *n* wok ɴᴇᴡ

kunti *n* edible root (red) ᴛs

kuntimarntu [kunti-marntu] *n* virgin; woman before having children ᴛs,ᴛᴍ

kuntipaitya [kunti-paitya] *n* mosquito ᴛs,ᴛᴍ,ᴡʏ

kuntipaitya kuya [kunti-paitya kuya] *n* mosquitofish *(Gambusia affinis/holbrooki)* ɴᴇᴡ

kuntu₁ *n* (1) chest (bodypart), associated with strong feelings such as courage, hatred and thirst ᴛs,ᴛᴍ,ɢᴀ,ᴡɪ,sᴛ,ᴋᴏ (2) anything that sticks out like the chest ᴛᴍ

kuntu manka striped scars on the chest ᴛs

kuntu pakurta round ornamental scars on the chest ᴛs

kuntu pamanthi [kuntu pama-nthi] *v-tr* hate; dislike ᴛᴍ

kuntu pungkunthi [kuntu pungku-nthi] *v-tr* hate; dislike ᴛᴍ

kuntu pungkurrinthi [kuntu pungku-rri-nthi] *v-intr* (1) be concerned about (someone) *Kuntu pungkurrinth'ai ngaityu yungaku.* 'I am concerned about (or long for) my brother.' ᴛᴍ (2) be sorry (for someone) ᴛᴍ (3) be anxious, uneasy, longing ᴛs (4) linger, mope, brood ᴛs

kuntu pungkurripurka [kuntu pungku-rri-purka] *n* anxious person ᴛs

kuntu warpu (1) *n* the chest bone *(sternum)* ᴛs,ᴡʏ (2) *adj* thirsty ᴛᴍ

kuntu warpurninthi [kuntu warpu-rni-nthi] *v-tr* (1) want, desire, wish or long for *Kauwitya kuntu warpurninth'ai.* 'I really want water.' ᴛs,ᴛᴍ (2) be thirsty, long for water ᴛᴍ

kuntu wilta *adj* brave, bold, courageous ᴛᴍ

kuntu wirri *n* scars on the chest ᴛs

kuntu yartarninthi [kuntu yarta-rni-nthi] *v-intr* be calm; be content; be comfortable *kuntu yartarninthi miyungka* 'to like someone's company' *Kuntu yartarninth'ai nintaityangka.* 'I feel comfortable with you.' ᴛᴍ

kuntu yartarrinthi [kuntu yarta-rri-nthi] *v-intr* be anxious, worried, concerned ᴛᴍ

kuntumuka [kuntu-muka] *n* chest of a man ᴛs

kunturrkinthi [kunturrki-nthi] *v-intr* be proud; stick your chest out ᴛᴍ

kuntu₂ *n* flood, deluge, very big inundation ᴛᴍ

kuntunthi [kuntu-nthi] *v-tr* (1) wash (something) ᴛs (2) beat the water with your hand, splashing it (on someone) ᴛᴍ

kunturrinthi [kuntu-rri-nthi] *v-intr* wash (oneself); bathe ᴛs,ᴛᴍ

kunturu [kuntu-ru] *n* rain ᴛs

kunturu katiti [kuntu-rdu kati-ti] *n* umbrella ᴛs

kuntuli *n* whale, blubber (from a whale) ᴛs,sᴛ,ᴡʏ,ᴡɪ

kuntuli kardlayirdi *n* oil lamp ᴛs

kuntuli paitpurla whale oil ᴛs

kuntyi *n* fringe worn around the waist ᴛs,ᴛᴍ,ᴄᴀ

kunyu *n* phyllium; leaf insect ᴡʏ

kupapinthi [kup(a)-(w)api-nthi] *v-tr* forsake; abandon ᴛs,ᴛᴍ

kupayinthi [kup(a)-(w)ayi-nthi] *v-intr* leave secretly; sneak off *naingu kupayinthi* 'to sneak away quietly' *Kutyunurlu miyurlu kupayi miitu wantinina.* 'After the other had gone to sleep he absconded.' ᴛs,ᴛᴍ

kupi *n* grub found in the redgum tree; bombyx ᴛs,ᴡʏ

kupiti *n* mattress; bedding ᴛs,ᴛᴍ

kupirdi! *intj* okay! go ahead! TS

kupurlu *n* (1) seawater, salt water TS, TM, GA, RO, WY (2) alcohol, grog, liquor, intoxicating spirits TS, WY, KO, CH

  kupurluwardli [kupurlu-wardli] *n* hotel NEW

kuraitya *n* mullet (fish) (*Aldrichetta forsteri*) WY

kuraka *n* white gum tree WY

kurda *loc* nearby; close; here *Nata ngai padnitha, niina kurda*. 'I will go now, you (stay) here.' *Kurda papaltu-arra tarralyi ngatpainga*. 'Put the fence alongside the stump.' TS, TM, RO, WY

  kurdakarra [kurda-karra] superficial, on the surface, in the shallows TS, TM

  kurdanta [kurda-nta] *loc* near; close by *Kurdanta padlu wanta*. 'He left (him) close by.' *Kurdantanta pa murinthi*. 'He quickly comes near.' TS, TM, WI, WY, ST

  kurda-kurdanthi [kurda-kurda-nthi] *v-tr* bring; deposit *Wakwaku padlu nintaitya kurdakurda*. 'He brought his child to you.' TM

  kurdantarninthi [kurda-nta-rni-nthi] *v-intr* come close; draw near *Kurdantarni'ngai*. 'I (will) draw nearer.' TM

  kurdanthi [kurda-nthi] *v-intr, v-tr* (1) approach, come near (to something) TS, WI (2) touch, feel (something) TS (3) bring (something) near TM, WI, ST

  kurdapurka [kurda-purka] *n* home body, person fond of staying home TS

  kurdarrinthi [kurda-rri-nthi] *v-intr* approach; come near TS

kurdaki *n* white cockatoo TS, CO, WI, ST

  kurdaki yuri *n* native flax *Kurdaki yuri-unungku turnki pingka* 'He has made the cloth of flax' TS

kurdana *n* noon; midday TS, TM

  kurdana mai *n* lunch; midday meal TS

kurdantana [kurda-nta-na] *adv* voluntarily; independently *Kurdantana ngathu yarltinthi*. 'on my own accord I forbid them.' TM

  kurdantarnangku [kurda-nta-na-ngku] *adv* of (his/her) own will TM

kurdanyi *n* (1) rainbow TS, TM, WY (2) colour NEW

  kurdanyi kuya *n* Murray rainbowfish (*Melanotaenia fluviatilis*) NEW

  kurdanyi mipurli *n* rainbow trout (*Oncorhynchus mykiss*) NEW

kurdi *n* (1) circle, compass TS (2) dance performed at ceremonies by 'wirra miyu' – men from the northern district (around Para river and Gawler) TS, TM, PI, WI, WY, ST (3) song performed by women at these ceremonies *Kurdirti! '*Don't sing! Be silent!' TS

  kurdimai [kurdi-mai] *n* pizza NEW

kurdingkainthi [kurdi-ngka-nthi] *v-intr* form a circle; sit in a circle TM

kurdinthi [kurdi-nthi] (var. **kuyinthi**) *v-tr* (1) surround, make a circle (around something), tie a rope or string (around something), gird *Kuyikuyirri pa*. 'He's tangled himself up (in a rope).' *Nganangka ngathu kurdikurditha mai?* 'What should I tie the food up with?' TS, TM (2) avoid mentioning the dead or certain words associated with them TM

kurdirri-apinthi [kurdi-rri-(w)api-nthi] *v-tr* (1) enclose; fence in TS, TM (2) cause to encircle or go around about (something) TM

kurdirrinthi [kurdi-rri-nthi] (var. **kuyirrinthi**) *v-intr* go around something TS, TM

kurditi [kurdi-ti] *n* perimeter fence NEW

kurdu *n* crown of the head; scalp TS, TM, WY

  kurdu-itya on account of shame TM

  kurdu-wiltarninthi [kurdu-wilta-rni-nthi] *v-intr* become cheeky or rude TS, TM

  kurdukarri [kurdu-karri] *n* shame or embarrassment TS

  kurdukarri-apinthi [kurdu-karri-(w)api-nthi] *v-tr* embarrass someone; make someone blush; shame someone TM

  kurdukarrinthi [kurdu-karri-nthi] *v-intr* blush; be embarrassed; feel ashamed TS, TM

  kurduthura [kurdu-tura] *n* parasol TS

  kurduwilta [kurdu-wilta] *adj* rude; cheeky TS, TM

  kurdu-anta [kurdu-anta] *n* globular vessel (shaped like a kurdu) TM

kuri-kuri *n* young emu WY

kurka *n* kangaroo rat TS, TM, PI, WY

kurla *adv* afterwards; alone; separate; empty; last TS, TM

  kurla-intyarlu [kurla-intya-rlu] *adj* later; more recent TS

  kurla-ityu [kurla-ityu] *adv* (1) quickly, fast TS (2) too quickly *Miyu kurlaityu padni ngai, niputina ngaityu. – Kupirdi, wantarrinthi niina*. 'The men go too fast for me, without a companion. – Ok, you stay behind.' TM **kurlakurlana** [kurla-kurla-na] (var. **kurlakurlanta**) *n* (1) youngest in the family TS, TM (2) favourite child TS

kurlana [kurla-na] (1) *adj* contemporary; recent; modern; new; later *kurlana miyu* 'a contemporary (peer)' TS (2) *n* child generation; youngest generation; progeny TM

kurlangka [kurla-ngka] *loc, temp* apart from; in someone's absence *Parnu kurlangka kuntu pungkurrinth'adlu*. 'In his absence we feel anxious and lonely.' TM

kurlantu [kurla-ntu] *n* stepfather ₜₛ,ₜₘ

kurlapulthu [kurla-pulthu] *n* emptiness *tii kurlapulthu* 'run out of tea' *Kurlapulthu niina wangkanthi.* 'You speak but no one listens to you.' ₜₘ

kurlinthi [kurli-nthi] *v-tr* rub; clean; erase ₜₛ,ₜₘ

kurliti [kurli-ti] *n* brush ₜₛ

Kurltataku *n* name of a Dreaming being ₜₛ

kurlti *n* (1) cough, cold ₜₛ,ₜₘ,ᴡʏ (2) sputum; phlegm that has been coughed up; expectorated matter ₜₛ

kurlti mingka a painful cough ᴡʏ

kurlti ngarntanthi [kurlti ngarnta-nthi] have a cold ₜₘ

kurltinthi [kurlti-nthi] *v-intr* cough ₜₛ,ₜₘ

kurltu *adj* (1) short, small, little *Wilya kurltungka tikanthi pa.* 'He is sitting amongst the short leaves.' ₜₛ,ₜₘ,ᴡʏ (2) in (two) pieces *kurltu wayinthi* 'to go to pieces' ₜₛ

kurltirntu [kurlt(u)-(th)irntu] *n* solstice (winter) ɴᴇᴡ

kurltu pakinthi [kurltu paki-nthi] *v-tr* cut something into short pieces ₜₘ

kurlturninthi [kurltu-rni-nthi] *v-intr* become short/small, decrease in size ₜₘ

kurlturru [kurltu-rru] *adj* very short *ngari kurlturrila* 'on a very short rope' ₜₘ

kurlu (var. **kurlyu**) *n* red kangaroo (female) ₜₛ,ₜₘ,ᴡɪ,ꜱᴛ

kurlutumi *n* periwinkle (shellfish) ᴘɪ,ᴡʏ

kurlwi *n* sheoak *(Casuarina)* ᴡʏ

kurnta₁ *n* wallaby ₜₛ

kurntanthi [kurnta-nthi] *v-tr* kill; beat; hit; cut; strike; fight *kardla kurntanthi* 'to cut firewood' *kurntanana yailtya!* '(I) thought (he) had been killed.' *Miyu ngadlu kurntanma, ngadlu pinti miyurlu mankuma padlu; titatitapimanta.* 'If we had killed a man, the white man would have seized us; hanged us even!' *Kurntaninyana ngai wangkanthi.* 'Because (they) have beaten (me) I am speaking.' ₜₛ,ₜₘ,ᴡɪ,ᴡʏ,ꜱᴛ,ᴄʜ

kurntarrinthi [kurnta-rri-nthi] *v-intr* beat (one's self; each other); cut (one's self; each other); kill (one's self; each other) ₜₘ

kurntarriti [kurnta-rri-ti] (var. **kurnta**₂) *n* beating *kurntarritingka* 'because of or on account of the beating' ʙʟ

kurraka *n* magpie ₜₛ,ᴄᴏ,ᴡɪ,ꜱᴛ,ᴡʏ

kurrayi *n* legless lizard ᴡʏ

kurrinthi [ku-(ka)-rri-nthi] (var. **ku(k)arrinthi**) *v-intr* steam ₜₛ,ₜₘ

kurrka *n* grey butcherbird *(Cracticus torquatus)* ᴄᴏ

kurrkinthi [kurrki-nthi] *v-tr* (1) swallow (something) ₜₛ,ₜₘ,ᴡʏ (2) devour, consume, scoff (something) down ₜₘ

kurrkintya *n* quail species ₜₛ,ʀᴏ

kurrkunthi [kurrku-nthi] *v-tr* (1) curse, wish evil on someone ₜₛ,ₜₘ (2) enchant, bewitch, conjure, cast a spell on someone ₜₘ

kurrkurrinthi [kurrku-rri-nthi] *v-intr* bewitch oneself, be enchanted ₜₘ

kurrkuti [kurrku-ti] *n* magical substance, spell ₜₘ

kurrkurla *n* (1) fat, grease ₜₛ (2) moisture or fat exuded by a corpse when it is left in the sun ₜₘ

kurrkurra *n* boy; young man ₜₛ

kurrkukurrkurra [kurrku-kurrkurra] *n* Orion (constellation) ₜₛ

kurrpu *n* stuff; furniture; tools; belongings ₜₛ

kurrunthi [kurru-nthi] (var. **kurrurrinthi**) *v-intr* blow ₜₛ,ₜₘ

kurruta [kurru-ta] *n* sneezing ₜₛ,ᴡʏ,ₜₘ

kurruti [kurru-ti] *n* breeze; wind ₜₛ

kurrutinthi [kurru-ta-nthi] (var. **kurrutunthi**) *v-intr* sneeze ₜₛ,ₜₘ,ᴡɪ,ꜱᴛ

kurruru *n* circle *kurruru mankunthi* 'to form a circle' ₜₛ,ₜₘ

kurru-angku [kurru-angku] *n* ceremony of the Murray people ₜₛ

kurta *n* (1) side, nearness, closeness (to something) *ninku kurtangka* 'near you, at your side, in your neighbourhood' ₜₛ,ₜₘ (2) protection, patronage *Parnu kurtangka ngadlu tikathi.* 'We have been living under his protection' ₜₘ

kurta-kurtarrinthi [kurta-kurta-rri-nthi] *v-tr* (1) leave, abandon, give-up (something) *yarlina kurta-kurtarrinthi* 'to leave one's husband' *yurlu kurta-kurtarrinthi* 'to turn your face away, to look away from something' ₜₘ (2) despise, look-down on, offend (someone) ₜₘ

kurtanthi [kurta-nthi] (1) *v-intr* lie on one side ₜₛ (2) *v-tr* leave (home), leave (someone) behind *Nganaitya nintu ngai kurta-kurtanthi? Parni kawai! Parni parni wanti!* 'Why are you leaving me? Come here! Stay here!' ₜₘ

kurtapiku [kurta-piku] *n* waist ₜₛ,ₜₘ

kurtarra padninthi [kurta-rra padni-nthi] pass close by someone ₜₘ

kurtarri-apinthi [kurta-rri-(w)api-nthi] *v-tr* direct a horse ₜₘ

kurtarrinthi [kurta-rri-nthi] *v-intr* be/feel left out ɴᴇᴡ

kurta-unyu *n* little finger ᴛs

kurtaka *n* joey; young kangaroo ᴛs,ᴡʏ

kurti *n* quandong; seedpod of pittosporum ᴡʏ,ᴛʀᴀᴅ

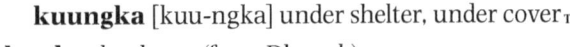
kurti

kurturrinthi [kurtu-rri-nthi] *v-intr* (1) mope; be sad ᴛs,ᴛᴍ (2) meditate ᴛᴍ (3) be dejected ᴛs,ᴛᴍ (4) be tired ᴛᴍ

kuru *n* (1) yakka or grass tree (*Xanthorrhoea*) ᴛs,ᴛᴍ (2) pot, bowl, cask, box (any vessel). kettle, container ᴛs,ᴛᴍ,ᴡɪ,ᴡʏ,sᴛ (3) fire-making tools (made from two sticks of the grass tree, each about 60cm long) ᴄᴀ

kuru (2)

  kuru yarnta a round, globular container ᴛᴍ

kutarri *n* older sister (deceased) ᴛᴍ

kutinthi [kuti-nthi] *v-tr* repeat ᴛs

  kutikutini [kuti-kuti-ni] *adv* repeatedly ᴛᴍ

  kutini [kuti-ni] *adv* again *Kutini pa pulthurni*. 'She had run off again.' ᴛᴍ,ᴡʏ

kutpanthi [kutpa-nthi] (var. **kutpakutpanthi**) *v-tr* shake; move; agitate *mara kutpakutpanthi* 'shake hands' ᴛs,ᴛᴍ

kutpi *n* toy spear; sham spear ᴛs,ᴛᴍ,ᴄᴀ,ᴡʏ

kutpuru [kutpuru] *adv* not yet ᴛs,ᴛᴍ

kutyu (1) *adj* little, few; remaining; some ᴛs,ᴛᴍ (2) *n* the rest, the remainder *Waa kutyu miyurna?* 'Where are the rest of the men?' *Kutyuarna parni warruwarruntu'rna!* 'Call the rest of the men!' **kutyunurla** 'the rest (dual)' **kutyuarna, kutyunurna** 'the rest (plural)' ᴛs,ᴛᴍ,ᴡʏ (3) *n* another *Kutyunila warlingka ngai wantithi*. 'I slept in another house.' ᴛᴍ

kutyunti [kutyu-nti] *adj* just a little; just a few; only a little; only a few ᴛs,ᴛᴍ

kuu (var. **kuukuu**) *n* (1) cover; shelter *Kuu yaku pudnituwayi panyiwartarlu*. '(I'm worried that) (he) might be without shelter in the morning.' ᴛs,ᴛᴍ (2) room ɴᴇᴡ

kuru (3)

kutpi

  kuu manyapiti [kuu many(a)-(w)api-ti] *n* fridge; refrigerator ɴᴇᴡ

  kuukuu yarltirrinthi [kuu-kuu yarlti-rri-nthi] *v-tr* prohibit; prevent ᴛᴍ

  kuukuu-arnkanthi [kuu-kuu-(k)arnka-nthi] screen the eyes from the sun with the hand ᴛᴍ

kuungka [kuu-ngka] under shelter, under cover ᴛᴍ

kuula *n* koala ɴᴇᴡ (from Dharuk)

kuuni *n* corn ɴᴇᴡ (from English 'corn')

kuupi *n* coffee ɴᴇᴡ (from English 'coffee')

kuwa *n* crow ᴛs,ᴛᴍ,ᴇʏ,ᴄᴏ,ʀᴏ

kuya *n* fish (in general) ᴛs,ᴛᴍ,ɢᴀ,ᴡɪ,ᴡʏ,sᴛ

  kuya ngani *n* place in the water where fish like to congregate, fishing spot ᴛᴍ

  kuya pirriwirrkinthi [kuya pirri-wirrki-nthi] *v-tr* go fishing ɴᴇᴡ

  kuyangari [kuya-ngarri] *n* fishing line ᴡɪ,sᴛ

  kuyaparra [kuya-parra] *n* fish scales ᴛs

  kuyapirri [kuya-pirri] *n* fish hook ᴡɪ,ᴡʏ,sᴛ

  kuyarnapinthi [kuya-rn(i)-(w)api-nthi] *v-intr* go fishing ᴛᴍ

kuyapirri

  kuyawika [kuya-wika] *n* fishing net ᴛᴍ

Kuyata *n* birth-order name: first born (male) ᴛs,ᴡʏ

kuyinthi => **kurdinthi**

kuyirrinthi => **kurdirrinthi**

kuyurra *n* grey currawong (*Strepera versicolor*) ᴛs,ᴄᴏ,ᴘɪ,ᴡʏ

L l

-la *suff* (on nouns) one who (agent) (See page 9 of grammar section; e.g. *kampalampala* 'baker'; 'cook)

-layi => **wayinthi**

-litya => **-itya**

-lityangka => **-ityangka**

-lityarnungku => **-ityarnungku**

M m

-ma (var. **-ama**) (1) *suff* indicates a question or uncertainty about a statement, e.g. that something might be true, that it is possible but not certain *Nala-alati-ama niina pudna-utha?* 'When will you return?' *Wanta-uthama nintu ngai?* 'Will you leave some meat for me?' *Nganaitya nintu yaku nayama?* 'Why haven't you been sewing?' *Nganaityarntama nintu wanta?* 'Why did you leave (it) there?' ᴛs,ᴛᴍ (2) *suff* (on verbs) mood marker: 'if' ... (subjunctive) *Kuinyunta mai Adamidlu yaku ngarkuma, yaku pa padluma*. 'If Adam had not eaten the forbidden fruit, he would not have died.' ᴛᴍ,ᴛs

maadlhu *n* snow ᴛᴍ

  maadlhupirrki [madlu-pirrki] *n* snow peas ɴᴇᴡ

maana *n* crosscut saw ᴛs,ᴛᴍ,ᴡɪ,sᴛ

  maana kurltu *n* hand saw ᴡɪ

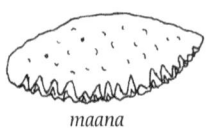
maana

madlala (var. **marlala**) *n* paternal grandfather (father's father) TS, TM, BA, WI, ST

   madlalatangkurla [madlala-ta-ngk(a)-(p)urla] (var. **madlatangkurla**) *n* two male grandchildren (of two brothers) TM

   madlanta [madla-nta] *n* grandchild of madlala (of father's father) TS, TM

madlara *n* droppings; excrement; poo (of herbivore) TS, TM

madli *n* swimmer TS, TM

   madlitina [madli-tina] *n* non-swimmer TS

Madli-thaltarni [madli-thaltarni] *n* name of a red star TS

madliarri *n* buttock muscle (*gluteous*) TS

madlu *n* mist; fog; darkness (weather) TS, TM

   madlu-adlurninthi [madlu-(m)adlu-rni-nthi] (var. **madlumadlurninthi**) *v-intr* get dark TS, TM

   madlumadlu [madlu-madlu] (var. **madluadlu**) *adj* dark; foggy; misty TS, TM

madlurta (var. **malurta**) *n* (1) possum (ring-tailed) WI, WY, ST (2) young possum TS

mai *n* food; vegetable *Padlu piiki mai-anta ngarki.* 'He even ate the pig food.' *Maimpi waa?* 'Where is some food?' TS, TM, BL, WI, WY, ST, KO

   mai karnkarnkati [mai karnka-karnka-ti] *n* spoon TS

   mai pudnapiti [mai pudna-(wa)pi-ti] *n* bait NEW

   mai wantawantati [mai wanta-wanta-ti] *n* plate. dish TS

   mai-idla (var. **maitidla**) without food *Mai-idlalya ngai madlitha.* 'I will die from lack of food' TM

   mai-itya [mai-itya] *adj* hungry WY, KO

maikudna [mai-kudna] *adj* stingy TS, TM

maikuntu [mai-kuntu] *n* skin; dingo hide TS, TM

maimarnguta [mai-marngu-ta] *adj* greedy (for food); gluttonous TS, TM, WY

maiminma [mai-minma] *adj* greedy (for food); gluttonous TS, TM

maimpi [mai-mpi] *adj* wanting food TS, WI, ST

maimunthu [mai-munthu] *adj* full or satisfied (after eating) TM

   maimunthu tikanthi [mai-munthu tika-nthi] *v-intr* have plenty; be well-stocked TM

mainthi [mai-nthi] *v-tr* (1) eat; live on (something); subsist on *maingka mainthi* 'to live on vegetables' *pardungka mainthi* 'to live on meat' TS (2) graze *Nanturla tuthangka mainthi.* 'The (two) horses are grazing' TS

maipadniti [mai-padni-ti] *n* (1) throat, oesophagus TS (2) gut, passage of the food TM

mairna [mai-rna] *n* provisions, foodstuffs, foods *Mairna kangkantu! – Mairna? – Mai parna!* 'Take the food (plural) with you! – Is that them (the food)? – That's them!' *Itu, ngangkurna mairna?* 'Whose provisions are these?' TS

maitidli [mai-tidli] (var. **mai'dli**) *adj* having food TS, TM

maitina [mai-tina] *adj* without food; destitute TS, TM

maikurru *n* breeze; wind TS, TM

mailtyanthi [mailtya-nthi] *v-tr* (1) try, experience, test the nature or quality (of something) *mailtyamailtyarri'rna* 'compare them' TS, TM (2) imitate, copy (something) *warra mailtyanthi* 'imitate someone's language or speech when they speak incorrectly' TS (3) taste or smell (something) *Mailtyantu!* 'Taste it!' TS, TM, WI

   mailtyamailtyarrina [mailtya-mailtya-rri-na] try; compare TM

   mailtyarri-apinthi [mailtya-rri-(wa)pi-nthi] *v-intr* explain; tell; communicate a message *Moserlu mailtyarri-apithi parnalityangka.* 'Moses has told them (the Laws).' TS, TM

   mailtyarrinthi [mailtya-rri-nthi] *v-intr* communicate; inform TS, TM

   mailtyarripurka [mailtya-rri-purka] *n* impersonator; tease TS, TM

maingki => **mingki**

maingkimaingkingka => **mingkimingkingka**

maitidla => **mai-idla**

maitkanthi [maitka-nthi] *v-intr* die TM

   maitkarrantinthi [maitka-rr(i)-anti-nthi] *v-intr* be newly deceased, only just passed away TM

   maitkarrira [maitka-rri-ra] *adj* dead, deceased TM

maityuka₁ [maityuka] *adj* active; lively; quick; attentive; diligent TS, TM

maityuka₂ *n* girl whose father has died TS

maityumaityu [maityu-maityu] *n* bat species (undefined) TS, PI, WY

   maityuwampi [maityu-wampi] *n* bicycle; bike NEW (inspired by Adnyamathanha *mika wiṟi* 'bat wing')

maiwaadli [mai-waadli] *adj* generous with food; hospitable TS, TM

maiwardli [mai-wardli] *n* greengrocer's; canteen NEW

makanthi [maka-nthi] *v-tr* (1) shake (something) TS (2) shake the legs while dancing *Warpurna wiltarninga, miyurna, nganta makatitya.* 'Men, let your bones be strong, so as to shake well (in dance performance)' TS, TM, GA, WI

maki *n* ice, glass, crystal, flint TS, TM, WI, WY, ST
   maki kuru *n* glass bottle WI, ST
   maki kuu *n* freezer NEW
   makirninthi [maki-rni-nthi] *v-intr* freeze TM
   makithau [maki-thau] *n* window TS, TM
   makithiya [maki-thiya] glass knife for cutting TM
   makithura [maki-thura] *n* mirror TS, TM
makiti *n* musket KO (from English 'musket')
maku *n* cloud *makurlaku wartingka* 'between two clouds' TS, TM, WI, WY, KO, ST
   maku mankunthi [maku manku-nthi] make or produce clouds TM
   maku manmarra night with light clouds, a good time for hunting possums TS, TM
   makutina [maku-tina] *adj* clear, cloudless (sky) TS
maltunthi [maltu-nthi] *v-tr* bring close together TM
   maltu mankunthi [maltu manku-nthi] *v-tr* press tightly together TM
   maltu mankurrinthi [maltu manku-rri-nthi] *v-intr* stick close together TM
   malturri-apinthi [maltu-rri-(w)api-nthi] *v-tr* gather; collect; assemble TS, TM
   malturrinthi [maltu-rri-nthi] *v-intr* stay together; remain in a group TS, TM
malurta => **madlurta**
malyu (1) *n* swelling, rise, undulation TS, TM (2) *adj* swollen, uneven, undulating (landscape) TS, TM
   malyurninthi [malyu-rni-nthi] *v-intr* (1) swell up, become large, become uneven or undulating TS, TM (2) be pregnant TS, TM
malyupartana [malyu-parta-na] *adj* funny TS
mamanthi [mama-nthi] *v-tr* (1) tie up TS (2) pick up and carry (a child) on your back TM
   mamanana [mama-nana] *n* released person TM
mampa *n* knee *mamparlaku wartingka* 'between the knees' TS, TM, GA, WY
   mampa tartarta kneeling, on one's knees TS, TM
mamparta *n* hairstyle for men TS, TM
mampinthi [mampi-nthi] *v-intr* (1) ripple TM (2) undulate TM, TS (3) waver; stagger TM, TS
mananya *adj* weak; not healthy; delicate TS, TM
manara *n* (1) crow's nest EY (2) name of a boy from about 10 to 12 years of age (possibly having changed from 'kuwa' (crow) after ceremony) EY
manarntu *n* lower arm; forearm TS
manga *n* (1) thread spun from hair or fur TS, TM (2) headband (worn in ceremony) TS, TM, CA, PI, WI, KO

manga

mangathata [manga-thata] *n* spindle (long vertical piece) TS, TM
mangayaingki [manga-yaingki] (var. **mangayaintya**) *n* spindle (horizontal cross piece) TM, WY

mangathata

mangalya *n* species of gum tree (undefined) TS
mangayaintya => **mangayaingki**
mangki-mangkinthi [mangki-mangki-nthi] *v-intr* gossip; talk about (someone behind their back) TS
   mangki-mangki-apinthi [mangki-mangki-(w)api-nthi] *v-tr* slander; dob on; tell on; gossip about; inform on TS, TM
mangkiti *n* finger BL
mangkulayinthi [mangku-layi-nthi] *v-intr* (1) be afraid, scared, fearful, full of dread TS, TM (2) be embarrassed TM
manimani *n* kestrel hawk, nankeen kestrel (*Falco cenchroides*) TS, WY, CO
manimaninya *n* swallow; welcome swallow TS, CO
manka (var. **mangka**) (see also: **mingka₂**) *n* scars; ceremonial scars; cicatrization TS, TM, CA, PI, WY
   manka pakinthi [manka paki-nthi] *v-tr* make 'manka' incisions on the body (ceremonial scarring) TS, TM
   manka-mankanthi [manka-manka-nthi] *v-tr* cicatrize WY
   mankamanka [manka-manka] *adj* striped TS, TM
   mankawitya [manka-witya] *n* initiand in 'wilyaru' stage after cermonial tattooing when the cuts begin to rise (when the keloid scars form) EY
   mankitya [mank(a)-itya] *n* scarred one KWP
mankarra [mankarra] *n* girl; unmarried young woman TS, TM, BL, RO, WI, WY, ST, CH
   Mankamankarrarna *n* girls; the Seven Sisters (a constellation) (Pleiades) TS, TM
mankunthi [manku-nthi] *v-tr* (1) touch, take, lay hold of *Manmantu!* 'Take it! (singular)' *Manmaingwa!* 'Take it! (dual)' *Manmainga!* 'Take it! (plural)' *Parni manmantu'rna kardlarna* 'Bring the firewood here' TS, TM, WI, WY, ST (2) tie *Wilta manmantu!* 'Tie it tighter!' TS (3) cause, produce, bring about TM (4) help *Ngathu parna ngaityu yungarna mankutha, yaku pia parna pilyurni-utha, wuingpatha ngai parna ngaityu yungarna* 'I shall help them, they are my brothers, they will perhaps not be content, they will challenge me, or demand of me (to assist them) my brothers' TM

manku-mankunthi [manku-manku-nthi] *v-tr* sharpen (a spear) ᴛᴍ

manku-mankurrinthi [manku-manku-rri-nthi] *v-intr* assemble; stay together *Mr Meyer, ngadli tapangka mankumankurrithi.* 'Mr Meyer and I have assisted each other (or 'stayed together') on the road.' ᴛᴍ

mankurri-apinthi [manku-rri-(w)api-nthi] *v-tr* (1) bring together, cause to meet at a point, unite, reconcile ᴛᴍ (2) surround (with something) ᴛᴍ

mankurrinthi [manku-rri-nthi] *v-tr* (1) take hold of, clasp (e.g. hands), hold on to *Kartaka mankurringkurti!* 'Don't grab on to my shoulder!' *tangka mankurrinthi* 'feel attached to, make friends with (someone)' ᴛꜱ,ᴛᴍ,ᴡʏ (2) reconcile, make up (with someone) *Ngadli nata mankurri.* 'We have now reconciled with each other.' ᴛᴍ

manmarra (var. **marmarra**) *n* moonlit night occasionally darkened by clouds ᴛꜱ,ᴛᴍ

manngimanngirrinthi [manngi-manngi-rri-nthi] *v-intr* glow, be red hot ᴛᴍ

manta *n* lie, untruth, fib ᴛꜱ,ᴛᴍ,ᴄʜ

manta kurrurrinthi [manta kurr(i)-(k)urri-nthi] (var. **manta kurrikurrinthi**; **manta kurrulyinthi**; **manta-urri-urrinthi**) *v-tr* accuse of lying; doubt someone; contradict; disprove *Ngai nintu manta kurrikurrinthi.* 'You accuse me of lying' ᴛꜱ,ᴛᴍ

manta kurrurripurka [manta kurr(i)-(k)urri-purka] (var. **manta kurrikurripurka**; **manta-urri-urripurka**) *n* person accusing someone of lying ᴛꜱ

manta wangkanthi [manta wangka-nthi] *v-intr* lie; deceive ᴛꜱ,ᴛᴍ,ᴡɪ,ꜱᴛ,ᴡʏ

manta warrawarra [manta warra-warra] *n* (1) lie, untruth ᴛᴍ (2) liar ᴛꜱ

manta warrawarrarninthi [manta warra-warra-rni-nthi] *v-intr* lie; pretend; deceive ᴛᴍ

manta-apinthi [manta-(w)api-nthi] (var. **mantapinthi**) *v-tr* misrepresent; fool someone into believing something ᴛꜱ,ᴛᴍ

mantapartana [manta-partana] (1) *adj* lying, full of lies ᴛꜱ (2) *n* liar, dishonest person ᴛᴍ

mantarti! [manta-rti] don't lie! ᴛꜱ,ᴛᴍ

mantharra [manth(i)-(th)arra] *n* string; handle ᴛꜱ,ᴛᴍ

manthi [ma-nthi] *v-tr* pull; draw out; take off *Tidnapaltha ninku mantu!* 'Take off your shoes!' *Ngari mantu!* 'Untie the rope!' *Padlu ngai murrka mama.* 'You had made me cry.' ᴛꜱ,ᴛᴍ

manti *adj, adv* unable, impotent *Manti yarltirrinth'ai.* 'I'm not able to pursuade them.' ᴛꜱ,ᴛᴍ,ᴡʏ

manti-apinthi [manti-(w)api-nthi] *v-intr* be unable to ᴛᴍ

manti-ngarrata slow, sluggish ᴛᴍ

mantikatpa [manti-katpa] *adj* slow; lazy ᴛꜱ,ᴛᴍ

mantikatparti! [manti-katpa-rti] *v-intr* hurry up! don't be slow! ᴛꜱ,ᴛᴍ

mantimantirrinthi [manti-manti-rri-nthi] *v-intr* be insufficient; be incapable; be unable ᴛᴍ

mantinguya [manti-nguya] *adj* slow; lazy; dull ᴛꜱ,ᴛᴍ

mantinta *n* skin, hide (of kangaroos and dogs) ᴛꜱ,ᴛᴍ

mantirri *n* muntrie berry, emu apple *(Kunzea pomifera)* ᴛꜱ,ᴄʜ

mantyi-mantyi *n* species of bird (undefined) ꜱᴛ

mantirri

manuwarta [manu-warta] *n* back of the head; nape of the neck ᴛꜱ,ᴛᴍ,ɢᴀ,ᴡʏ,ᴋᴏ

manuwarta warpu [manu-wartu warpu] *n* neck bone ᴡɪ

manuwartarninthi [manu-warta-rni-nthi] *v-intr* bow the head; bend the neck forwards ᴛᴍ

manya (1) *n* rain, cold, cold and rainy weather *Manya nalati pudni.* 'The rain is starting right now.' ᴛꜱ,ᴛᴍ,ʙʟ,ᴘɪ,ʀᴏ,ᴡɪ,ᴡʏ (2) *adj* rainy, cold *Manya-artungka ngathu kampatha?* 'Shall I boil it in cold (water)?' ᴛꜱ,ᴛᴍ

manya kuu *n* fridge; refrigerator ɴᴇᴡ

manya mankunthi [manya-manku-nthi] produce rain, cause it to rain ᴛᴍ

manya nurnpu-nhurnpurri [manya nhurnpu-nhurnpu-rri] rain approaches suddenly ᴛᴍ

manya parltarrinthi [manya parlta-rri-nthi] *v-intr* rain *manyarlu parltarrinthi* 'it rains' ᴛꜱ,ᴛᴍ

manya payarnantinthi [manya paya-rna-nti-nthi] *v-intr* freeze; get cold *mika manya payarrinthi* 'the face is bitten by the cold' ᴛᴍ

manya pudnanthi [manya pudna-nthi] *v-intr Manya pudna-intyidla tirnturlu, nganparritha naa.* 'If it has been raining tomorrow, you (plural) will stay home.' ᴛᴍ

manya wardninthi [manya wardni-nthi] *v-intr* rain is falling ᴛᴍ

manya warri-warri sudden rain ᴛᴍ

manyapartana [manya-partana] *n* rain-maker ᴛᴍ

manyapayana [manya-paya-na] *adj* very cold

weather; chilly *Manya payana pakirri.* 'The cold is cutting.' TS,TM

manyarrinthi [manya-rri-nthi] *v-intr* **(1)** be cold; feel cold *Manyarrinth'ai.* 'I'm cold.' TS,TM,WI,WY,ST **(2)** be rainy, raining *manyarrinthurlu ninku kunturu katiti manmantu* 'when it rains then get your umbrella' TM

manyarrinthurlu [manya-rri-nth(i)-urlu] during the rain; when it rains TM

manyinthi [manyi-nthi] **(1)** *v-tr* soften, yield, soften fibres (by rubbing them between the fingers) TM **(2)** *v-intr* compose one's self TM

manyurrinthi [manyu-rri-nthi] *v-intr* smoke; smoulder TM

mapa *n* rubbish; dirt *Kutyu-arnani piti mapartarna manku'athu'rna.* 'I will just get some rubbish first.' TS,TM

mapakuru [mapa-kuru] *n* rubbish bin NEW

mapapurtu [mapa-purtu] *adj* full of rubbish TS,TM

maparra [mapa-rra] *adj* dirty TS,TM

mapu *n* quoll TS,TM,BL,PI,WI,WY,ST

mara *n* **(1)** hand; finger *mararlu pingkanthi* 'to lift up or raise the hand' *mararlu warrunthi* 'to beckon with the hand (to get someone to come towards you)' *mararlu yarltinthi* 'to shoo someone away with the hand (to get them to go away)' TS,TM,BL,EA,GA,WI,WY,ST,KO **(2)** paw NEW

mara kutpakutpanthi [mara kutpa-kutpa-nthi] shake hands TS

mara-angki [mara-(ng)angki] *n* thumb TS,WY

marakurta-unyu [mara-kurta-unyu] *n* little finger; pinky finger TS

marangka padninthi [mara-ngka padni-nthi] *v-intr* accompany, go along with someone TS,TM

maranthi [mara-nthi] *v-intr* crawl TS

maraparkana [mara-parkana] *n* grub species TS

marapina [mara-pina] **(1)** *n* boxer, fighter, person who fights a lot TM **(2)** *adj, n* fighting often, violent, pugnacious TS

marapirri [mara-pirri] *n* fingernail TS,KO

maratha [mara-tha] *n* palm of the hand TS

marathangka [mara-thangka] *n* palm of the hand TM,WY

marawaadli [mara-waadli] *adj* **(1)** generous, liberal TM **(2)** stingy, not generous TS **(3)** covetous, envying TS **(4)** filthy, dirty TS

marawaka [mara-waka] *n* cupped hand(s) TS,TM

marawakanthi [mara-waka-nthi] *v-tr* cup the hands (to drink or catch something) TS

marawardli [mara-wardli] *n* palm of the hand TS

marawari [mara-wari] *n* fingertip TS

marawiti [mara-witi] *n* octopus NEW

marayarli [mara-yarli] *n* index finger TS,WY

mardla (var. **marla**) **(1)** *adv* only, merely, just, simply *mardla kauwi* 'only water' *Mardla nintu namuntya yailtyanthi.* 'You just think so.' TS,TM,WY **(2)** *adv* indifferently, without a real intention *mardla padninthi* 'just walking (for the sake of it, not going anywhere)' TM **(3)** *n* zero NEW

mardlaitirra [mardla-itirra] (var. **mardlatirra**) **(1)** *adv* accidentally, unintentionally, without a cause *mardlaitirra martamartanthi* 'to suspect or accuse (someone) without a cause' TM **(2)** *adj* indifferent, not concerned *Mardlatirra'ai tiki.* 'I had nothing to do with it.' TS,WI **(3)** *intj* never mind, anyway TS,WI,ST

mardlana [mardla-na] *adj, adv* **(1)** not *Mardlanarni ngainti-alya murithi.* 'Without anyone I went alone.' TS,TM,RO,WI,WY,KO **(2)** no, none TS,TM,RO,WI,WY,ST,KO,CH

mardlananta [mardla-na-nta] none at all TM

mardlarninthi [mardla-rni-nthi] *v-intr* become nothing; dead WI

mardlarri-apinthi [mardla-rri-(w)api-nthi] (var. **marlarri-apinthi**) *v-tr* stop (make); complete TS,TM

mardlarrinthi [mardla-rri-nthi] *v-intr* stop; get over; recover *Manya nata mardlarri.* 'The rain has stopped now.' TS,TM,WI

mardla-mardlarrinthi [mardla-mardla-rri-nthi] *v-intr* stop completely TM

mardlinthi [mardli-nthi] *v-intr* die *Mardli pa.* 'He is dead.' TS,TM,WY

mardlimardlinya *v-intr* drawing near to death, dying TM

marilana *n* mullet (fish) (*Aldrichetta forsteri*) TS,WI,ST

marka *n* **(1)** mark, trace, track TM **(2)** slate (used by school students for writing on) TS,TM

marka wayinthi [marka wayi-nthi] **(1)** *v-intr* come first, try or strive to be first, press forward to get in front of someone else *Ngai ngunukunyanta marka wayithi. Nata maitidla taityu tikanthi.* 'He got here before me (and got all the food). Now I'm going to be hungry.' TM **(2)** *v-tr* urge, encourage, push (someone to do something) TM

marka wayipina [marka wayi-pina] *n* winner NEW

marka-apinthi [marka-(w)api-nthi] *v-tr* imitate; impersonate *Nganaitya nintu ngai marka-apinthi* 'Why are you imitating me?' TM

marka-markanthi [marka-marka-nthi] *v-tr* **(1)** count, number (something) TS,TM **(2)** mark out, measure, delineate, trace (something) TM **(3)** track (something) *tidnangka markamarkanthi* 'to follow (something's) tracks, to track something' TM

markanthi [marka-nthi] *v-tr* (1) trace, imitate TS,TM (2) guess, approximate (something) TS

markaparkana [marka-parna] *n* whiteboard NEW

markapulyuna [marka-pulyuna] *n* blackboard NEW

markarrinthi [marka-rri-nthi] *v-intr* (1) trace, guess, approximate (something) TS (2) beat the time (as in music) TM,KO

marla => **mardla**

marlala => **madlala**

marlarri-apinthi => **mardlarri-apinthi**

marlta *n* (1) beard, whiskers TS,TM,GA,EA,WI,WY,ST,KO,CH (2) edge (of something) *kauwa marlta* 'edge of a cliff, precipice' TM

  marlta mankurrinthi [marlta manku-rri-nthi] *v-intr* stick close, tight together TM

  marlta pirranthi [marlta pirra-nthi] *v-tr* shave TS

  marlta pirralirrala [marlta pirra-l(a)-(p)irra-la] *n* barber TS

  marlta pirrati [marlta pirra-ti] *n* razor TS

  marlta purnkipurnki [marlta purnki-purnki] *adj* red-bearded (used as an insult) TS

  marlta titparra a good, correct speaker TM

  marlta warpu *n* cheek bone, jaw bone TS,TM,WY

  marlta warta *n* cheek TS,TM,GA,KO,WI,ST

  marltaitya [marlta-itya] *n* cheek TS,TM

  marltangaitya [marlta-ngaitya] *adj* speaking badly, incorrectly, not eloquent TS,TM

  marltawilta [marlta-wilta] *adj* fluent; eloquent *Marlta-yartpaniantingka niina wangkanthi, tarrkarri niina wangkatha marltawiltarningka.* 'You only speak (our language) in its basic form, (but) in the future you will speak fluently.' TS,TM

  marltayartpana [marlta-yartpa-na] *adj* speaking incorrectly, not speaking fluently TM

marltarra *n* species of gum tree (similar to stringy bark) TS

marmarra => **manmarra**

marna *n* firstborn child; eldest child in family (male or female) TM

marngu₁ *n* envy; anger; jealousy TS,TM

  -marnguta [marngu-ta] *suff (on nouns)* desiring; wanting; greedy for *pardumarnguta* 'desiring meat' TS,TM,WY

  marngu yungkunthi [marngu yungku-nthi] cause anger, make someone cross TM

  marngungkinthi [marngu-ngka-nthi] *v-intr* be angry, envious, offended, annoyed *Nintu ngai yaku mai yungki, marngungkinth'ai.* 'You didn't give me any food, I'm angry (or offended).' TS,TM

  marngupina [marngu-pina] *n* grumpy person; angry person; jealous person TS,TM

  marngutanthi [marngu-ta-nthi] *v-intr* be greedy for, jealous, envy TM

marngu₂ *n* knob; button; heel; knot TS,TM,KO

  marngu-marngu [marngu-marngu] *adj* (1) speckled, spotty, polka-dot TM (2) uneven, bumpy, knobbly TS

  marngu-marngu waitku *n* purple-spotted gudgeon (fish) *(Mogurnda adspersa)* NEW

marni (1) *n* fat, grease TS,TM (2) *adj* good TS,TM,GA,RO,WI,WY,ST,CH

  marni tiwita very good, really great TM

  marninthi [marni-nthi] (1) *v-intr* be fat TS (2) *v-tr* grease, anoint (someone/something) TS,TM

  marnirninthi [marni-rni-nthi] *v-intr* become fat TM

  marnirrinthi [marni-rri-nthi] *v-intr* grease; anoint TS,TM

  marniti [marni-ti] *n* (1) grease TS (2) boy greased and painted with red ochre (part of initiation ceremony of 'the eastern tribes') TS

  tawarri marni very good TM

marnka *n* prayer NEW

  marnkalarnkala [marnka-l(a)-(m)arnka-la] *n* beggar TM

  marnkanthi [marnka-nthi] *v-tr* (1) beg, request, ask, plead, petition, apply (to someone) *Ngathu niina marnkathi.* 'I asked you (for it).' TS,TM (2) pray, supplicate (ask God for something) KL

  marnkarri-purka [marnka-rri-purka] *n* (1) beggar TS,TM (2) person who wants something, desirer TM

  marnkarrinthi [marnka-rri-nthi] *v-intr* beg; request; ask *Ngai nintaitya marnkarrithi.* 'I requested of you.' TS,TM

marnkutyi *num* three TS,TM,BL,GA,WY

  Marnku-irntu [marnku(tyi)-(th)irntu] *n* Wednesday NEW

  marnkuawata [marnku-(th)awata] *num* three thousand NEW

  Marnkuiki [marnku(tyi)-(p)iki] *n* March NEW

  marnkuirrka [marnku(tyi)-irrka] *num* thirty NEW

  marnkuirrka kuma [marnku(tyi)-irrka kuma] *num* thirty one NEW

  marnkuiwurra [marnku(tyi)-(wi)wurra] *num* three million NEW

  marnkurluku [marnku(tyi)-rluku] *adv* three times TS

  marnkutyi partirrka [marnkutyi partu-irrka] *num* three hundred NEW

marnpi *n* bronzewing pigeon TM, CO, PI, WI, WY, ST

marntu (var. **marnu**) *n* uncircumcised boy TS, TM

marranthi [marra-nthi] *v-tr* pour; spill; scatter; spread around *kaaru marrarninthi* 'spilling blood' *Ngathu kauwi marratha? Marrantu!* 'Shall I pour the water? Pour it!' TS, TM, WI, WY, ST

   marra yuwati [marra-yuwa-ti] *n* tap (water etc) NEW

   marrarrinthi [marra-rri-nthi] *v-intr* (1) spill TS (2) boil over WY

marraka [marra-ka] *adj* without; lacking *turnki marraka* 'naked, without clothing' TS, TM

marri *n* east *marri-ana* '(going) towards the east' TS, TM, WY

   marrarta [marri-(y)arta] *n* east country, Peramangk lands TM

   marri miyurna [marri miyu-rna] name of a north-eastern tribe, Peramangk people TS

   marriku [marri-ku] (var. **marrika**) *dir* easterly TM

   marrikurlu [marri-k(u)-(ng)urlu] in the east TM

   marrimarrirlu [marri-marri-rlu] towards the east TM

marrinthi [ma-rri-nthi] *v-intr, v-tr* (1) undress; take off, slip off, put off TS, TM (2) separate oneself, go off by oneself *Tawatila miyungka pa marrinthi.* 'Because of all the people he goes off by himself.' TM

marriru *n* (1) moon TM, WY (2) month WY

   marrmarrila [marr-marr-ila] in the moonlight TM

marrkarri-apinthi [marrka-rri-(w)api-nthi] (1) *v-intr* complain, grumble, be dissatisfied (with something) TS (2) *v-tr* tell, inform, communicate with (someone) TM

   marrkarripurka [marrka-rri-purka] *n* grumbling, complaining, argumentative person TS

marrku *n* (1) use, application, purpose, function (of something) TM (2) action of passing something from hand to hand in order to use it TM

   marrkunthi [marrku-nthi] *v-tr* use; apply TM

   marrkurri-apinthi [marrku-rri-(w)api-nthi] *v-tr* used (cause to be); employ *Ngaityu kurutila ngathu marrkurri-apinthi ninku kuru.* 'I use your pot instead of my own pot.' TM

marrpu (var. **murtpu**) *n* murder *marrpu ngartirrinthi* 'enquire into the murder' TM

   marrpuna [marrpu-na] *n* murderer TS, TM, WI, WY, ST

   marrpurrinthi [marrpu-rri-nthi] *v-tr* murder; kill TM

marru *num* six NEW

marrawata [marr(u)-(th)awata] *num* six thousand NEW

marrirrka [marru-irrka] *num* sixty NEW

marriwurra [marru-(w)iwurra] *num* six million NEW

marru partirrka [marru part(u)-irrka] *num* six hundred NEW

Marruartu [marru-(k)artu] (var. **Marruyu**) *n* birth-order name: sixth born (female) TS, TM, EY

Marruiki [marru-(p)iki] *n* June NEW

Marrutya [marru-tya] *n* birth-order name: sixth born (male) TS, EY, WY

Marruyu => **Marruartu**

marta *n* (1) suspicion, accusation, slander TM (2) anticipation, idea TM

   marta-martanthi [marta-marta-nthi] *v-tr* falsely accuse TM

   martalartala [marta-l(a)-(m)arta-la] *n* accuser; slanderer TS

   martanthi [marta-nthi] *v-tr* (1) accuse, suspect, slander (someone) TS, TM (2) imagine, suppose, suspect (something) *mardlaitirra martanthi* 'to merely imagine (something)' TM

   martarrinthi [marta-rri-nthi] *v-tr* pretend; expect *mai martarrinthi* 'to pretend that there is food' TM

martarninthi [marta-rni-nthi] *v-intr* (1) be cold *Nguy'athu'rla tidnarla, martarninthi purla, manyarrinthi ngai.* 'I will warm the feet, they are cold, I am cold.' TS, TM (2) be hungry, starving TM, TS

marti *n* bandicoot TS

martinthi [marti-nthi] *v-tr* embrace; hold onto; clasp TS, TM

   martirrinthi [marti-rri-nthi] *v-intr* embrace TS, TM

martu *n* (1) taste, flavour, smell, scent TS, TM, WY (2) essence (of something) TS, TM (3) revenge TS

   martu mailtyanthi [martu mailtya-nthi] *v-tr* smell; taste TS, WY

   martu-alya favourite one TS

   martulayinthi [martu-layi-nthi] *v-intr* smell TM

martu-itya [martu-itya] (1) on behalf of; for (the sake of) *Ngadluku martu-itya madli Kirritu.* 'Christ died on our behalf (or for us).' TS (2) instead of, in place of TM

   martungka [martu-ngka] (1) because of, on account of, in remembrance of (something) *pukiana turla martungka* 'in remembrance of an old fight' TS (2) instead of *mai martungka* 'instead of food' TM (3) for (someone) *ngadluku martungka* 'for us' TM

maru *n* species of red ant TS

marungayu *n* freshwater turtle ᴡʏ

matamudlu *n* toy spear ᴀɴ,ᴄᴀ

matha *n* knee ᴛꜱ,ᴛᴍ,ᴇᴀ,ᴡɪ,ᴡʏ,ꜱᴛ,ᴋᴏ

   matha tararta tikanthi [matha tararta tika-nthi] kneel ᴛꜱ,ᴛᴍ

   mathanya [matha-nya] *n* owner; master *wardli mathanya* 'the owner of the house' *yangarra mathanya* 'husband, owner of the wife' ᴛꜱ,ᴛᴍ,ᴄᴀ,ᴇʏ

Mathari *n* name of one of the two Kaurna moieties ᴛɪ

matinyi *n* constellation (uncertain) ᴛꜱ

matpinthi [matpi-nthi] *v-intr* be sleepy, tired ᴛꜱ,ᴛᴍ

matpu *n* venereal disease ᴛꜱ

matu *n* plain; flat land ᴛᴍ

   matumidla [matu-midla] *n* spleen ᴛꜱ,ᴛᴍ

   matunthi [matu-nthi] *v-tr* stroke; pat ᴛᴍ,ᴋᴏ

   maturrinthi [matu-rri-nthi] *v-intr* crawl ᴛᴍ

   matu-maturrinthi [matu-matu-rri-nthi] crawl up onto the body like insects do ᴛᴍ

   maturta [matu-rta] *adj* level; smooth; straight; even ᴛꜱ,ᴛᴍ,ᴡʏ

midla (var. **mila**₁) *n* **(1)** spear-thrower, woomera ᴛꜱ,ᴛᴍ,ᴄᴀ,ᴡɪ,ᴡʏ,ᴋᴏ,ꜱᴛ **(2)** force, violence, power, strength, might *midla mankunthi* 'to take a wife by force' ᴛꜱ,ᴛᴍ **(3)** wife who was taken by force ᴛꜱ,ᴛᴍ

   midla mailtyanthi [midla mailtya-nthia] put the spear into the midla and try it out ᴛᴍ

   midla mankunthi [midla-manku-nthi] take a wife by force ᴛᴍ

Midlaitya [midla-itya] *n* birth-order name: fifth born (male) ᴛꜱ,ᴇʏ,ᴡɪ,ᴡʏ,ꜱᴛ

Midlartu [midla-(ka)rtu] *n* birth-order name: fifth born (female) ᴛꜱ,ᴇʏ,ᴡɪ,ꜱᴛ

midlinthi [midli-nthi] (var. **milinthi**) *v-tr* **(1)** pinch, crush, grind *Tadlanya mili-milinthi.* 'It pinches the tongue.' ᴛꜱ,ᴛᴍ,ᴡʏ **(2)** strangle, choke, suffocate ᴛꜱ

   midli kurntanthi [midli kurnta-nthi] *v-tr* cut up; beat (into bits) ᴛᴍ

   midli mankunthi [midli manku-nthi] *v-tr* crush *Paitya nintu midli manki.* 'You have crushed an insect' ᴛᴍ

   midli-midli pakinthi *v-tr* cut (something) into small pieces ᴛᴍ

   midlimidli [midli-midli] *adv* *Midlimidli ngadli-utha.* 'It may burn small or through'

   midlimidlinthi [midli-midli-nthi] *v-intr* stick to; adhere to *Tadlanya midlimidlinthi.* 'The tongue sticks to the gums.' ᴛᴍ

midla

mii *n* eye ᴛꜱ,ᴛᴍ

   mii wiltarninthi [mii wilta-rni-nthi] fix your eye on something, pay close attention to something ᴛᴍ

   mii-angki [mii-(ng)angki] eyebrow ᴋᴏ

   mii-thurtpu [mii-thurtpu] *adj* sleepy; tired ᴛᴍ

   miikauwi [mii-kauwi] *n* tears *Miikauwi parltarrinthi.* 'The tears are flowing.' ᴛꜱ,ᴛᴍ,ᴡʏ

   miikuamarti! [mii-kua-marti] *intj* a curse: 'may the crows pick out (your) eyes!' ᴛꜱ,ᴛᴍ

   miimaintya [mii-maintya] (var. **miimuntya**) *n* iris (of eye) ᴛꜱ,ᴛᴍ

   miimaki [mii-maki] *n* glasses (for eyes) ᴛꜱ,ᴛᴍ

   miimunthu [mii-munthu] *n* eyeball ᴛꜱ,ᴛᴍ

   miimurrka [mii-murrka] *n* tears; crying ᴛꜱ,ᴛᴍ

   miinantinthi [miina-nti-nthi] *v-intr* look (in a certain direction) ᴛᴍ

   miingarramarti! [mii-ngarra-marti] *intj* (a curse) 'may (your) eyes be poked out with a burning stick!' ᴛꜱ,ᴛᴍ

   miipadlu [mii-padlu] *n* eyelashes ᴛꜱ,ᴛᴍ

   miipaltha [mii-paltha] *n* eyelid ᴛꜱ,ᴛᴍ

   miiparkana [mii-parkana] *n* white of the eye (sclera) ᴛꜱ,ᴛᴍ

   miipayinthi [mii-payi-nthi] *v-tr* search for; look for ᴛᴍ

   miipirrkiparrati! [mii-pirrki-parra-ti] *intj* (a curse) ᴛꜱ

   miipirrkipati! [mii-pirrki-pati] *intj* (a curse) ᴛᴍ

   miipirrkitana! [mii-pirrki-tana] *intj* (a curse) ᴛꜱ

   miipudlunthi [mii-pudlu-nthi] *v-tr* show; reveal; represent ᴛꜱ,ᴛᴍ

   miipudnanthi [mii-pudna-nthi] *v-intr* **(1)** wake up ᴛᴍ **(2)** stare, open the eyes widely ᴛꜱ,ᴛᴍ

   miipulyuna [mii-pulyuna] *n* pupil (of eye) ᴛꜱ

   miiputhi [mii-puthi] *n* eyelashes ᴛꜱ,ᴛᴍ,ᴡɪ,ᴡʏ,ꜱᴛ,ᴋᴏ

   miiwardli [mii-wardli] *n* eyelid ʙʟ,ᴋᴏ

   miiwartarninthi [mii-warta-rni-nthi] *v-intr* squint; look at (sideways) ᴛᴍ

miina *n* eye *Miina turtpurninthi.* 'The eyes close (because of sleepiness).' *Miina warrungka tarn(arn) ingku* 'bulging eyes, staring' ᴛꜱ,ᴛᴍ,ʙʟ,ᴇᴀ,ɢᴀ,ᴘɪ,ᴡɪ,ᴡʏ,ꜱᴛ,ᴋᴏ,ᴄʜ

   miinurla two eyes ᴛᴍ

miita (1) *n* flame, blaze, fire ᴛꜱ,ᴛᴍ **(2)** *n* heat ᴛᴍ **(3)** *adj* hot, heated, warm *warli miitangka* 'in a warm house' *kauwi miitarlu* 'by or with hot water' ᴛᴍ,ʀᴏ

   miita nguyuti [miita nguyu-ti] *n* gas heater ɴᴇᴡ

   miitarninthi [miita-rni-nthi] *v-intr* warm up; get hot ᴛᴍ

   miitayapa [miita-yapa] *n* gas oven ɴᴇᴡ

miitu *n* sleep *Miiturti!* 'Don't sleep!' ᴛꜱ,ᴛᴍ,ᴡɪ,ᴡʏ,ᴋᴏ,ꜱᴛ
  miitu kadlunthi [miitu kadlu-(rri)-nthi] (var. **miitu kadlurrinthi**) *v-intr* be sleepy, falling asleep ᴛꜱ,ᴛᴍ
  miitu kuu [miitu kuu] *n* bedroom ɴᴇᴡ
  miitu mutyarta *n* pyjamas; pjs ɴᴇᴡ
  miitu padlunthi [miitu padlu-nthi] *v-intr* be sleepy ᴛꜱ,ᴛᴍ
  miitu parltanthi [miitu parlta-nthi] *v-intr* wake up ᴛᴍ
  miitu patinthi [miitu pati-nthi] *v-intr* wake up ᴛᴍ
  miitu payirrinthi [mitu payi-rri-nthi] *v-intr* be sleepy ᴛꜱ
  miitu puulti *adj* dead, deceased (euphemistic) ᴛꜱ,ᴛᴍ
  miitu tungki *n* deep sleep ᴛᴍ
  miitu wantinthi [miitu wanti-nthi] *v-intr* lie down asleep ᴛꜱ,ᴛᴍ
  miitu-anarlu [miitu-ana-rlu] while going to sleep ᴛᴍ
  miitu-itya [miitu-itya] *adj* sleepy; falling asleep ᴛᴍ
  miituanangka [miitu-ana-ngka] up until going to sleep ᴛᴍ
  miitumpi [miitu-mpi] *adj* sleepy, needing sleep ᴛꜱ
  miiturninthi [miitu-rni-nthi] *v-intr* (1) become sleepy, fall asleep ᴛᴍ,ᴛꜱ (2) die ᴛᴍ
  miituthirntu [miitu-thirntu] *n* bedtime ɴᴇᴡ
  miituthirntu palti [miitu-thirntu palti] *n* bedtime song ɴᴇᴡ
  miituthirntu pirrku [miitu-thirntu pirrku] *n* bedtime story ɴᴇᴡ
  miituthungki [miitu-thungki] *adj* (1) soundly asleep, sleeping heavily ᴛᴍ (2) disorientated and confused after waking from a deep sleep ᴛᴍ
  miituthurnki [miitu-thurnki] *n* sheet; bedsheet ɴᴇᴡ
  miitutina [miitu-tina] *adj* sleepless, not sleepy or tired ᴛꜱ,ᴛᴍ

mika (see also: **minkarra**) *n* (1) face (of a person) ᴛᴍ (2) presence (of a person) *parni mika murinthi* 'to go before someone' *nurnti mika murinthi* 'to leave someone's presence' ᴛꜱ,ᴛᴍ
  mikangka [mika-ngka] (var. **mikamikangka**) *loc* in front of *ngaityu mikangka* 'in my presence, before me' ᴛꜱ,ᴛᴍ
  mikangkanthi [mi(i)-kangka-nthi] *v-tr* show; point out *Ngathu niina mikangka-itha.* 'I'll show it to you. I'll point it out to you.' ᴛᴍ
  mikarri-apinthi [mika-rri-(w)api-nthi] *v-tr* direct; steer; guide ᴛᴍ
  mikarrinthi [mika-rri-nthi] (var. **mikamikarrinthi**) *v-intr* turn; change direction ᴛᴍ

mila₁ => **midla**
mila₂ *num* five ɴᴇᴡ
  mila partirrka [mila part(u)-irrka] *num* five hundred ɴᴇᴡ
  milauwata [mil(a)-(th)awata] *num* five thousand ɴᴇᴡ
  Miliki [mil(a)-(p)iki] *n* May ɴᴇᴡ
  Milikirntu [milik(i)-(th)irntu] *n* May Day ɴᴇᴡ
  Milirntu [mil(a)-(th)irntu] *n* Friday ɴᴇᴡ
  milirntu warta [mil(i)-(th)irntu warta] *n* weekend *Marni milirntu warta!* 'Have a good weekend!' ɴᴇᴡ
  milirrka [mil(a)-irrka] *num* fifty ɴᴇᴡ
  miliwurra [mil(a)-(w)iwurra] *num* five million ɴᴇᴡ

mili *n* elbow ᴡʏ
milinthi => **midlinthi**
milthi (1) *n* red ochre ᴛꜱ (2) *adj* red colour ɴᴇᴡ
mingka₁ *n* seedpod of wattle or acacia tree ᴛꜱ,ᴡʏ
mingka₂ (see also: **manka**) *n* (1) cut, wound, sore ᴛꜱ,ᴛᴍ,ɢᴀ,ᴡɪ,ᴡʏ,ꜱᴛ (2) tear, hole in clothing ᴛꜱ,ᴛᴍ
  mingka pakinthi [mingka paki-nthi] cut someone's skin to make decorative scars ᴡɪ
  mingka parrkulinthi [mingka parrku-l(ay)i-nthi] open a sore ᴛᴍ
  mingka parrkumanthi wound (someone) ᴛᴍ
  mingkamingka [mingka-mingka] *adj* (1) hurt, wounded, sore ᴛꜱ,ᴛᴍ,ᴡɪ,ꜱᴛ (2) broken, damaged, full of holes ᴛꜱ,ᴛᴍ
  mingkarninthi [mingka-rni-nthi] *v-intr* get hurt; get cut *Niina nganarlu mingkarni? – Kudla ngai mingkarni.* 'What were you wounded by? – I got hurt by accident.' ᴛᴍ,ᴛꜱ

mingki (var. **maingki**) *n* (1) joy, happiness ᴛꜱ,ᴛᴍ (2) laughter, smiling ᴛꜱ,ᴛᴍ,ᴘɪ,ᴡɪ,ꜱᴛ,ᴡʏ,ᴋᴏ (3) joke, teasing, jocularity ᴛꜱ
  mingki warnirntu! [mingki warn(i)-(th)irntu] *intj* Happy Birthday! ɴᴇᴡ
  mingkilayinthi [mingki-layi-nthi] *v-intr* laugh, rejoice, be happy *Maingkilayinina ngathu nakuthi.* 'I saw that they laughed/were happy.' ᴛꜱ,ᴛᴍ
  mingkimingkingka (var. **maingkimaingkingka**) in jest, as a joke ᴛꜱ,ᴛᴍ
  mingkinthi [mingki-nthi] *v-intr* laugh, be happy *Mingkirti!* 'Don't laugh!' ᴛᴍ
  mingkipina [mingki-pina] (1) *adj, n* someone who laughs a lot, happy person ᴛꜱ (2) *n* kookaburra ᴛᴍ

minhi *n* vagina; female genitals ᴛꜱ,ᴛᴍ
mininta *n* egg yolk ᴛꜱ,ᴡɪ,ꜱᴛ
minkarra [minka-rra] (var. **minkaminkarra**) (see

also: **mika**) *loc* in front of, in someone's presence *ninku minkarra* 'in your presence' ᴛꜱ,ᴛᴍ

minkarrantinthi [minka-rra-nti-nthi] be in someone's presence ᴛᴍ

minkuminku [minku-minku] *adv* softly; gently; slowly; easily ᴛꜱ,ᴛᴍ

Minkirntu [minku-(th)irntu] *n* Sunday ɴᴇᴡ

minpi (var. **mingpi**) *n* flint ᴛꜱ,ᴛᴍ,ᴡɪ,ᴡʏ

mintamintarrinthi [minta-minta-rri-nthi] *v-intr* (1) suffer, hurt, be in pain *Kurdukila ngathu mintamintarrinthi*. 'I feel pain on the top of my head.' ᴛᴍ (2) be tired *Kati mintamintarrinth'ai*. 'I'm tired' ᴛᴍ,ᴛꜱ

mintawarta [minta-warta] (var. **mintuwarta**) *n* navel; belly-button ᴛꜱ,ᴛᴍ,ᴡɪ,ᴡʏ,ꜱᴛ

mintawarta wirrkanthi [minta-warta wirrka-nthi] rub the navel (healing technique used by traditional doctors to remove pain from the abdomen) ᴛᴍ

minthi *n* net ᴛꜱ,ᴛᴍ,ᴡʏ

minti *n* scar ᴛꜱ,ᴛᴍ

mintirninthi [minti-rni-nthi] *v-intr* heal *Nalati mintirningkutha?* 'When will it heal up?' ᴛᴍ

mintuna [mintu-na] *adj* shrivelled up; wrinkled ᴛᴍ

minturninthi [mintu-rni-nthi] (var. **mintuminturninthi**) *v-intr* shrink; shrivel up; contract ᴛᴍ

minunthi [minu-nthi] *v-tr* make; build ᴛꜱ,ᴛᴍ

minukura *n* roots of reeds ᴡʏ

minyangkayinthi [minyangkayi-nthi] (var. **minyarrangkinthi**) *v-intr* talk; chatter *Minyarrangkingurti, munthu mingkayinya!* 'Don't talk so noisily, speak from the belly!' ᴛꜱ,ᴛᴍ

mipurli *n* (1) trout (fish) ᴡʏ (2) common jollytail (fish) (*Galaxias maculatus*) ɴᴇᴡ

mirdilta (var. **mirdinta**) *n* leech species ᴛꜱ,ᴛᴍ

mirdilyayinthi [mirdi-layi-nthi] (var. **mirdimirdilyayinthi**) *v-intr* shine; glow ᴛᴍ

miri *n* (1) hail stones ᴛꜱ,ᴛᴍ,ᴡɪ,ᴡʏ,ꜱᴛ (2) salt crystals ᴛꜱ

mirnu *n* (1) wattle tree, golden wattle (*Acacia*) ᴛꜱ,ᴛᴍ,ᴡɪ,ᴡʏ,ꜱᴛ (2) gum or sap which people drank during the summer (wattle gum) ᴛꜱ,ᴡʏ,ᴋᴏ

mirnu purrumpa *n* flower of the wattle tree ᴛᴍ

mirnunirnuna [mirnu-(m)irnu-na] *adj* shining; glittering; slippery ᴛꜱ,ᴛᴍ

mirnurrinthi [mirnu-rri-nthi] *v-intr* glitter; shine ᴛꜱ,ᴛᴍ,ᴡʏ

mirrka *n* penis ᴛꜱ,ᴛᴍ

miti *n* (1) upper leg, thigh, hip ᴛꜱ,ᴡɪ,ꜱᴛ (2) climber, person that climbs well ᴛꜱ,ᴛᴍ

miti warpu *n* hip bone ᴡɪ,ꜱᴛ

mititina someone that can't climb well, poor climber ᴛꜱ

mitika *n* flower ᴛꜱ

mitinthi [miti-nthi] (var. **mitimitinthi**) *v-tr* steal; take away *Padlu mitinana yailtya*. 'He thought it had been stolen.' *Nintu nganaitya miti'tithi?* 'Why did you steal (the bread)?' *Ngantu'aityu mititthi mudlirna? Itu-intya pia! 'athu malatirra kati*. 'Who has stolen my things? Those here! I took them by mistake (without any bad intention)' ᴛꜱ,ᴛᴍ,ᴡɪ,ꜱᴛ

mitilitila [miti-l(a)-(m)iti-la] *n* thief; robber ᴛꜱ,ᴛᴍ

mitirrinthi [miti-rri-nthi] *v-tr* steal; take away *mitimitirringka* 'because of the theft, on account of stealing' (var. **mitimitirrinthi**) ᴛꜱ,ᴛᴍ,ᴡɪ,ꜱᴛ

mitirritingka [miti-rri-ti-ngka] (live) on stolen goods ᴛᴍ

mitirripurka [miti-rri-purka] *n* thief; robber ᴛꜱ,ᴛᴍ

mititya *n* snake species ᴛꜱ,ᴡʏ

mityi *n* name ᴛᴍ

miya *n* 'soft spot' on the top of the head (*anterior fontanelle*) ᴛꜱ

miya yurlanthi [miya-yurla-nthi] *v-intr* (1) be sleepy, nodding off ᴛꜱ (2) have a headache ᴛᴍ

miyu [miyu] *n* man; person *Miyurti!* 'No men! Be without men!' *miyu'angki* 'man and wife' *miyu pulyuna* 'blackfellow' ᴛꜱ,ᴛᴍ,ʙʟ,ʙᴀ,ɢᴀ,ʀᴏ,ᴡʏ,ᴋᴏ,ᴄʜ

miyu kumpu *n* the male or outer rainbow ᴡʏ

miyu maimaingka [miyu mai-mai-ngka] *n* cannibal ᴛᴍ

miyu paityarri [miyu paitya-rri] *n* cannibal ᴛᴍ

miyu trruku-ana [miyu trruku-ana] *n* cannibal ᴛᴍ

miyu-katha [miyu-katha] *n* fighter; argumentative person ᴛꜱ,ᴛᴍ

miyurna [miyu-rna] *n* men; people ᴛꜱ

Miyurna [miyu-rna] *n* alternative name for Kaurna people, the people of the Adelaide Plains ᴡʏ

miyuti [miyu-ti(na)] *adj* single (woman) ᴛꜱ

miyutidlu [miyu-tidlu] alone, without a companion ᴛᴍ

miyutila [miyu-ti(na)-la] *adv* in the absence of men; with no men around, women only ᴛᴍ

miyuwarta [miyu-warta] *n* countryman; compatriot ᴛꜱ,ᴛᴍ

-mpi *suff (on nouns)* lacking, wanting *pardumpi* 'without meat' *maimpi* 'lacking food' *Nalatimpi tirntu ngatpi.* 'The sun set without haste.' TS, TM

mudlha *n* nose *mudlhatarra* 'through the nostrils' TS, TM, EA, GA, WI, WY, ST, KO, CH

  mudlha-iku [mudlha-iku] *n* point; end; tip TS, TM

  mudlhakanthi *n* side of the nose TS

  Mudlhangga *n* Le Fevre Peninsula WI

  mudlhanthi [mudlha-nthi] *v-tr* smell (something) TS, TM, GA, WY

  mudlharninthi [mudlha-rni-nthi] *v-intr* point with your nose TM

  mudlharrangki *adj* drowned TS

  mudlharrangkinthi [mudlha-(ta)rra-ngki-nthi] *v-intr* drown *Miyu mudlharangki! Kawainga! Ngatpa'dlu kauwingka!* 'A man has drowned! Come here (you mob)! Let's dive in the water!' TS, TM

  mudlharta [mudlha-rta] *n* nose piercing TS, TM, CA, WI, WY, ST

  mudlhayala [mudlha-yala] *n* (1) septum of the nose, cartilage and skin separating the two nostrils TS (2) hole, piercing in the septum of the nose where a bone, stick or reed could be worn WY

mudlharta

  mudlhayapa [mudlha-yapa] *n* nostrils *mudlhayapa-tarra* 'through the nostrils' TS, TM, WY

mudli (var. **murli**) *n* (1) tool, furniture, implement, thing, object, belonging *Ngangkurna mudlirna? Ngaityurna.* 'Whose are these things? Mine.' TS, TM, CA (2) rubbish TS

  mudliwaadli [mudli-waadli] useless thing TM

  mudliwarra *n* noun NEW

mudnu *n* uncircumcised person TS

muinmu (var. **muyinmu**) *adj, adv* more; again *Nganaitya nintu warra muinmu pingkanthi?* 'Why are you making more words?' *Nganaitya naa muinmu kurntarrinthi? Nata pirdi, tikainga!* 'Why are you all still fighting with each other? That's enough, sit down!' TS, TM, WY

  muinmu piltapilturru more layers (folded onto each other) TM

  muinmurninthi [muinmu-rni-nthi] *v-intr* continue; keep on *Muinmurti!* 'Cut it out! No more! No further! Stop it!' TS, TM

muinyi munthu *n* newborn baby TM

muiyu *n* affection; love; feelings; desire *Ngu'athu muiyu mankunthi, parni kaityantu.* 'I like that woman, send her here.' TS, TM

muiyu kapanthi [muiyu kapa-nthi] hate, feel spite towards (someone) TS, TM

muiyu karrinthi [muiyu karri-nthi] wish (someone) would go away TM

muiyu mankunthi [muiyu manku-nthi] *v-tr* love, fall in love with, take a fancy to *Yaku nintu muiyu manki ngaityu wardli? Ngathu niina turrku yalarra ngaityu wardlingka niina wantititya.* 'Didn't you like my house? I told you already that you should sleep in my house.' TS, TM

muiyu wakinharninthi [muiyu wakinha-rni-nthi] *v-intr* be/feel guilty NEW

muiyu yungkunthi [muiyu yungku-nthi] *v-intr* be/feel grateful NEW

muiyuminti [muiyu-minti] *n* depression below the sternum *(scrobiculus cordis/epigastric fossa)* WY

muiyupinti [muiyu-pinti] *n* pit of the stomach TS, TM

muka *n* (1) egg TS, TM, WI, WY, ST (2) round or oval shaped (thing) TS

  muka wangkawangkanthi [muka wangka-wangka-nthi] *v-intr* meditate; think deeply TM

  mukamuka [muka-muka] *n* (1) brain TS, TM, WI, ST (2) thought, mental faculties, power of thinking TM

  mukamukarninthi [muka-muka-rni-nthi] *v-intr* (1) be alone, lonely, isolated, solitary TS

  mukanta-wantanthi [muka-nta-wanta-nthi] *v-tr* forget; abandon; leave behind TM

  mukantarri-apinthi [muka-nta-rri-(w)api-nthi] *v-tr* forget; lose; leave behind TS, TM

  mukantarrinthi [muka-nta-rri-nthi] *v-tr* (1) forget *ngai mukantarri* 'I forgot' *Niina yaku mukantarri?* 'Have you not forgotten it?' TM, TS, RO, WY (2) be ignorant (of something) WY

  mukapanthi [muka-pa(a)-nthi] *v-tr* (1) know, remember, think of *Tarrkarri ngathu mukapatha.* 'Later I will think about it.' *Nintu puru mukapanthi?* 'Do you still remember?' TS, TM (2) show, point out, represent TS, TM

  mukapapanthi [muka-pa(a)-pa(a)-nthi] *v-intr* think deeply; meditate TM

  mukaparrinthi [muka-pa(a)-rri-nthi] *v-intr* remember; think to oneself TS, TM

  mukarntu [muka-(ka)rntu] *n* computer NEW

  mukarta [muka-rta] *n* (1) head, crown of the head, skull TS, TM, GA, WI, WY, KO (2) round piece of bark (used as a target for spear practice) WY

  mukarta karra-yarnkanthi [muka-rta karra-yarnka-nthi] *v-intr* think; contemplate *Niina nganaitya mukarta karra-yarnkanthi?* 'What are you thinking about?' TM

  mukarta marni [muka-rta marni] *adj* intelligent;

good at learning; smart ₜₛ,ₜₘ

mukarta partarninthi [muka-rta parta-rni-nthi] *v-intr* be clever, sensible, witty ₜₘ

mukarta tawutawu [muka-rta tawu-tawu] *adj* clear-headed; open-minded ₜₘ

mukarta walara [muka-rta walara] *adj* intelligent; clear-headed ₜₛ,ₜₘ

mukarta wangkiwangki [muka-rta wangki-wangki] *adj* forgetful; inattentive ₜₘ

mukarta warpu [muka-rta warpu] *adj* intelligent; good at remembering ₜₛ,ₜₘ

mukartantinthi [muka-rta-nti-nthi] *v-intr* (1) turn the head ₜₘ (2) stick out your head, appear with your head first (e.g. looking around a corner) ₜₘ

mukartatana [muka-rta-tana] *adj* stupid; slow-witted ₜₛ

mukarti-ana [muka-rta-ana] *n* hat; cap ₜₛ,ₜₘ,ᵂʸ

mukatina [muka-tina] *adj* stupid; silly ₜₛ,ₜₘ

mukanthi [muka-nthi] (var. **mukarrinthi**) *v-intr* play, sing, dance, perform ceremony ₜₛ,ᴿᴼ,ᵂʸ

mukamukarninthi [muka-muka-rni-nthi] *v-intr* (2) be glad, happy, lively, animated ₜₘ

mukamukarrinthi [muka-muka-rri-nthi] *v-intr* celebrate; play ₜₘ

mukati [muka-ti] *n* game (fun/sport) ɴᴇᵂ

mukumukurru *adj* round; globular ₜₛ,ₜₘ

mukurniti [muku-rni-ti] *adj* bent; arched ₜₘ

mukurrinthi [muku-rri-nthi] *v-intr* (1) move, hurry, hasten ₜₛ,ₜₘ (2) be uneasy, anxious, uncomfortable ₜₘ,ɴᴇᵂ (3) break up ₜₛ

mukurripurka [muku-rri-purka] *n* person who moves around a lot ₜₛ,ₜₘ

mukurta *n* hill; mountain *mukurtila* 'in the hills' *mukurtarra* 'along the hills' ₜₛ,ₜₘ,ᴿᴼ,ᵂᴵ,ᵂʸ,ˢᵀ

mularta *n* stick; rod; fishing rod ₜₛ,ₜₘ,ᵂᴵ,ᵂʸ,ˢᵀ

mularta parntu *n* hockey ɴᴇᵂ

mularta wikatidli parntu [mularta wika-tidli parntu] *n* lacrosse ɴᴇᵂ

multinthi [multi-nthi] *v-intr* (1) melt ₜₛ,ₜₘ (2) rot, go off, putrify ₜₛ,ₜₘ

multyu *n* fruit of pigface plant ₜₛ,ₜₘ,ᵂʸ

multyumultyu [multyu-multyu] *n* bowels and excrement of kangaroo; excrement and bowels of kangaroo ₜₛ

mulyirrinthi [mulyi-rri-nthi] *v-tr Tirnturlu mii mulyirrinthi.* 'The sun blinds the eye.' ₜₘ

muna *adv* first, beforehand *Muna padni!* 'Go first! / Go ahead!' ₜₛ,ₜₘ

munaintya [muna-intya] *n* (1) before, sooner, earlier (than something else) ₜₛ,ₜₘ (2) beginning, creation ɴᴇᵂ (3) 'Dreaming', 'Dreamtime' ɴᴇᵂ

munaintya pirrku [muna-intya pirrku] Dreaming story ɴᴇᵂ

munaintyarlintya [muna-intya-rl(u)-intya] in the beginning, earliest, soonest, very long time ago ₜₘ

munaintyarlu [muna-intya-rlu] long time ago, sooner (than something else) ₜₛ,ₜₘ

Munaintyarlu [muna-intya-rlu] *n* Creator ᵂʸ

munampi [muna-mpi] *adj* ambitious ₜₘ

munana [muna-na] *adj* ancient, former, late, of the ancestors ₜₛ,ₜₘ

munangka [muna-ngka] *adv* first; beforehand *Nganaitya padlu yaku ngaityu munangka wanta?* 'Why hasn't he/she saved any for me?' *Munangka karla parr'athu.* 'I'll light the fire first' ₜₛ,ₜₘ

munarra [muna-arra] *adv* before; first *munarra padninthi* 'to go before, go ahead' ₜₛ

Munaitya *n* birth-order name: fourth born (male) ₜₛ,ᴱʸ,ᵂʸ,ᵂᴵ,ˢᵀ

Munartu [muna-(k)artu] *n* birth-order name: fourth born (female) ₜₛ,ᴱʸ,ᵂᴵ,ᵂʸ,ᴷᴼ,ˢᵀ

munkaka *n* hawk ˢᵀ,ᵀᴵ

munta *n* net (for large game) ₜₛ,ₜₘ

munta

muntangka pungkunthi [munta-ngka pungku-nthi] catch (something) in a 'munta' ₜₘ

munthu (var. **murlu**) *n* belly; stomach; abdomen *mai munthu tikanthi* 'to be well off, and have plenty (of food)' *munthu 'iwi ngai* 'to stick in your throat' *munthurlu wantinthi* 'to lie on your stomach' ₜₛ,ₜₘ,ᴳᴬ,ᵂᴵ,ᵂʸ,ˢᵀ

munthu padlunintyarla [munthu padlu-intyarla] *n* glutton ₜₘ

munthu pakurta decorative scarring on the abdomen ₜₛ

munthu partu *adj* (1) overweight, having a big belly ₜₘ (2) full (of food), satisfied ₜₘ

munthu tawata *adj* full (of food); stuffed (with food) ᵂᴵ,ˢᵀ

munthu wayirrinthi [munthu wayi-rri-nthi] *v-intr* give birth; labour (be in) ᵂᴵ,ˢᵀ

munthungka padlunthi [munthu-ngka padlu-nthi] *v-intr* miscarry, be still-born ᵂʸ

munthurntu [munthu-(pa)rntu] *adj* pregnant ₜₘ

munthurntu-antinthi [munthu-(pa)rntu-(w)anti-nthi] *v-intr* become pregnant ₜₘ

munthuthakana [munthu-thakana] *n* goat ₜₛ
munthuwirri [munthu-wirri] *n* cuts on the abdomen ₜₛ
munti *n* drumming on cloaks during ceremony ₜₛ,ᵂʸ
munu *n* point; tip; end of something ₜₘ
munyarrinthi [munya-rri-nthi] *v-intr* pant (like a dog) ᵂʸ
murdanyi *n* mother whose child has died ₜₛ,ᵂʸ
murdu *n* dust, ashes (cold) ₜₛ,ₜₘ,ᵂʸ
  murdumurdu [murdu-murdu] *n* (1) flour ₜₛ,ᵂʸ (2) bread ₜₛ,ᵂʸ
  murdu-murdurla [murdu-murdu-rla] *n* sandwich ɴᴇᴡ
  murdumurdu kampati [murdu-murdu kampa-ti] *n* toaster ɴᴇᴡ
  murdurninthi [murdu-rni-nthi] *v-intr* turn to dust, ashes ₜₘ
murinthi [muri-nthi] (var. **muyinthi**) (1) *v-intr* go, walk, run, travel, move (from one place to another) *Muritha ngai?* 'Shall I go?' *Muringk'ai parni!* 'Come here to me!' *Niina wanti muritha? – Karra ngai muritha Yultiwirra- ana.* 'Where are you going? – I am going up to the Stringy-bark Forest.' ₜₛ,ₜₘ,ɢᴀ,ʀᴏ,ᴡɪ,ꜱᴛ (2) *v-tr* remove, take away *Nuki murintu!* 'Clean your nose!' *Nuki muyintu!* 'Wipe your nose!' ₜₘ,ₜₛ
  muri-murinya [muri-muri-nya] *adj* creeping; slow-moving ₜₛ
  muringkayinthi [muri-ngka-(w)ayi-nthi] *v-intr* run to; go (somewhere) quickly ₜₘ
murki *n* face; forehead ₜₛ,ₜₘ
  murkipaltha [murki-paltha] *n* face mask ɴᴇᴡ
murla *adj* dry ₜₛ,ₜₘ
  murla parltanthi [murla parlta-nthi] *v-tr* finish, complete *murla parlta nungkurrinthi* 'return to finish each other off (in a fight)' ₜₘ
  murla-ityarri-apinthi [murla-itya-rri-(w)api-nthi] *v-tr* dry (something) ₜₘ
  murlamurla [murla-murla] *n* towel ɴᴇᴡ
  murlanthi [murla-nthi] *v-intr* (1) dry out, become dry ₜₛ,ₜₘ (2) be dead (and drying out) ᴡɪ,ꜱᴛ
  murlapaka [murla-paka] *n* shield ₜₛ,ₜₘ,ᴄᴀ,ᵂʸ,ᴋᴏ
  murlapiti [murla-(wa)pi-ti] *n* dryer; clothes dryer ɴᴇᴡ
  murlarninthi [murla-rni-nthi] *v-intr* dry out, become parched *wangki mularni* 'thirsty' ₜₛ,ₜₘ

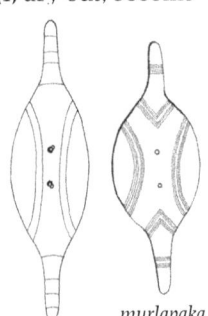
murlapaka

murlarrinthi [murla-rri-nthi] *v-intr* be finished, done with, over *Miitu murla-murlarri, yangadli karri-karringki!* 'Stop sleeping, soon you must get up!' ₜₘ
Murlayaki (var. **Murdlayaki**) *n* Great Para River ₜₘ
murli => **mudli**
murltarra *n* female emu ᵂʸ
murlu => **munthu**
murluwarta *n* belly button; navel ᵂʸ
murntu *n* buttocks; bottom; anus ₜₛ,ₜₘ,ɢᴀ
  murntu padlunthi [murntu padlu-nthi] *v-intr* desire women, be horny ₜₘ
  murntu padlurnintyarla [murnthu padlu-rni-(i)ntyarla] person who has a strong desire for women, horny person ₜₘ
  murntu warra *n* swearing; bad language; obscene language ₜₛ,ₜₘ
  murntuwaadli [murntu-waadli] *adj* chaste; celibate ₜₘ
murrka *n* crying ₜₛ,ₜₘ,ᵂʸ,ᴋᴏ
  murrka yungkunthi [murrka yungku-nthi] *v-intr* cry over; lament over ₜₘ
  murrkamanthi [murka-ma-nthi] *v-tr* make someone cry *Padlu ngai murrkamama.* 'He has made me cry.' ₜₘ
  murrkanthi [murrka-nthi] *v-intr* lament; cry *Murrkarti!* 'Don't cry!' ₜₛ,ₜₘ,ʀᴏ,ᴡɪ,ꜱᴛ
murrmarninthi [murrma-rni-nthi] *v-intr* (1) decrease, shrink *Nintunti nganmantu! Tangka ngai murrmarninthi, mairnanti ngaityurna.* 'You go ahead and eat alone. My appetite is gone, never mind that the food is mine.' ₜₘ (2) go bald ₜₘ
murta *n* animal droppings, poo, manure ₜₛ,ₜₘ,ɢᴀ
  murta-ana-itya [murta-ana-itya] *n* chicken; hen ₜₘ,ᴡɪ,ꜱᴛ
  murtatinthi [murta-ti-nthi] *v-tr* defecate ₜₛ,ₜₘ
murtana [murta-na] *adj* (1) hurt, injured, deformed *tidna murtana* 'having a deformed foot' ₜₛ,ₜₘ (2) broken, defective, no good *warti murtana* 'dock-tailed horse' ₜₛ,ₜₘ
  murta-wardninthi [murta wardni-nthi] *v-intr* (1) get hurt, injured ₜₘ (2) become broken, defective ₜₘ (3) become frail ₜₘ
  murtarrinthi [murta-rri-nthi] *v-intr* hurt oneself *Kudla pa murtarri.* 'It broke on its own.' ₜₘ
murtpanthi [murtpa-nthi] *v-intr* (1) leap, jump ₜₛ (2) hop ₜₘ
  murtpamanku [murtpa-manku(nthi)] *n* mark (in football) *Murtpamanmantu!* 'Take the mark!' ɴᴇᴡ

murtpu => **marrpu**

mutanthi [muta-nthi] *v-tr* (1) eat, drink, enjoy, feast on (something) TS,TM,RO,WI,WY,CH (2) eat quickly, eat during a journey, eat a snack while on the way to somewhere TS

 muta-mutanya kuu [muta-muta-nya] *n* dining room NEW

 muta-mutarru [muta-muta-rru] *n* take-away; snack; fast food TM

 mutarru wardli [muta-rru wardli] *n* take-away shop NEW

 mutarta [muta-rta] (var. **murtata**; **mutata**) *adj* (1) edible, cooked, well done, ready to eat, not raw TS,TM (2) soft TS (3) brittle TS

mutyarta *n* shirt; clothing *mutyartila* 'wearing the clothes' *mutyartina* 'naked, without clothes' *mutyarturti* 'naked, without clothes' *mutyartutana* 'naked, without clothes' *mutyarta yaki-ana nudnu-nudnu-apinthi* 'wrap a corpse in clothing' TS,TM,BL,WI,WY,CH (from English 'my shirt')

 mutyarta kuru *n* clothes container NEW

 mutyarta tainkyadli *n* clothes basket NEW

 mutyarta tita *n* clothes peg NEW

 mutyarta wardli *n* clothes shop, boutique NEW

muyinmu => **muinmu**

muyinthi => **murinthi**

N n

-na adjectival suffix

naa [nhaa] (var. **-nhaa**) *pro* you mob; you (plural nominative/accusative) *Naa waa wanti?* 'Where are you mob camped?' TS,TM,BL

 naaku [nhaa-ku] *pro* your(s); you mob's (plural possessive) *Yaku ngaityu yunga kamparritiwarta naaku tikatha.* 'My brother will not be your cook.' TS,TM,WY

 naalitya [nhaa-litya] *pro* (1) for you mob; on account of you mob (purposive) TS,TM (2) to you mob (allative)

 naalityangka [nhaa-litya-ngka] with you, beside you (plural comitative) TM

 naanti [nhaa-nti] only you TM

naawi? [nhaawi] *inter* how many? TS,TM,WY

 naawi tirnturna? [nhaawi thirntu-rna] How long? *Naawi tirnturna wartingka ninkurna?* 'How long have you been on the road?' *Naawi naaku tirnturna?* 'How long will you stay?' TS

 naawirluku? [nhaawi-rluku] *adv* how often?; how many times? *Naawirluku? – Purlarluku.* 'How many times? - Twice.' TS,TM

nadlarrinthi [nhadla-rri-nthi] *v-tr* shrink; warp; change shape *taa nadlarrinthi* 'to sulk, stick out the bottom lip' TS

 nadla-nhadlarrinthi [nhadla-nhadla-rri-nthi] (var. **nala-nhalarrinthi**) *v-intr* (1) stretch oneself (as when waking up) TM (2) shrink, warp, distort, change shape (like meat does when it cooks) TM

nadlati => **nalati**

nadli [nhadli] *n* short, compact person or thing TM

Nadnu (var. **Nanu**) *n* Creation being CA

naingu [nhaingu] *adv* softly; gently *naingu kupayinthi* 'to sneak away quietly' TM

 nainguta [nhaingu-ta] *adj* soft; pliable; elastic TS,TM

nakudla [nhakudla] *n* shark TS,TM,WI,WY,ST

nakunthi [nhaku-nthi] *v-intr, v-tr* (1) see, look *Wardli ngathu kurda nakuntyidla tirnturlu ngai pudna-itha yaintya.* 'After I have seen my house, tomorrow I will come here.' TRAD,TS,TM,PI,CH (2) know, be aware of, understand, remember *Waa'adli kauwi kampatha? – Yaku'athu naki.* 'Where will we boil the water? – I don't know.' TM,WI,WY (3) meet (someone) *Yalakanta ngathu nanga.* 'I met him quite recently.' TM

 nakarra [nhak(u)-arra] *adj* awake TS,TM

 nakarrantinthi [nhak(u)-arra-nti-nthi] *v-intr* wake up TM

 naku-nhakunthi [nhaku-nhaku-nthi] *v-tr* look at; inspect; examine *Naku-naku'athu.* 'I'll have a look at it.' TM

 Nakupirntu [nhaku-(a)pi-(th)irntu] *n* Show Day NEW

 nakurni-apinthi [nhaku-rni-(w)api-nthi] (var. **nakulyarni-apinthi**) *v-tr* instruct; teach; educate; cause to see *Nintu ngadlu nintini pipangka nakulyarni-apinthi?* 'Will you let us look at the paper again? Will you teach us again?' TM

 nakurninthi [nhaku-rni-nthi] *v-intr* perceive; consider *Ngaityu warrarna nakurninga!* 'Consider my words!' *Wantaka nakurni'adlu'rna.* 'We will definitely see them.' TM

 nakurri-apinthi [nhaku-rri-(w)api-nthi] *v-tr* see (cause to); appear; reveal oneself TS,TM

 nakurrinthi [nhaku-rri-nthi] *v-intr* (1) be awake TS,TM (2) see TM,KO

 nakutha! [nhaku-tha] *intj* goodbye! NEW

nala-nhalarrinthi => **nadla-nhadlarrinthi**

nalati (var. **nadlati**) (1) *adv* quickly, hastily *Nalatimpi tirntu ngatpi.* 'The sun set without haste.' TS,TM (2) *inter* when?; at what time? *Nalatintya?* 'At what time then? (expressing impatience)' TM

nala-alati when? at what time? ᴛꜱ,ᴛᴍ,ᴡʏ

namanthi [nhama-nthi] *v-tr* (1) carry (something) on your back *wakwaku ngurrungka namanthi* 'to carry a child on your back' ᴛꜱ,ᴛᴍ (2) take up, pick up (in order to carry) ᴛᴍ

   namarrinthi [nha-ma-rri-nthi] *v-tr* carry; pull; draw out/up ᴛᴍ,ᴋᴏ

namu [nhamu] (var. **-amu**) *adj, adv* like this; thus; like this one; so *Wingku ngai namutarnaintya.* 'I want some like this one/these ones.' *namu tura-turana* 'like this/that one, similar to this/that one' *Namurlinya'rna ngaityurna madli.* 'Such were my children when they died.' ᴛꜱ,ᴛᴍ

   namu-amu [nhamu-(nh)amu] that's the right way, like that ᴛᴍ

   namudlinyarnanthi [nhamu-dli-nya-rna-nthi] (var. **namudliarnanthi**) *v-intr* become like (these ones); become similar to (these ones) ᴛᴍ

   namuntirlinthi [nhamu-nti-rli-nthi] *v-intr* just do it like this ᴛᴍ

   namuntya [nhamu-ntya] *adv* just like this ᴛꜱ,ᴛᴍ

   namuntyanta [nhamu-ntya-nta] only like this, exclusively in this way (and no other) ᴛᴍ

   namurli [nhamu-rli] (var. **namudli**) *adv* in this way, like this *Namurli ngaityurna madli.* 'My (children) were the same (age) when they died.' ᴛꜱ,ᴛᴍ

   namutaku wayinthi [nhamu-ta-ku wayi-nthi] act or do something in this way ᴛᴍ

   namutarla? [nhamu-ta-rla] *inter* then?; about that time? *Namutarlaintya niina pudni? – Mardlana, puru ngai namutarlaintya tapangkanti padnithi.* 'Did you arrive at that time? – No, at that time I was just on the road coming.' ᴛᴍ

   namutarna [nhamu-ta-rna] like these (ones) (plural) ᴛꜱ

   namutarnaintyanthi [nhamu-ta-rna-ntya-nthi] *v-intr* be like; resemble ᴛᴍ,ᴛꜱ

-nana *suff (on verbs)* (1) denoting an action has been completed (past perfect) *Ngathu parltanana.* 'I have hit (something).' *Mitinana padlu pudlu.* 'He said it had been stolen' ᴛᴍ (2) denoting an action had been completed (when talking about a time in the past) (pluperfect) *Painingka, ngathu parltanana.* 'Previously, I had hit (something).' ᴛᴍ (3) denoting an action that has been done to someone *Ngai parltanana.* 'I have been beaten.' ᴛᴍ

   nanganthi [nhanga-nthi] *v-tr* see; look *Nangantu!* 'Look!, Behold!' ᴛꜱ,ᴛᴍ

nangkarra [nhangka-arra] defiance; resistance *nangka-angkanthi padlu* '[uncertain]' ᴛᴍ

   nangkarrinthi [nhangka-rri-nthi] *v-intr* (1) be boastful, haughty, defiant, resistant ᴛᴍ (2) insist upon, depend upon ᴛᴍ

nangku => **nungku** *adv*

-nangku => **-nungku** *suff (on nouns)*

nantanthi [nhanta-nthi] *v-tr* (1) stick or join (something) together (with something else) ᴛᴍ (2) eat vegetable food and meat together ᴛꜱ

   nantarla [nhanta-rla] *n* twins, two together ᴛᴍ

   nantarri-apinthi [nhanta-rri-(w)api-nthi] *v-tr* (1) put (things) together, pile (things) up *Nantarri-apinama.* 'I have been piling things up.' ᴛᴍ (2) mend (something), sew (something) together ᴛᴍ

   nantarti [nhanta-rti] *n* (1) something joined or put together with something else ᴛᴍ (2) dish containing vegetable food along with meat ᴛꜱ

nanti-nhantina [nhanti-nhanti-na] *adj* grown-up; adult; mature ᴛꜱ,ᴛᴍ

nantu *n* (1) grey kangaroo (male) ᴛꜱ,ᴛᴍ,ᴡʏ,ʙʟ (2) horse, pony *Nanturlu pa katinthi.* 'The horse carries him' *Nanturla tuthangka mainthi purla* 'Both the horses are grazing.' *Nantungka pa padninthi.* 'He goes on horseback.' ᴛꜱ (3) large animal (e.g. kangaroo, horse, bullock) ᴡʏ,ᴡɪ,ꜱᴛ

   Nantu Purka *n* (1) kangaroo (male grey) elder; kangaroo totem group belonging to Adelaide ʙᴀ,ʀᴏ (2) old, grey-haired male kangaroo ᴡʏ

   nantuwarta [nhantu-warta] cart ᴛꜱ,ᴡɪ

Nanu => **Nadnu**

naparta *n* mouth; roof of the mouth ᴛꜱ,ᴡɪ,ᴡʏ

nari *n* name *Ngaintya niina nari?* 'What's your name?' *Ngana nari ninku?* 'What's your name?' *Niina nari ngaintya?* 'What's your name?' *Ninku nari ngaintya?* 'What's your name?' *Purlaku ngaintya narirla?* 'What are their (two) names?' ᴛꜱ,ᴛᴍ,ᴡʏ

   nari-nharitpina [nhari-nhari-(y)itpi-na] possibly 'named after the child' (uncertain) ᴛᴍ

   nari-yungkurri [nhari-yungku-rri] someone who has the same name as you ᴛᴍ,ᴛꜱ

   naritina [nhari-tina] *n* no-name (person whose regular name can't be used) ɴᴇᴡ

narna *n* door *Narna tartantu!* 'Shut the door!' ᴛꜱ

narni *n* nightjar (bird) ᴘʟ,ꜱᴛ

narnta *adj* rough ᴡʏ

narntangka *n* pigeon (bronze, yellow legs) ᴡʏ

narntu *n* upper arm ᴛꜱ,ᴛᴍ,ɢᴀ,ᴡɪ

   narntu ngaitya *adj* weak-armed, tired, not powerful (person) ᴛꜱ,ᴛᴍ

narnturla [nharntu-rla] *n* jacket ᴡʏ

narnu *n* native pine *(Callitris)* ᴛs, ᴛᴍ

  narnu yaku *n* gum, resin from native pine tree (used to make knives) ᴛs

narrka *n* eyelash ᴋᴏ

narrpa *n* rat species ᴛs, ᴡɪ, sᴛ

nata *temp* now *Nat'adlu!* 'Let's go!' *Nata nurnt'idli!* 'Let's (us two) go!' *Natama?* 'Now?' ᴛs, ᴛᴍ, ᴡɪ, sᴛ ᴡʏ

  natampi [nhata-mpi] *adv* quickly, in a hurry ᴛs, ᴛᴍ

  natapirdi! [nhata-pirdi] *intj* enough!; no more! *natapirdanta* 'that's just enough now' ᴛᴍ, ᴡʏ

nayanthi [nhaya-nthi] *v-tr* **(1)** sew, fasten, attach (something) ᴛs, ᴛᴍ, ᴡʏ **(2)** shut (something) ᴛs

  nayarrinthi [nhaya-rri-nthi] *v-intr* sew; shut ᴛs

  nayati [nhaya-ti] *n* glue ɴᴇᴡ

nayinmanthi [nhayin-ma-nthi] *v-tr* press together; hold together; keep together; compact ᴛs, ᴛᴍ

  nayinma-nhayinmarri taikunthi speaking in the abbreviated, contracted form of the language, which is how Kaurna people usually spoke ᴛᴍ

  nayinmarrinthi [nhayin-ma-rri-nthi] *v-intr* stick together, be pressed together ᴛs, ᴛᴍ

  nayinmayinmati [nhayin-ma-(nha)yin-ma-ti] *n* scissors; pincers ᴛs

nga? *inter* who?; what? *Nga? – Iya!* 'Who? – Him/her?' ᴛᴍ

  ngaintya? [nga-intya] *inter* **(1)** what? *Niina nari ngaintya?* 'What is your name?' *Ngaintya pa wangki?* 'What did he say?' ᴛs, ᴛᴍ, ᴡʏ **(2)** how? in what way? *Ngaintya'athu wapirna?* 'What should I do? How should I act?' *Ngaintya ngai parnuku?* 'What am I to him? (what sort of relation)' ᴛs, ᴛᴍ **(3)** how many? *Ngaintya tirnturna mai-itya?* 'How many day's food is there?' ᴛᴍ

  ngaintyarlu? [nga-intya-rlu] *inter* how? in what way? ᴛᴍ

  ngaintyatana? [nga-intya-ta-na] *inter* **(1)** of what kind? of what description? what sort? ᴛs **(2)** how long? of what length of time? *Ngaintyatanama tawarra padlu ngarki? Yaku pardu-alya!* 'How long has he been eating like that for? There might be no more meat!' ᴛᴍ

  ngangku? [nga-ngku] *inter* whose? ᴛs, ᴡɪ, ᴡʏ, sᴛ

  ngantaityangka? [nganthu-itya-ngka] *inter* because of whom? *Ngantaityangka miyurna turlalayinthi?* 'Who are the men so angry over?' *Ngantaityangka miyungka maingki-maingkithi?* 'Who have they been laughing at?' ᴛᴍ

  ngantu? *inter* who? (ergative singular) *Ngantu pirrki-pirrkitirna ngarkuthi?* 'Who ate the biscuits?' *Ngantu kadli ngaityu parlta?* 'Who struck my dog?' ᴛs, ᴛᴍ, ʙʟ

ngadla *n* stepfather ᴛs, ᴛᴍ

Ngadlaitya [ngadla-itya] *n* birth-order name: eighth born (male) ᴛs, ᴇʏ

Ngadlartu [ngadl(a)-(k)artu] *n* birth-order name: eighth born (female) ᴛs

ngadli (var. **'adli**; **'dli**) *pro* we (two); us (two) (dual nominative/accusative) ᴛs, ᴛᴍ, ᴡɪ, ᴡʏ

  ngadliku *pro* our(s) (dual possessive) *ngadliku yunga* 'our brother (the brother of us two)' ᴛs, ᴛᴍ, ᴡʏ

  ngadlilitya *pro* **(1)** to us two (dual allative) **(2)** for us two (dual purposive)

ngadlu (var. **'adlu**; **'dlu**) *pro* we; us mob (plural nominative/accusative) *Ngadlulityangka ninku yunga nintu pudnanyapi.* 'You have made your brother come to us.' *ngadlu purrutyi ngarnta-anthi* 'we are all ill' ᴛs, ᴛᴍ, ᴡʏ

  ngadluku *pro* our(s) (plural possessive) ᴛs, ᴡʏ

  Ngadluku Tirntu *n* Australia Day ɴᴇᴡ

  ngadlulitya [ngadlu-litya] *pro* **(1)** for us (plural purposive) ᴛs **(2)** to us (plural allative)

ngai (var. **'ai**) *pro* I, me (nominative/accusative) *Nintu ngai nganapira wuinpanthi?* 'Why are you angry with me?' *Ngaini kuma yungkuntu!* 'Give (it) to me too!' *Ngai-ma? – Niina kuma.* 'Me too? – Yes, you too.' *ngai ngarnta-anthi* 'I am ill' ᴛs, ᴛᴍ, ʙʟ, ᴡʏ

ngaikinta *n* little toe ᴛs

ngaingku *n* expert; specialist; a person knowing anything well ᴛs

  ngaingkurni-apinthi [ngaingku-rni-(w)api-nthi] *v-intr* be/become knowledgeable, an expert ᴛᴍ

-ngaitya *suff (on nouns)* weak-, faint- *narntu-ngaitya* 'weak-armed' *yarku-ngaitya* 'not strong on foot' ᴛs, ᴛᴍ

  ngaityana [ngaitya-na] *adj* **(1)** weak, feeble, not strong ᴛs, ᴛᴍ **(2)** tired, faint, weary ᴛs

  ngaityarni-apinthi [ngaitya-rni-(w)api-nthi] *v-tr* weaken (someone); tire (someone) out ᴛs, ᴛᴍ

  ngaityarni-purka [ngaitya-rni-purka] *n* weak person; someone who tires easily ᴛᴍ

  ngaityarninthi [ngaitya-rni-nthi] *v-intr* **(1)** be/become weak, faint, weary, feeble ᴛs, ᴛᴍ **(2)** be/become tired, worn out ᴛs, ᴡʏ

ngaityu *pro* my; mine (singular) *Ngaityurna-alya mairna; kauwi ngaityu karnkantu pa!* 'Draw my water for my food plants!' *ngaityu yangarra* 'my wife' ᴛs, ᴛᴍ, ʙʟ, ʙᴀ, ʀᴏ, ᴡʏ, ᴡɪ, sᴛ, ᴋᴏ, ᴄʜ

ngaityai *n* (1) mum, my mother, mummy ᴛꜱ,ᴛᴍ,ᴘɪ,ʀᴏ,ᴡʏ,ᴄʜ (2) father-in-law ᴛᴍ

ngaityaingkula [ngaityai-ngku-la] *adj* mother relationship ᴛᴍ

Ngaityairntu [ngaityai-(thi)rntu] *n* Mother's Day *Ngunya Ngaityaithirntu!* 'Happy Mother's day!' ɴᴇᴡ

ngaityaita [ngaityai-ta] *n* with my mum ᴛᴍ

ngaityalya [ngaity(u)-alya] *intj* thanks ɴᴇᴡ

ngaityarli [ngaity(u)-(y)arli] *n* dad; my father ᴛꜱ,ᴛᴍ,ʙᴀ,ɢᴀ,ᴘɪ,ʀᴏ,ᴡɪ,ᴡʏ,ꜱᴛ,ᴄʜ

ngaityu'rla [ngaityu-rla] *adj* my; mine (dual) ᴛᴍ

ngaityu'rna [ngaityu-rna] *adj* my; mine (plural) *Namurlinyarna ngaityurna madli* 'Of such (age) were mine (children) when they died' ᴛᴍ

ngaityurtila [ngaityu-rti-la] *adv* without me, in my absence ᴛᴍ

ngakala *n* rainbow lorikeet ᴛꜱ,ᴛᴍ,ᴄᴏ,ᴘɪ,ᴡʏ

ngakalamurdu [ngakala-murdu] *n* Magellanic Cloud (galaxy) ᴛꜱ

ngakirra *n* duck species ᴛᴍ

Ngalta *n* Murray River ᴛᴍ

ngalta yawitya *n* eel-tailed catfish (*Tandanus tandanus*) ɴᴇᴡ

ngaltaitya [ngalta-(pa)itya] *n* yabby, freshwater crayfish (*Cheerax destructor*) ᴛꜱ,ᴛᴍ,ᴡʏ

ngaltaityapinthi [ngalta-(pa)itya-(w)api-nthi] *v-tr* catch yabbies ᴛꜱ,ᴛᴍ

ngama *adj* heavy; bulky; stout ᴛꜱ,ᴛᴍ

ngama-ngamaityarntinthi [ngama-ngama-itya-rni-nthi] *v-intr* become a woman, come of age (females) ᴛᴍ

ngamaitya [ngama-itya] (var. **ngama-ngamaitya**) *n* (1) woman, adult female ᴛꜱ,ᴛᴍ,ɢᴀ,ʀᴏ,ᴡɪ,ᴡʏ,ᴄʜ (2) wife ᴛᴍ,ɢᴀ,ʀᴏ,ᴡɪ,ᴡʏ

ngamaitya kumpu [ngama-itya kumpu] *n* inner or female rainbow ᴡʏ

Ngamatyi *n* name of the site where the GPO stands ʙᴀ,ɢʀ

ngami *n* breast (female) ᴛꜱ,ᴛᴍ,ɢᴀ,ᴡɪ,ᴡʏ,ꜱᴛ,ᴋᴏ,ᴛʀᴀᴅ

ngamingaru [ngami-ngaru] *n* milk *Niina nganaitya pudni? – Ngamingaru-urna.* 'What have you come for? – For milk.' ᴛꜱ,ᴛᴍ,ɢᴀ,ᴡɪ,ᴡʏ,ꜱᴛ

ngamipaltha [ngami-paltha] *n* bra ɴᴇᴡ

ngampa *n* edible root ᴛꜱ,ᴛᴍ,ᴡʏ

ngana? *inter* what? which? ᴛᴍ,ᴡʏ,ᴡɪ,ꜱᴛ,ᴄʜ

nganaitya? [ngana-itya] *inter* why? what for? *Niina nganaitya yalarra yaku piipa-itya pudni?* 'Why didn't you come to school today?' *Nganaitya iyarntama nintu wanta?* 'Why have you left it here?' *Nganaitya nintu pinti miyu kurntanthi?* 'Why do you kill the Europeans?' ᴛꜱ,ᴛᴍ

nganalalitya? [ngana-lalitya] *inter* for whom?; to whom? ᴛᴍ

nganalalityangka? [ngana-lalitya-ngka] *inter* with whom? ᴛᴍ

nganangka? [ngana-ngka] *inter* (1) for how much? *Nganangka nintu manki?* 'How much did you get it for?' ᴛꜱ,ᴛᴍ (2) in what? on account of what? ᴛꜱ,ᴛᴍ

nganangku? [ngana-(na)ngku] *inter* from whom?; from where? ᴛꜱ,ᴛᴍ

nganapira? [ngana-pira] *inter* why?; what for? ᴛꜱ,ᴛᴍ

nganapurtu-itya? [ngana-purtu-itya] *inter* why?; because of what?; for what reason? *Nintu ngai nganapurtuitya nakunthi?* 'What are you looking at me for?' ᴛᴍ

nganapurtu? [ngana-purtu] *inter* what's wrong? ᴛꜱ,ᴛᴍ

nganarlu? [ngana-rlu] *inter* (1) how? by what means? ᴛꜱ,ᴛᴍ (2) when? around what time? ᴛᴍ

ngangaitya (var. **ngangaityi**) *n* (1) mother-in-law ᴛꜱ,ᴛᴍ (2) father's older brother ᴛᴍ

ngangka *n* obstacle; hinderance; barrier ᴛꜱ

ngangka mankunthi [ngangka manku-nthi] interfere in a fight ᴛꜱ

ngangki *n* (1) woman ᴛꜱ,ᴛᴍ,ʙᴀ,ʙʟ (2) female (animal etc) ᴛꜱ,ɢᴀ,ᴡʏ,ᴡɪ,ꜱᴛ

-ngangki *suff* (on nouns) mother of *Kadli-ngangki* 'Kadli's mum' ᴇʏ

ngangkarti [ngangk(i)-(p)arti] *n* grub species ᴛꜱ

ngangki-miyu [ngangki-miyu] *n* female parent ᴛꜱ,ᴛᴍ

ngangki-munthu [ngangki-munthu] *n* stomach ᴛꜱ,ᴛᴍ

ngangki-pardu [ngangki-pardu] *n* carnal person ᴛᴍ

ngangki-pina [ngangki-pina] ladies' man, someone who likes to be around women ᴛꜱ,ᴛᴍ

ngangkiku [ngangki-ku] *n* mother's (possessive) ᴛᴍ

Ngangkipari [ngangki-pari] *n* women's river (Onkaparinga) ᴛᴍ

Ngangkiparingga [ngangki-pari-ngka] *n* Onkaparinga ᴛᴍ

ngangkipurka [ngangki-purka] *n* queen ɴᴇᴡ

Ngangkirntu [ngangk(i)-(th)irntu] *n* Women's Day ɴᴇᴡ

ngangkita [ngangki-ta] *n* mother ᴛꜱ,ᴛᴍ,ᴡɪ,ᴡʏ,ꜱᴛ

ngangkitarla [ngangki-ta-rla] mother and child, animal and its young ᴛᴍ

ngangkiwaadli [ngangki-waadli] someone who doesn't like female company, or is not interested in women ᴛs, ᴛᴍ

ngangki *n* pigface (plant) ᴛs

ngani *n* gathering place *kuya ngani* 'place in the water where fish like to congregate (fishing spot)' ᴛᴍ

ngangki

nganparrinthi [nganpa-rri-nthi] *v-intr* be indisposed; unable to go out ᴛs, ᴛᴍ

nganparri-apinthi [nganpa-rri-(w)api-nthi] *v-tr* make someone blush, shame someone ᴛᴍ, ᴡʏ

nganta *adv* (1) much, a great deal, a lot *Nganaitya nintu ngai ngarnta nakunthi?* 'Why are you staring at me so hard?' ᴛs, ᴛᴍ (2) well, ably ᴛs, ᴛᴍ (3) quickly, swiftly, vigorously ᴛs, ᴛᴍ, ᴡɪ, sᴛ

nganta padninthi [nganta padni-nthi] *v-intr* hurry; walk quickly ᴛs

nganta-ngantanya [nganta-nganta-nya] *n* bird species (undefined) ᴛᴍ

ngantamanu [nganta-manu] *n* wrist ᴡʏ

ngantara *n* proper marriage ʙᴀ

Nganu *n* Dreaming being, sea monster ᴛs

ngapapi *n* paternal grandmother (father's mother) ᴛs, ᴛᴍ, ʙᴀ, ᴡɪ

ngapitya *n* grandchild of ngapapi (of father's mother) ᴛs, ᴛᴍ

ngapidlu *pro* someone; something (indefinite) ᴛs, ᴛᴍ

ngapidlurlu *pro* someone, something; also used like English 'I say!' (indefinite, ergative) ᴛᴍ

ngapurlantinthi [ngapurla-nti-nthi] *v-intr* become damp, moist; become cool ᴛᴍ

ngar *intj* call of the 'kuinyu' ᴛs

ngaraitya [ngara-itya] *n* plenty; many; enough; abundance *ngaraityaku tirntuitya* 'for many days' ᴛs, ᴛᴍ, ᴡɪ, ɢᴀ, ᴡʏ, sᴛ

ngaraityintyarla [ngara-ity(a)-intya-rla] *most* ɴᴇᴡ

ngararluku [ngara-rluku] *adv* many times; often ᴛs, ᴛᴍ

ngarawaadli [ngara-waadli] *adj* half full, not full ᴛs

ngaranthi [ngara-nthi] (var. **ngara-ngaranthi**) *v-intr* (1) wait *Ngaini ngara-ngarantu!* 'Wait for me!' *Ngaini ngara-ngarantu! Ngadli puru padni'adli.* 'Wait for me! Let's go together in due course.' ᴛs, ᴛᴍ (2) hide, conceal, withhold *Ngaintya pa wangkathi, pudluntu ngai! Ngarangara-urti!* 'Tell me what he has said! Don't conceal it!' ᴛs, ᴛᴍ

ngararaka [ngara-(nga)ra-ka] *adv* secretly; sneakily; covertly; stealthily; treacherously; hidden ᴛs, ᴛᴍ

ngardlinthi [ngarli-nthi] *v-intr* burn; catch fire; boil *Kudla ngardlingku.* 'It might burn by itself.' *Kuntu warpu ngardlinthi.* 'The thirst is burning.' ᴛs, ᴛᴍ, ᴡɪ, ᴡʏ, sᴛ

ngari *n* string; rope *ngaritangkurla* 'two bullocks tied together' ᴛs, ᴛᴍ, ɢᴀ, ᴡʏ

ngari patinthi [ngari pati-nthi] *v-tr* cast (a line) (fishing) ɴᴇᴡ

ngari warrinya *n* son of hanged person ᴛs

ngari wikarnti *n* father of hanged person ᴛs

ngari wilu *n* brother of hanged person ᴛs

ngarimai [ngari-mai] *n* spaghetti ɴᴇᴡ

ngarimurdu [ngari-murdu] *n* pretzel ɴᴇᴡ

ngaritya [ngari-itya] *n* hanged person ᴛs, ᴛᴍ

ngarilta *n* bachelor; unmarried young man ᴛs, ᴛᴍ, ᴡʏ

ngarkunthi [ngarku-nthi] *v-tr* (1) eat, drink, consume (something) *kawi ngark'athu* 'give me water' ᴛs, ᴛᴍ, ᴡɪ, ᴡʏ, sᴛ (2) enjoy (something) *kurdi ngarkunthi* 'to sing or enjoy the kurdi ceremony' ᴛs, ᴛᴍ

nganmainga! *v-imp* eat! (plural) ᴛs, ᴛᴍ

nganmaingwa! *v-imp* eat! (dual) ᴛs, ᴛᴍ

nganmantu! *v-imp* eat! (singular) ᴛs, ᴛᴍ

ngarku-ngarkunya [ngarku-ngarku-nya] *n* edible foods ᴛs

ngarkularkula [ngarku-l(a)-(ng)arku-la] *n* eater *pardu ngarkularkula* 'fond of meat' ᴛs

ngarla *num* eight ɴᴇᴡ

ngarla partirrka [ngarla part(u)-irrka] *num* eight hundred ɴᴇᴡ

ngarlauwata [ngarl(a)-(th)awata] *num* eight thousand ɴᴇᴡ

Ngarliki [ngarl(a)-(p)iki] *n* August ɴᴇᴡ

ngarlirrka [ngarl(a)-irrka] *num* eighty ɴᴇᴡ

ngarliwurra [ngarl(a)-(wi)wurra] *num* eight million ɴᴇᴡ

ngarlawirri [ngarla-wirri] *n* long and heavy club ᴛs

ngarna *n* sister; female relative ᴛs, ᴘɪ

ngarnarnawartarna [ngarna-rna-warta-rna] *n* siblings; children with a family (same mother) ᴛᴍ

ngarnataurla [ngarna-ta-(p)urla] *n* two siblings (same mother) ᴛᴍ

ngarlawirri

ngarnta *n* sickness; suffering; pain ᴛᴍ

ngarnta-ngarntanya [ngarnta-ngarnta-nya] *n* (1) suffering, illness, pain ᴛᴍ (2) sick person, someone experiencing pain or suffering ᴛᴍ

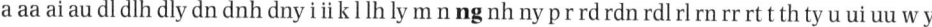

ngarnta-ngarntayana [ngarnta-ngarnta-(n)ya-na] *adj* having become sick ᴛꜱ

ngarntana [ngarnta-na] *adj* (1) sick, unwell ᴛꜱ,ᴛᴍ (2) painful ᴛꜱ,ᴛᴍ

ngarntanthi [ngarnta-nthi] *v-intr* (1) be sick, suffer an illness ᴛꜱ,ᴛᴍ,ʀᴏ,ᴡɪ,ᴡʏ,ꜱᴛ,ᴄʜ (2) feel pain, ache, experience an unpleasant sensation *Niina mukarta ngarntanthi? Tiati ngai kuma.* 'Do you have a headache? Yes, me too.' ᴛꜱ,ᴛᴍ

ngarntarrinthi [ngarnta-rri-nthi] *v-intr* be unwell, sick ᴛꜱ,ᴛᴍ

ngarnta warnga *adj* (1) shallow, not deep ᴛᴍ (2) not yet physically mature (in reference to a girl) ᴛᴍ

ngarra *n* (1) burnt tree stump ᴛꜱ,ᴛᴍ (2) burnt stick ᴛꜱ,ᴛᴍ (3) piece of wood ᴛꜱ,ᴛᴍ

ngarra-kuinyu *n* burning firesticks, carried during funerals (they are carried by a man 'in both his hands … at a native funeral … he holds it close to his ears, walking in a stooping posture.' ᴛꜱ,ᴛᴍ

ngarra-kupa *n* burning firesticks, carried during funerals and circumcision ceremonies ᴛꜱ,ᴛᴍ

ngarra-papaltu *n* tree stump, block of wood used as a stool ᴛꜱ,ᴛᴍ

ngarra-ngarra tika! *intj* move away! ᴛᴍ

ngarrakultu *n* maggot species (large) ᴛꜱ

ngarrampulanthi *v-intr* (1) be tired, fatigued, sluggish *Ngarrampulanthi ngai, karla ngarnta parrantu!* 'I'm tired. Light a big fire!' ᴛꜱ,ᴛᴍ (2) be lazy, idle ᴛꜱ

ngarrarrinthi [ngarra-rri-nthi] *v-intr* hide (oneself) *Karra wartangka ngarrarri.* 'He is hiding behind the karra (redgum) tree.' ᴛꜱ,ᴛᴍ

ngarrata [ngarra-ta] *n* spine, backbone *manti-ngarrata* 'slow, sluggish' ᴛꜱ,ᴛᴍ

ngarrata-watpana quick, swift, active ᴛᴍ

ngarri *n* blue mountain parrot ᴡʏ,ᴘɪ

ngarrinthi [ngarri-nthi] (var. **ngarri-ngarrinthi**) *v-intr* (1) cry, groan, whine, moan ᴛᴍ,ᴛᴍ (2) sing (to soothe pain or to comfort a child) ᴛꜱ

ngarrka *n* hunter ᴛᴍ,ɴᴇᴡ

Ngarrkata *n* Dreaming being ᴛꜱ,ᴛᴍ

ngarrkata palti hunter's song (perhaps a hunting ceremony) ᴛꜱ

ngarrkiarru *n* beard ᴛꜱ,ᴛᴍ,ᴡʏ

ngarrpa *n* species of mouse (large, brown) ᴛᴍ

ngarrpadla *n* aunt; father's sister ᴛꜱ

ngarrparrinthi [ngarrpa-(ng)arrpa-rri-nthi] (var. **ngarrparrparrinthi**) *v-intr* stutter, not speak well ᴛᴍ

ngarrparrpa [ngarrpa-(nga)rrpa] *adj* stammering; stuttering; speaking poorly ᴛꜱ,ᴛᴍ

ngarrparrparringka wangkanthi [ngarrp(a)-(ng)arrpa-rri-ngka wangka-nthi] speak incorrectly, with difficulty; speak like a child who has not yet mastered the language ᴛꜱ,ᴛᴍ

ngarrparrpu *n* father-in-law (of man) ᴛꜱ,ᴛᴍ

ngarrputya *n* (1) son-in-law (of man) ᴛꜱ,ᴛᴍ (2) nephew (man's younger sister's son) ᴛᴍ

ngarrputyata [ngarrputya-ta] *n* son-in-law relation ᴛꜱ,ᴛᴍ

ngarrurrinthi [ngarru-rri-nthi] *v-intr* shorten (oneself); pluck off *ngarru pakinthi* 'to pluck (something) off' ᴛᴍ

ngarta *n* pubic area (female) ᴛꜱ,ᴛᴍ

ngarta yarri *n* pubic hair ᴛᴍ

ngartarrinthi [ngarta-rri-nthi] *v-intr* scream; cry ᴛꜱ,ᴛᴍ

ngartinthi [ngarti-(rri)-nthi] (var. **ngartirrinthi**) *v-tr* ask about; enquire after; inquire into *Warritya pukilyarlu ninku ngartirrithi.* 'Warritya asked after you yesterday.' ᴛꜱ,ᴛᴍ

ngartilartila [ngarti-l(a)-(ng)arti-la] *n* inquirer; someone who asks questions ᴛꜱ,ᴛᴍ

ngartirri-purka [ngarti-rri-purka] *n* someone who asks lots of questions ᴛꜱ,ᴛᴍ

ngartiti [ngarti-ti] *n* question ɴᴇᴡ

ngartu *n* child; baby *ngartu-itya ngadluku* 'for our children' ᴛꜱ,ᴛᴍ,ʀᴏ

ngartu-arla [ngartu-(inty)a-rla] *adj* smaller (child) ᴛᴍ

ngaru *n* (1) any white substance such as white ochre, chalk, lime, pipe clay ᴛꜱ,ᴛᴍ (2) milk ᴛꜱ,ᴛᴍ (3) downy part of a feather ᴛᴍ

ngaru wardli *n* whitewashed house ᴛꜱ

ngarumuka [ngaru-muka] *n* brain ᴛꜱ,ᴛᴍ

ngaruta (var. **ngarruta**) *n* centipede species (undefined) ᴛꜱ,ᴛᴍ,ᴡʏ

ngathu (var. **'athu**) *pro* I (ergative) *ngathu parlta ninku kadli* 'I struck your dog' *ngathu niina naki* 'I see you' *yangadli'athu'ina nakutha* 'I will see you later' ᴛꜱ,ʙʟ

ngathaitya [ngatha-itya] *pro* (1) to me (allative) ᴛꜱ (2) for me (purposive)

ngathaityangka [ngatha-itya-ngka] *pro* with me (comitative) ᴛꜱ

ngathaityanungku morphology [ngath-itya-nungku] *pro* from me (ablative) ᴛꜱ

ngathunti [ngathu-nti] *pro* only I, I alone (did it to someone, something) ᴛꜱ

ngatpanthi [ngatpa-nthi] (1) *v-intr* go into, enter (the water, a room, an item of clothing) *Parni ngatpantu!* 'Come in!' TS, TM (2) *v-intr* set, go down (e.g. the sun) *tirntu ngatparninthidla* 'while the sun is setting' TS, TM (3) *v-intr* dip into, dive into (e.g. water) *Mara munu ngatpantu kauwi-ana!* 'Dip the tip of your finger in the water.' TM (4) *v-intr* flow into e.g. a larger body of water as a river does when it enters the sea or a lake *Pari warta ngatpanthi.* 'The river flows out (into the sea).' TM (5) *v-tr* put (something) into TS, TM, WI, ST

  ngatpa murlarta [ngatpa murla-rta] *n* goal posts NEW

  ngatpa! *n, intj* goal! (sport) *Ngatpa manmantu!* 'Go for goal!' NEW

  ngatparrinthi [ngatpa-rri-nthi] *v-intr* (1) sink TS (2) enter, put oneself into *Ngatparri-ngai?* 'Shall I go in (to the room)? Shall I get into (these pants)?' TM

  ngatparriti [ngatpa-rri-ti] *n* sinker (fishing) NEW

ngauwa (var. **ngawaka**) *n* (1) fire, flame TM (2) firewood, kindling, fuel *ngauwakila* 'instead of firewood, for firewood' TM (3) heat TM (4) light TM

  ngauwaka *n* (1) red hot coal, glowing ember TS (2) species of parrot (blue head and red breast) TS

ngauwalyu *n* mother-in-law (man's) TS, TM

  ngauwadli *n* niece (man's brother's daughter) TS, WY

  ngauwaitya [ngauwa-itya] *n* father-in-law (uncertain) TS

  ngauwalyata *n* parent-in-law relation TM

ngauwinthi [ngauwi-nthi] *v-intr* pass by TM

ngayanthi [nunyangaya-nthi] (var. **ngayarrinthi**) (1) *v-intr, v-tr* play at; act out *kurdi ngayanthi* 'act out the Kurdi (ceremony)' *Wakwaku ngayanthi ngunyawayitidlu.* 'the child is playing at dancing' TS, TM (2) *v-intr* sing (oneself) to sleep TM (3) *v-intr, v-tr* tease TS, TM

ngayirda *n* (1) sky, air, firmament *ngayirdila* 'in the air' TS, TM (2) space *ngayirdapira, tirntupira wangkanthi* 'talking about space and time' NEW (3) white of egg WI

-ngga => **-ngka** *suff (on nouns)*

ngintirrinthi [nginti-rri-nthi] *v-intr* crackle; snap TS

ngirlinthi [ngirli-nthi] (var. **ngirtinthi**) (1) *v-intr* stumble; limp TS, TM (2) break down (car) NEW *Yaka! Padnipadniti ngirlinthi.* 'Oh no! The car's breaking down.'

  ngirla *adj* broken WY

ngirrinthi [ngirri-nthi] *v-tr* (1) collect, gather *Ngaityu-anti mai ngirri'athu.* 'I will only collect food for myself.' TM (2) heap up, put in a pile *karla ngirrinthi* 'to put the fire in a heap, pile it up' TM (3) pick up (a date) *Kutyunurnanta yangarrarna ngirrinthi!* 'He even picks up other people's wives!' TM, NEW

ngirrirrinthi [ngirri-rri-nthi] *v-intr* assemble, form a group TM

-ngka (var. **-ngga**) *suff (on nouns)* (1) at, on, in (locative) *Ngangki-pari-ngga* 'At the women's river (Onkaparinga)' TM (2) on account of, because of, for the purpose of (causal/purposive) *Pamarringka parna pudna.* 'They have come in order to spear each other.' TM (*NB: Use '-ngga' on proper nouns (i.e. names of people and places) and '-nkga' for common nouns*)

-ngkurti => **-rti**

-ngkutha => **-ngutha**

ngu *dem* that (person, thing); there *Ngunhaintya pia mitithi, piipawardlingka parnu wantinthi.* 'Those (children) might have stolen it, them living in the school house.' *Piltirtirdla ngu!* 'Don't separate them both!' *Wantanthi'ai padlu, nguntya'ai yungkungki!* '(That which) he left for me, give me that!' *Ngu! Niina kukathi ngu.* 'There, where you have been digging there.' TS, TM

  ngu-arra *loc* along there *Ngu-arra padni!* 'Go around!' TS

  nguntya [ngu-ntya] *loc, temp* there; then *Nguntya ngathu wanta.* 'I left it just there.' *Nguntya ngaityu munangka tikaingka. Namu ngai pudlurnintu: nii – namu ngai pudlurrirniutha. – Yaintya tikanthi ngadlu parnu munangka; yaintya pa wangkathi pudnititya.* 'You mob sit there in front of me. Say to them from me: yes – I will speak to them in this way. – We are sitting here in front of him, he has said that he will come here.' TS, TM

  ngununtya *loc* over there; thither *Ngununty'athu wantatha.* 'I'll put it over there.' TS

  ngurna [ngu-rna] *dem* those over there TM, TS

  ngurnaintya [ngu-rna-intya] (var. **ngurnintya**) *pro* those over there (plural) TS, TM

ngudli *n* pouch (e.g. of a kangaroo) TS, TM

  ngudli wantiti [ngudli wanti-ti] *n* sleeping bag NEW

  ngudlitidli nuinpi [ngudli-tidli nuinpi] *n* pouched lamprey (fish) (*Geotria australis*) NEW

  ngudli wayirrinthi [ngudli waya-rri-nthi] (var. **ngudli wayarrinthi**) *v-intr* miss; long for; worry about (someone) TM

nguimpayinthi [nguimpa-(wa)yi-nthi] *v-intr* withdraw; retract; creep back TM

nguitkurra [nguitku-rra] *n* whistling TS, TM

  nguitkurrinthi [nguitku-rri-nthi] (var. **nguiku-ikurrinthi**) *v-intr* whistle TS, TM

nguiya => **nguya**

nguiyunthi => **nguyunthi**

nguku *n* owl species ₜₛ

ngukurda *n* shoulder joint ₜₛ, ₜₘ

ngulta *n* **(1)** cuts made on a man's back and chest during the final initiation *ngulta pakinthi* 'to make this type of cut or incision' (var. **ngulti**)ₜₘ **(2)** man who has undergone the last initiation and received 'ngulti' cuts ₜₛ, ₜₘ, ₑʏ

ngulthi *n* **(1)** night *Ngulthi puru ngai wayitha.* 'When it is dark I will still work.' ₜₛ, ₜₘ, ʀᴏ, ᴡʏ, ᴡɪ, ɢᴀ **(2)** darkness ₜₘ

   ngulthi-mai *n* evening meal; dinner; supper ɴᴇᴡ

   ngulthi-puru [ngulti-puru] *temp* early morning; still dark ₜₛ

   ngulthi-warta [ngulthi-warta] *n* evening ₜₛ, ₜₘ

   ngulthingka [ngulthi-ngka] *temp* **(1)** at night, during the night ₜₛ, ₜₘ, ᴡɪ, ₛₜ **(2)** last night ᴡʏ **(3)** tonight ₜₛ

   ngulthinthi [ngulthi-nthi] *v-intr* be dark ₜₛ

   ngulthirlu [ngulthi-rlu] *temp* at night, during the night ₜₘ

   ngulthirninthi [ngulthi-rni-nthi] *v-intr* get dark ₜₛ, ₜₘ

ngulti => **ngulta**

ngulya-ngulya *n* sweat of a dying person ₜₘ

ngumunta *n* shrub (with yellow flowers) ₜₛ, ᴡʏ

   ngumunta parti *n* grub that lives in the ngumunta bush ₜₛ

nguna *n* marshmallow plant; root of marshmallow plant ₜₘ

ngunata *n* plant with small, yellow flowers (uncertain) ᴡʏ

ngungana *n* kookaburra ₜₛ, ₜₘ, ᴄᴏ

ngungulurdu *n* **(1)** burp; belch ₜₘ **(2)** hiccup ₜₘ

ngunirrinthi [nguni-rri-nthi] *v-intr* **(1)** walk unsteadily, limp, be lame ₜₛ, ₜₘ **(2)** be loose, shake, wobble ₜₘ

ngunkunya *n* ashes ₜₛ

ngunta *loc, dem* over there somewhere, indefinite pronoun *ngunta tirntu ...* 'When the sun is about there ...' ₜₛ, ₜₘ

   nguntarlu [ngunta-rlu] *loc* somewhere in that direction *Wantidlu naa nurntidlu padni? – Nguntarluntya, Nurtumputarra.* 'Where are you mob leaving for? – Over there, towards Nurtumpu.' ₜₘ

   nguntarta [ngunta-rta] *loc* behind; beyond; on the other side *wardli nguntarta* 'behind the house' *Ninku nguntarta pa karla.* 'The wood is behind you.' ₜₛ, ₜₘ

   nguntartinyarlangka [ngunta-rt(a)-in(t)yarla-ngka] *loc* farther away on the other side ₜₘ

   nguntartinyarna [ngunta-rta-ntya-rna] *dem* those over there ₜₘ

nguntarninthi [ngunta-rni-nthi] *v-intr* become tired; become lazy ₜₘ

   nguntarni-purka [ngunta-rni-purka] lazy person ₜₘ

nguntinthi [ngunti-nthi] *v-tr* look for ₜₛ, ₜₘ

   ngunti-apinthi [ngunti-(w)api-nthi] *v-tr* look into; examine; inspect ₜₛ, ₜₘ

ngunyakurla [ngunya-kurla] *n* arm string ornament ₜₛ

ngunyinthi [ngunyi-nthi] *v-intr* laugh, be happy ₜₛ, ₜₘ

   ngunya (var. **ngunyi**) *n* joy; pleasure ₜₛ, ₜₘ, ᴡʏ

   ngunya mankunthi [ngunya manku-nthi] *v-tr* take pleasure in, enjoy (something) ₜₛ

   Ngunya Yiityuku Warnirntu! [ngunya yiityu-ku warn(i)-(th)irntu] *intj* Happy Christmas! ɴᴇᴡ

   ngunya-wayinthi [ngunya-wayi-nthi] *v-intr* **(1)** play ₜₛ **(2)** dance, perform ceremony ₜₛ

   ngunyawayiti [ngunya-wayi-ti] *n* **(1)** dance, ceremony, performance ₜₛ, ᴡʏ **(2)** toy ₜₘ

   ngunyawayiti wardli [ngunya-wayi-ti wardli] *n* toy shop ɴᴇᴡ

   ngunyirntu [nguny(a)-(th)irntu] *n* holiday ɴᴇᴡ

   Ngunya Ngaityairntu! [ngunya ngaityai-(thi)rntu] *intj* Happy Mother's Day! ɴᴇᴡ

   Ngunya Yarli Tirntu! *intj* Happy Father's Day! ɴᴇᴡ

   Ngunya Yiitya! *intj* Happy Easter! ɴᴇᴡ

ngupa *n* husband ₜₛ, ₜₘ

nguputa *adj* feeble ₜₘ

ngurdanya *n* armpit *(axilla)* ₜₛ

ngurika *n* flower; blossom ₜₛ, ₜₘ, ᴡʏ

ngurinthi [nguri-nthi] *v-tr* throw (with a spear thrower) *ngurinthi pardu* 'throw sticks at birds (in trees)' ₜₛ, ₜₘ, ᴡʏ, ᴡɪ, ₛₜ

ngurlu (1) *dem* that (person/thing) (ergative) *Ngurla-ityangka-ntya pia padlu kurta-kurtanthi, painingka ngathu parnuku mudlirna miti. Ngurla-ityangka pia ngai padlu kurta-kurtanthi.* 'Perhaps he is avoiding me because of that, previously I stole his stuff. Perhaps that is why he's avoiding me.' ₜₛ, ₜₘ **(2)** *dir* in that direction *Ngadli padnitha ngurlu Wirramu-ana* 'We (two) will go that way to Encounter Bay.' ₜₛ

   ngurlu-urla [ngurlu-(p)urla] *pro* those two ₜₛ, ₜₘ

   ngurluntya [ngurlu-ntya] *pro* **(1)** someone, anyone (ergative) ₜₛ, ₜₘ **(2)** in that case-, then- *Manya parltarri-utha ngurlu kurda. Manya yaku wadni-utha ngurluntya muri-utha.* 'If it rains then (we will stay) at home. If it doesn't rain, then (we will) go out.' ₜₘ

ngurra *n* ceremonial scar or cut ₜₘ
  ngurratinthi [ngurra-ti-nthi] *v-intr* heal (cut) ₜₘ

ngurrku *n* tuft of grass ₜₛ,ₜₘ

ngurru *n* **(1)** back *ngurrungka* ₜₛ,ₜₘ **(2)** rear, back side (of something) *wardli ngurrungka* 'at the back of the house' *ninku ngurrungka* 'behind your back' ₜₛ,ₜₘ
  ngurru warpu back bone ᴡʏ

ngurrumpayinthi [ngurru-mp(i)-(w)ayi-nthi] *v-intr* swim underwater ₜₘ

ngurrunturru *n* stout person; fat person ₜₘ

-ngurti => **-rti**

ngurtu *n* frog species (undefined) ᴡʏ,ʀᴏ

ngurtuwarta *n* chin ₜₛ,ₜₘ,ᴡʏ,ᴡɪ,ꜱᴛ,ᴋᴏ

ngutanthi [nguta-nthi] *v-tr* **(1)** frighten, scare (someone) by telling them stories ₜₛ,ₜₘ **(2)** threaten, intimidate (someone) ₜₛ,ₜₘ

-ngutha (var. **-ngkutha**; **-tha**; **-utha**) *suff (on verbs)* going to-; just about to- (immediate future) *Inaintya ngai katpirrirni-utha.* 'I will wait for you right here.' *Kangkarringkutha pa!* 'It (the dog) is going to give birth (to puppies)!' ₜₘ

ngutu [ngutu] *n* knowledge ɴᴇᴡ (derived from Kaurna *ngutu-atpanthi*)
  ngutu-atpanthi [ngutu-(ng)atpa-nthi] *v-tr* teach; instruct ₜₘ

nguya (var. **nguiya**) *n* **(1)** pustule, boil, ulcer, sore ₜₛ,ₜₘ **(2)** smallpox disease ₜₛ,ₜₘ,ᴡɪ,ᴡʏ,ꜱᴛ
  nguyanguya [nguya-nguya] *n* **(1)** disagreement, grievance, fight, falling out (between people) *Painingka purlaku nguya-nguya tikathi. Nata purla pia turla warti warltu wanta.* 'Previously they had a fight. Now it seems they have let go of their anger.' ₜₘ **(2)** opponent (sport) ɴᴇᴡ
  nguyanguya muri [nguya-nguya-muri(nthi)] *n* reconciliation ɴᴇᴡ
  nguyanguya wantanthi [nguya-nguya wanti-nthi] make up, give up a grievance with someone ₜₘ
  nguyapalti [nguya-palti] *n* smallpox song (ceremony) ₜₛ

nguyunthi [nguyu-nthi] (var. **nguiyunthi**) *v-tr* warm; heat up *Nguyu'athu'rla tidnarla, martantinthi purla, manyarrinthi ngai.* '(I) will warm the feet, they are cold, I am cold.' *Tidnarla nguyu'athu purla.* 'The feet, I will warm them.' *Nguyu'athu'rla* 'I will warm them (the feet)' *Tidnarla nguyu'athu'rla* 'I will warm my feet (dual)' ₜₛ,ₜₘ
  nguyurrinthi [nguyu-rri-nthi] *v-intr* warm (oneself) up *Nguyurringai?* 'Shall I warm myself up?' *Nguyurrinth'ai.* 'I am warming up.' ₜₛ,ₜₘ

nguyuti [nguyu-ti] *n* heater ɴᴇᴡ

-ni => **-rni** *suff (on verbs)*

nidlanthi [nhidla-nthi] *v-intr* **(1)** stop (somewhere and not go further) ₜₛ **(2)** remain, stay at home (when others are going out) ₜₛ

nii *intj* yes ₜₛ,ₜₘ

niina *pro* you (singular nominative/accusative) *Wanti niina?* 'Where are you going to?' *Niina ngaintya wapi ngu?* 'What did you do then?' (var. 'ina) ₜₛ,ₜₘ,ʙʟ,ᴡʏ

niipu *n* mate; neighbour; friend; companion ₜₛ,ₜₘ
  niipu-tina [nhiipu-tina] *adj* alone; solitary ₜₛ
  niipunthi [nhiipu-nthi] *v-tr* accompany; be a neighbour to someone *Nintu'adlu niipuntu!* 'Accompany us!' *Niipu ngai!* 'Accompany me!' ₜₛ,ₜₘ
  niipurrinthi [nhiipu-rri-nthi] *v-intr* accompany, go with each other *Nganaitya niwa niipurringwa?* 'Why are you two going around with him?' ₜₛ,ₜₘ

niku *n* joke ₜₛ,ₜₘ
  niki-nhiki slang ₜₘ
  nikunikungka [nhiku-nhiku-ngka] *adv* jokingly, as a joke *nikunikungka wayinthi* 'play around' ₜₛ
  nikupina [nhiku-pina] *n* joker ɴᴇᴡ
  nikurninthi [nhiku-rni-nthi] *v-intr* joke; mess around *Nikurti!* 'Don't joke! Be serious!' ₜₛ
  nikurrinthi [nhiku-rri-nthi] *v-intr* joke; mess around ₜₛ

nilti *n* rush species ₜₛ,ₜₘ

-nina *suff (on verbs)* tense/aspect marker (past continuous) *Painingka ngathu parltathi, numa pa mururithi ngathu parlti-nina.* 'When I split (the wood) before, it ran well when I was hitting (it).' ₜₘ

ningka *adv* nearly; almost *Ningka padlu'ai pama.* 'He nearly speared me.' *Ningk'ai warni.* 'I nearly fell.' *yuku ningkama* 'almost crooked' *Ngai padlu ningka parlta, ngaityu tukutyurlu.* 'He nearly hit me, my little one.' ₜₛ,ₜₘ
  ningkatpa [nhingk(a)-(ng)atpa] *n* point (football) ɴᴇᴡ

ninku *pro* your(s) (singular, possessive) *Wanti niina muritha? Warli-ana, ninku-ana? – Nii, ngaityu-ana.* 'Where are you going? To the house, to yours? – Yes, to mine.' *Painingka ngai kuntu pungkurrithi ninkurtila. Nata ngai kuntu yartarninthi nintaityangka, niina pudnaintyidla.* 'Before, I felt uneasy in your absence, but now with you I feel comfortable, because you came.' *ninku kadli* 'thy (your) dog' ᴛs,ᴛᴍ,ʙʟ,ʙᴀ,ʀo,ᴡɪ,ᴡʏ,sᴛ,ᴋo,ᴄʜ

ninkai [nhink(u)-ai] *n* your mother ᴛs

ninkarli [nhink(u)-(y)arli] *n* your father *Ngantu katitha ninkarlitya piipa? – Yukurlu.* 'Who will take the letter to your father? – The ship will.' ᴛs,ᴡʏ

ninku pulthu [nhinku pulthu] (var. **ninku pulthungka**) *n, loc* (1) after you, in your tracks ᴛᴍ,ᴛs (2) instead of you, in your place ᴛs

ninkunti [nhinku-nti] (var. **ninku-anti**) only yours, your alone ᴛᴍ

ninkurtila *adv* in your absence (singular) ᴛᴍ

nintini *adv* again ᴛᴍ

nintu (var. **'ntu**) *pro* you (singular ergative) *Wathangku padlu-urlaitya turti-anurla? Miti pirdi nintu purla!* 'Where's that jacket from? You probably stole it!' *nintu ngaityu kadli kurnta* 'you beat my dog' ᴛs,ᴛᴍ,ʙʟ

nintaitya *pro* (1) to you (the destination) (singular allative) *Wanti niina muri-utha? – Nintaitya.* 'Where are you going? – To you.' *Nintaitya padningai* 'I'll come to you.' ᴛs,ᴛᴍ (2) for you (singular purposive) (3) for you (the beneficiary of an action) *Ngai yaku nintaitya warpulai.* 'I have not worked for you.' ᴛs,ᴛᴍ

nintaityangka *pro* with you, at you (singular comitative) *Nintaityangka ngadluku warra wantinthi.* 'You now understand our language.' *Nintaityangka ngai marnkarri.* 'I have queried this with you' ᴛᴍ,ᴛs

nintaityanungku [nhint(u)-itya-nungku] *pro* away from you (singular ablative) ᴛᴍ

nintunti [nhintu-nti] you alone, only you (did it to someone/something) ᴛᴍ

nipa (var. **niparra**) *n* (1) wrinkle; fold; pleat ᴛs,ᴛᴍ (2) membrane ᴛᴍ (3) ornamental headband ᴋo,ᴡʏ

nipa-nhipa [nhipa-nhipa] *adj* wrinkly; creased ᴛs,ᴛᴍ

nirdiana *n* nephew ᴛs,ᴛᴍ

nirrkinya *n* nits; lice eggs ᴛs

nita *n* (1) stiffness, laziness ᴛᴍ (2) erection, lust (resulting in stiffness) ᴛᴍ

nitati-purka [nhita-ti-purka] *n* lazy person ᴛs,ᴛᴍ

nitatinthi [nhita-ti-nthi] *v-intr* be lazy ᴛs

niwa [nhiwa-dli] *pro* you two (dual nominative/accusative) *Niwa waa murithi?* 'Where did you two go?' ᴛs,ᴛᴍ

niwadlitya [nhiwa-dl(u)-itya] *pro* (1) to you (two) (dual allative) ᴛᴍ (2) for you two (dual purposive) ᴛᴍ

niwadluku [nhiwa-dlu-ku] *pro* your(s), of you two (dual possessive) ᴛs

-nta₁ => **-anta₁**

-nta₂ => **-anta₂**

-nthi *suff (on verbs)* tense marker (present) ᴛs

-nti => **-anta₁**

'ntu => **nintu** *pro*

-ntya (see also: **-intya**) *suff* (1) denotes emphasis *iya – yaintya* 'here, this – this one right here' *nalati? – nalatintya?* 'when? – at what time then? (impatiently)' ᴛs,ᴛᴍ (2) more, -er (comparative/superlative) *muna – munaintya* 'first – beforehand, earlier (than something else)' ᴛᴍ

nudnu (var. **nunu**) *n* (1) body, flesh ᴛs,ᴛᴍ (2) corpse, carcass, dead body (not skeleton) *Nunu-unangku pa tarni, warpurnanti kurlangka.* 'The flesh rose again, (but) the bones remained (in the grave).' ᴛs,ᴛᴍ,ᴡʏ

nudnu wanganthi [nhudnu wanga-nthi] *v-intr* bury a corpse ᴛᴍ

nudnu-nhudnu-apinthi [nhudnu-nhudnu-(w)api-nthi] (var. **nunu-nhunu-apinthi**) *v-intr* prepare a corpse *mutyarta yaki-ana nudnu-nudnu-apinthi* 'wrap a corpse in clothing' *puiyu yaki-ana nudnu-nudnu-apinthi* 'envelop with smoke (as was done with the dead body during Kaurna funeral ceremonies)' ᴛᴍ

nuinpa [nhuinpa] *adj* burnt ᴛᴍ

nuinpinthi [nhuinpi-nthi] *v-tr* (1) suck *kaaru nuingpinthi* 'to suck out the blood' (var. **nuingpinthi**) ᴛs (2) breastfeed, suckle ᴛᴍ

nuinpirrinthi [nhuinpi-rri-nthi] *v-intr* leak ᴛᴍ

nuinpiti [nhuinpi-ti] *n* nipple ɴᴇᴡ

nuinyanthi [nhuinya-nthi] (1) *v-intr* misbehave, be naughty ᴛᴍ (2) *v-intr* grumble, be dissatisfied ᴛs,ᴛᴍ (3) *v-tr* spoil, destroy, throw around (something) ᴛs,ᴛᴍ (4) *v-tr* tell (someone) off, rebuke or chide (someone) ᴛᴍ

nuinyarri-purka [nhuinya-rri-purka] *n* naughty, destructive person *Nuinyarripurka!* 'Naughty boy! Naughty girl!' ᴛs,ᴛᴍ

nuinyarrinthi [nhuinya-rri-nthi] *v-intr* (1) misbehave, be naughty, be disobedient *Nuinyarringurti ngu!* 'Now don't you be naughty!' ᴛs,ᴛᴍ (2) don't be destructive, cause damage *Nuinyarringurti ngu!* 'Now don't you be destructive!' ᴛs,ᴛᴍ

nuki *n* snot; mucus *Nuki kumpantu!* 'Clean your nose!' *Nuki murintu!* 'Clean your nose!' ᴛs,ᴛᴍ,ᴡʏ,ᴋo

nuki ngarntanthi [nuki ngarnta-nthi] *v-intr* have a cold ᴛᴍ

nuki winturrinthi [nuki wintu-rri-nthi] *v-intr* sniff/snort mucus back up your nose ᴛᴍ

nuki wirrkiti [nuki wirrki-ti] *n* handkerchief, tissue ᴡʏ

nukiana [nuki-ana] *n* handkerchief; tissue ᴛs

nukuna *n* (1) assassin~TS~ (2) evil being that sneaks up on someone in the night and kills them~TS,WY~ (3) locust (small wingless)~WY~

numa (1) *adj* good, right, correct, skillful~TS,TM~ (2) *adv* well, correctly, skillfully,~TS,TM~

    numa wangka-wangkanthi [numa wangka-wangka-nthi] chat in a friendly way~TM~

    numa-nhakunthi [nhuma-nhaku-nthi] *v-tr* like, love, be pleased with (someone/something)~TS,TM~

    numarninthi [numa-rni-nthi] *v-intr* be kind~NEW~

nunanthi [nhuna-nthi] *v-tr* scratch; prick; touch *Nuna-urti, murrkanthi pa.* 'Don't touch him, he cries.'~TM~

    nunarrinthi [nhuna-rri-nthi] (var. **nuna-nhunarrinthi**) *v-intr* (1) scratch/rub oneself where it itches~TM~ (2) roll around on the back like horses or dogs do when they scratch themselves~TM~

nungata *n* rat species~TS,TM~

nungku (var. **nangku**) *adv* back again; returning *nungkuanta* 'back for good' *nungkuana* 'on the way back, returning'~TS,TM~

    -nungku (var. **-anangku**; **-nangku**; **-unungku**) *suff (on nouns)* from; away from; coming from (ablative) *Niina wathangku? – Wardlinangku.* 'Where are you coming from? – From home.' *pinti-nungku* 'from the grave' *Tarntanyanungku* 'from Adelaide'~TS,TM,BL~

    -nungkurrinthi [nhungku-rri-nthi] *suff (on verbs)* each other *kurnta-nhungkurrinthi* 'to beat each other' *pama- nhungkurrinthi* 'to spear each other'~TM~

    nungku-nhungkurninthi [nhungku-nhungku-rni-nthi] *v-intr* return; come back again~TM~

    nungkumanthi [nhungku-ma-nthi] *v-tr* take back again~TS~

nungurru (var. **nungnurru**) *adj* wet; damp; moist~TS,TM,WI,ST~

    nungurru-antinthi [nhungurru-(w)anti-nthi] (var. **nungnurru-antinthi**) *v-intr* get wet; become damp or moist~TM~

nunu => **nudnu**

nunu-nhunu-apinthi => **nudnu-nhudnu-apinthi**

nunyanthi [nhunya-nthi] (var. **nunya-nhunyanthi**) *v-tr* scold; criticise; tell off~TM~

nurlu *n* (1) corner, curvature *nurlungka* 'on the bend'~TS,TM~ (2) bend in a river *Nurlungga* 'Noarlunga = river bend'~TM~

nurlimai [nhurli-mai] *n* banana~NEW~

nurlinthi [nhurli-nthi] *v-tr* turn; twist; spin~TS,TM~

nurliti [nhurli-ti] (var. **taa nurliti**₁; **wilta nurliti**) *n* key *wardli nurliti* 'house key'~TS,TM~

nurluta [nhurlu-ta] *n* corner; angle *nurlutila* 'in the corner'~TS,TM~

nurnpurrinthi [nhurnpu-rri-nthi] *v-intr* (1) push in line, press to the front (e.g. of a crowd of people), push oneself forward~TM~ (2) be forward, cheeky, pushy, demanding, insistent, dogged *Nurnpurrithi'urla* 'They were both cheeky/forward.'~TM~

    nurnpurringka [nhurnpu-rri-ngka] in the press (of people), amongst a crowd~TM~

nurnti *adv* away; far off; distant *Nurnti padni.* 'Go away!' *Nurnti talapinku.* 'Let him be off then. Let him go.' *Nata nurnti'dli.* 'We're off now (us two).' *Nata nurnti'dli* 'Let's go! (us (2)'~TS,TM~

    nurnti-anta [nhurnti-anta] (1) *loc* far away, entirely off~TS~ (2) *adv* not moving, staying still~TM~

    nurnti kurtarrinthi withdraw from, forsake (something)~TM~

    nurnti-nhurnti [nhurnti-nhurnti] (var. **nurnti-urnti**) (1) *intj* out of the way! get out of here!~TM,WY~ (2) *loc* beyond, behind, on the other side (of something) *pari nurnti-nhurnti* 'beyond (on the far side of) the river'~TS~

    nurntidlu [nhurnti-rlu] (var. **nurntirlu**) *loc* far away from *Ninku nurntirlu.* '(Hold it) away from you.'~TM~

    nurntiki [nhurnti-ki] (1) *loc* farther away, farther still *Nurntikirti.* 'No farther! Stop!'~TS,TM~ (2) *adv* continually, longer, further, more *nurntiki purrutitina* 'immortal, living continually or indefinitely'~TM~

    nurntina [nhurnti-na] *adv* forward; onward; continuing~TM~

    nurntirdlu-arra [nhurnti-rlu-arra] (var. **nurntirluarra**) *adv* continually; constantly~TM~

nurrunthi [nhurru-nthi] *v-tr* (1) enchant, charm, put a spell on (something)~TS,TM~ (2) hunt, chase (something)~TS~

    nurru-nhurru [nhurru-nhurru] *adj* bent; stooping~TM~

    nurrulurrula [nhurru-l(a)-(nh)urru-la] *n* sorcerer~TS~

    nurruti [nhurru-ti] *n* spell; charm; enchantment~TS,TM~

nurtunthi [nhurtu-nthi] *v-tr* have sex (man)~TS,TM~

    nurturrinthi [nhurtu-rri-nthi] *v-intr* have sex (with each other)~TS~

nuunthi [nhu-(nh)u-nthi] (var. **nununthi**) *v-tr* (1) point or indicate something with the hand or finger ᴛs,ᴛᴍ (2) stir (e.g. the fire, or in a possum hole) *Karlakiri nuununtu! Purtapurta-ingku!* 'Stir the fire up! Let it really blaze!' ᴛs,ᴛᴍ

  nuuti [nhu-(nh)u-ti] *n* showing; pointing; pointing thing (i.e. forefinger) ᴛs,ᴛᴍ

nuyi blow ᴋᴏ

-nya *suff (on nouns)* (1) person who does or undergoes an action (nominaliser: v-intr) *pukanthi – puka-pukanya* 'to bathe – someone who bathes a lot (i.e. bath(e)-er)' *ngarntanthi – ngarnta-ngarntanya* 'to suffer or hurt – a sick person (i.e. suffer-er)' ᴛᴍ (2) forms a noun for an action (nominaliser: reduplicated v-intr) *karltanthi – karlta-karltanya* 'to cry or shout – the calling, the shouting' *ngarntanthi – ngarnta-ngarntanya* 'to suffer or hurt – the suffering, pain, illness' ᴛᴍ

nyaani (see also: **wauwi**) *n* sheep ɴᴇᴡ (from Nukunu, onomatopeic)

-nyarla => **-intyarla**

nyurrkarda *n* wrong marriage ʙᴀ

P p

pa (1) *pro* he/him, she/her, it (nominative/accusative) *Pa waa wanti?* 'Where is he camped?' *Ngaityai! Ityamai pa warru-warruntu!* 'Mum! Ityamaii, go call her!' *Pa ngarnta-anthi* 'he or she is ill' ᴛs,ᴛᴍ (2) *loc* there *Waa? – Paintya!* 'Where? – There!' *pa pa* 'just there' ᴛᴍ

  padlaitya *pro* (1) to him/her/it (allative) *Padlaitya padni!* 'Go to him!' ᴛs,ᴛᴍ (2) for him/her/it (purposive) ᴛs,ᴛᴍ

  padlaityangka [padlaitya-ngka] *pro* with him/her/it; at him/her/it *Padlaityangka pidna!* 'Stay with him!' ᴛᴍ

  padlaityanungku [padlaitya-nungku] *pro* away from him/her/it (ablative) *Padlaityanungku padni!* 'Go away from him!' ᴛs,ᴛᴍ

  padlu *pro* he; she; it (ergative) ᴛs,ᴛᴍ,ʙʟ

  padluntya [padlu-ntya] *pro* with him/her/it; by means of him/her/it ᴛᴍ

  padlu-urla-ntya with or by means of those two ᴛs,ᴛᴍ

  panta towards there, to that place (not as far away as 'ngunta') ᴛᴍ

  pantaintya? towards there? to that place? ᴛᴍ

paanthi [paa-nthi] (1) *v-intr* shine, radiate (like the sun or a fire) *tirntu paanthi* 'the sun shines' *Tirntu karlarlu paanthi.* 'The sun is burning.' ᴛs,ᴛᴍ (2) *v-tr* put on, apply, smear, spread, scatter (something onto something else) *taapaanthi* 'to kiss (someone)' *Tupurrarlu pardi paanthi.* 'The blow fly puts maggots (in the meat).' ᴛs,ᴛᴍ

  paarrinthi [paa-rri-nthi] *v-intr* shine; radiate (heat, light) *Tirntu kardla ngarnta paarrinthi.* 'The heat of the sun is really oppressive.' ᴛᴍ

paapa *n* teenage boy; youth ᴛs,ᴛᴍ,ᴡɪ

  paapa tumpu *n* smoking incense (ceremony) ᴛᴍ

  paapa yuwanthi [papa yuwa-nthi] *v-intr* undergo circumcision ᴛs,ᴛᴍ

  paapa-mathanya *n* person directing circumcision (ceremony) ᴛs

paatya *n* bus ɴᴇᴡ (from English 'bus')

padlunthi [padlu-nthi] *v-intr* die *Maitidla kurla padlu-ingku.* '(He) is without food and will die on his own.' *Karla padlunthi.* 'The fire is dying.' ᴛs,ᴛᴍ,ᴡɪ,ᴡʏ,ɢᴀ,sᴛ

  padli *adj* dead ᴛᴍ

  padlu-apinthi [padlu-(w)api-nthi] *v-tr* kill ᴛs,ᴛᴍ

  padlu-kurntanthi [padlu-kurnta-nthi] *v-tr* beat to death ᴛs,ᴛᴍ

  padlu-padlunya [padlu-padlu-nya] *n* old, dying person; person who is dying ᴛs,ᴛᴍ

  padlu-parltanthi [padlu-parlta-nthi] *v-tr* (1) kill (something) by throwing it ᴛs,ᴛᴍ (2) beat out the fire ᴛᴍ

  padluntyila [padlu-nty(a)-ila] *n* dead person ᴛs

  padlunyana [padlu-nya-na] *adj* dying ᴛᴍ

  padlurninthi [padlu-rni-nthi] *v-tr* want, desire, long for, covet (something) *Mai padlurninth'ai.* 'I want food.' ᴛs,ᴛᴍ,ᴡɪ,sᴛ

  padlurnintyarla [padlu-rni-ntyarla] (1) *adj* strongly desiring, longing, wanting (something) ᴛs (2) *n* someone who strongly desires or wants (something) *murntu padlurnintyarla* 'someone who likes physical pleasures, a sensuous or hedonistic person' ᴛᴍ

padminthi [padmi-nthi] *v-intr* jump; skip; leap ᴛs,ᴛᴍ,ᴡɪ,sᴛ,ᴋᴏ

  padmi-padminya [padmi-padmi-nya] *n* (1) jumping, skipping ᴛs,ᴛᴍ (2) someone who jumps or skips ᴛs,ᴛᴍ

padna₁ => **parna₁**

padna₂ => **parna₂**

padnaintya => **parnaintya**

padni-apinthi => **parni-apinthi**

padninthi [padni-nthi] *v-intr* go; walk; run; travel *Mardla purla padnirninyana naki.* '(They) only saw that they were going.' *Padni-padningka! Mai niina yungkungki.* 'Run quick! You will get food.' ᴛs,ᴛᴍ,ᴡʏ,ᴋᴏ

padni-padninya [padni-padni-nya] *n* running; going quickly ᴛꜱ,ᴋᴏ,ᴡɪ,ꜱᴛ

Padnipadninyirntu [padni-padni-ny(a)-(th)irntu] *n* Saturday ɴᴇᴡ

padnipadniti [padni-padni-ti] *n* car ɴᴇᴡ

painingka [paini-ngka] *temp* previously, in the past ᴛꜱ,ᴛᴍ,ᴡʏ,ꜱᴛ

  paini-painingka [paini-paini-ngka] *temp* very long ago ᴛᴍ

  painingka-intyarla [paini-ngka-intyarla] (var. **painingka-intyardla**) *temp* long ago ᴛꜱ,ᴛᴍ

  painingkiana [paini-ngk(a)-na] *adj* former; previous ᴛꜱ

  painingkiarna [paini-ngk(a)-rna] *n* ancestors; people who lived long ago ᴛᴍ

paintya [paintya] (1) *dem* that one, this one *Wantanthi paintya ngathu.* 'I keep that one in reserve.' *Paintya ngai ngaityarlirlu yungkungki.* 'My father will give me this.' *Ngaityu panya* 'That is mine' ᴛꜱ,ᴛᴍ,ʙᴀ (2) *loc, dem* here, there *Paintya wayinga niipurna! Turlarlu'ai pungkutuwayi. Ngulthi madlu-adlu.* 'Play with each other over there! Otherwise I might get cross. It's a really dark night.' ᴛꜱ,ᴛᴍ

  paintyangka in that, on that ᴛᴍ

  paintyarra along there ᴛᴍ

paintya-yaintya [pa-intya-(i)ya-intya] *adj* scattered; dispersed ᴡʏ

paintyanthi => **pantyinthi**

paintyi => **pantyi**

paitpurla *n* fat, oil, grease, tallow, whale blubber ᴛꜱ,ᴡʏ,ᴘɪ,ɢᴀ

  paitpurla kardlayirdi candle ᴛꜱ

paitpurtu [pait(ya)-purtu] *adj* grumpy; irritable; argumentative ᴛꜱ

paitpurturti! [pait(ya)-purtu-rti] *intj* settle down! ᴛꜱ

paitya *n* (1) monster ᴛꜱ (2) reptile ᴛꜱ (3) brown snake ᴡʏ,ᴘɪ (4) any biting or stinging animal or insect ᴛꜱ,ᴛᴍ,ᴡʏ (5) any animal that is not fit for eating, vermin, grasshoppers, locusts ᴛꜱ,ᴛᴍ,ᴡɪ

  paitya! *intj* deadly!; wow! ᴛꜱ,ᴛᴍ

  paityakudna [paitya-kudna] *n* blood (used in ceremony) ᴛᴍ

  paityamurdu [paitya-murdu] *n* poison dust (ceremony) ᴡʏ

  paityapuulti [paitya-puulti] *n* (1) old woman ᴛꜱ,ᴛᴍ,ᴡɪ,ᴡʏ,ʀᴏ,ꜱᴛ (2) old witch ᴛᴍ

  Paityapuulti Warnirntu [paitya-puulti warn(i)-(th)irntu] *n* Queen's Birthday ɴᴇᴡ

  paityarri *adj* very (comparative affix) *paityarri marni* 'very good' *paityarri tawarra* 'very big' ᴛᴍ

paitya-marrinthi [paitya-marri-nthi] *v-intr* run fast; flee ᴛᴍ

paityuti *n* blind person *paityutipurka* 'old blind man' *Paityutiluama pa karku-arra kangkithi.* 'Perhaps it was in blindness that he led (the oxen) past the Sheoak.' ᴛꜱ,ᴛᴍ,ᴡʏ,ᴡɪ,ɢᴀ,ᴋᴏ,ꜱᴛ

  paityuti-antinthi [paityuti-anti-nthi] *v-intr* go blind ᴛᴍ

  paityutina [paityuti-na] *adj* blind *Paityutiana niina?* 'Are you blind?' ᴛᴍ

  paityuwarti [paityu-warti] *n* sorcerer's instrument used to cause blindness ᴛꜱ,ᴛᴍ

paka *n* (1) dry bark ᴛꜱ,ᴛᴍ,ᴡʏ,ᴡɪ,ᴋᴏ,ꜱᴛ (2) skin ᴛᴍ,ᴡʏ,ᴡɪ (3) peel, husk of something ᴛꜱ,ᴛᴍ (4) scab ᴡʏ,ᴡɪ

  pakadla *n* (1) hoar frost, tiny ice crystals that form on surfaces during cold, clear nights ᴛꜱ,ᴛᴍ (2) salt ᴛꜱ

  pakamanthi [paka-ma-nthi] *v-tr* peel ᴛꜱ,ᴛᴍ,ᴡʏ,ᴡɪ

  pakamati *n* vegetable peeler ɴᴇᴡ

  pakapaltha *n* bandaid ɴᴇᴡ

  pakapuru *adj* unpeeled ᴛꜱ,ᴛᴍ

  pakapuruti *adj* peeled, without skin ᴛꜱ,ᴛᴍ

  pakayuku [paka-yuku] *n* bark canoe ᴡʏ,ᴡɪ,ꜱᴛ

pakanthi [paka-nthi] *v-tr* dig up ᴛꜱ,ᴛᴍ

  paka-pakanthi [paka-paka-nthi] *v-intr* trot ᴛꜱ

  Paka-pakirntu [paka-pak(a)-(th)irntu] *n* Adelaide Cup Day ɴᴇᴡ

pakinthi [paki-nthi] *v-tr* cut ᴛꜱ,ᴛᴍ,ᴡɪ,ᴡʏ,ᴋᴏ,ꜱᴛ

  paki-tharralyi *n* cutting board ɴᴇᴡ

  pakipakiti [paki-paki-ti] *n* knife ᴛꜱ,ᴛᴍ,ᴡʏ,ᴡɪ

  pakirrinthi [paki-rri-nthi] *v-intr* (1) cut (oneself) *Pakirringa! Pakirringa! Purku tawarra.* 'Cut yourself! Cut yourself! (There is) lots of dew.' ᴛꜱ,ᴛᴍ (2) be very cold, (as when water feels 'bitingly' cold) *Kauwi pakirri.* 'The water is "cutting" (cold).' ᴛᴍ,ɢᴀ,ʀᴏ

paku-paku *n* butcherbird ᴘɪ

pakurta *n* (1) ceremonial scars ᴛᴍ (2) dots on the chest and back ᴛꜱ

palangkita *n* blanket ɴᴇᴡ (from English 'blanket')

paltha *n* covering (of a bodypart) *tidnapaltha* 'boot/shoe' *miipaltha* 'eyelid' ᴛᴍ,ᴛꜱ,ꜱᴛ,ᴡʏ

palti₁ *n* (1) ceremony, 'corroborree' belonging to the Karnu Miyurna (hill people) ᴛꜱ,ᴛᴍ,ᴄᴀ,ᴡʏ (2) song, dance, performance ᴛꜱ,ᴛᴍ

  palti makanthi shake the legs while performing 'palti' ᴛᴍ,ᴡʏ

  palti mutanthi sing and enjoy 'palti' ᴛꜱ

  palti ngarkunthi sing and enjoy 'palti' ᴛꜱ

palti tarkanthi sing 'palti' TS, TM

palti waatu ceremonial shout in unison TM

palti₂ (var. **paltiwalti**; **paltiwarltu**) n groin TS, TM, KO

palti-palti n parrot CO, PI, WY

palya n (1) shrub (similar to myrtle) TS, TM (2) hook made from the palya shrub which is used to get grubs out of the ground or holes in trees TS, TM, CA, WY, AN

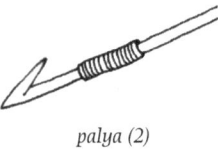
palya (2)

palyathata n cross-wise sticks (ceremony) PI

pamanthi [pama-nthi] v-tr (1) spear, pierce, stab (something) TS, TM, WI, WY, ST, KO (2) touch, border on (something) (as when two countries touch or border on each other) TS, TM

   pama-nungkurrinthi spear each other TM

   pamalyarninthi [pama-alya-rni-nthi] v-tr continue spearing TM

   pamaparti [pama-parti] n wasp NEW

   pamarrinthi [pama-rri-nthi] v-intr (1) spear, pierce, hit (each other) *Wirntarna yartarli'arna, nata padni'adlu. Tirntu-arra pamarrinthi'adlu.* 'The spears are broken, let's go now. We'll be spearing again tomorrow.' *Pamarringka ngai pudni. Mukarta kurntangka! Kurdu karrinth'ai.* 'I came for spearing. (But since it is not going to happen now) Strike my head! I feel ashamed.' TS, TM (2) touch against, border on (each other) TS, TM

pampayi n lizard GA

pangka n (1) lake, lagoon TS (2) Lake Alexandrina TS, TM

   Pangka miyurna [pangka miyu-rna] n people from Lake Alexandrina area TS, TM

pangkarra n district, country (inherited land) *Ngarraitya pardu'aitya pangkarrila.* 'There is lots of game in my country.' TS, TM

pangkawirri n club (Ngarrindjeri) TS

panminthi [panmi-nthi] v-intr dive; jump WY, KO

pangkawirri

panpa-panpalya [panpa-panpa-lya] n conference; meeting NEW

   panpa-panpalyarninthi [panpa-panpa-lya-rni-nthi] v-intr introduce (groups of people) TM

pantyi (var. **paintyi**; **pantya**) n side *piiki warli paintyi-ana* 'to the side of the pig sty' *ninku pantyingka* 'at your side, on the side of you' TS, TM

   paintyi warpu the area of the ribs TM

pantyapinthi [pantyi-(w)api-nthi] v-tr (1) cause to touch, feel *Yaku ngaii paintyapitha.* '(He) will not touch me.' *Paintyapirritha purla.* 'They will touch each other.' TM (2) cause to lie on the side, make (someone) lie on their side TS

pantyinthi [pantyi-nthi] (var. **paintyanthi**) v-intr lie on the side TS

panya n younger sibling (brother or sister) *ngaityu panyaku* 'my brother's, (belonging to my brother)' TM

   panyapi n (1) younger sibling, little brother or sister TS, WY, WI, KO (2) deceased younger sibling TM

   panyarla n deceased younger sibling TM

panyi n early morning *panyipuru* 'early in the morning' TM, RO

   panyimai n breakfast NEW

   panyingkurlu [panyi-ngka-rlu] n tomorrow TM, WI, ST

   panyiwarta n morning (after sunrise) TS, TM, GA

   panyiwartarlu [panyi-warta-rlu] temp in the morning TM

papaltu n tree stump; stump *papaltu-arra* 'passing by, or along the side of a tree stump' TS, TM

   papaltu-kuinyu men carrying burning firesticks during circumcision ceremony TM

papanthi [papa-nthi] v-tr dry a skin by stretching it on the ground TM, TS

pardi n (1) maggot TS, TM (2) rice TS, TM, WY, WI, ST

pardlu n hair, fur, feathers, plumage TS, TM, WI, WY, GA, KO, ST

pardni-mankunthi => **parni mankunthi**

pardu n (1) meat, flesh, food from an animal *pardungka mainthi* 'to live on or subsist on meat' TS, TM, WY, WI, ST (2) animal, game TS, TM

   pardu mulartila n kebab NEW

   Pardu Paitya n man's name WY

   pardu-apinthi [paru-paru-(w)api-nthi] v-tr challenge; threaten *kurntatina pardu-apinthi* 'to threaten with a fight' (var. **pardu-pardu-apinthi**) TS, TM

   pardu-pamamati [pardu-pama-(pa)ma-ti] n fork TS

   pardu-wirrka n curry NEW

   pardurninthi [pardu-rni-nthi] v-intr turn into an animal TS, TM

   parduwardli [pardu-wardli] n butcher's shop NEW

pardurdu [pardu-(pa)rdu] n uncircumcised person TS, TM

pari n river; creek; gully (with creek bed) *paringka* 'in or on the river' TS, TM, BL, GA, WI, WY, ST

   pari pulyuna kuya n river blackfish (*Gadopsis marmoratus*) NEW

parinthi [pari-nthi] (var. **pathinthi**) *v-intr* swim ₜₛ,ₜₘ,ᴡɪ,ᴡʏ

paripardu [pari-pardu] *n* waterfowl, river birds ₜₛ

pariparinya [pari-pari-nya] *n* swimming ɴᴇᴡ

parkana [parka-na] *adj* white; light-coloured; bright *parkana miyu* 'white man' ₜₛ,ₜₘ,ᴡʏ,ᴡɪ,ꜱᴛ,ᴄʜ

  parka-ityinthi [parka-ity(a)-(way)i-nthi] (var. **parka-ityayinthi**) (1) *v-tr* white-wash, whiten (something) ₜₘ (2) *v-intr* get white on oneself *Niina parkaityayi.* 'You've gotten white on yourself.' ₜₘ

  parkananti-apinthi [parka-na-nti-(w)api-nthi] *v-tr* whiten, make white ₜₘ

  parkarninthi [parka(na)-rni-nthi] (var. **parkanthi**) *v-intr* (1) be white, be clear ₜₛ (2) shine *Tirntu parkarni-utha ...* 'When the sun is shining ...' ₜₛ,ₜₘ

parkanarntinthi [parka-na-rni-nthi] *v-intr* turn white ₜₘ

parltanthi [parlta-nthi] (1) *v-tr* hit, push, knock, beat, strike (someone or something), throw, split (wood) *kardla padlu- parltanthi* 'to beat the fire out' *Painingka ngathu parltathi, numa pa mururrithi ngathu parlta-nana.* 'When I split (the wood) before, it ran well when I was hitting (it).' *Ngai parltanana.* 'I am the one who has been beaten.' ₜₛ,ₜₘ,ʙʟ,ᴋᴏ (2) *v-tr* pull out, pluck off (something) ₜₛ,ₜₘ (3) *v-tr* rip, tear (something) ɢᴀ (4) *v-tr* break (something) ᴡʏ (5) *v-intr, v-tr* fall heavily, beat upon (something) *Manyarlu parltanthi.* 'The rain is beating down heavily.' *Mirnu purrumpamparltanthi.* 'The wattle flower is falling.' ₜₘ (6) *v-tr* beget, impregnate (someone), get (someone) pregnant ₜₘ (7) *v-intr, v-tr* beat the time (during a song) ᴡʏ

parlta-parlta *n* knocking ₜₛ

  parlta-parltarriti [parlta-parlta-rri-ti] *n* stretching oneself ₜₛ,ₜₘ

  parltanyarninthi [parlta-nya-rni-nthi] *v-intr* become stretched ₜₘ

  parltarri-apinthi [parlta-rri-(w)api-nthi] *v-tr* pull off; pluck; break off ₜₛ,ₜₘ

  parltarrinthi [parlta-rri-nthi] (var. **parlta-parltarrinthi**) *v-intr* (1) stretch (oneself) (as people do when they wake up) ₜₛ,ₜₘ (2) wear out, decay, fall apart, crumble *Turnki ngathaityangka parltarrinthi.* 'The coat is wearing out on my body.' *Yitpi parltarrinthi kathi-urlu.* 'My soul is wearing out from exhaustion.' *Tangka parltarrinthi warltarlu tawarrarlu.* 'My heart is wearing out from the heat.' ₜₘ (3) fall *Manya parltarrinthi.* 'It is raining.' ₜₛ,ₜₘ

parltarta [parlta-rta] (var. **parltarti**) *adj* (1) not heavy, light ₜₛ,ₜₘ (2) weak, feeble, not strong (object) *Parltarta niina.* 'You are weak.' ₜₘ

  parltarta kapa [parlta-rta kapa] weak, feeble, not strong ₜₘ

parna₁ [pa-rna] (var. **'rna**; **padna₁**) *pro* (1) they (plural nominative) ₜₛ,ₜₘ,ʙʟ (2) them (plural accusative) ₜₛ,ₜₘ

  parnaintya [pa-rna-intya] (var. **padnaintya**) *pro* those there ₜₛ,ₜₘ

  parnaku [pa-rna-ku] *pro* their(s) (plural possessive) ₜₛ,ₜₘ,ᴡʏ

  parnaku-anti [pa-rna-ku-anti] theirs alone, belonging only to them ₜₘ

  parnakurtila [pa-rna-ku-rtila] *adv* in their absence ɴᴇᴡ

  Parnakuyarli [Pa-rna-ku-yarli] *n* star name ₜₛ

  parnalitya [pa-rna-litya] *pro* (1) for them (plural purposive) ₜₛ,ₜₘ (2) to them (plural allative) ₜₛ,ₜₘ

  parnalityangka [pa-rna-litya-ngka] with them, on account of them, because of them (plural locative/causative) ₜₘ

  parnalityanungku [pa-rna-litya-nungku] (away) from them (plural ablative) ₜₘ

  parnarlu *pro* they (plural ergative) ɴᴇᴡ

parna₂ (var. **padna₂**) *n* (1) star indicating the autumn (undefined) ₜₛ,ₜₘ (2) one of two men who lead the procession and stand at either side of the line which participants form during the circumcision ceremony ₜₛ,ₜₘ

  parnati₂ [parna-ti] *n* autumn ₜₛ,ₜₘ

parnapi *n* mushroom species ₜₛ,ₜₘ,ᴡɪ,ᴡʏ,ꜱᴛ

parnata (var. **parnati₁**) *loc* on this side *Pathawilya parnati* 'On this side of Holdfast Bay' *pari parnata* 'on this side of the river' ₜₛ,ₜₘ

  parnatinya'rna [parnat(a)-inya (pa)rna] those on this side ₜₘ

parnga *n* club; fighting stick ₜₘ

parnguta *n* (1) edible root (bulbous) ₜₛ,ₜₘ,ᴄʜ (2) potato ₜₛ,ₜₘ,ᴡʏ,ᴄʜ (3) yam ᴄʜ

parni *dir* towards here; to here (allative) *Parni kawai!* 'Come here!' *Kauwi parni!* 'Give me water!' *Parni katintu'rna!* 'Fetch them! Bring them here!' *Parni ngatpantu!* 'Come in!' ₜₛ,ₜₘ,ʙʟ

  parni mankunthi [parni-manku-nthi] (var. **pardni-mankunthi**) *v-tr* give; pass; hand (something) *parni manmantu!* 'Give it here! Pass it to me!' ₜₛ,ₜₘ

  parni-api kurda [parni-(w)api kurda] *n* short pass (football) ɴᴇᴡ

  parni-apinthi [parni-(w)api-nthi] (var.

padni-apinthi) *v-tr* give; pass; hand (to someone) *Parni-apintu!* 'Give it here! Hand it to me!' TS, TM

parnidlu [parni-rlu] *loc* close by; nearby TM

parnpanthi [parnpa-nthi] *v-tr* prevent (someone) from doing something, deter, dissuade, hold back (someone) *Mai yungkutuwayi parnpapi.* 'He convinced me not to give you food.' TS, TM

  parnpa-parnpanya [parnpa-parnpa-nya] *n* dissuading; preventing from doing something; deterring; holding (someone) back TS

parnta *n* (1) limestone TS, TM, WY (2) brick *Parntarlu ngathu wardli tayitha.* 'I shall build the house with bricks.' WI, TS

  parntawardli *n* mud hut WY

parnta-midla *n* spear thrower TM, WY

parntakarla [parnti-karla] *n* rifle KO

  parntapurdi [parnti-purdi] *n* (1) gun, musket, *tukutya parntapurdi* 'pistol' TS, WI, WY, ST (2) bullet, ball, shot (for a gun) TS

parntala (var. **parntadla**) *n* spine; lumbar region TS, TM, WI, ST, KO

parntanthi [parnta-nthi] *v-tr* wring out; squeeze *kauwi parntanthi* 'to wring the water out (of something)' TS, TM

parntinthi [parnti-nthi] *v-intr* crackle (fire); sparkle; spark TS, TM

parntu *n* Murray cod (*Maccullochella peelii*) TS, TM

parntu *n* (1) ball NEW (2) leather ball TS, TM, WY, CA

parntu mukarta waitku *n* big-headed/flat-headed gudgeon (*Philypnodon grandiceps*) NEW

parnu (var. **parnuku**) *pro* his; hers; its (possessive) TS, TM, WI, ST

  parnuku-anti [parnu-ku-anti] only his, hers or its, exclusively belonging to him, her or it TM

  parnukuntya [parnu-ku-ntya] *pro* his, hers, its, 'the indefinite possessive TM

  parnukurlu [parnu-ku-rlu] he, she, it (the agent in the sentence), third person singular ergative TM

  parnukurni [parnu-ku-rni] for him, her, it, third person singular dative TM

parpunta *n* plains WY

parra *n* branch TS

  parrarra [parr(a)-(p)arra] *n* big branch *parrarraila* 'on the big branch' TM

  parrarratangkurla [parr(a)-(p)arra-tangk(a)-(p)urla] *n* rip or tear (into two large pieces) TS

parraitpa (var. **parraipa**) *n* grasshopper; locust TS, TM, WY

parraitya *n* seaweed TS, TM

parranthi [parra-nthi] *v-tr* (1) chew (something) TS, TM (2) light a fire (by rubbing two sticks together) *karla parranthi* 'to light a fire' *kardla parranthi* 'to kindle a fire OR to light a fire' TS, TM, WY (3) marry (someone) *yangarra parranthi* 'to obtain a wife' *Nintu parratha ninku miyuwarta?* 'Will you marry your countrywoman? OR Will you marry your countryman?' TS, TM

parrka (var. **parrka-widlu**; **parrka-wilu**) *n* person whose older sister has died TS, TM

parrku *n* sound, noise TS, TM, WY

  parrku-manthi [parrku-ma-nthi] *v-tr* make a noise TM

  parrkulayinthi [parrku-layi-nthi] *v-intr* (1) make a noise, make a sound TS, TM (2) sound out the letters in spelling TM

  parrkunthi [parrku-nthi] *v-intr* make a sound TS, TM

parrpa *n* (1) (human) skin TS, TM, WI (2) foreskin TM

parru-parru *n* bird of the cuckoo family WY

parruntayinthi [parru-nta-(wai)yi-nthi] *v-intr* move to and fro; bend TM

parta *n* sex TS, TM

  parta mankunthi [parta manku-nthi] *v-intr* have sex (woman) TM

  parta yungkunthi [parta yungku-nthi] *v-intr* have sex (man) TM

  partamu *n* initiate (at a certain stage) EY

  partatangkurla [parta-ta-ngk(a)-(p)urla] *n* couple; husband and wife TM

partana (var. **-partana**) *adj* (1) many, much, lots TS, TM, WY (2) entirely-, nothing but- *mukarta partana* 'nothing but heads, many war-like men -' *manta partana* 'nothing but lies, all lies' TM (3) full of-, characterised by- *mantapartana* 'full of lies, a liar, constantly lying' TS (4) maker of-, instigator of- (e.g. rain-) *Pulyuna miyurna manya partana pudlurrinthi.* 'The black men call themselves rain makers.' TM

partarluku [parta-rluku] *adv* every time; often TM

partarrinthi [parta-rri-nthi] *v-intr* remain still *Tiwi ngai tirntu partarri-utha.* 'Often I will stay there all day.' TM

parti *n* (1) grub TS, TM (2) insects in general TS

partu *adj* big; large; thick *munthu partu* 'big belly, full and not hungry anymore' TS, TM

  partu tita-wardli supermarket NEW

  partu-yuri *n* cauliflower NEW

patha *n* gum tree species; swamp gum TS, TM, WY

pathinthi [pathi-nthi] => **parinthi**

patinthi [pati-nthi] (var. **pati-patinthi**) *v-tr* **(1)** throw, hurl *kadliadli patinthi* 'to accuse or suspect (someone) of causing a death' *Nintu 'iti ngai yurirlu patinthi.* 'You address me first. (literally: 'You first throw me your face')' *Warru-ana patintu!* 'Throw it outside!' TS,TM **(2)** direct, send, cause (something) to go somewhere *Ninku warrarna ngathu pati-patiutha.* 'I will deliver your message.' *Nintu ngai yitpi tungkinana pati-patinthi* 'You hate me. ('You throw bad spirit towards me')' TM **(3)** release, let go, untie TM **(4)** thrust into the ground WY **(5)** push or knock down WI,ST

    pati-apinthi [pati-(w)api-nthi] *v-tr* release; untie; let go TS

    patirrinthi [pati-rri-nthi] *v-intr* throw (oneself/each other) *wingku patirrinthi* 'to breathe, respire' TS,TM

patpa *n* south TS,TM,WY

    patpa kupi *n* Swan River goby (fish) (*Pseudogobius olorum*) NEW

    patpa-ana to the south TM

    patpaintyarla further south TM

    patpangka in the south TS,TM

    patparta southerly TS,TM

pauwa *num* nine NEW

    pauwa partirrka [pauwa part(u)-irrka] *num* nine hundred NEW

    Pauwani *n* ninth-born (male or female) TS,EY

    pauwata [pauw(a)-(taw)ata] *num* nine thousand NEW

    Pauwiki [pauw(a)-(p)iki] *n* September NEW

    pauwirrka [pauw(a)-irrka] *num* ninety NEW

    pauwiwurra [pauw(a)-(w)iwurra] *num* nine million NEW

pawunthi [pawu-nthi] *v-tr* stoke, put wood on the fire, feed the fire wood *Karla purta-purta-ingku! Pawu'ngathu, manyarrinth'ai.* 'Let the fire blaze! I will add wood to it, I'm cold.' TS,TM

paya! *intj* wow! An expression of wonder, surprise or astonishment. TS,TM

payanthi [paya-nthi] *v-tr* **(1)** bite, chew, eat (something) *mirnu payanthi* 'to chew gum' *kadli payanthi* 'to eat dog' TS,TM,WY,WI,PI,KO,CH **(2)** understand *warra payanthi* 'to understand a language or someone's speech' *Kardlarlu payayarnana.* '(He) has been bitten by the fire (i.e. burned).' TS,TM

    payanantinthi [paya-na-nti-nthi] *v-intr* be bitingly cold, very cold *Manya payanantinthi.* 'It's becoming really cold.' TS

payarrinthi [paya-rri-nthi] *v-tr* **(1)** bite, chew on (something) TS,WY **(2)** understand (language) *ngaityu nintu payarri warra?* 'did you understand my language?' RO

payati [paya-ti] *n* biting insect NEW

payinthi [payi-nthi] (var. **payirrinthi**) *v-tr* **(1)** search for, seek, look for (something) *Niina nganapurtu-itya payirrinthi?* 'What are you looking for?' TS,WY,WI,ST **(2)** examine, think about, consider TS

    payirri-apinthi [payi-rri-(w)api-nthi] *v-tr* consider (make someone); look for (make someone); investigate (make someone) TS

-pi => **-api**

pia *aux* Particle expressing uncertainty; perhaps; maybe *Pia waa ngaityu yunga? Madli pia pa.* 'Where is my brother I wonder? Perhaps he has died.' *Waa ngaityu tantu waa? Waa alya pia?* 'Where is my bag? Where is it?' *Pia waa- waa?* 'Where is (he)?' *Pia ngaintya pia, yararrinth'ai.* 'Whatever it is, I am not certain.' TS,TM

piarrinthi [pia-rri-nthi] *v-intr* **(1)** separate (from each other), stray (from the group) TS,TM **(2)** be scattered TS

    piarri-apinthi [pia-rri-(w)api-nthi] *v-tr* scatter; disperse TS,TM

pidlanthi [pidla-nthi] (var. **pidlarrinthi**) *v-intr* (undefined obscenity) TS,TM

    pidlingka [pidli-ngka] *adj* selfish; stingy *Naa pidlingkarna.* 'You mob are stingy.' *pardu pidlingka* 'unwilling to give meat' (var. **-pidlingka**) TS,TM

pidna *n* charcoal TS,TM,WI,KO,ST,KO

    pidnanthi [pidna-nthi] *v-intr* **(1)** stay; wait, remain TM **(2)** delay, hesitate TM

    pidnarninthi [pidna-rni-nthi] *v-intr* turn into charcoal TM

    pidnarri-purka [pidna-rri-purka] *n* lazy person; loiterer TS

    pidnarrinthi [pidna-rri-nthi] *v-intr* loiter; walk slowly; dawdle *Pidna-pidnarringurti!* 'Don't dawdle!' (var. **pidna-pidnarrinthi**) TM

piidna *n* Adam's apple (*laryngeal prominence*) WY

piiki *n* pig TM (from English 'pig')

piipa *n* paper; letter; book TS,TM (from English 'paper')

    piipakaityawardli [piipa-kaitya-wardli] *n* post office NEW

    piipamudlirna [piipa-mudli-rna] *n* print-based resources NEW

    piipathitawardli [piipa-thita-wardli] *n* newsagent NEW

    piipawardli [piipa-wardli] *n* schoolhouse TM

piipawarpulayi kuu [piipa-warpu-(w)ayi kuu] (var. **piipawarpulayi-wardli**) *n* office NEW

pika *adj* soft; flexible TS,TM
   pika-pika *adj* very soft, pliable, flexible TM,TS
   pika-pikarninthi [pika-pika-rni-nthi] *v-intr* become soft, flexible TS

piki *n* (1) moon TS,TM,KO (2) month NEW

piku (var. **piku-puthi**) *n* eyebrow *Pikurdla* 'two eyebrows' TS,TM,WI,WY,ST,KO

pila *n* eagle species (undefined) TS

pilki *n* fungus species TS

pilta *n* (1) hip, side of the body TS,TM (2) side of something *piltarlu wanti-apinthi* 'to lay (something) on its side' TM
   pilta-muka *n* buttocks TS
   pilta-mukurta *n* hip bone TM
   pilta-pilunthi [pilta-pilu-nthi] (var. **pila-pilunthi**) *v-intr* turn over; turn inside out *warra pilta-pilunthi* 'interpret (a language)' TM
   pilta-warpu *n* hip bone TS
   pilta-wuingki *adj* weak; fragile TM
   pilta-yurlu *n* (1) hip bone TM (2) hip (the entire hip) TM (3) glenoid cavity (part of the shoulder joint) TS
   piltangka [pilta-ngka] at the hip; at the side TS

pilta-pilta *n* mouse species (undefined) TS

piltilainthi [pilti-layi-nthi] *v-intr* crackle (fire); sparkle TM

piltilinthi [pilti-l(ay)i-nthi] *v-intr* break; collapse TS

piltinthi [pilti-nthi] *v-tr* cut off; cut through; pinch off *yuka piltinthi* 'to cut hair' TS,TM
   piltiti [pilti-ti] *n* scissors TS,TM,WI,ST

pilunthi [pilu-nthi] *v-tr* roll over; turn over TS,TM

pilupiluna [pilu-pilu-na] *n* tip of the sternum (ensiform cartilage) TS

pilyapilya *n* butterfly; moth WI,ST

pilyapilya *n* chatter; noise (of talking) *Pilyapilyarti!* 'Stop talking!' *Pilyapilyarti tikainga!* 'Sit quietly you lot!' TS,TM

pilyunthi [pilyu-nthi] *v-tr* scold; criticise; tell off TS
   pilyu *n* peace NEW
   pilyurni-apinthi [pilyu-rni-(w)api-nthi] *v-tr* (1) pacify, persuade (someone) TM (2) invite, entreat (someone) TM
   pilyurninthi [pilyu-rni-nthi] *v-intr* become calm, compose oneself TM

pimpina *n* finch TS

pina *n* man; adult TS

pinanapinthi [pina-na-(wa)pi-nthi] *v-tr* bring up, raise (child) TM

pinarninthi [pina-rni-nthi] *v-intr* grow up, become an adult TM

-pina *suff* (on nouns) characterised by, in the habit of, liking *maingki-pina* 'someone who laughs a lot' *warra-pina* 'chatterbox' *turla-pina* 'short-tempered person, fighter' *marngu-pina* 'envious, jealous person' TS,TM

pingkanthi => **pintyanthi**

pingkarninthi => **pintyarninthi**

pingkarrinthi *v-intr* flashing with lightning WY

pingki$_1$ *n* bag (for magic objects) TS,TM,WY

pingki$_2$ *n* grass shirt WY

pingku *n* bilby TS

pingkya-lingkyala => **pintyalintyala**

pingyanthi => **pintyanthi**

pingyarri-apinthi => **pintyarri-apinthi**

pinkanthi => **pintyanthi**

pinkya => **pintya**

pinkya-pinkya! (var. **pintya-pintya!**) *intj* slow down! *Ngai padlu pintya pintya.* 'He kept calling me back.' TS

pinkyapinkyarti! => **pintya-pintyarti!**

pinkyarrinthi$_1$ [pinkya-rri-nthi] (var. **pintyarrinthi**$_2$) *v-intr, v-tr* flash; illuminate TS,WI,WY,GA,ST

pintapinta *adj* (1) bald, hairless TS,TM (2) sleek, smooth TS,TM
   Pinta kurltu-kurltu *n* salt water lakes (placename – undefined) TM
   pintarni-apinthi [pinta-rni-(w)api-nthi] (var. **pintapintarni-apinthi**) *v-tr* cut off (someone's) hair, (make someone) bald TS,TM
   pintarninthi [pinta-rni-nthi] *v-intr* go bald TM

pinti (1) *n* grave, place where souls reside before birth and after death TS,TM (2) *n* pit, hole in the ground, ditch *muiyu-pinti* 'the pit of the stomach' TS,TM,WI,ST (3) *adj* European, foreign *pinti mai* 'European food' *pinti miyu* 'white man' *pintiyu warli* 'white man's house' TS,TM,WY,KO
   pinti kudlu *n* European flea TS,TM
   pinti miyu *n* European person TS,TM,BL,RO,KO
   pinti nantu *n* horse TS
   pinti pita *n* European goose TM
   pinti tupurra English drone bee WY
   pinti-wanga grave; tomb TS,TM
   Pintingka [pinti-ngka] *n* Kangaroo Island WY

pintinungku [pinti-nungku] *adj* (1) from the grave ᴛꜱ,ᴛᴍ (2) from Europe; European ᴛꜱ

pintirninthi [pinti-rni-nthi] *v-intr* go downwards; sink inwards; form a hole ᴛᴍ

pintiti [pinti-ti] *adj* unborn ᴛᴍ

pintiwaadli *n* old woman ᴛꜱ,ᴛᴍ

pintiwaadlirninthi [pinti-wadli-rni-nthi] *v-intr* become an old woman ᴛᴍ

pintya (var. **pinkya**) *adv* slowly; softly; gently *Pintya ngai pithi!* 'Slow down, I'm (not ready) yet!' *Pintya'ithi ngai tikarningutha. Kuntu pungkurrinth'ai kumarnurlu yartarlu. Yalakanth'ai padnithi karradlu kuma yarta-nangku.* 'Not so fast! I will stay here for a bit. I felt uneasy at another place. I just came from another distant place.' ᴛꜱ,ᴛᴍ

pintya-pintya! => **pinkya-pinkya!**

pintya-pintyarti! [pintya-pintya-rti] (var. **pinkyapinkyarti!**) *intj* hurry up! ᴛꜱ,ᴛᴍ

pintyanthi [pintya-nthi] (var. **pingkanthi**; **pingyanthi**; **pinkanthi**) *v-tr* (1) make, create, produce, form *pinty'athu karla* 'I'll make a fire' *Ngai nintu kuma panyapi pingkanthi.* 'You are making me your younger sibling.' ᴛꜱ,ᴛᴍ,ᴡʏ,ʙʟ (2) build, erect, raise, lift up ᴛᴍ,ᴡʏ (3) turn around, fold back on itself (e.g. clothes) ᴛꜱ,ᴡʏ (4) write ᴡʏ,ᴡɪ

pintya-pintya! => **pinkya-pinkya!**

pintyalintyala [pintya-l(a)-(p)intya-la] (var. **pingkya-lingkyala**) *n* (1) creator, maker ᴛꜱ,ᴛᴍ (2) God the Creator ᴛꜱ,ᴛᴍ

pintyarninthi [pintya-rni-nthi] (var. **pingkarninthi**) *v-intr* turn around, be lifted up *Nata niina pintyarni.* 'Now you are lifted up / turned around.' ᴛᴍ

pintyarri-apinthi [pintya-rri-(w)api-nthi] (var. **pingyarri-apinthi**) *v-tr* turn around; lift up ᴛꜱ,ᴛᴍ

pintyarrinthi₁ [pintya-rri-nthi] (var. **pinkyarrinthi**₂) *v-intr* turn around, turn back (when you were going somewhere) ᴛꜱ,ᴛᴍ,ꜱᴛ,ᴡɪ

pintyarrinthi₂ => **pinkyarrinthi**₁

pinyanthi [pinya-nthi] *v-tr* do magic; curse (something) *kauwi pinyanthi* 'curse or poison water' ᴡʏ

pinyata (1) *n* nectar from the grass tree ᴛꜱ,ᴛᴍ (2) *n* sugar, lollies ᴛꜱ,ᴡʏ,ᴡɪ,ꜱᴛ,ᴄʜ (3) *adj* sweet ᴄʜ,ᴡʏ

pinyamai *n* fruit ɴᴇᴡ

pinyatutana [pinyatu-tana] *adj* (1) savoury; without sugar ᴛꜱ (2) sour ɴᴇᴡ

-pira *suff* (on nouns) because of; for *Nganapira? – Maipira.* 'What for? – For/on account of food.' *ngaityu wakwakupira* 'for (or about) my child'

Ngaityu wakwakupira kuntu pungkurrinth'ai. 'I am very worried for my child.' ᴛꜱ,ᴛᴍ

pirdi (var. **pirdina**) (1) *adv* however, still, yet, but *Mardlatirra, pirdi manmantu!* 'Never mind, take it anyway!' ᴛꜱ,ᴛᴍ (2) *adv* now *Pirdi wantangki Kartamirurna!* 'Now finish up (dealing) with Kartamiru's (business).' ᴛᴍ (3) *adv* probably, surely, most likely ᴛꜱ (4) *adj* enough, sufficient *Natapirdi!* 'That's enough now!' *Pirdi-anta!* 'That's enough! That will do!' *Nurutirti; nata pirdi. Maitidli pinti piyu nurntirlu tikama. Pirdinta ngurlu-urlaintya miyurla titapi – miyu kumartarna'adlu.* 'Don't work sorcery! It is enough now! The white man has food and sits (giving it) away. Enough that these two men have been hanged – we are other men' ᴛᴍ (5) *adv* only, just *Warrarti pirdi tikatika!* 'Just sit quietly!' *Pirdi kawaingwa nata!* 'Only you two come now!' ᴛᴍ

pirdi-anta enough, sufficient ᴛꜱ,ᴛᴍ

pirdipirdi *adj* old; past child-bearing age ᴛꜱ

piri *n* scaffold *karra piri* 'bedstead' ᴛᴍ

pirira *n* (1) leafy vegetable ᴛꜱ,ᴛᴍ (2) cabbage ɴᴇᴡ

pirirarli [pirira-rli] *n* lettuce ɴᴇᴡ

pirku *n* group (of people) ᴛꜱ,ᴛᴍ

pirlta *n* possum (brush-tailed) ᴛꜱ,ᴛᴍ,ᴡʏ,ᴡɪ,ʀᴏ,ꜱᴛ

pirra *n* lungs *miyurna pirrangku* 'for the people' *pirra padninthi* 'go in anger' *pirra wangkanthi* 'fight with passion and determination' ᴛᴍ

pirra-pina (1) *adj* angry; having an inclination for fighting ᴛᴍ (2) *n* angry person inclined to fight ᴛᴍ

pirra-pirrarninthi [pirra-pirra-rni-nthi] *v-intr* become angry; feel like fighting ᴛᴍ

pirrapina => **irrapina**

pirranthi [pirra-nthi] *v-tr* (1) pluck, pull out (hair) ᴛꜱ,ᴛᴍ (2) shave, scratch ᴛꜱ,ᴛᴍ

pirra-pirrala [pirra-pirra-la] *n* barber ᴛꜱ

pirrarrinthi [pirra-rri-nthi] *v-tr* pluck; shave (each other) ᴛꜱ

pirri *n* (1) fingernail, toenail, claw, talon ᴛꜱ,ᴡʏ,ɢᴀ (2) hook, e.g. fish hook, thin hooked twig used for getting grubs out of holes *kuya pirri* 'fish hook' ᴛᴍ,ᴀɴ,ɢᴀ

pirri-wirrkinthi [pirri wirrki-nthi] *v-tr* catch fish; go fishing ᴡɪ,ꜱᴛ

pirriwarta [pirri-warta] *n* grasshopper (short-winged) ᴡʏ

pirrki *n* bit, small piece, fragment *Mai pirrki-urlu nintu ngai yungkuma.* 'You've given me less food (than them).' ᴛꜱ,ᴛᴍ

pirrki pakinthi [pirrki paki-nthi] *v-tr* cut into pieces ᴛꜱ,ᴛᴍ

pirrki parltanthi [pirrki parlta-nthi] *v-tr* beat or pound (into pieces)ᴛѕ

pirrki warninthi [pirrki warni-nthi] fall apart, fall to bitsᴛᴍ

pirrki wayinthi [pirrki wayi-nthi] *v-intr* (1) break, fall apart, go to pieces *Makitau pirrki wayituwayi* 'Lest the window breaks'ᴛѕ,ᴛᴍ (2) separate from each other into smaller groupsᴛᴍ

pirrki-apinthi₁ [pirrki-(w)api-nthi] *v-tr* (1) break (something) into bits, tear (something) apartᴛѕ (2) divide, distribute (something)ᴛᴍ

pirrki-apinthi₂ [pirrki-(w)api-nthi] *v-tr* shootᴛѕ,ᴛᴍ,ᴡɪ

pirrki-apirninthi [pirrki-(w)api-rni-nthi] *v-intr* be shot *Ngaityarli pudluntu, puru ngai wartarra padnitha. Pirrki-apirnama ngai yailtyatuwayi tulyarlu.* 'Tell my dad that I will come after (later). Otherwise he might think the police have shot me.'ᴛᴍ

pirrkiparltaparltanya [pirrki-parlta-parlta-nya] *adj* fragile; brittle; breakableᴛѕ

pirrkipirrki *n* peasᴛѕ,ᴡɪ,ᴡʏ

pirrkirna [pirrki-rna] *n* change (money)ɴᴇᴡ

pirrkiti [pirrki-ti] *n* biscuit *pirrkiti tanturna katinga Munaityurna! – Kauwainga!* 'Fetch Munaitya's biscuit bags! – Come on now!'ᴛѕ,ᴋᴏ (unlikely to be from English 'biscuit')

pirrkirna *n* baby 'wati-wati'ᴛѕ

pirrku *n* story, report, news, message *pirrku padninthi* 'to go and carry a message' *pirrku pudnanthi* 'to come with a message' *pirrku tikanthi* 'to wait for a message' *pirrku mankunthi* 'to go get (fetch) a message'ᴛᴍ,ᴛѕ,ᴡʏ

pirrku mankulankula [pirrku manku-l(a)-(m)anku-la] *n* (1) messenger, ambassador, someone who brings a reportᴛᴍ (2) angelᴛᴍ

pirrku mankunthi [pirrku manku-nthi] *v-tr* accompany; escort; fetchᴛѕ

pirrku tirntu *n* storytimeɴᴇᴡ

pirrku-piipa *n* newspaperɴᴇᴡ

pirrkunthi [pirrku-nthi] *v-intr* give a report or messageᴛѕ

pirrkupiipawardli [pirrku-piipa-wardli] *n* newsagentɴᴇᴡ

pirrkurninthi [pirrku-rni-nthi] *v-intr* make a loud noiseᴛᴍ

pirrkuwarta [pirrku-warta] *n* person who accompanies a messengerᴛᴍ

pita *n* (1) Cape Barren goose (*Cereopsis novaehollandiae*)ᴛѕ,ᴛᴍ,ᴡɪ,ѕᴛ (2) name for Aboriginal people from the Murray riverᴛѕ,ᴛᴍ

pita miyu *n* person from the Murray river; Ngayawangᴛѕ

pita warra *n* language spoken by Murray river people (Ngayawang)ᴛѕ

pita yarta *n* land of the Murray river people (Ngayawang)ᴛѕ

pithapitha *adj* smoothᴛᴍ

pithapitharni-apinthi [pitha-pitha-rni-(w)api-nthi] *v-tr* iron (clothing etc)ᴛᴍ

piti (var. '**iti**') *adv* (1) first, before, sooner *Padni'adlu 'iti naku'adlu 'iti, mai pudlurrinthi.* 'Let's go and see first, (they) say there is food.' *Pintya ngai piti!* 'Slow down, I'm (not ready) yet!'ᴛѕ,ᴛᴍ (2) in first place, in winning placeɴᴇᴡ

piti *n* bowels; entrailsᴛᴍ,ᴡɪ,ѕᴛ

pitpa *n* (1) thorn, prickle or briarᴛѕ,ᴛᴍ (2) man's name (Old Tommy)ᴡʏ

pitpauwi [pitpa-(k)auwi] *n* (1) sweet, flowering part of the 'tarnma' (banksia, honeysuckle tree) which is soaked in water and sucked onᴛѕ (2) water that has been sweetened with banksia flowersᴛᴍ

Pitpauwitpina [pitp(a)-(k)auwi-(yi)tpi-na] *n* father of Pitpauwiᴡʏ

pitpayinthi [pitpa-(wai)yi-nthi] *v-intr* (1) close the eyesᴛᴍ (2) twinkle the eyesᴛᴍ

pitunthi [pitu-nthi] *v-tr* (1) touch, press, gently squeeze (something)ᴛѕ,ᴛᴍ (2) fondle, caress, touch (someone) in a sexual wayᴛᴍ

pituka *adj* (1) soft, pliableᴛѕ (2) swampyᴛᴍ

piturru *n* thunder or lightningᴛѕ,ᴛᴍ

pityarra *n* marshmallow plant (edible root)ᴛᴍ,ᴡʏ

pudlunthi [pudlu-nthi] *v-intr, v-tr* tell; inform; say; report *Parnuku padlu pudlunthi.* 'He says it is his.' *Kurdu wilta padlu ngai pudlunthi.* 'He says I am rude.' *Ngathu niina kaitya pudlurrinki* 'Say I sent you.'ᴛѕ,ᴛᴍ

pudlurri-apinthi [pudlu-rri-(w)api-nthi] *v-tr* send a message *Yalarra nintu pudlurri-apithi ngatha-ityangka.* 'You told me a while ago.'ᴛѕ

pudlurrinthi [pudlu-rri-nthi] *v-intr, v-tr* tell, inform (each other) *Ngai nintaityangka pudlurrinthi.* 'I tell you.' *Pudlurringwa ngathaitya!* 'Tell me (you two)!'ᴛѕ,ᴛᴍ

pudna *n* waterhole; soak; spring; well (water source)ᴛѕ,ᴛᴍ,ᴡʏ

pudnanthi [pudna-nthi] *v-intr* (1) come *Pa painingka pudnarnima, padlu ngadlu nurntiki purti-apithi.*

'When he used to come, he would always make us happy.' ᴛᴍ (2) arrive, appear *Yalakinyanta ngai pudni.* 'I have just now arrived.' *Yaintya pudna'ina. Yalarra ngadlu naki.* 'He has come. We just saw him.' ᴛs, ᴛᴍ (3) return *Niina pudna- intyidla, nintu ngai pardu yungkutha?* 'When you return will you give me meat?' ᴛs (4) extend ᴛs

   pudnapinthi [pudna-(w)api-nthi] (var. **pudnanyapinthi**) *v-tr* (1) fetch, bring (something), make (something) come ᴛs, ᴛᴍ (2) return, restore (something) ᴛs

pudni *n* malleefowl (*Leipoa ocellata*) ᴛs, ᴄᴏ

pudniwarta *n* cart; buggy; gig ᴛᴍ

puikurrinthi [puiku-rri-nthi] *v-intr* (1) be liquid, be wet ᴛs, ᴛᴍ (2) melt, moulder ᴛs, ᴛᴍ

puingurru *n* bone (for ceremony) ᴛs, ᴛᴍ, ᴄᴀ

puinyu *n* young possum ᴛs, ᴛᴍ

puiyu => **puyu**

pukanthi [puka-nthi] *v-intr* swim; bathe ᴛs, ᴛᴍ, ᴡʏ, ᴋᴏ, ꜱᴛ

   puka-pukanya [puka-puka-nya] *n* someone who swims a lot; someone who bathes a lot ᴛs, ᴛᴍ

pukarra *n* north-westerly wind ᴛs, ᴛᴍ

puki (1) *adj* former, ancient, from a long time ago ᴛs, ᴛᴍ (2) *temp* formerly, in the past ᴛs, ᴛᴍ

   pukiana [puki-ana] (1) *adj* old, ancient ᴛs, ᴛᴍ (2) *n* ancestors, forefathers *pukiana miyu* ᴛs, ᴛᴍ

   pukilya *n* deceased father ᴛs, ᴛᴍ

   pukilyarlu [puki-lya-rlu] *temp* yesterday *kuma pukilyarlu* 'the day before yesterday' ᴛs, ᴛᴍ, ᴡʏ

   pukintyarlintya [puki-ntyarla-ntya] *temp* most ancient; from very long ago ᴛᴍ

   pukintyarlu [puki-(i)ntya-rlu] (var. **pukinyadlu**) *temp* more ancient ᴛs, ᴛᴍ

   pukipuki *temp* very long ago ᴛs, ᴛᴍ

puku *adj* bare; naked *yarta puku* 'the bare ground' ᴛᴍ

   pukupuku *adj* bald; hairless ᴛs, ᴛᴍ, ᴡʏ

pukuli *n* preying mantis ᴡʏ

pultha *n* heart (of a person or animal) *Pultha tuturtayinthi kathiurlu.* 'The heart is beating quickly from exhaustion.' ᴛs, ᴛᴍ, ᴋᴏ

   pulthawarta [pultha-warta] *n* dorsal vertebrae ᴛs

   pulthawilta [pultha-wilta] *adj* brave; courageous; fearless ᴛᴍ, ᴛs

pulthu *n* (1) mark, trace, evidence, vestige, track *kudla pulthu* 'the mere traces, only the remains' *miyu pulthu* 'the signs of former human habitation' *Puki piti pa padni. Pulthu puru.* 'He left long ago. Only traces (remain).' ᴛs, ᴛᴍ (2) place where something used to be *Kudla pulthu niina wangkanthi.* 'You are speaking to the air. (i.e. no one is here to listen)' *tii kurla pulthu* 'run out of tea' *Mai pulthurna.* 'They have no food.' *wardli pulthu* 'place where a camp used to be' *pulthu-nungku; pulthu-anungku* 'coming from the place (where something used to be)' ᴛs, ᴛᴍ

   pulthu purruna fresh evidence (of someone that was here just recently) ᴛᴍ

   pulthu-arra [pulthu-arra] *loc* along ᴛs

   pulthu-arrapinthi [pulthu-arr(a)-(w)api-nthi] *v-intr* trace an outline; draw (following pre-marked lines) ᴛᴍ

   pulthupuru *adv* first; before hand; prior to ᴛs, ᴡʏ

   pulthurni-apinthi [pulthu-rni-(w)api-nthi] *v-tr* (1) go straight on ᴛs (2) cause to sneak off; allow to escape ᴛᴍ

   pulthurninthi [pulthu-rni-nthi] *v-intr* (1) be absent, gone away ᴛᴍ (2) escape, sneak away, abscond, disappear *Pulthurninth'ai tawarninyana.* 'I will go off secretly because (I) have been scolded.' *Kutini pa pulthurni.* 'She had run off again.' ᴛs, ᴛᴍ

pulti-ulti *adj* grumpy; irritable; argumentative ᴛs, ᴛᴍ

pultu-pultu *n* wattle parrot ꜱᴛ

pulturru (1) *adj* dry ᴛs, ᴡɪ, ꜱᴛ (2) *n* dry wind, dry air ᴛs, ᴛᴍ

-pulyu *suff* (on nouns) without-; lacking- *kardla-pulyu* 'without fire' *Warra-pulyu tikarti! Wangkanthi'adlu!* 'Don't sit there without talking! Let's talk!' *Nganaitya nintu ngai warra-pulyu wantanthi, ngaitya yunga?* 'Why do you pass me without speaking to me, my brother?' ᴛs, ᴛᴍ

pulyuna [pulyu-na] *adj* black; dark coloured *pulyuna miyu* 'black man, Aboriginal person' *kadli pulyuna* 'black dog' ᴛs, ᴛᴍ, ᴡʏ, ᴡɪ, ʙʟ, ʀᴏ, ɢᴀ, ᴋᴏ, ꜱᴛ, ᴄʜ

   pulyu-ulyapinthi [pulyu-(p)ulyu-(w)api-nthi] *v-tr* cause to become black, dark or dirty *karla pulyu-ulyapi* '[uncertain]' ᴛᴍ

   pulyurrinthi [pulyu-rri-nthi] *v-intr* (1) be/become black, dark coloured ᴛs, ᴛᴍ, ᴡʏ (2) be/become dirty, soiled ᴛs, ᴛᴍ (3) be/become dark and cloudy ᴡɪ, ꜱᴛ

punga *n* (1) shade, shadow *karra pungangka* 'in the shade of a gum tree' *wardli pungangka* 'in the shadow of the house' ᴛs, ᴛᴍ, ᴡʏ, ᴋᴏ (2) reflection (in water) ᴡʏ

pungkunthi [pungku-nthi] *v-tr* (1) pierce, thread through, prick (something) *taingkyadli pungkunthi* 'to make 'taingkyadli' (rush bags)' *mangka pungkunthi* 'to make 'mangka' cuts to create scarring' ᴛs, ᴛᴍ, ᴡʏ (2) make 'wikatyi' net bags ᴛᴍ (3) beat, fight, stab, kill *pardu pungkunthi* 'to kill or catch game animals' ᴛs, ᴛᴍ, ᴡʏ, ɢᴀ (4) bother, stab or beat in a metaphorical sense *Pungkuthi ngai yalarra.* '(He) has urged me a little while ago.' *maingkidlu pungkunthi* 'to be moved to laughter' *kuntu pungkunthi* 'to be uneasy, to dislike' TM

  pungki *adj* pierced; stabbed; killed TM

  pungku-arninthi [pungku-arni-nthi] *v-tr* continue stabbing, piercing, killing TM

  pungku-nungkurrinthi [pungku-nungku-rri-nthi] beat or stab each other TM

  pungkurrinthi [pungku-rri-nthi] *v-intr* (1) stab, beat, kill, fight (each other) TS, WI, ST (2) cut oneself *Mangka pa pungkurri.* 'He made 'mangka' cuts on himself.' TS (3) bother (oneself), stab or beat in a metaphorical sense *kuntu pungkurrinthi* 'to be very concerned or anxious' TM

puntulti *n* kangaroo tooth (in spear thrower) WY

puntunthi [puntu-nthi] *v-tr* blow (with mouth) TS, TM, WI, WY, KO, ST

  puntu-untu *n* dragonfly (large) WY

  puntuntu *n* helicopter NEW (inspired by Tiwi *pipirriwini* 'dragonfly')

puntunya *n* goanna species (undefined) TS

punturrpa *n* blister TS, TM

purakali *n* broccoli NEW (from English 'broccoli')

purdi *n* (1) stone *purdi-untu* 'stony ground' TS, TM, WI, GA, ST (2) sandstone (used for scoring animal skins) WY

  purdilya *n* kneecap TM

  purdita *n* kidneys *karrku purdita* 'smooth oval stone used for preparing red ochre' TS, TM

  purditarli [purdita-rli] *n* mango NEW

purirntu [pur(u)-(th)irntu] *n* minute (unit of time) NEW

purka (1) *n* old man, fully initiated man; Elder TS, TM, WY, CA, RO, EY (2) *n* king NEW (3) *adj* old *purka ngamaityarninthi* 'to become an old woman and pass the age of child-bearing' TS, WI, WY, ST

  -purka *suff* (on nouns) (1) man who often does that action *nitatipurka* 'lazy bones, idle person' *pidnarripurka* 'loiterer, someone who hangs around' *mitirripurka* 'thief' TS, TM (2) attached to a person's name: Father of that person *Karrkalapurka* 'Karrkala's dad' *Ngulthipurka* 'Ngulthi's dad' TS, TM (3) attached to a place name: 'Man from-' or 'Owner of-' that place *Murlawirrapurka* 'Dry forest man, (King John)' *Karrawirrapurka* 'Red-gum forest man' *wardlipurka* 'inhabitant of the house' TS, TM

  purkalainthi [purka-layi-nthi] *v-intr* become old; age TM

  purkarninthi [purka-rni-nthi] *v-intr* be/become old TS

purku *adj* heavy; tiring TS, TM

  purkurninthi [purku-rni-nthi] *v-intr* (1) become heavy TS, TM (2) become tired, weary TS

purkupurku *n* common grey mouse TS, TM, WI, WY, ST

purla [purla] (var. **'rla**) *pro* those two; they/them (dual nominative/accusative) TS, TM, GA

  purla pilta-pilturru [purla pilta-pilu-rru] *adj* two ply; doubled over *muinmu pilta-pilturru* 'more ply, more layers' TM

  purlaintya [purla-intya] those two (emphatic form) TS, TM

  purlaityi *num* two *purlaityinti* 'only two' *Purlaityidla-ityangka parra-parrantu! Kumantarlu pukutirlu yaku pilu-pilurnituwayi. Kuru tawarra warrunangkantu, kathi pakirrituwayi.* 'Get me two! So I don't have to go back and forth all the time with just one bucket. The container is very big, I might get exhausted.' TS, TM, WI, WY, BL, ST, KO, CH

  purlaityi kuma *num* three KO

  purlaityi partirrka [purlaityi part(u)-irrka] *num* two hundred NEW

  purlaityi purlaityi *num* four KO

  purlaityi purlaityi kuma *num* five KO

  purlaityi purlaityi purlaityi *num* six KO

  purlaityidlaku [purlaityi-rla-ku] *pro* their; theirs (dual genitive) TM

  purlaityidlu [purla-itya-dlu] *pro* with those two; with both (dual instrumental) TM

  purlakarli [purla-k(u)-(y)arli] *n* their father (dual) WY

  purlaku [purla-ku] *pro* their(s) (dual possessive) TS, TM, WY

  purlalitya [purla-itya] *pro* (1) to them two (dual allative) TS, TM (2) for them two (dual purposive) TS, TM

  purlarlu *pro* they (two) (dual ergative) NEW

  purlarluku [purla-rluku] *adv* twice *purlarlukunti* 'only twice' TS, TM

  purlawata [purl(a)-(th)awata] *num* two thousand NEW

  Purliki [purl(a)-(p)iki] *n* February NEW

  Purlirntu [purl(a)-(th)irntu] *n* Tuesday NEW

  purlirrka [purl(a)-irrka] *num* twenty NEW

  purlirrka kuma *num* twenty one NEW

  purliwurra [purl(a)-(wi)wurra] *num* two million NEW

purli *n* star TS, TM, WY, GA, RO, KO

purlinthi [purli-nthi] *v-intr* be full; be satisfied; satiated (after eating) *Niina purli? – Nii.* 'Are you full? – Yes.' TS, TM, WY

purninthi [purni-nthi] *v-tr* wet; sprinkle with water ᴛꜱ

purnkipurnki *adj* reddish brown; brownish coloured *marlta purnki-purnki* 'red-bearded (used as an insult)' ᴛꜱ,ᴛᴍ

   purnkipurnki mipurli *n* brown trout (*Salmo trutta*) ɴᴇᴡ

purnkuta *n* species of small bird ᴛꜱ

purnpunthi [purnpu-nthi] *v-tr* (1) surround, enclose (something) ᴛꜱ (2) grab (someone) from behind to stop them fighting ᴛᴍ (3) wrestle (someone) ᴛᴍ

   purnpurrinthi *v-tr* wrestle with; hold onto (each other) ᴛꜱ,ᴛᴍ

purnu *n* net bag ᴛꜱ,ᴛᴍ

purpurta *n* sparrow hawk ᴡʏ

purrku *n* dew ᴛꜱ,ᴛᴍ

purru *n* whole; all *ngadli purru* 'we both, together' *Ngarra purru warnintuwayi.* 'Or else I will fall together with the (burnt out) tree.' ᴛᴍ

   purrumanthi [purru-ma-nthi] *v-tr* (1) make (someone) alive; revive ᴛᴍ (2) raise (someone) from death ᴛᴍ

   purruna [purru-na] (1) *adj* alive, living ᴛꜱ,ᴛᴍ,ᴡɪ,ᴡʏ,ꜱᴛ (2) *adj* whole, complete, sound *Miyu purruna tarni.* 'The whole, entire man rose.' ᴛᴍ (3) *adj* well, healthy ᴛᴍ (4) *n* life *Purruna tikatha kaaru-urlu.* 'Life resides in the blood.' or 'We live by blood.' ᴛᴍ

   purrunantinthi [purruna-nti-nthi] *v-intr* be alive *Purrunantinthi kaarungka.* 'Life exists in the blood.' ᴛᴍ

   purrunatina [purru-na-tina] *adj* lifeless ɴᴇᴡ

   purruti-apinthi [purru-ti-(w)api-nthi] *v-tr* (1) make (someone) alive, raise (someone) to life ᴛꜱ,ᴛᴍ (2) make (someone) whole or healthy, heal (someone) ᴛᴍ

   purrutinthi [purru-ti-nthi] *v-intr* (1) live, be alive ᴛꜱ,ᴛᴍ (2) survive, revive, recover ᴛꜱ,ᴛᴍ

   purrutyi [purru-tyi] *adj, n* all; whole amount *ngadlu purrutyi ngarnta-anthi* 'we are all ill' ᴛꜱ,ᴛᴍ

purrumpa *n* flower, blossom *Mirnu purrumpa parltanthi.* 'The wattle flowers are falling.' ᴛꜱ,ᴛᴍ,ᴡʏ

purta *n* (1) burning embers, fire, flame *purturlu* 'with (by means of) a burning fire stick' ᴛᴍ (2) ashes ᴛꜱ

   purtamanthi [purta-ma-nthi] *v-tr* stoke the fire *kardla purtamanthi* 'make the fire blaze' ᴛꜱ

   purtanthi [purta-nthi] *v-intr* (1) burn, blaze *kurnta karla purtanthi* 'to be burning with thirst, really thirsty' ᴛꜱ,ᴛᴍ (2) rage (like a big storm) ᴛᴍ

   purtarti [purta-rti] *adj* roasted; baked; boiled ᴛꜱ,ᴛᴍ

purtinthi [purti-nthi] *v-intr* (1) rejoice, be happy *Purtipurti nata!* 'Now rejoice!' ᴛꜱ,ᴛᴍ (2) shout for joy ᴛꜱ,ᴛᴍ (3) be excited ɴᴇᴡ

   purti-apinthi [purti-(w)api-nthi] *v-tr* (1) make (someone) happy, cheer up *Padlu ngadlu nurntiki purti-apirnima.* 'He always made us really happy.' ᴛꜱ,ᴛᴍ (2) salute ᴛꜱ

purtpunthi [purtpu-nthi] *v-intr kuinyu purtpunthi* 'to mention or talk about death' ᴛᴍ

   purtpurninthi [purtpu-(alya)-rni-nthi] (var. **purtpulyarninthi**) *v-intr kuinyu purtpurninthi* 'to often mention or talk about death, to remind people of death' ᴛᴍ

purtpurrinthi [purtpu-rri-nthi] *v-intr* jump (like a kangaroo) ᴛꜱ,ᴛᴍ

-purtu *suff (on nouns)* (1) full of-, impregnated with- *yartapurtu* 'full of dirt, dirty' *kauwipurtu* 'wet, full of water' ᴛꜱ,ᴛᴍ (2) characterised by-, having the quality of- *turlapurtu* 'wrathful, angry' ᴛꜱ,ᴛᴍ

   purturninthi [purtu-rni-nthi] *v-intr* become full of; get covered in *yarta purturninthi* 'to become full of dirt, to get dirty' ᴛꜱ,ᴛᴍ

purtu pari *n* dry riverbed ᴛᴍ

purtultu *n* burnt tree stump ᴛꜱ,ᴛᴍ

   purtultu kuinyu *n* firesticks (ceremony) ᴛᴍ

purtuna [purtu-na] *adj* old; aged; worn out; grown up ᴛꜱ,ᴛᴍ

   purtunantinthi [purtu-na-rni-nthi] (var. **purtunarntinthi**) *v-intr* become old; become worn out looking ᴛᴍ

purtunthi [purtu-nthi] *v-tr* cut off *Pityarra ngadlu purturti.* 'We have cut off the marshmallow plants.' ᴛᴍ

puru *adv* still, yet *Yaku padlu puru nakunthi.* 'He doesn't know yet.' *Pa puru ngarntanthi.* 'He is still sick.' *Puru'ai tika-tikanthi* 'I will still remain' ᴛꜱ,ᴛᴍ

   puru-iti (var. **puru-piti**) (1) *adv* before, first ᴛꜱ (2) *intj* not yet!, wait! ᴛꜱ,ᴛᴍ

   purumpi *adv, intj* not yet!; wait! ᴛᴍ

   purupuru *adv* soon; not yet *Parni kawai! – Purupuru!* 'Come here! – Not yet! (I'm not ready)' ᴛꜱ,ᴛᴍ,ᴡɪ,ᴡʏ,ꜱᴛ,ᴄʜ

puruti *n* flying ant ᴘɪ

putaputa *n* sponge (bottle-shaped) ᴡʏ

puthi *adj* hairy ᴛꜱ,ᴛᴍ

putpa *adj* fertile, good quality ᴛꜱ,ᴛᴍ

   putpa yarta *n* good fertile land; farmland ᴛꜱ,ᴛᴍ

   putpayartawardli [putpa-yarta-wardli] *n* farmhouse ɴᴇᴡ

putyi *n* drizzling rain; dense fog *ngarntana putyilyurlu* 'sick from the drizzling rain' ₜₘ

putyita *n* dog ₜₘ

putyurra *adj* thin; lean; skinny ₜₛ,ₜₘ

puulti *adj* asleep *miitu puultu* 'dead' ₜₛ,ₜₘ

puwa *n* stink; bad smell ₜₛ,ₜₘ

puyu (var. **puiyu**) *n* **(1)** smoke *puiyu yaki-ana nudnu-nudnu-apinthi* 'envelop with smoke (as was done with the dead body during Kaurna funeral ceremonies)' ₜₛ,ₜₘ,ᴡɪ,ᴡʏ,ʀᴏ,ᴋᴏ,ₛₜ **(2)** pipe for smoking tobacco ₜₛ **(3)** cigarette or cigar ᴋᴏ

  puyurri-apinthi [puyu-rri-(w)api-nthi] *v-intr* smoke (tobacco) ₜₛ

  puyurrinthi [puyu-rri-nthi] *v-intr* smoke *yurlu puyurringka yarltinthi* 'to scold and tell off really strongly' ₜₛ,ₜₘ

puyumara *n* young woman (before childbearing) ₜₛ,ₜₘ

R r

-rla (var. **-dla**) *n* dual suffix

'rla => **purla** *pro*

-rli *suff* (on nouns) resemble; -like; be similar to *wakwakurli* 'Like, in the same way as a child' ₜₘ

-rlu (var. **-dlu**; **-urlu**) *suff* (on nouns) **(1)** identifies the agent (subject of a transitive verb) (ergative) ₜₘ,ₜₛ **(2)** with, by means of (instrumental) ₜₛ **(3)** at, on, in (temporal) ₜₛ

-rluku *suff* (on nouns) times *purlarluku* 'twice' *marnkurluku* 'three times' ₜₘ

-rna *suff* (on nouns)(var. **-dna**) *n* plural marker

'rna => **parna₁** *pro*

-rni (var. **-ni**; **-rnti**) *suff* (on verbs) be, become (inchoative) *kuku – kukurninthi* 'sick – to become sick' *maki – makirnnthi* 'ice – to freeze' ₜₛ,ₜₘ

-rnti => **-rni** *suff* (on verbs)

-rri *suff* (on verbs) each other, (one)self (reflexive/ reciprocal) ₜₛ,ₜₘ

-rrka *suff* (on nouns) like; similar to *kaiya – kaiyarrka* 'spear – tall and skinny' *tia – tiarrka* 'tooth – sharp, pointy' ₜₘ

-rta *suff* (on nouns) -like; similar to *muka – mukarta* 'egg – head' *paka – pakurta* 'dry bark – ceremonial scars' ₜₘ

-rti [(wi)rti] (var. **-ngkurti**; **-ngurti**; **-urti**; **wirti**) *suff* (on verbs) do not, may not (prohibitive) *Warrarti!* 'Be quiet! Don't talk!' *Ngunyarringurti!* 'Don't be naughty!' *Miti-urti!* 'Don't steal!' *Wirti ngai nangantu, kurdu karrinth'ai.* 'Don't stare at me, I'm blushing' *Wirti yakaninga!* 'Don't (you plural) chase!' ₜₛ,ₜₘ

-rtila *suff* (on nouns) in the absence of (with pronouns)

S s

shiipi kangkalangkala [shiipi kanga-l(a)-(k)anga-la] *n* one who tends or raises sheep; shepherd ₜₛ

Sunday warli *n* church *tapangkanth'ai sunday warli kurtarra* 'I went close by the Church' ₜₘ,ɴᴇᴡ

T t

-ta *suff* (on nouns) denoting relationship (dyadic) *taru – taruta* 'man's wife's brother – man's sister's husband' ₜₘ

  -tangkurla [ta-ngk(a)-(p)urla] *suff* (on nouns) couple, pair ₜₛ,ₜₘ

taa *n* **(1)** mouth *taangka* 'in the mouth' ₜₛ,ₜₘ,ɢᴀ **(2)** hole, opening ₜₘ

  taa nayanthi [thaa naya-nthi] *v-tr* shut the door ₜₘ

  taa nurliti [thaa nhurli-ti] *n* key ₜₘ

  taa pidlanthi [thaa pidla-rri-nthi] (var. **taa pidlarrinthi**) *v-intr* be sulky, stick one's lip out ₜₛ,ₜₘ

  taa pidlarri-purka [thaa pidla-rri-purka] *n* sulky person; discontented person ₜₛ,ₜₘ

  taa pingkanthi [thaa pingka-nthi] *v-tr* open the door ₜₘ,ₜₛ

  taa pirrikayinthi [thaa pirri-kayi-nthi] *v-intr* be sulky, stick one's lip out ₜₘ

  taa purta-purtanthi [thaa purta-purta-nthi] *v-intr* be full up *Taa purta-purta-ingku.* 'It will be full (of fire).' ₜₘ

  taa purti-purti [thaa purti-purti] *adj* full (as in a vessel full of water) ₜₘ,ₜₛ

  taa tarrkinthi [thaa tharrki-nthi; ta] *v-intr* **(1)** yawn ₜₛ,ₜₘ,ᴡʏ,ᴋᴏ **(2)** be open; gape *Tarrkinthi pa.* 'It is open.' ₜₛ,ₜₘ

  taa tartanthi [thaa tharta-nthi] *v-tr* **(1)** shut, close (something) ₜₛ,ₜₘ **(2)** cover over (a hole) ₜₘ

  taa tartati [thaa tharta-ti] *n* lid; cover ₜₛ,ₜₘ

taa-nhurlu *n* corner of the mouth ₜₛ,ₜₘ

taa-partu *adj* thick lipped ₜₘ

taakanthi [thaaka-nthi] *v-tr* say (someone's name); name (someone); mention (someone); call (someone) *palti taakanthi* 'to perform (say, call) the 'palti' ceremony' *wirila taakanthi* 'to speak quickly, chatter' ₜₛ,ₜₘ,ᴡʏ

taakarrinthi [thaaka-rri-nthi] *v-intr* say (someone's name); name (someone); mention (someone); call (someone); sing (someone) TS, WY, GA

taamanti *n* (1) lip (lower) TS, TM, PI, GA, KO (2) beak GA

taaminu [thaa-mi(r)nu] *n* upper lip TS, TM, WY

taamiti *n* moustache TS, TM, WY, KO

taapa *n* kiss NEW

taapa nakunthi [thaapa nhaku-nthi] *v-tr* penetrate; examine TM

taapa ngurinthi [thaapa nguri-nthi] *v-tr* make a hole (by throwing something) TM

taapa nuunthi [tapa nhu(nh)u-nthi] *v-tr* pierce, open (with a pointed object) TM

taapa pakinthi [thaapa paki-nthi] *v-tr* cut open; cut a hole (in something) TM

taapaanthi [thaa-paa-nthi] *v-tr* kiss TS, TM, WI, WY, ST

taaparrinthi₁ [thaa-pa-rri-nthi] *v-intr* open up, be open TS

taaparrinthi₂ [thaapa-rri-nthi] *v-intr* kiss TM

taarrka [thaa-rrka] *adj* not full TS

taawu *n* breath (in cold weather) TS, TM

taayapa [thaa-yapa] *n* mouth (hole) *Taa-yaparnalityanungku ngathu yurikaitya.* 'I have heard it from (out of) his own mouth.' TS, TM, WY, ST, KO

taara *n* net worn by men around the loins (in battle) CA

tadlanya (var. **tadlanyi**) *n* tongue *Tadlanya milimilinthi.* 'It pinches the tongue.' TS, TM, EA, GA, WI, WY, ST, KO

tadli *n* spit; froth; foam TS, TM, WI, KO, ST

  tadlaitpurla [thadl(i)-(p)aitpurla] *n* shampoo NEW

  tadli-patinthi [thadli-pati-nthi] *v-intr* spit; spit out TS, TM

  tadli-thadli [thadli-thadli] *n* frying pan; cooking pot TS

  tadlimurdu [thadli-murdu] *n* washing powder NEW

  tadlipanthi [thadli-pa(a)-nthi] *v-tr* spit at/on TS, TM

  tadlipurdi [thadli-purdi] *n* soap NEW

  tadlirrkantinthi [tadl(i)-irrka-nti-nthi] *v-intr* salivate; drool TM

  tadliwirrka *n* washing liquid NEW

tadlta => **tarlta**

tadnunthi [tha(a)-nhu(nhu)-nthi] *v-tr* search; look for TM

taikunthi [thaiku-nthi] *v-tr* join; unite; partner TM

  taikamanthi [thaiku-ma-nthi] *v-intr* participate; join in *taikamatuwayi* 'lest he take part' TM

  taikurra [thaiku-arra] *loc* (1) near, at, alongside of *wita taikurra* 'near or alongside of the Peppermint Gum tree' TS, TM (2) together, along with TM

  taikurri [thaiku-rri] *adv* with; along with; accompanying TS, TM

  taikurri-apinthi [thaiku-rri-(w)api-nthi] *v-tr* (1) mix (things) together TS (2) do (something) in company, along with someone else TS

  taikurringka [thaiku-rri-ngka] (1) *adj* shared in common, belonging to everyone *ngadliku taikurringka mai* 'food that belongs to us two, our food' TS (2) *adv* together, with company TM

  taikurrinthi [thaiku-rri-nthi] *v-intr* (1) be mixed together, be all mixed up TS, TM (2) be united, together, in a partnership TS, TM

  taikurti [thaiku-rti] *n* (1) relative, family member TM (2) side of, area beside (someone/something) *Ninku taikurti ngathu nakunthi.* 'I look past you.' TM

  taikurtiata [thaiku-rti-ta] *n* relative; neighbour *taikurtiaturla* '(two) family members (dual form)' TM

  taikurtirna [thaiku-rti-rna] *n* family; relatives *Taikurtinna* 'Name of Kaurna dance troupe formed by Stephen Gadlabarti Goldsmith' NEW

tainga *n* footprint; track TS, TM

taingi *n* (1) muscle, sinew TS (2) strength, power TM

  taingipartana [thaingi-parta-na] *adj* muscular; strong TS, TM

  taingiwilta *adj* strong; powerful TS, TM

taingila *n* grub species (large, edible) TS, TM

tainkyadli *n* (1) woven rush bag TS, TM (2) mat NEW

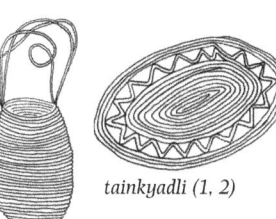
tainkyadli (1, 2)

  tainkyadli mukartiana [thainkyadli mukart(a)-iana] *n* straw hat TS

tainmunta *n* mistletoe TS, TM, WY

tainmunta

taitpa *n* adult TM

taitya *n* female emu WY

taityu₁ *adj* hungry TS, TM, WI, WY, GA, CH

taityu₂ *adv* immediately; instantly; straight away *Taityu ngari patipati.* 'He has released him immediately.' TM

  taityirntu [thaity(u)-(th)irntu] *n* second (unit of time) NEW

takana₁ *n* unmarried woman; single woman; virgin (female) *takana padninthi* 'to live as a single woman' TS, TM, WI

takana₂ (1) *adj* wide, broad, spacious, extensive *yarrka takana* 'open plain' TS, TM (2) *n* bright, clear evening sky TM

taltanthi [thalta-nthi] *v-intr* be stubborn, unkind, unhelpful, naughty *tangka taltanthi* 'long to be off someplace' TM

    taltaitpi [thalta-(y)itpi] *adj* stubborn; unkind; unhelpful; naughty *Taltaitpirti!* 'Don't be stubborn and unhelpful!' TS, TM

    taltapinthi [thalta-(wa)pi-nthi] *v-tr* go off somewhere; escape; run away *Nurnti taltapintu!* 'Go away! Get out of here!' *Parni taltapintu!* 'Come here! Get over here!' *Nurnti taltapingku.* TS, TM

talthu (var. **tarltu**) *n* red hot embers; glowing coals TM

    talthaityai [thaltha-itya] *adj* red hot; glowing TM

    taltharni [thalta-rni] (1) *adj* red, yellowish red TS, TM, WI, WY (2) *n* something red or yellowish red TS, TM, WI, WY

    taltharnirla [thaltha-rni-rla] *n* red shirt TS, WY

    taltharni parra [thaltha-rni parra] *n* redfin (fish) (*Perca fluviatilis*) NEW

talyarla *n* name for a relative (undefined) TS, TM

tamamu [tham(u)-(th)amu] *n* maternal grandfather (mother's father) TS, TM, WY, BA

    tamamuta [tham(u)-(th)amu-ta] *n* grandfather relationship (to daughter's child) TS, TM

    tamu *n* grandchild of tamamu (of mother's father) TS, TM, WY

    tamuta [thamu-ta] *n* grandson relationship (to mother's father) TS

tamartu [thaa-martu] *n* taste *tamartu ngarkurrinthi* 'to taste (something)' TS, TM

tami *adj* flat; plate-like TM

    tamiami [thami-(th)ami] *n* plate TS

    tamianta [thami-(th)anta] *n* playing card NEW

    tamikuru [thami-kuru] (var. **tamuru**) *n* bowl NEW

tamiaku *n* tomahawk; axe *tamiaku marri* 'the axe slipped off' TS

tamingka *n* white gum WI, ST

tampa *n* plain; flat land *Tampawardli* 'Emigration Square' TS

tampinthi [thampi-nthi] *v-tr* know; understand; recognise; perceive; acknowledge; be acquainted with TS, TM, WY

    tampithirkanthi [thampi-thirka-nthi] *v-intr* read NEW

tamurti! *intj* oh no!; oh dear! TS, TM

-tana₁ => **-tina**

-tana₂ => **-ana** *suff (on nouns)*

tamiaku

tangaka *n* snake species TS

tangka *n* (1) liver TS, TM, WY, WI (2) part of the body where you experience strong emotions like desire and longing, the 'heart' TS, TM (3) inner part of something *tidna tangka* 'hollow of foot' *mara tangka* 'hollow (or palm) of the hand' TS (4) back of the body *tangkarlu wantinthi* 'lie on the back' *tangkarlu padminthi* 'jump backwards' *tangkarlu wardninthi* 'fall backwards' TS, TM, KO

    tangka mampinthi [thangka mampi-nthi] *v-intr* mourn; grieve over TM

    tangka mankunthi [thangka manku-nthi] *v-tr* (1) win someone's trust; get into favour with someone; ingratiate oneself; TS (2) insinuate TS

    tangka mankurrinthi₁ [thangka manku-rri-nthi] *v-intr* compassion for (have); make friends with; feel attached to TM

    tangka mankurrinthi₂ [thangka manku-rri-nthi] *v-tr* (1) get sympathy from (someone), make (someone) feel sorry for you TM (2) ingratiate oneself with (someone), get on (someone's) good side TM

    tangka marnirninthi [thangka marni-rni-nthi] *v-intr* (1) regain your appetite TM (2) get in the mood for (something), get an appetite for (something), improve your opinion of (something) TM

    tangka martulayinthi [thangka martu-layi-nthi] *v-intr* long for; miss TM

    tangka murrmarninthi [thangka murrma-rni-nthi] *v-intr* lose your appetite TM

    tangka pardu *n* mean person; cruel person TM

    tangka taltanthi [thangka thalta-nthi] long to be off someplace TM

    tangka wayinthi [thangka wayi-(rri)-nthi] (var. **tangka wayirrinthi**) *v-intr* sympathise; have compassion; condole TS, TM

    tangka wiltarninthi [thangka wilta-rni-nthi] *v-intr* (1) calm down, relax, feel at ease TM (2) finish mourning for someone who has died TM (3) become mean, cruel, ungenerous TM

    tangka-artarta [thangka-(k)art(a)-(k)arta] *n* diaphragm; membrane separating organs from intestines TM

    tangka-umpu [thangka-(k)umpu] *n* gall bladder; gall; bile TS, TM

    tangkalurdu [thangka-(ku)lurdu] (var. **tangka kulurdu**) *n* (1) burp, belching TS, TM (2) hiccup WY

    tangkarninthi [thangka-rni-nthi] (var. **tangka-angkarninthi**) *v-intr* (1) want *Parngutaitya ngai tangkarninthi.* 'I feel like (have an appetite for) potatoes.' *Tangkarninth'ai ngaityu yungaku.* 'I long for my older brother.' *yartana tangka-angkarninthi* 'to long for another country, miss your homeland' ᴛᴍ (2) be/feel hopeful ɴᴇᴡ

tangkaru [thangka-(kaa)ru] *n* (1) fright, fear, terror, horror ᴛᴍ (2) rage, great anger ᴛs,ᴋᴏ

tangkaru parltanthi [thangka-(kaa)ru parlta-nthi] *v-tr* strike with terror; terrify ᴛᴍ

tangkaru wilta [thangka-(kaa)ru wilta] *adj* fearless; brave; courageous ᴛᴍ

tangkarurninthi [thangka-(kaa)ru-rni-nthi] *v-intr* (1) be terrified, be very frightened, be horror struck ᴛᴍ (2) become very angry, get into a rage ᴛs

tangkawilta *adj* hard-hearted; cruel; mean; ungenerous ᴛᴍ

tangkairda *n* fungus species ᴛs

tangku *n* snake species ᴛs,ᴛᴍ,ᴡʏ

tangkuinya [thangk(a)-(th)uinya] *n* dream ᴛs,ᴛᴍ

tangkuinyapinthi [thangk(a)-(th)ui-nya-(wa)pi-nthi] *v-tr* cause to dream ᴛᴍ

tangkuinyinthi [thangk(a)-(th)ui-nya-nthi] *v-intr* dream ᴛᴍ

tanparriti => **tarnparriti**

tanta *n* (1) exchange, barter, trade ᴛᴍ (2) place where trading happens ᴛᴍ

tantapinthi [thanta-(wa)pi-nthi] *v-tr* (1) invite, order, hire, draft, employ, engage (someone to do something) ᴛs,ᴛᴍ (2) promise, swear and oath, give one's word ᴛᴍ

tantanaku *n* fighting stick ᴛs,ᴛᴍ,ᴄᴀ

tantu *n* (1) leather bag *tantungka* 'in the bag' *tantu purruna* 'a whole bag full' *Pirrkiti tanturna katinga Munaityurna! Kawainga!* 'Fetch Munaitya's biscuit bags! Come on! (you lot)' ᴛs,ᴛᴍ,ᴡɪ,ᴡʏ,ɢᴀ,sᴛ (2) bag ɴᴇᴡ

tantuthita [thantu-thita] *n* string for carrying 'tantu' ᴛs

tanturlatina [thanturla-tina] *n* deceased brother-in-law ᴛᴍ

tantutiti *n* native lilac (*Hardenbergia violacae*) ᴡʏ

tantyalu *n* rush basket ᴄᴀ,ᴡɪ

tantyalu-parntu *n* basketball ɴᴇᴡ

tapa *n* (1) path, road *tapangka* 'on the road' *taparra* 'along the road' ᴛs,ᴛᴍ,ᴡʏ,ᴡɪ,sᴛ (2) lifestyle, way of behaving and living, 'path' in a moral sense *tapa marnirni-apinthi* 'to improve your way of living, take a 'better path' in life' *tapa wadli-apinthi* 'to take a 'bad path' in life' ᴛᴍ (3) walk, conversation, stroll ᴛᴍ

tapa ngardlinthi [thapa ngardli-nthi] *v-tr* burn holes through ᴛᴍ

tapa warunthi [thapa waru-nthi] *v-intr* go on ahead; leave (someone) behind ᴛᴍ

tapalayinthi [thapa-layi-nthi] *v-intr* come out; break through; emerge *mainkingka tapalaiyinthi* 'to burst out laughing' *Tapa-tapalaingka ngardlitha.* 'It will burn through (by itself).' (var. **tapa-thapalayinthi**) ᴛᴍ

tapangkanthi [thapa-ngka-nthi] *v-intr* be on/go on the road *Tapangkanth'ai Sunday-wardli kurtarra.* 'I went (on the road) close by the church.' ᴛᴍ

taparninthi [thapa-rni-nthi] *v-intr* be on/go on the road ᴛᴍ

tapu *n* (1) common black fly ᴛs,ᴛᴍ,ʙʟ,ᴡɪ,ᴡʏ,sᴛ (2) one of the two men who lead the procession during the circumcision ceremony ᴛs,ᴛᴍ

tapurru *n* possum skin drum ᴛs,ᴛᴍ,ᴄᴀ

tapurta *n* blood relatives ʙᴀ

tarana *n* duck species ᴛs

tararta *n* row; series *matha tararta tikanthi* 'kneel' ᴛs,ᴛᴍ

tarka *n* grey kangaroo (male) ᴛᴍ,ᴡʏ,ᴡɪ,ʀᴏ

tarka-arka *adv* softly; lamely *tarka-arka padninthi* 'to walk softly, as though lame, or like someone who has Syphilis' ᴛs,ᴛᴍ

tarlta (var. **tadlta**) *n* large hail stone (large) ᴛs,ᴛᴍ

tarlta wardli *n* well-built hut to protect against hail ᴛs

tarlti *n* (1) feather ᴛs,ᴛᴍ (2) wing of large birds ᴛs,ᴛᴍ,ᴋᴏ (3) quill pen; pen ᴛs,ᴡɪ,sᴛ,ɴᴇᴡ

tarltirninthi [tharlti-rni-nthi] *v-intr* get wings ᴛᴍ

tarltu => **talthu**

tarma *n* manna gum, white gum, ribbon gum (tree) (*Eucalyptus viminalis*) ᴡʏ

tarna *n* back (of something) ᴛs,ᴛᴍ

tarnangka [tharna-ngka] *adj* rude ᴛᴍ

tarni *n* sea; ocean; surf; breakers ᴛs,ᴛᴍ

tarnanthi [tharna-nthi] (var. **tarninthi**) *v-intr* rise, come forth, spring up, appear *Miyu purruna tarni.* 'The whole man rose (from the grave).' ᴛs,ᴛᴍ

tarnanta *n* pool; pond ᴛᴍ

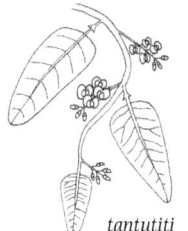
tarlti (3)

tarni warra the sound of waves ᴛꜱ

tarni-kungkurla *n* prawn ɴᴇᴡ

tarnipaitya [tharni-paitya] *n* crab ᴛꜱ

Tarnirntu [tharn(i)-(th)irntu] *n* Easter Sunday ɴᴇᴡ

tarnkunthi [tharnku-nthi] *v-tr* devour; stuff oneself with; binge on; eat greedily ᴛꜱ, ᴛᴍ

tarnma *n* banksia; native honeysuckle (*Banksia marginata*) ᴛꜱ, ᴛᴍ

tarnpanthi [tharnpa-nthi] *v-tr* fasten; glue; stick onto ᴛꜱ, ᴛᴍ

  tarnpa-tharnparni [tharnpa-tharnpa-rni] *adj* hard; firm *Tarnpa-tharnparni kadlutha* 'He will trample it firm or hard.' ᴛᴍ

  tarnparri-apinthi [tharnp(a)-rri-(w)api-nthi] (1) *v-tr* attach, fasten, stick (things) together, paste ᴛᴍ (2) *v-intr* attach oneself, hold onto, stick (to something) ᴛꜱ, ᴛᴍ

  tarnparrinthi [tharnpa-rri-nthi] *v-intr* adhere; stick to *kudna tarnparrinthi* 'dirtied with faeces (poo)' *Matumidla tarnparrinthi kudnangka.* 'The spleen is attached to the guts.' ᴛꜱ, ᴛᴍ

  tarnparriti [tharnpa-rri-ti] (var. **tanparriti**) *n* anchor ɴᴇᴡ

tarnta *n* (1) red kangaroo (male) ᴛꜱ, ᴛᴍ, ᴡɪ, ꜱᴛ (2) name of the dreaming ancestor who introduced initiation ceremonies and who was transformed into a kangaroo ᴛꜱ

  Tarntanya [tharnt(a)-(k)anya] *n* male red kangaroo rock, Adelaide ʙᴀ

  Tarntanya Pari [tharnt(a)-(k)anya pari] *n* male red kangaroo rock river; River Torrens ᴡɪ

  Tarntanyangga [tharnt(a)-(k)anya-ngka] *n* male red kangaroo rock place; Victoria Square ᴡɪ

  tarntarninthi [tharnta-rni-nthi] *v-intr* be/become a male red kangaroo ᴛꜱ

tarntinthi [tharnti-nthi] *v-intr, v-tr* (1) crackle ᴛꜱ, ᴛᴍ (2) pretend to fight ᴛꜱ, ᴛᴍ

tarra *n* (1) handle of a basket, bag, kettle, etc; something that joins or links two points *waadlatarra* 'a tree fallen across a river, used as a bridge' *tarrangka wikatyi tarranthi* 'to carry a "wikatyi" net bag by stringing it over the shoulder' ᴛᴍ (2) string girdle worn around the waist (women's) ᴛꜱ, ᴡɪ, ꜱᴛ

tarra (2)

  tarraitpapinthi [tharra-itpa-(wa)pi-nthi] (var. **tarra-arraitpapinthi; tarra-tharraitpapinthi**) *v-tr* (1) hand over; pass from hand to hand ᴛꜱ, ᴛᴍ (2) take turns ᴛꜱ, ᴛᴍ

  tarraitpayinthi [tharra-itpa-(wai)yi-nthi] *v-tr* join together; link; connect ᴛᴍ

  tarranthi [tharra-nthi] *v-tr* (1) carry (something) by hanging it over your shoulder *Ngathu yaku purnu tarrathi.* 'I didn't carry a net bag.' ᴛᴍ (2) strap (something) onto someone, put on (equipment) ᴛꜱ, ᴛᴍ

-tarra => **-arra** *suff* (on nouns)

tarralyi *n* (1) plank of wood, piece of timber ᴛꜱ, ᴛᴍ, ᴡʏ, ᴡɪ, ꜱᴛ (2) anything made from a piece of wood: bench, shelf, table, board ᴛꜱ, ᴛᴍ, ɴᴇᴡ (3) splinter, chip of wood ᴛꜱ (4) spear-thrower ᴛᴍ (5) fence *Kurda papaltu-arra tarralyi ngatpainga.* 'Put the fence alongside the stump.' ᴛꜱ (6) cross, wooden cross ᴛꜱ

tarrarrinthi [tharra-rri-nthi] *v-intr* be angry, grumpy, rude ᴛᴍ

  tarra-tarrarrinthi [tharra-tharra-rri-nthi] *v-intr* be proud ᴛᴍ

  tarrarri-purka [tharrarri-purka] *n* proud person ᴛᴍ

tarrinthi [tharri-nthi] *v-tr* get dressed; put on clothes ᴛᴍ, ᴛꜱ

tarrka *n* eggshell ᴛꜱ, ᴛᴍ, ᴡɪ, ꜱᴛ

  tarrkarta [tarrka-rta] *n* bark of gum tree ᴛꜱ, ᴛᴍ

tarrkanyi *n* man (at initiation stage) ᴛꜱ, ᴇʏ

tarrkarri *temp* in the distant future *Nala-alati wantatha? – Tarrkarrina. Muinmu kadlutha.* 'When will you bury (the corpse)? – Later. (We) will inquire further (first).' ᴛꜱ, ᴛᴍ, ᴡɪ, ᴡʏ, ꜱᴛ

  tarrkalyarlu [tharrka-(rri)-alya-rlu] (var. **tarrkarrilyarlu**) *temp* tomorrow *tarrkalyarluitya, tarrkarrilyarluitya* 'for or until tomorrow' ᴛꜱ, ᴡʏ, ᴛᴍ

  tarrkarrinthi [tarrkarri-nthi] (var. **tarrkarrantinthi**) *v-intr* be present *Ngai tarrkarringkutha.* 'I will come (at a future time).' ᴛᴍ

  tarrkarrintyarlu [tarrkarri-nyta-rlu] (var. **tarrkarrintyarla; tarrkarrinyadlu**) *temp* further in the future, a very long time from ᴛꜱ, ᴛᴍ

tarrki *dir* away *tarrki wantarrinthi* 'to run away' *tarrki wantarrinthi kauwitya* 'to run off for water' ᴛꜱ

tarrkinthi [tharrki-nthi; ta] *v-intr* be open *Tarrkinthi pa.* 'It is open.' ᴛꜱ, ᴛᴍ

tartanthi [tharta-nthi] *v-tr* cover; close over; shut up *Wardlidlu tartanthi.* 'The house covers (the sound). i.e. it muffles the noise' *Wingku ngai tarta.* 'The breath holds me back.' *Yarlurlu tirra tartanthi.* 'The sea covers over (the sun).' ᴛꜱ, ᴛᴍ

  tarta wardli *n* covered house ᴛᴍ

tartarrinthi [tharta-rri-nthi] *v-intr* cover over ₜₛ,ₜₘ

tartu *n* swampy land ₜₛ

taru *n* brother-in-law (man's) ₜₛ,ₜₘ,ᴡʏ

   taruta [tharu-ta] *n* brother-in-law (man's) ₜₛ,ₜₘ,ᴡʏ,ᴡɪ,ꜱᴛ

   tarutangkurla [tharu-ta-ngk(a)-(p)urla] (var. **tarutaurla**) *adj* brothers-in-law (dual) ₜₛ,ₜₘ

taru-tharu *n* (1) lizard (small) ₜₛ,ₜₘ (2) name of a Dreaming Ancestor ₜₛ,ₜₘ

tatarrinthi [tata-rri-nthi] *v-intr* grumble; complain; begrudge ₜₛ,ₜₘ

tatarta *n* stick; club ₜₛ

tatayaingki [(manga)tata-(manga)yaingki] *n* cross (Christian) ɴᴇᴡ

tatinthi [tati-nthi] *v-intr* (1) climb, ascend, go up ₜₛ,ₜₘ,ᴡʏ,ᴡɪ,ᴋᴏ,ꜱᴛ (2) go towards *Parni tati pa.* 'He is coming here.' ₜₘ

   tati mipurli *n* climbing galaxias (fish) (*Galaxias brevipinnis*) ɴᴇᴡ

   tati-apinthi [tati-(w)api-nthi] *v-tr* make (someone) climb ₜₛ,ₜₘ

tatunthi [tatu-nthi] *v-tr* kick ₜₛ,ₜₘ,ᴡɪ,ᴡʏ,ꜱᴛ

   taturrinthi [tatu-rri-nthi] *v-intr* (1) stretch your legs out ₜₛ (2) kick and move around *Taturringurti!* 'Don't kick! Lie still!' ₜₛ (3) draw your legs back quickly after stretching them out ₜₘ

tau *n* hole; opening; passage through ₜₛ,ₜₘ

   taunthi [thau-nthi] *v-tr* penetrate; go through ₜₛ

taulta *n* fungus species ₜₛ

tawanta *n* (1) duck ɴᴇᴡ (2) blue-winged shoveler (duck) (*Spatula rhynchotis*) ₜₛ,ₜₘ,ᴄᴏ,ᴡʏ,ᴘɪ,ɢᴀ

tawanthi [thawa-nthi] *v-tr* (1) push, knock over (something) ₜₛ,ᴡʏ (2) scold, criticise, verbally abuse (someone) *Tawarninyana ngai wangkanthi.* 'I am speaking because (they) have scolded me.' ₜₛ,ₜₘ

   tawarrinthi [thawa-rri-nthi] *v-intr* argue (with each other); fight (with each other) *Tawarringkurti ngu tikainga!* 'Don't argue! Sit there without arguing!' ₜₛ,ₜₘ,ᴡʏ

   tawarriti [thawa-rri-ti] *n* argument; quarrel; abusive language *tawarritingka* 'because of an argument, on account of a quarrel' ₜₛ,ₜₘ

tawarra [thawa-arra] (1) *adj* big, tall, large, great ₜₛ,ₜₘ,ᴡʏ,ʀᴏ,ɢᴀ (2) *adv* very, extremely, much ₜₛ,ₜₘ,ᴄʜ

   tawarluku [thawa-rluku] *adv* often; frequently ₜₛ,ₜₘ

   tawarrantinthi [thawa-arra-nti-nthi] *v-intr* become big; grow up *Kauwadlangga pa tawarrantithi.* 'He grew up at Kauwadla.' ₜₘ

tawata *adj* many *Miyu tawaturlu kukathi.* 'Many men have been digging.' ₜₛ,ₜₘ,ᴡʏ,ᴡɪ

tawatantinthi [thawata-nti-nthi] *v-intr* multiply ₜₘ

tawinthi [thawi-nthi] *v-tr* (1) sharpen, grind (something) ₜₘ (2) score, scrape (skins) ᴡʏ

   tawiti [thawi-ti] *n* grinding stone ₜₘ

tawu *n* evening; dusk *tawurlu* 'towards evening' ₜₛ,ₜₘ

   tawu-mai *n* dinner ɴᴇᴡ

   tawurnunthi [thawu-rni-nthi] *v-intr* be overtaken by darkness ₜₘ

   tawurri [thawu-rri] *n* (1) redness of the evening sky ₜₘ (2) dusk, evening breeze ₜₛ

tawiti

tawulawati *n* quail (undefined) ꜱᴛ

tayinthi [thayi-nthi] *v-tr* build; raise; put up; erect *wardli tayinthi* 'to build a house' *Parntarlu ngathu wardli tayitha]* 'I shall build the house with bricks' (var. **tayirrinthi**) ₜₛ,ₜₘ,ᴡɪ,ꜱᴛ

   tayilayila [thayi-l(a)-(th)ayi-la] *n* builder ɴᴇᴡ

-tha => -ngutha

-thi *suff (on verbs)* tense marker (past) *Ngu, nintu kukathi ngu.* 'There, where you dug.' ₜₘ

-ti₁ *suff (on nouns)* nominaliser *tikanthi – tikatikati* 'to sit – a chair' *yuwanthi – yuwati* 'to stop – a tap' ɴᴇᴡ

-ti₂ *suff* verbaliser (for bodily functions) *kumputinthi* 'to pass urine'

tidla *n* (1) edible bulbous root ₜₛ (2) carrot ɴᴇᴡ

-tidla (var. **-idla**) *suff (on nouns)* without *Mai-idla-alya ngai padlutha.* 'I will likely die from lack of food.' *Maitidla kudla padlu-ingku.* 'Let him die by himself without food.' ₜₘ

tidli (1) *n* abdomen, waist, stomach ₜₛ,ₜₘ,ᴋᴏ (2) *adj* hungry *Tidlila ngai marnkarrinthi.* 'I beg because of hunger.' *Tidli paka ngai.* 'I'm hungry' *Mai ngaini yungainga! Tidli yarta ngai, karradlu-anangku ngai pudnithi.* 'Give me food! I'm hungry and have come a long way.' ₜₛ,ₜₘ,ᴡʏ

tidli-kurriti [thidli-kurri-ti] *n* girdle for waist ₜₛ,ₜₘ

   tidli-paka hungry ₜₘ

   tidli-umpu (var. **tidli-kumpu**) *n* bladder ₜₛ,ₜₘ,ᴡɪ,ꜱᴛ

   tidlirni-apinthi [thidli-rni-(w)api-nthi] *v-tr* supply; provide with *Yiuwarlu yarlu kuyarna tidlirni-api.* 'Jehova has supplied the sea with fish.' ₜₘ

-tidli (var. **-idli**) *suff (on nouns)* having, provided with *maitidli* 'having food' *yangarratidli* 'married, having a wife' TS, TM

tidli *n* green bark; fresh tree bark TS, TM

    tidli warli bark-roofed hut TM

tidna *n* (1) foot TS, TM, WI, WY, EA, GA, BL, ST, KO (2) tracks, footprint *ngaityu tidna pulthu-arra* 'in my footsteps, along my tracks' TM

    tidna murtana *n* deformed foot TM

    tidna-ana *n* socks NEW

    tidnakuntu *n* ball of foot; sole TS, TM

    tidnangangki *n* big toe WY

    tidnapaltha *n* shoe; boot TS, WI, WY, ST

    tidnapalthatina *adj* [thidna-paltha-tina] *n* barefoot, without shoes TS

    tidnaparntu *n* football NEW

    tidnapultha *n* instep; inner side of foot WY

    tidnarla *n* feet (dual) TS

    tidnatangka [thidna-thangka] *n* arch (of foot) TS, TM, WY, KO

    tidnatidnanthi [thidna-thidna-nthi] *v-intr* (1) tread, step TM (2) enter *Niwa nganaitya wardli tidna-tidnanthi?* 'Why are you two going into the house?' TM

    tidnawarru *n* heel WY

    tidnawarta *n* heel; back of ankle TS, TM, WY

    tidnayarli *n* big toe WI, WY, ST, KO

tidngi *n* elbow TS, TM, WI, WY, EA, KO

tii *n* tea *tii kurla pulthu* 'empty of tea' TM (from English)

tiintinti *n* kingfisher PI

tiitha *n* star finch WY

tikanthi [thika-nthi] *v-intr* (1) sit *Warrarti tika!* 'Sit still and be quiet!' *Tika-iti! Yangadli muringki.* 'Sit down (for a while)! Later you can leave.' *Tikaiti! Namu ngai wangkathi.* 'Sit down (with me)! That's what I have said.' TS, TM, BL, WI, WY, RO, GA, PI, ST, KO (2) live, stay, reside, remain (at a place) *Tikantitha'ai.* 'I will still stay.' *Parna kumpanintyirdla, niinani parni padningki! Parna tikarni-utha, warta puru padni-padningka!* 'If they leave, then you come alone! (But) if they stay, then all come together!' *Waa'ina tikanthi? Ngai tikanthi Tarntanyangka* 'Where do you live? I live in Adelaide.' *Puru'ai tika-tikanthi.* 'I will still remain.' TS, TM, PI, BL

    tikanyapinthi [thika-nya-(w)api-nthi] *v-tr* put; put down; place TM

    tikapinthi [thika-(wa)pi-nthi] *v-tr* sit (make someone); sit (someone) down TM

    tikapirrinthi [thika-(wa)pi-rri-nthi] *v-intr* sit down TM

    tikathikati [thika-thika-ti] *n* chair; seat TS

tiki *n* side (of the body) TS, TM, WY, KO

    tikiana [thiki-ana] *n* waistcoat; vest TS, TM

-tila *suff (on nouns)* instead of; in the absence of *Ngaityu kurutila ngathu marrkurri-apinthi ninku kuru.* 'I use your pot instead of my own pot.' *miyutila* 'with no men around, only women' TM

tililya *n* wattle *(Acacia saligna)* WY

tilti *n* (1) native cherry tree, cherry ballart *(Exocarpos cupressiformis)* TS, TM, WY (2) cherry NEW

tiltya *n* (1) sinew TS, TM (2) strength, power, might *tiltya mailtya-mailtyanthi* 'to try or test (someone/something's) strength' TM (3) vein TS

    tiltyalayinthi [thiltya-layi-nthi] (var. **tiltyalinthi**) *v-intr* disentangle; get away (from someone); extricate oneself TS, TM

    tiltyapartana [thiltya-parta-na] *adj* muscular; strong; powerful TS

tilti

timana [thima-na] *adj* (1) raw; uncooked *Pardi puru timana.* 'The rice isn't ready yet.' TS, TM, GA, WI (2) green (unripe) TM, TS

-tina (var. **-tana₁**) (1) *suff (on nouns)* without; lacking (privative) *maitina* 'without food' *kardlatina* 'without wood or fire' TS, TM

tininya *n* (1) rib TS, TM, WY, WI, ST (2) iron; steel TS, TM, WY

    tininya ngaruta *n* train (railway) NEW

    tininya parti *n* tram NEW

    tininya tapa *n* railway line NEW

    Tininyarrarna *n* Orion (constellation) TS, TM

    tininyawardli the iron store (which once stood in the parklands north of the Torrens) TS, TM

tinkunthi [thinku-nthi] *v-intr* put your hand into a gap TM

tinkyadla *n* stubble quail *(Coturnix pectoralis)* TS, WY, WI, RO, ST

tinkyu *n* dry leaf, dry leaves and sticks TS, TM, WI, WY, ST, KO

    tinkyuwardli [thinkyu-wardli] small hut made from branches WI

    tinkyuwatu [thinkyu-watu] *n* branches WI, ST

    tinkyuyuri [thinkyu-yuri] *n* brussels sprout NEW

tinta-inta *n* rainbow bee-eater *(Merops ornatus)* WY

tintanthi [thinta-nthi] *v-intr* (1) be stuck fast, immovable TM, TS, WY (2) be narrow, tight TS

tintyi *n* tench (fish) *(Tinca tinca)* NEW (from English 'tench')

tintyu-thintyu *adj* young; raw; unripe TS, TM

tintyurninthi [thintyu-rni-nthi] *v-intr* become young; raw (become) ᴛᴍ

tinyarra *n* young man; boy (8 to 20 years) ᴛꜱ, ᴛᴍ, ᴡɪ, ᴡʏ, ʙʟ, ʀᴏ, ꜱᴛ, ᴄʜ

tipanthi [thipa-nthi] *v-tr* support ᴛᴍ

    tiparrinthi [thipa-rri-nthi] (var. **titparrinthi**) *v-intr* (1) feel pain, ache ᴛꜱ, ᴛᴍ (2) offend; hurt (each other's) feelings ᴛᴍ

tipu *n* (1) spark (fire) ᴛꜱ, ᴛᴍ (2) gas lighter ɴᴇᴡ

    tipu-ngatpa-ngatpati [thipu-ngatpa-ngatpa-ti] *n* ramrod (for a musket) ᴛꜱ

    tipukardla [thipu-kardla] *n* (1) gunpowder ᴛꜱ (2) matches ᴛꜱ

    tipumarngu [thipu-marngu] *n* switch (electric) ɴᴇᴡ

tirdinthi [thirdi-nthi] *v-intr* (1) squat down ᴛꜱ, ᴛᴍ (2) crawl *Painingka ngai tirdithi*. 'Formerly (when I was a child) I crawled.' ᴛᴍ (3) move along (while in a squatting position) *Piti paintya-ana piti tirdi'ngai.* 'First I will draw nearer (to the table).' ᴛᴍ

    tirdi-apinthi [thirdi-(w)api-nthi] *v-tr* draw nearer, come closer ᴛᴍ

tirkanthi [thirka-nthi] *v-intr* know; understand; perceive; learn ᴛꜱ, ᴛᴍ, ᴡɪ, ꜱᴛ

    tirkalirkala [thirka-l(a)-(th)irka-la] *n* (1) wise person; intelligent person ᴛꜱ (2) student; pupil ɴᴇᴡ

    tirkati [thirka-ti] *n* bier (for corpse) ᴛꜱ, ᴛᴍ, ᴇʏ

tirkura *n* budgerigar ᴡʏ

tirntu [thirntu] *n* (1) sun *Tirntu parni tarnina …* 'When the sun has risen …' *Tirntu nata wangkarta.* 'The sun is in the west. (i.e.: it is afternoon)' ᴛꜱ, ᴛᴍ, ɢᴀ, ᴡɪ, ᴡʏ, ʀᴏ, ꜱᴛ, ᴋᴏ, ᴄʜ (2) time ᴋᴏ (3) day *Naawi tirnturna ninkurna?* 'How many days will (your journey) last for?' *Tirntu-arra naku'athu'rna.* 'During the day I will look (at them).' ᴛꜱ, ᴛᴍ, ᴡʏ, ᴋᴏ (4) clock, watch ᴛꜱ, ᴋᴏ

    tirntu kamparrinthi [thirntu kampa-rri-nthi] *v-intr* be sultry, hot and calm (weather) ᴛꜱ

    tirntu parka-parka *n* sunrise ᴛᴍ

    tirntu tukutya morning, just after sunrise ᴡʏ

    tirntu yurlurrinthi [thirntu yurlu-rri-nthi] *v-intr* sunrise ᴘɪ

    tirntu-irntu [thirntu-(th)irntu] *temp* everyday *tirntu-irntu warrarna* 'everyday expressions' ɴᴇᴡ

    tirntu-karla *n* (1) sunshine *Tirntu karlarlu …* 'When the sun is rising …' ᴛꜱ, ᴛᴍ (2) sun's light and heat ᴛᴍ

    tirntu-umpu [thirntu-(k)umpu] *n* dawn ᴛᴍ

    tirntumiyu [thirntu-miyu] watch maker ᴛꜱ

    tirnturlu [thirntu-rlu] *temp* tomorrow, the next day ᴛᴍ, ᴡʏ

    tirntuthirra [thirntu-thirra] *n* sunscreen ɴᴇᴡ

    tirntu-mata *n* shell (small, freshwater univalve) ᴛꜱ, ᴡʏ

tirra *n* obstacle, hindrance, barrier, screen, something that gets in your way ᴛꜱ, ᴛᴍ

    tirra mankulankula [thirra manku-l(a)-(m)anku-la] *n* saviour; deliverer; mediator; protector *nungku tirra mankulankula* 'returning saviour' ᴛᴍ

    tirra mankunthi [thirra manku-nthi] *v-tr* mediate; interfere in a fight ᴛꜱ, ᴛᴍ

    tirra tartanthi [thirra tharta-nthi] *v-tr* hide; cover; shelter; obscure *Yarlurlu tirntu tirra tartanthi.* 'The sea blocks the sun from view. (i.e. when it sets)' ᴛᴍ

    tirra-apinthi [thirra-(w)api-nthi] *v-tr* (1) screen, hide, conceal (something) ᴛꜱ (2) protect, shelter (something) ᴛꜱ, ᴛᴍ

    tirrangka [thirra-ngka] *adj* hidden; concealed *tirrangka wantinthi* 'lying in ambush', *tirrangka tikanthi* 'sitting in ambush' ᴛꜱ, ᴛᴍ

    tirranthi [thirra-nthi] *v-intr* hide, conceal (oneself) *Tirrarti!* 'Don't hide! Come out! Show yourself!' ᴛꜱ, ᴛᴍ

    tirrapina [thirra-pina] *n* defender (in sport) ɴᴇᴡ

tirritpa *n* lark species (*Grallina cyanoleuca*) ᴛꜱ, ᴛᴍ, ᴡʏ, ᴄᴏ

tita *n* (1) fastener, anything that joins two things together, (e.g. a string, knot, tie, button, handle) ᴛꜱ, ᴛᴍ (2) exchange, barter, swap ᴛꜱ, ᴛᴍ

    tita trruku *n* a centre where exchange takes place ɴᴇᴡ

    tita-wardli *n* shop ɴᴇᴡ

    titangka [thita-ngka] in exchange; as a transaction ᴛꜱ, ᴛᴍ

    titangka mankunthi [thita-ngka manku-nthi] *v-tr* take in exchange; buy; purchase ᴛꜱ, ᴛᴍ

    titangka yungkunthi [thita-ngka yungku-nthi] *v-tr* give in exchange, sell ᴛᴍ

    titapina [thita-pina] *n* trader ᴛꜱ, ᴛᴍ

    titapinthi [thita-(wa)pi-nthi] *v-tr* (1) fasten, tie (something) ᴛꜱ, ᴛᴍ, ᴡɪ, ꜱᴛ (2) tie up, put (someone) in chains or shackles *Titapinyana miti.* '(They) are tied up because (they) have stolen.' *Titapina'rla.* 'They are both chained.' *Titapinana'urla.* 'They have both been chained.' ᴛꜱ, ᴛᴍ, ᴡɪ, ꜱᴛ (3) hang (someone) to death *Painingka purlaityinti miyurla titapi. Nata pirdianta. Kutini titapi-urti, kutini pirrki-api-urti nurutuwayi'adlu, purrutyi'adlu padlituwayi.* 'Up till now only two men have been hanged. Now it is enough. Don't hang again, don't shoot again lest we be sorcerised, lest we all die.' ᴛꜱ

Titapirntu [thita-(wa)pi-(thi)rntu] *n* Good Friday ₙₑw

titatina [thita-tina] *adj* without fetters; free ₙₑw

titinta *n* hair (above pubes) ₜₛ,ₜₘ

titita *n* whistling (inwards) ₜₛ

    titayinthi [thita-(wai)yi-nthi] *v-intr* whistle ₜₛ,ₜₘ

    tititayinthi [thitita-(wai)yi-nthi] *v-intr* whistle (like birds); twitter; chirp ₜₘ

    titititya *n* parakeet species ₜₛ

titpanthi [thitpa-nthi] *v-tr* hurt ₜₘ

    titparrinthi [thitpa-rri-nthi] *v-intr* (1) ache; feel pain; hurt ₜₛ,ₜₘ (2) offend, hurt (each other's) feelings ₜₘ

titparra [thitpa-arra] *adj* tough; firm; fibrous ₜₛ,ₜₘ

-titya => **-itya**

tiwa *n* native honey, sugarbag ₜₛ,ₜₘ

tiwi *adv* (1) often, frequently, repeatedly *tiwi kurntanthi* 'to fight often' ₜₛ,ₜₘ (2) continually, still, for a long time *tiwi tikanthi* 'to sit for a long time' *Nganaitya pa tikanthi tiwi? Yala yala pa tiki. – Kudla pa tikanthi, nganparrinthi pa.* 'Why is he constantly sitting? He was sitting there just before. – He's just sitting (alone, or for no reason), he's not up to going out.' ₜₘ

    tiwirti! [thiwi-rti] *intj* no more!; cut it out! ₜₛ

    tiwita [thiwi-ta] *adv* often; repeatedly ₜₛ

tiwu *n* yellow-tailed black cockatoo ₜₛ,ₜₘ,ᴄᴏ,ᴘɪ,ᴡʏ

tiya *n* tooth; row of teeth ₜₛ,ₜₘ,ᴡʏ,ᴡɪ,ᴇᴀ,ᴋᴏ

    tiya turruti [thiya thurru-ti] (var. **tiya turruta**) *n* hand saw ₜₛ,ₜₘ

    tiya wirruti [thiya wirru-ti] (var. **tiya wirruta**) *n* crosscut saw ₜₛ,ₜₘ

    tiya-tina *adj* blunt; toothless ₜₘ

    tiya-wirrkarriti [thiya-wirrka-rri-ti] (var. **tiyawirrkati**) *n* toothbrush ₙₑw

    tiyangari [thiya-ngari] *n* dental floss ₙₑw

    tiyangaru [thiya-ngaru] *n* toothpaste ₙₑw

    tiyaningka [thiya-ningka] *n* gums ᴋᴏ

    tiyarla [tiya-rla] teeth in the mouth, the upper and lower rows of teeth ₜₛ,ₜₘ,ᴋᴏ,ᴄʜ

    tiyarla-tharnparrinthi [thiya-rla tharnpa-rri-nthi] *v-intr* clench the teeth ₜₘ

    tiyarrka (1) *adj* sharp ₜₛ,ₜₘ (2) *adj* grumpy, bad tempered, sour *Tiyarrkurti!* 'Don't be grumpy!' ₜₛ (3) *n* toothpick ₜₛ,ₜₘ

    tiyarrku *n* headdress ᴄᴀ

tiyapi *n* chewed (fibre of pityarra mallow) ᴡʏ

tiyarra (var. **tiyangarra**) *n* shrub species ₜₛ

tiyarrarti [tiyarr(a)-(p)arti] *n* species of grub (uncertain) ₜₛ

tiyati *intj, adv* (1) yes, certainly, correct ₜₛ,ₜₘ,ᴡɪ,ᴡʏ,ᴋᴏ,ₛₜ,ᴄʜ (2) true, correct ₜₘ

    tiyati wangkanthi [thiya-ti wangka-nthi] *v-intr* tell the truth ₜₛ,ₜₘ,ᴡʏ

    tiyati warra [thiya-ti warra] *n* truth ₜₘ

    tiyati yailtyanthi [thiya-ti yailtya-nthi] *v-intr* believe (to be true); accept (as a fact) ₜₘ

trrukanthi [t(u)rruka-nthi] (var. **turrukanthi**) (1) *v-intr* fall down ₜₘ (2) *v-tr* drop, dribble, lower (something) ₜₛ,ₜₘ (3) *v-intr, v-tr* descend ₜₘ

    trrukarrinthi [t(u)rruka-rri-nthi] *v-intr* descend; lower oneself; go downwards *Trrukarri! Trrukarri!* 'Come down!' ₜₘ

trruku *n* (1) inside, interior, centre (of something) *trrukungka* 'in the middle, inside, within' *Ngai miyu trruku-ana* 'I am surrounded by people. I am in the midst of people.' ₜₛ,ₜₘ (2) mall, shopping centre ₙₑw

trrunga (var. **trrunga-trrunga**) *adj* dirty; soiled; filthy ₜₛ,ₜₘ

trrungku *n* species of bird (uncertain) ₜₛ

tudlyu (var. **tulyu**) *n* Adelaide rosella ₜₛ

tudna₁ *n* pubic covering, loin covering (men's) ᴄᴀ

tudna₂ *n* posterior ₜₘ

tudnu₁ *adv* permanently; continually; forever; entirely *Tudnu pa padni.* 'He has left entirely.' ₜₘ

    tudnurru the back (of something), the posterior ₜₘ

tudnu₂ => **turdnu**

tudnu-ununya *n* snake species (small) ₜₛ

tuinya *n* widow *tuinyangka* 'on account of the widow, because of the widow' ₜₛ,ₜₘ,ᴡɪ,ᴡʏ,ₛₜ

tuiyunthi => **tuyunthi**

tuka *n* (1) mud, clay, wet dirt *tuka wayinthi* 'to get muddy' ₜₛ,ₜₘ,ᴡɪ,ᴡʏ,ₛₜ (2) mortar ₜₛ,ₜₘ

    tukapina [thuka-pina] *n* European carp (fish) (*Cyprinus carpio*) ₙₑw

    tukapina waitku [thuka-pina waitku] *n* western carp gudgeon (fish) (*Hypseleotris klunzingeri*) ₙₑw

    tukayarta *n* swampy land ᴡʏ

tuki *n* slant ₜₘ

    tuki-thukinthi [thuki-thuki-nthi] *v-intr* flutter ₜₘ

    tuki-apinthi [thuki-(w)api-nthi] *v-intr* perform ceremony (undefined) ₜₘ

    tukinthi [thuki-nthi] *v-intr* hang; lean (to the side) ₜₛ

tukini *n* zucchini ₙₑw (from English 'zucchini')

tuku₁ *adj* small, little ₜₘ (2) *n* child *tuku parta-partana* 'a mother of many children' ₜₘ

tukami [thuk(utya)-(th)ami] *n* saucer (plate) NEW

tukirntu [thuk(u)-(th)irntu] *n* hour NEW

tuku-angki [thuku-(ng)angki] *n* mother of many children; prolific woman TS, TM

tuku-angkirninthi [thuku-(ng)angki-rni-nthi] *v-intr* become fertile, have many children TM

tuku-kungkurla [thuku(tya)-kungkurla] *n* prawn NEW

tuku-purlaitya [thuku-purla-itya] *adj* having two children TS

tukuparka [thuku-parka] *n* (1) grown up female TS, TM (2) daughter TM

tukupitina [thukupi-tina] *adj* barren; childless TS

tukurruru [tuk(u)-(k)urruru] (var. **tukukuru**) *n* ring (jewellery) NEW

tukuru [thuk(utya)-(k)uru] (var. **tukukuru**) *n* cup NEW

tukuthaa kuya [thuku(tya)-thaa kuya] *n* small-mouthed hardyhead (fish) (*Atherinosoma microstoma*) NEW

tukutya [thuku-tya] (1) *adj* small, little, few *tukutyarla* 'smaller, littler' TS, TM, WY, WI, RO (2) *n* child, baby *tukutya- tana* 'without children' TS, TM

tukutya parntapurdi pistol TS

tukutya pulyuna [thuku-tya-pulyu-na] twilight, early morning before sunrise PI

tukutyarninthi [thuku-tya-rni-nthi] (var. **tukutyarntinthi**) *v-intr* shrink; decrease: decrease (numbers); get thinner; diminish, become smaller TS, TM

tukuwingkura [thuku-(tya)-wingkura] *n* microwave NEW

tuku₂ *n* spade; shovel (wooden) CA

tulturlu tikananthi [thultu-rlu tika-na-nthi] *v-intr* kneel TM

tultyunthi [thultyu-nthi] *v-tr* assemble; bring together; fetch TM

tultyurri-apinthi [thultyu-rri-(w)api-nthi] *v-tr* collect TM

tultyurrinthi [thultyu-rri-nthi] *v-intr* assemble; come together TM

tulya *n* soldier; police officer JB, WI, ST (from English 'soldier')

tulyawardli [thulya-wardli] *n* police station NEW

tulyu => **tudlyu**

tumatu *n* tomato NEW (from English)

tumpu *n* smoke; something that is smoking; incense TM

tumpu mankunthi smoke something (e.g meat or fish) TM

tumpunthi [thumpu-nthi] *v-tr* (1) suffocate with smoke TM (2) smoke out (e.g. a possum out of a hole) TM

tumpula *n* gadfly WY

tungki *adj* smelly; stinky; rotten TS, TM

tungki warturrinthi [thungki wartu-rri-nthi] *v-intr* collapse, faint (from suffocating) TM

tungkirninthi [thungki-rni-nthi] *v-intr* rot; decay; go off TS, TM

tunkunthi [thunku-nthi] *v-tr* provoke; incite; stir up; agitate *Ngantu niina tunkurrithi pudlu?* 'Who has told you that they have been provoked?' TM

tunkurta *n* shrub – Swainsona WY

tuntanta [thunta-(thu)nta] (var. **tuntuntu**) *n* heel; ankle bone TS, TM

tunta-untarlayinthi [thunta-(th)unta-rlayi-nthi] *v-intr* kick with the heels TM

tuntarri [thunta-rri] *adv* always; repeatedly TS

tunurti *n* grub species TS

tupa *n* everything; all; entirety *tupa ngarkunthi* 'to eat everything' *Tupa tuiyu-tuiyunthi!* 'Picking it all up!' TS, TM

tuparra *n* lizard (small, black bands) TS, TM, WY

tupurra *n* blowfly TS, TM, WI, WY, ST

tupurra pardi maggot of the blowfly WI

tura *n* (1) shadow, shade *turangka tikanthi* 'to sit in the shade' TS, TM, WY (2) reflection, likeness, image TS, WY

tura nakunhakurriti [thura nhaku-nhaku-rri-ti] *n* mirror TM, WI, WY, ST

tura-thurarni-apiti [thura-thura-rni-(w)api-ti] *n* photocopier NEW

turaityati [thur(a)-(k)aitya-ti] *n* television NEW

turalayinthi [thura-layi-nthi] (1) *v-intr* reflect (e.g. light) TS, TM (2) *v-tr* cast a shadow TS, TM (3) *v-intr* look at your reflection (e.g. in a mirror) TS

turapati [thura-pa-ti] *n* data projector NEW

turarna [thura-rna] *n* movies, pictures NEW

turathurana [thura-thura-na] (1) *adj* similar to, equal to, the same as TS, TM (2) *adv* in the same way as, thus, like this *Ngadluku turathuramurli tikainga.* 'You must live in the same way as us.' TM

turathurana ngulthi [thura-thura-na ngulthi] *n* equinox NEW

turawardli [thura-wardli] *n* cinema NEW

turdi-thurdi *adv* (1) alone, by oneself, separately *turdi tikanthi* 'to sit or to live alone' TS, TM (2) in spite of, nevertheless, anyway, regardless, even so *Yaku ngai madlitha, turdi-thurdi padnitha.* 'I won't die, but will live regardless.' TM

turdi-thurdirninthi [thurdi-thurdi-rni-nthi] *v-intr* waste time, delay, be stubborn/uncooperative ™

turdlunthi [thurdlu-nthi] (var. **turlunthi**) *v-tr* (1) roll, roll away ts,™ (2) stoke the fire ts

turdnu (var. **tudnu₂**; **turnu**) *n* species of grey snake ts,™,wi,st

turla (1) *n* anger, hostility, fight *turlangka* 'in anger' *turlaitya* 'to the fight' ™ (2) *adj* angry, provoked, hostile *Turlarna pia ngaityu ituntya.* 'These (people) might be angry with me.' ts,™,wy,jk (3) *adv* seriously, in earnest, sincerely *Turlapurtungka nintu pa kangki?* 'Have you brought him here sincerely?' ts,™

    turla mardlarrinthi [thurla-mardla-rri-nthi] *v-intr* stop being angry; get over being angry ™

    turla minunthi [thurla minu-nthi] *v-tr* be angry with, accuse ™

    turla ngarkunthi [thurla ngarku-nthi] *v-tr* (1) eat (something) hungrily ts (2) fight, argue, quarrel (with someone) ts

    turla pintyanthi [thurla pintya-nthi] *v-tr* be angry with, accuse ™

    turla warpurninthi [thurla warpu-rni-nthi] *v-intr* be/become serious or solemn ™

    turla yakarrinthi [thurla yaka-rri-nthi] *v-intr* attack; start a fight ts

    turla-parrku *n* anger; wrath ™

    turla-yiira *n* lamellicorn beetle wy

turlalayinthi [thurla-layi-nthi] *v-intr* be angry, mad, provoked *Nintu ngathaitya turlalayinthi.* 'You are angry with me.' *Ngadlukupira pa turlalayithi parkana miyu.* 'He argued with the Europeans on our account.' ts,™

turlapina [thurla-pina] (1) *n, adj* feisty, argumentative, short-tempered person, someone who fights a lot, pugnacious ™ (2) *n* attacker (in sport) new

turlapurtu [thurla-purtu] *adj* hostile; full of anger ts,™

turlarninthi [thurla-rni-nthi] *v-intr* be/become angry or provoked *turlarninthi padlaitya* 'to be or become angry with someone' ts,™

turlarti! [thurla-rti] *intj* don't fight! ts

turlatarri (var. **turlarri**) over the anger ™

turlatina [thurla-tina] *adj* calm; peaceful; placid ts

turlawarpu [thurla-warpu] *adj* (1) bad tempered, argumentative, quarrelsome *Turlawarpurti!* 'Don't fight! Stop arguing! Be quiet!' ts (2) very serious, grave, solemn ™

turlawingku [thurla-wingku] *n* anger; wrath; rage; fury ts,™

turlta *n* girlfriend; lover ™,wi,st

    Turlta Tirntu *n* St Valentine's Day new

    turltata tikanthi [thurlta-ta tika-nthi] *v-intr* be in a relationship, lovers ™

    turltatangkurla [thurlta-ta-ngk(a)-(p)urla] two lovers, a couple ™

turlu *n* person who performs circumcision ts,™

    turlu-yakanthi (var. **turlu-yakarrinthi**) catch the 'turlu' when he tries to escape ts,™

turlu *n* swift or swallow (bird) wy

turluka *n* large edible grub species ts,pi

turlunthi => **turdlunthi**

turluntyaru *n* water beetle (*Gyrinus*) wy

turngu *n* shrikethrush (large, slate-coloured) wy

turnki *n* (1) clothing, covering for the body, cloak ts,™,pi,wy (2) cloth ts,wy (3) sails of a ship wy

    turnki marngu *n* button ts,™

    turnki marraka *adj* naked; uncovered ts,™

    turnkithita [thurnki-thita] *n* button ts,™

    turnkitina [thurnki-tina] naked, without clothing or covering ™

    turnkiwardli [thurnki-wardli] *n* tent wy,pi

turnta *adj* leaky; full of holes ts,™

turnu => **turdnu**

turrku *n* backside; posterior *ninku turrkungka* 'behind you' ts,™

turrkunthi [thurrku-nthi] *v-tr* tell; inform *Ngarra-ngarra-urti, mardla turrkuntu!* 'Don't keep it a secret, just tell it!' *Turrku'athu? Turrku'athu.* 'Shall I tell it? I will tell it.' ts,™

    turrkurrinthi [thurrku-rri-nthi] *v-tr* tell (each other); inform (each other) ts

turru *n* (1) ridge, top of a range of hills *turrungka padminthi* 'to travel on the ridge of a range of hills' ts,™,wi,st (2) back *ninku turrungka* 'on your back' ts,™

turrukanthi => **trrukanthi**

turrunthi [thurru-nthi] *v-tr* saw; shave; grind; rub; sharpen *Karla ninku turrungkathu?* 'Shall I cut your wood?' ts,™,wy

turtanthi₁ [thurta-nthi] (var. **turtarrinthi**) *v-intr* (1) pretend, feign *mai turtanthi* 'to pretend to have food (when you don't)' *Wakwakurna tangka ngarkutitya turtanthi.* 'He threatens to eat the children's heart.' ™ (2) be lazy, sluggish ™

    turtarri-purka *n* a lazy, sluggish person ™

turtanthi₂ [thurta-nthi] *v-intr* open (a sore or wound) ™

turtapinthi [turta-(a)pi-nthi] *v-tr* open (a sore or wound) ᴛᴍ

turti *n* **(1)** arm ᴛs,ᴛᴍ,ᴇᴀ,ᴡɪ,ᴡʏ,ᴋᴏ **(2)** bird's wing ᴛs,ᴛᴍ **(3)** tree branch ᴛᴍ

  turti waru-warunthi [thurti waru-waru-nthi] *v-tr* beckon with the hand ᴛᴍ

  turti-ana *n* jacket; coat; shirt ᴛs,ᴛᴍ

  turti-anurla [thurti-an(a)-(p)urla] *n* **(1)** jacket, coat, shirt, clothing that covers the arms *Wathangku padlu'urlaintya turti-anurla? Miti pirdi nintu purla … Yungki ngai padlu, yaku ngathu miti.* 'Where is that jacket from? Most likely you have stolen it … He gave it to me, I didn't steal it.' ᴛᴍ,ᴡʏ **(2)** sleeves ᴡʏ

  turti-murla *adj* weak-armed; withered-armed ᴛᴍ

  turtipumanthi [thurti-puma-nthi] *v-tr* strike; hit ᴋᴏ

  turtirninthi [thurti-rni-nthi] *v-intr* stretch out your hand; reach with your hand ᴛᴍ

turtpa (var. **turtpu**) *adj* narrow and long; tight (space) ᴛs,ᴛᴍ

  turtpa-thurtpanthi [thurtpa-thurtpa-nthi] *v-intr* stretch ᴛs

  turtpanthi [thurtpa-nthi] *v-intr* **(1)** stretch, extend, reach, continue ᴛs,ᴛᴍ **(2)** stretch out the legs with the feet together ᴛᴍ

  turtpapinthi [thurtpa-(w)api-nthi] *v-tr* stretch, extend, continue ᴛᴍ

  turtparninthi [thurtpa-rni-nthi] *v-intr* **(1)** be or become narrow and long, small, tight *Turtparningku.* 'It will become smaller.' ᴛs,ᴛᴍ **(2)** fold together ᴛs

turtu (var. **yarta turtu**) *n* clod; lump of dirt; lump of earth ᴛs,ᴛᴍ

  turtu mara a fist ᴛᴍ

turtu-artu *n* scorpion species ᴛᴍ

turturninthi [thurtu-rni-nthi] *v-intr* be/become tired ᴛs

turturntu *n* **(1)** right hand *turturntukana* 'towards the right hand' ᴛs,ᴛᴍ,ᴡʏ,ᴡɪ **(2)** right (side) *turturnturlu* 'on the right' ᴛs,ᴡɪ,ѕᴛ

tutha *n* grass; hay; straw *tuthangka warkanthi* 'to graze on grass' ᴛs,ᴛᴍ,ᴡʏ,ᴋᴏ

  tutha-ipiti *n* native robin (*Petroica*) ᴛs,ᴛᴍ,ᴄᴏ

  tutha-kuinyu *n* woman in funeral ceremony ᴛs

  Tutha-piki *n* November ɴᴇᴡ

  tuthilti [[thuth(a)-(t)ilti] *n* strawberry ɴᴇᴡ

tutu **(1)** *adj* straight, upright, perpendicular ᴛᴍ **(2)** *adj* on guard, watching, alert, vigilant ᴛs **(3)** *adv* directly, without ceremony, pointedly *tutu tarkanthi* 'to speak to someone in a direct and straight forward manner, to address someone without ceremony' ᴛᴍ

  tutu tikanthi [tutu tika-nthi] *v-intr* **(1)** be on watch (during the night) ᴛs,ᴛᴍ **(2)** lie in ambush, lie in wait ᴛᴍ **(3)** sit up straight and attentively ᴛᴍ

  tutuangkanthi *v-intr* walk right up to someone ᴛᴍ

  tutumpurri **(1)** *adj* straight, upright ᴛs **(2)** *adv* directly, straight on ᴛs

  tutuwari [tutu-wari] *adv* straight *Iya nurnti tutuwaritya.* 'Along here in a straight line.' ᴛᴍ

tuturtu *n* circle; compass; wheel ᴛs

  tuturtu tidnapaltharla [tuturtu thidna-paltha-rla] *n* roller blades ɴᴇᴡ

tuwarri [thuwa-rri] **(1)** *n* dead body, corpse ᴛᴍ **(2)** *adj* dead, lifeless ᴛᴍ

  tuwa-thuwarrinthi [thuwa-thuwa-rri-nthi] *v-intr* sit with legs outstretched (like a corpse) ᴛs,ᴛᴍ

  tuwarrinthi [thuwa-rri-nthi] *v-intr* die, expire ᴛs,ᴛᴍ

-tuwayi *suff* (on verbs) lest (aversive) *Turlapurtu miyu; nurutuwayi nunyarritinga!* 'Full of anger is the man; Be silent, lest he work sorcery on you.' ᴛs

tuwila *n* **(1)** spirit ᴛs,ᴛᴍ **(2)** ghost ᴛs,ᴛᴍ **(3)** soul *Tuwilurlu nudnu purruti-apinthi.* 'The soul makes the body live.' ᴛs,ᴛᴍ

  tuwilatana without spirit ᴛᴍ

tuwina *adj* long; stretched out ᴛs,ᴛᴍ,ɢᴀ,ᴡʏ

  tuwimanthi [thuwi-ma-nthi] (var. **tuwirunthi**) *v-tr* stretch out ᴛs,ᴛᴍ

  tuwinarntinthi [thuwina-rni-nthi] *v-intr* extend; stretch out; become long ᴛᴍ

  tuwinirntu [thuwin(a)-(th)irntu] *n* solstice (summer) ɴᴇᴡ

  tuwiruti *adj* stretched ᴛs

tuyunthi [thuyu-nthi] (var. **tuiyunthi**) *v-tr* **(1)** pick (something) up *tupa tuiyu-tuiyunthi* 'to pick everything up' ᴛs,ᴛᴍ **(2)** gather, collect (something) ᴛs,ᴛᴍ

tuyurrinthi [thuyu-rri-nthi] *v-intr* gather ᴛs

U u

-unungku => **-nungku** *suff* (on nouns)

-urlu => **-rlu**

-urti => **-rti**

-utha => **-ngutha**

W w

waa *inter* where? *Waa pa?* 'Where is he?' *Waa pia?* 'I wonder where (he is).' *Waa alya pia pa?* 'Where on earth can he be?' TS, TM, BL, RO, WI, WY

waa'rna [waa-rna] *inter* which ones? TM

waamu [waa-(na)mu] *inter* whereabouts? along where? TS, TM

waangka [waa-ngka] *inter* in what?; in where? *Waangka 'athu katitha? – Tantungka.* 'What shall I fetch it in? – In a bag.' TS, TM

waapurti? [waa-purti] *intj* what's wrong? TS, TM

waardlu [waa-rlu] (var. **waarlu**) *inter* with what?; using what? TS, TM

waatha (var. **waatha-waatha**) *inter* where?; which place? TS, TM

waatha-intyarla [waatha-intya-rla] *inter* where? *Waathaintyarla warlingka?* 'At what place?' TM

waatha-intyarna [waatha-intya-rna] *inter* which ones? *Waathaintyarna niina ngartirrinthi?* 'Which people are you asking about?' TM

waathangku? [waatha-(nu)ngku] *inter* where from? *waathangkuta'rna* 'Where are they from?' TS, TM, BL

waadla *n* (1) tree lying on the ground TS, TM, WY, KO (2) block of wood TS, TM

waadlakatha [waadla-katha] *n* fallen tree across a river; bridge TS

waadlaparti [waadla-parti] *n* grub species WY

waadlatarra [waadla-tarra] *n* bridge TM

waadlawarnka [waadla-warnka] *n* fallen tree TM

waadlawarnkati [waadla-warnka-ti] *n* mid-autumn TS

waadli (1) *adj* wrong, incorrect TS, TM (2) *n* foul (in sport) NEW (3) *adj* bad, imperfect *waadli martu* 'bad smell' *waadli warra* 'bad language' TS, TM (4) *adv* badly, poorly, awkwardly, incorrectly, imperfectly *waadli parltanthi* 'to throw badly, to miss the target' *waadli payanthi, waadli wayinthi* 'to not understand' TS, TM

-waadli *suff (on nouns)* disliking, opposed to *marawaadli* 'generous' *maiwaadli* 'disliking food, generous' *puyuwaadli* 'disliking smoking, a non-smoker' *murntuwaadli* 'chaste, not into chasing women' TS, TM

waadli kudnanthi [waadli kudna-nthi] (var. **wadli kudna-kudnanthi**) *v-intr* be cross, dissatisfied *Waadli kudna-unangku ngai padlu kaitya.* 'He has sent me away out of dissatisfaction.' *Waadli kudna-kudnarti!* 'Don't be angry!' TM

waadli nakunthi [waadli nhaku-nthi] *v-tr* hate; detest TS, TM

waadli ngarntanthi [waadli ngarnta-nthi] (var. **waadli-arntanthi**) *v-intr* not want to; not feel like TM

waadli parltanthi [waadli parlta-nthi] *v-tr* miss, throw badly TS

waadli yarrurrina [waadli yarru-rri-na] *adj* broken TS

waadli-apinthi [waadli-(w)api-nthi] *v-tr* spoil; corrupt; make (something) bad *Pulyuna miyu tapa waadli-api.* 'The black men have corrupted their way (or path).' TM

waadli-mara stingy, greedy, covetous TS, TM

waadlirninthi [waadli-rni-nthi] *v-intr* be/become bad TM

waadlirrinthi [waadli-rri-nthi] *v-intr* be tired of, dislike, hate *Ninku ngai waadlirrinthi.* 'I'm tired of you.' TS, TM

waarki *n* holes in ground (animal burrows) TS, TM

waatu *n* (1) noise *yaki waatu* 'a deep, roaring noise' *palti waatu* 'ceremonial shout in unison' TS (2) low, deep shout, made during a pause or at the end of a song performed by the Marri Miyurna (Eastern people) TM

waatu *adv* together; in partnership *Parnu partata waatu mankunthi.* 'They are having sex.' TM

waaturlayinthi [waatu-rla-(wa)yinthi] *v-intr* lie down together (dual) TM

wadlala *n* rush of water TS, TM

wadlha *n* wallaby WI, ST

wadli kudna-kudnanthi => **waadli kudnanthi**

wadlu pumanthi [wadlu puma-nthi] *v-tr* wrap in; cover with TS

wadlu warta *adj* slow; lazy; idle *Wadlu wartarti!* 'Don't be lazy! Hurry up!' TS

wadlunthi₁ [wadlu-nthi] (var. **wadlu-wadlunthi**) *v-intr* be loaded down, carry lots TM

wadlunthi₂ [wadlu-nthi] *v-tr* (1) glare, stare, scowl at (someone) TS, TM (2) put smoke up inside a hollow tree to get possums out TM

wadna *n* (1) stick for tree climbing TS, TM, CA, EY, WY, KO (2) boomerang (as found in all other Thura-Yura languages) NEW

wadna-wadna *n* inquest into death TS, TM

wadna-wadna warra the verdict or answer reached by means of the inquest TM

wadna (1)   wadna (2)

wadni *n* red or green native fruit (undefined) TS, TM

wai! *intj* hey! NEW

waikurta *n* string; girdle TS, TM

wailyu *n* leaves of 'kantara' TM, WY

waipiti [wai-(wa)pi-ti] *n* motor NEW

waitku *n* fish species TS, WI

waitpi *n* cold wind TS, WY

wakanthi [waka-nthi] *v-tr* (1) step into (someone's) way *mara-wakanthi* 'catch (something) in your cupped hands' TS, TM (2) wait in ambush to catch animals (that are being driven towards you by another group of hunters) TM

    wakalti [waka-lti] *n* bark shield WY, CA

    wakarri-apinthi [waka-rri-(w)api-nthi] *v-tr* (1) forget (something) and leave it behind or lose it TS, TM (2) spoil (something) and make it useless TM

    wakarrinthi [waka-rri-nthi] *v-intr* (1) be ignorant, stupid, foolish, out of your mind, not understand *Wakarrithi.* 'He is out of his mind (crazy).' TS, TM, WY (2) be lost, on a wrong path *wakarringka tikanthi* 'to live in a 'lost, forlorn, lonely or wrong place' TS, TM, RO (3) forget *Wakarrintitha pa.* 'He will forget it.' TM (4) be drunk, tipsy *kupurlu wakarrinthi* 'to be intoxicated' WI, ST (5) giddy TS, WI

    wakarripurka [waka-rri-purka] *n* stupid person; ignorant person; fool TS, TM

wakinha (1) *adj* bad, wrong, evil, immoral, wicked *Wakinha warraintya!* 'That's a bad word!' TS, TM, WY, WI, RO, ST, CH (2) *n* sin *Ngadluku wakinhila madli'pa.* 'He died on account of our sins.' TM (3) *adj* naughty *Maingkirti! Wakinha-urti!* 'Don't laugh! Don't behave badly!' TS (4) *n* penalty (in sports) NEW

    wakinhanti-apinthi [wakinha-nti-(w)api-nthi] (var. **wakinhantapinthi**) *v-tr* (1) make (something) become bad, cause (something) to deteriorate TS, TM (2) make (someone) act immorally TM

    wakinharninthi [wakinha-rni-nthi] (var. **wakinhantinthi**) *v-intr* become bad, immoral TS, TM

waku *n* spider TS, TM, WY

    waku ngari (var. **waku-ari**) *n* spider web TM

wakuinya *n* barter; exchange; trade TS, TM

    wakuinyapinthi [wakuinya-(wa)pi-nthi] *v-tr* barter; exchange; trade TS, TM

wakurri *n* lizard species (undefined) TS

wakurti (var. **'akurti**) *adv* perhaps; probably *Ngai-akurti.* 'Me too most likely.' *Nguntaintya-akurti ngaityu wangatha.* 'Perhaps I will plant my (potatoes) over there.' *Nguntaintya-akurti, ngunta-unta.* 'Over there probably, there.' *Yarntaintya-akurti, yarnta-arnta.* 'Over here probably, here.' TM

wakwaku [wak(u)-waku] *n* child; baby; offspring TS, TM, WI, WY, GA, BL

    wakwakurli [wak(u)-waku-rli] like, in the same way as a child TM

walara *adj* (1) clear, bright, light *walara-urlu* 'in the day time, early in the morning' TM (2) clear headed, intelligent, clever TM

    walarantinthi [walara-nti-nthi] *v-intr* shine, give light, become daylight TM

waltha *n* bustard, wild turkey (*Ardeotis australis*) TS, TM, WY, WI, CO

walyu *n* (1) white edible root resembling a radish TS (2) white radish NEW

wama₁ *n* (1) plain; flat country *wamangka* 'on the plain' TS, TM, WY, RO (2) empty space *wama wangkanthi* 'to speak 'into the air', to no one in particular' TM

wama₂ *n* index finger; forefinger WY

wamanyu *n* venereal disease TS, TM

wamina *intj* what (is it)? *Wamina? Naku'athu, parni-apintu!* 'What is it? Let me see, give it to me!' TS

wampi (var. **wampiti**) *n* (1) wing of a large bird TS, TM (2) fan TM

    wampinthi [wampi-nthi] *v-intr, v-tr* (1) fly TM (2) fan, wave, swing, move (something) in a way that resembles a bird flapping its wings TS, TM

wana-wana *n* movements during funeral (ceremony) WY

wanga *n* grave (burial) TS, TM

    wanganthi [wanga-nthi] (var. **wangarrinthi**) *v-tr* bury; inter TS, WI

    wangayarta [wanga-yarta] *n* graveyard; cemetery NEW

wangardi *n* niece or nephew (older sister's child) TM, WY

wangka *n* west TS, TM

    wangka-intyarla [wangka-intya-rla] most westerly, far to the west TM

    wangkaku (var. **wangkaka**) towards the west, westward TS, TM **wangkakurlu** [wangkaku-rlu] when (it's) in the west (e.g. sun) TM

    wangkalti [wangka-lti] further west TM

    wangkangka [wangka-ngka] in the west TM

    wangkarta [wangka-rta] westerly TS, TM

wangki *n* throat; gullet TS, TM, WY

    wangkanthi [wangka-nthi] *v-intr* say; speak; talk; chat *Ngaintya pa wangki?* 'What did he say?' *Ngai tangka wayirrinthi manti niina wangkanintyarla.* 'I am sorry that you can't speak (the language).' *Ngadluku warra nintu payarnintyidla nintu, warra miyu pulyunarlu wangkainki.* 'Whenever you understand our language, you must speak in the black man's language.' *Namu pa wangkathi ...* 'This is how he spoke/what he said ...' *Wangkanina niina ngathu yailyathi. – Yaku ngaii wangkithi.* 'I thought you had said something. – I didn't say anything.' ᴛꜱ, ᴛᴍ, ᴡʏ, ᴡɪ, ʀᴏ, ᴄʜ

wangkalyarninthi [wangk(a)-alya-rni-nthi] *v-intr* keep talking, keep going on (about something) *Ngana niina warti warra wangkalyarni?* 'Why do you still continue making words between?' ᴛᴍ

wangki murlarni [wangki murla-rni] thirsty ᴛᴍ

wangku *n* possum species, possibly pygmy possum, feathertail glider, sugar glider or ringtail (small) ᴛꜱ, ᴡʏ, ᴡɪ, ʀᴏ, ꜱᴛ

wangkurrinthi [wangku-rri-nthi] *v-intr* ascend; climb; go up *kauwangka wangkurrinthi* 'to ascend a cliff face' ᴛꜱ, ᴛᴍ

wangkurti *n* corner; alcove; niche; nook *wangkurila* 'in the corner' ᴛᴍ

wangu *num* seven ɴᴇᴡ

wangauwata [wang(u)-(th)awata] *num* seven thousand ɴᴇᴡ

wangirntu [wang(u)-(th)irntu] (var. **wanguirntu**) *n* week ɴᴇᴡ

wangirrka [wang(u)-irrka] *num* seventy ɴᴇᴡ

wangiwurra [wang(u)-(w)iwurra] *num* seven million ɴᴇᴡ

wangu partirrka [wangu part(u)-irrka] *num* seven hundred ɴᴇᴡ

wangu tirnturna [wangu thirntu-rna] *n* seven days or a week ɴᴇᴡ

Wanguartu [wangu-(k)artu] *n* birth-order name: seventh-born (female) ᴇʏ

Wanguiki [wang(u)-(p)iki] *n* July ɴᴇᴡ

Wangutya [wangu-tya] *n* birth-order name: seventh-born (male) ᴡʏ, ᴇʏ

wanpa *n* number ɴᴇᴡ

wanpa-wanpanthi [wanpa-wanpa-nthi] *v-tr* count; number ᴛꜱ, ᴛᴍ

wanpanapinthi [wanpa-na-(w)api-nthi] *v-tr* summon; call; invite *Nganaitya nintu ngai mardla wanpanapi?* 'Why have you summoned me here for no reason?' ᴛᴍ

wanpanapilyarninthi [wanpana-(wa)pi-lya-rni-nthi] *v-intr* invite persistently ᴛᴍ

wantaka *adv* **(1)** definitely, absolutely, for sure, positively *Wantaka nanganturna, mitituwayi nintu.* 'You will definitely see them, but don't steal them.' ᴛꜱ, ᴛᴍ **(2)** immediately, straight away *Wantaka ngathu niina pardu yungku-yungkutha.* 'I will give you meat right away.' ᴛᴍ

wantaka nakunthi [wantaka nhaku-nthi] know for sure ᴛꜱ

wantanthi [wanta-nthi] *v-tr* **(1)** put down, leave, stop working on (something) *Wantantu!* 'Leave it alone! Let it be! Cut it out!' ᴛꜱ, ᴛᴍ, ᴡɪ, ᴡʏ, ꜱᴛ **(2)** leave behind, leave (something) for later *Yaku wantaningwa ngaityu, niwani nganmaingwa.* 'Don't leave any food for me, you two eat it.' ᴛꜱ, ᴛᴍ

wanta-wantanthi [wanta-wanta-nthi] forsake, abandon (something) ᴛᴍ

wantapinthi [wanta-(wa)pi-nthi] *v-tr* cause to put down, leave or stop working on (something) ᴛᴍ

wantarni-apinthi [wanta-rni-(w)api-nthi] *v-tr* put down (cause to be); left behind (cause to be); given up on (cause to be) ᴛᴍ

wantarrinthi [wanta-rri-nthi] *v-tr* leave behind; put down; forsake *Ngaityu wantarringkurti!* 'Don't leave me behind!' ᴛꜱ, ᴛᴍ

wantawu *n* flycatcher ꜱᴛ

wanti *inter* where to? *Wanti niina?* 'Where are you going?' ᴛꜱ, ᴛᴍ

wanti-ana? in what direction? ᴛᴍ

wanti-arlu? in what direction? ᴛꜱ

wantinthi [wanti-nthi] *v-intr* **(1)** lie down *Miitu wantingku wakwaku.* 'The child will lie down to sleep.' *Yartana wantinina naki Ngarparla.* 'Auntie found it lying on the ground.' ᴛꜱ, ᴛᴍ, ᴡɪ, ᴡʏ, ɢᴀ, ʀᴏ, ᴋᴏ **(2)** live, exist, be (somewhere) *Kudla wanti-ana pinti miyu. Tidlina pinti miyu. Parnaku niiupu pudni, ngadlu titapituwayi. Miyu pulyuna kudla wantinthi.* 'Let the white man live alone. The white man is opulent. He has come (to be) their neighbour, or else we will be chained. Let the black man live separately.' ᴛꜱ, ᴛᴍ

wanti-apinthi [wanti-(w)api-nthi] *v-tr* **(1)** make (someone) lie down, allow (someone) to lie down ᴛꜱ, ᴛᴍ **(2)** live with (someone) ᴛꜱ

wanti-apirrinthi [wanti-(w)api-rri-nthi] *v-tr* lie down (make each other) ᴛᴍ

wapa *n* feather ᴛꜱ, ᴛᴍ

wapayinthi [wapa-(wai)yi-nthi] *v-intr* leave secretly; abscond; sneak off ᴛᴍ

wapinthi [wapi-nthi] *v-tr* **(1)** do, make, act, perform *Wapi-urti!* 'Don't do that!' *Ngathunti wapiutha.* 'I will do it by myself.' *Yungkuntu! Wapi'athu.* 'Give it to me!

I'll do it.'ₜₛ,ₜₘ **(2)** intend to (do something) *Ngulthi mankatitya parna wapithi.* 'They intended to carry off the 'ngulthi'.'ₜₘ **(3)** tell, say *Niina purla wapi-wapi.* 'They have both told you.' *murntu warra wapinthi* 'to say a bad word, to use dirty language'ₜₘ

   wapirna [wapi-rna] *intj* Amen!ɴᴇᴡ

   wapituwayi [wapi-tuwayi] *n* warningɴᴇᴡ

   wapiwarra [wapi-warra] *n* verbɴᴇᴡ

   wapiwarrarla karrpa [wapi-warra-rla karrpa] *n* complex sentenceɴᴇᴡ

wapu *n* mother-in-lawₜₛ,ₜₘ

wara *n* sandₜₛ,ₜₘ

   warapina [wara-pina] *n* congolli, tupong (fish) *(Pseudaphritis urvilli)* ɴᴇᴡ

   warati [wara-ti] *n* tadpoleʀᴏ

wara-wantaka *loc* across; side-on to; on the side of (something)ₜₛ,ₜₘ

warda *n* bandicootʀᴏ

wardli (var. **warli**) *n* house; hut; building; home *wardlirdlaku wartingka* 'between the two houses'ₜₛ,ₜₘ,ᴄᴀ,ʙʟ,ɢᴀ,ᴡɪ,ᴡʏ,ʀᴏ,ᴄʜ

   wardli nurliti [wardli nurli-ti] house keyₜₛ

   wardli pulthu *n* abandoned house; ruin; place where a house was *Warrityarna warlipulthungka tikanthi* 'to live in Waritya's old house or in the place where Waritya's house used to be'ₜₘ

   Wardlipari [wardli-pari] *n* Milky Wayₜₛ,ₜₘ

   wardlipurka [wardli-purka] *n* resident; householderₜₛ

   wardliwardli [wardli-wardli] *n* town; townshipɴᴇᴡ

   wardliwitya [wardli-witya] (var. **warliwitya**) *n* **(1)** armpitₜₘ **(2)** side of the ribsₜₛ

   wardliyapa [wardli-yapa] *n* inside of a house; interior of a house *wardliyapangka* 'inside a house' *wardliyapa- ana* 'into the inside of a house'ₜₛ,ₜₘ

   warli takana a spacious houseₜₘ

   warli wangku-wangkurtu a high but narrow houseₜₘ

wardninthi [wardni-nthi] (var. **warninthi**) *v-intr* **(1)** fall down, fall, drop *Madlu-adlu wardni-utha ngai.* 'It is very dark, I might fall.'ₜₛ,ₜₘ,ᴡʏ **(2)** be born *Yaku niina purka wardni.* 'You were not born as a grown man.'ₜₛ,ₜₘ,ᴡʏ **(3)** appear, become (used in relation to the phases of the moon) *Niina nata purka wardni.* 'You are now a grown man'ₜₘ **(4)** originate *Pulyuna miyurna waathangku wardni?* 'Where did the black men originate from?'ₜₘ

   wardni-apinthi [wardni-(w)api-nthi] *v-tr* **(1)** drop, let (something) fallₜₛ,ₜₘ **(2)** cause (something) to fall down, throw (something) downₜₛ **(3)** lose (something) *ngathu wardni-apinina.* 'if I had lost it ...'ₜₛ,ₜₘ

   wardni-wardninya [wardni-wardni-nya] *adj* not good in a fight; falling; stumblingₜₛ,ₜₘ

   warnirntu [warn(i)-(th)irntu] *n* birthdayɴᴇᴡ

wardu *adj* warmₜₛ

   wardunthi [wardu-nthi] *v-tr* roast (in the ashes)ₜₘ

wari *n* point; tip; end (of object); extremityₜₛ

   wariparti [wari-parti] *n* circumcised personₜₛ

warka *adj* bent overₜₛ,ₜₘ

   warka-warkarrinthi [warka-warka-rri-nthi] *v-intr* walk slowly; drag your feetₜₘ

   warkanta [warka-nta] *n* cascade; waterfallₜₛ

   warkanthi [warka-nthi] *v-intr* **(1)** bend down, stoopₜₛ,ₜₘ **(2)** graze (bending forward like a horse)ₜₛ,ₜₘ

   warkarninthi [warka-rni-nthi] *v-intr* get venereal diseaseₜₘ

warki (var. **warkiti**) *n* pincersₜₛ,ₜₘ

   warkinthi [warki-nthi] *v-tr* **(1)** clasp (something) in talons like a bird of preyₜₛ,ₜₘ **(2)** pinch, take hold of (something) with a pair of tongsₜₛ,ₜₘ

warli => **wardli**

warliarri *n* person whose father's wife is deadₜₘ

warliwitya => **wardliwitya**

warlta **(1)** *adj* warm, hot, clear (weather)ₜₛ,ₜₘ,ᴡɪ,ᴡʏ,ɢᴀ **(2)** *n* constellation that governs the summer seasonₜₘ

   warltarninthi [warlta-rni-nthi] *v-intr* become hotɢᴀ

   warltati [warlta-ti] *n* **(1)** summer, hot seasonₜₛ,ₜₘ,ᴡʏ **(2)** yearᴡʏ

   warltawingkura [warlta-wingkura] *n* heatwaveɴᴇᴡ

warltu (var. **warti warltu**) *n* **(1)** nape of the neck, where the spine meets the headₜₛ,ₜₘ,ᴡʏ **(2)** gap, space between two things *Yaku ngathu warti warltu nakunthi.* 'I can't see (or don't know of) any exit or escape route.'ₜₛ,ₜₘ **(3)** valleyₜₘ **(4)** difference (between two things), argument or disagreement (between two people) *Warti warlturna ngai payirrinthi.* 'I examine the difference.' *Painingka purlaku nguya-nguya tikathi. Nata purla pia turla warti warltu wanta.* 'Previously they were fighting. (But) now it seems they have put their differences aside.'ₜₘ **(5)** line, stripe, rowₜₛ

warki

warltu-arri [warltu-(ng)arri] *n* Adelaide rosella co

warlturninthi [warltu-rni-nthi] *v-intr* go through a valley, go between two things TM

warlturri-apinthi [warltu-rri-(w)api-nthi] *v-tr* clear a passage; make a path between things TM

warlturrinthi [warltu-rri-nthi] *v-intr* run through a gap; pass between *Tapa warlturrinthi.* 'The road runs along, through (the valley).' TM

warlutina nuinpi [warltu-tina nuinpi] *n* short-headed lamprey (fish) (*Mordacia mordax*) NEW

warninhari *n* birth-order name NEW

warninthi => **wardninthi**

warnka₁ (var. **warnkata**) (1) *n, loc* front or space in front of something TS, TM (2) *n* omentum, layer of fat at the front of the belly which covers the intestines TS

warnkangka [warnka-ngka] *loc* in front of *kardla warnkangka* 'in front of the fire' TS

warnkarlu [warnka-rlu] *loc* towards or along the front TM

warnkarrinthi [warnka-rri-nthi] *v-intr* protrude; poke out in front TM

warnka₂ *n* venereal disease TS, TM

warnka-warnka *n* fungus species TS

warnpa *n* bullrush root (*Typha*) TS, TM

warnpi *n* fatherless person; orphan TS, TM, WY

warnta-ingki [warnta-ingki] *adj* describes different quarters of the moon (uncertain) TM

warntalinthi [warnta-li-nthi] *v-intr* have hiccups; burp TM

warntanthi [warnta-nthi] *v-intr* (1) hover, soar (like a bird) TS, TM (2) flap (like a bird) TS

warntapinthi [warnta-(wa)pi-nthi] *v-tr* (1) hang (something) up TM, WI (2) make (something) soar (like a bird) TM

warntu *n* black honeyeater (bird) (*Sugomel niger*) WY, CO

warnu *n* bottom; bum; buttocks TS, KO

warnupaltha [warnu-paltha] *n* nappy NEW

warnutina [warnu-tina] *adj* restless; annoying; troublesome TS

warpu (var. **wartpu**) *n* (1) bone TS, TM, WY (2) hard centre of something (e.g. stone in a fruit, hard part of a plant or tree) TS, TM (3) wooden dagger CA

warpu-warpulayinthi [warpu-warpu-(w)ayi-nthi] *v-intr* hurry TM

warpu-warpurru [warpu-warpu-rru] *adv* quickly; hastily TM

warpu-wilta (var. **warpu-wiltu**) *adj* (1) strong, powerful TS, TM (2) brave TM

warnpa

warpularra *adj* unpleasant; argumentative; irritable; annoying TS

warpulayi [warpu-layi] *n* work; job NEW

warpulayi tarralyi [warpu-layi tarralyi] *n* workbench NEW

Warpulayi-layila Tirntu [warpu-layi-l(a)-(l)ayi-la thirntu] *n* Labour day NEW

warpulayinthi [warpu-layi-nthi] *v-intr* (1) work, exert oneself TS, TM (2) be active or busy TS, TM (3) serve, care for (someone) TM

warpulayitina [warpu-layi-tina] *adj* unemployed NEW

warpurninthi [warpu-rni-nthi] *v-intr* be/become hard, dry, lean TM

warpurti [warpu-(pa)rti] *n* grub species TS, PI

warputina [warpu-tina] *adj* boneless; ghostly; not solid TS

warpuwiltarninthi [warpu-wilta-rni-nthi] *v-intr* become strong, powerful, brave TM

warpuwiltarrinthi [warpu-wilta-rri-nthi] *v-intr* try hard; exert oneself TM

warra *n* (1) language TS, TM, WI, BL (2) speech, act of talking TS, TM, WY (3) voice TS, TM (4) word TS, TM (5) message TM (6) throat TS, TM

warra ingkarninthi [warra ingka-rni-nthi] *v-tr* pay attention to, listen to, or wait for (someone's words) TM

warra inpanthi [warra inpa-nthi] *v-tr* reply; respond; answer TM

warra katinthi [warra kati-nthi] *v-tr* bring a message; inform; report; proclaim TM

warra kumpanthi [warra kumpa-nthi] *v-intr* stop speaking, be silent *Warra kumpi.* 'He is silent.' TM

warra mailtyanthi [warra mailtya-nthi] *v-tr* imitate someone's speech TM

warra mankunthi [warra manku-nthi] *v-tr* (1) repeat what someone else said TS (2) answer, reply to (someone) *Warra nintu nganaitya yaku manki?* 'Why didn't you answer?' *Yaku ngai padlu warra mankunthi.* 'He doesn't answer me.' TM

warra markanthi [warra marka-nthi] (1) be attentive, listen carefully TS (2) imitate (someone's) speech TM

warra nakunthi [warra nhaku-nthi] *v-intr* understand (what was said) WI

warra padniti [warra padni-ti] *n* windpipe; trachea TS, TM

warra parltanthi [warra parlta-nthi] *v-tr* inform; fetch permission (from someone) *Ngathu ngaityu miyu* *wartarna warra parltatha. Naa miyuwartatina.* 'I will tell my countrymen (to take care of you). You are without countrymen.' ᴛᴍ

warra payanthi [warra paya-nthi] *v-tr* understand (a language); understand (what was said) ᴛᴍ

warra pilta-pilunthi [warra pilta-pilu-nthi] interpret (a language) ᴛᴍ

warra tarra-tharra-itpapinthi interpret language ᴛꜱ,ᴛᴍ

warra tatarta *n* message stick ɴᴇᴡ

warra wardninthi [warra wardni-nthi] *v-intr* it is said ...; they say ...; (the) rumour is ... ᴛᴍ

warra wartangka [warra warta-ngka] according to the word or order ᴛꜱ,ᴛᴍ

warra wikinthi [warra wiki-nthi] despise (someone's) words ᴛꜱ,ᴛᴍ

warra yungkunthi [warra yungku-nthi] *v-tr* inform; tell; communicate to ᴛꜱ,ᴛᴍ

warra yungkurrinthi [warra yungku-rri-nthi] inform, give information (to someone) ᴛꜱ

warraityati [warra-(ka)itya-ti] *n* telephone ɴᴇᴡ

warramankuti [warra-manku-ti] *n* voice recorder ɴᴇᴡ

warranthi [warra-nthi] *v-intr* speak; say; talk *Warrarti!* 'Be silent!' ᴛꜱ,ᴛᴍ

warrapanthi [warra-pa(a)-nthi] (1) *v-intr* chat, converse with (someone) ᴛꜱ,ᴛᴍ (2) *v-intr, v-tr* speak to, address (someone) ᴛꜱ,ᴛᴍ

warrapiipa [warra-piipa] *n* dictionary ɴᴇᴡ (inspired by German *wörterbuch* 'word book')

warrapina [warra-pina] *n* talkative person; chatterbox ᴛᴍ

warrapulyu [warra-pulyu] *adj* silent; reserved (person); quiet ᴛᴍ

warrarra [warra-(wa)rra] (var. **warra-warra**) *n* (1) spell cast by a sorcerer; (magic) curse ᴛᴍ (2) sorcerer; traditional healer (extended to modern day doctors) ᴛꜱ,ᴛᴍ,ᴄᴀ

warrarti! *intj* be quiet! shut up! ɴᴇᴡ

warratina [warra-tina] *adj* speechless; dumb ᴛꜱ,ᴛᴍ

warrawiilta [warra-wiilta] *n* windpipe; trachea ᴡʏ

warrangku [warra-ngku] (1) *adj* sick, unwell ᴛᴍ (2) *n* illness, disease *Warrangkurlu pa madli.* 'He died from a disease.' ᴛᴍ

warrangkurninthi [warrangku-rni-nthi] *v-intr* (1) get sick ᴛꜱ (2) die (from a disease) *warrangkurnintyarla* 'in case he dies' ᴛᴍ

warra-tatarta

warranka *n* parrot ꜱᴛ

warrarrinthi [warra-rri-nthi] *v-intr* hesitate, tarry; or to turn back, wander around without a permanent home *mantikatpa warrarrinthi* 'to hesitate, tarry; or to turn back, wander around without a permanent home' ᴛꜱ,ᴛᴍ

warrarruka => **warru-warruka**

warri *n* (1) wind *Murla warridlu parltatha.* 'When a dry wind will blow.' ᴛꜱ,ᴛᴍ,ᴡʏ,ᴡɪ,ɢᴀ,ʀᴏ (2) airconditioner ɴᴇᴡ

warri parltanthi [warri parlta-nthi] the wind blows ᴛᴍ

warri turrunthi [warri turru-nthi] the wind blows ᴛᴍ

warri wangkanthi [warri wangka-nthi] the wind blows ᴛꜱ

Warripari [warri-pari] *n* wind river (Sturt River) ᴡɪ,ᴛꜱ

Warri-artu [warri-(k)artu] *n* birth-order name: second born (female) ᴇʏ,ᴡɪ

warrinthi [warri-nthi] *v-tr* seek; look for ᴛꜱ,ᴛᴍ

warri-apinthi [warri-(w)api-nthi] (var. **warri-warri-apinthi**) *v-tr* find; pick up ᴛꜱ,ᴛᴍ

warrinya [warri-nya] *n* fatherless orphan ᴛꜱ,ᴛᴍ

warrirninthi [warri-rni-nthi] (var. **warrirntinthi**) *v-intr* be-; become-; gain a characteristic, acquire a quality *Yama warrintitha'rna.* 'They are crazy.' *Kudla murla warrirningku nungurru.* 'The moisture will evaporate (become dry) on its own.' ᴛᴍ

Warritya [warri-tya] *n* birth-order name: second-born (male) ᴡʏ,ᴇʏ,ᴡɪ,ꜱᴛ

warru *n* (1) exterior; outside (of something) *warrungka* 'outside (of the house), somewhere away from home' *Warru- ana padni!* 'Get out!' *warrungka wayinthi* 'to be out, not at home' *warru-arra wantinthi* 'to lie (sleep) outside' *warru-ana kangkanthi* 'to pull, drag' *Warru-ana patintu!* 'Throw it outside!' ᴛꜱ,ᴛᴍ,ᴡʏ (2) abroad, overseas ᴡʏ

warru-kadli *n* wild dog; untamed dingo ᴛꜱ,ᴛᴍ,ᴡʏ

warru-marngu *n* ankle ᴛꜱ,ᴛᴍ,ᴡʏ

warru-mpi *adj* not going out; staying at home ᴛꜱ

warru-thirntu *n* time out ɴᴇᴡ

warru-warruka (var. **warrarruka**) *n* barking (dogs) ᴛꜱ,ᴛᴍ,ᴋᴏ

warru-warrukanthi [warru-warruka-nthi] *v-intr* bark (dog) ᴛꜱ,ᴛᴍ

warrukapinthi [warruka-(wa)pi-nthi] *v-tr* bark at *Ngana miyungka kadlidlu warrukapinthi?* 'Who is the dog barking at?' ᴛᴍ

warrukayinthi [warruka-(wa)yi-nthi] *v-intr* bark ᴛᴍ,ᴋᴏ

warrukiti *n* barking owl (*Ninox connivens*) ᴛs

warrulyi [warru-(tarra)lyi] *n* outboard motor ɴᴇᴡ

warrumarngu [warru-marngu] *n* ankle bone ᴛᴍ,ᴋᴏ

warrumpa *n* grub species ᴛs

Warruyu *n* birth-order name: second born (female) ᴡʏ

warta (1) *n* back of something, place behind something ᴛs,ᴛᴍ (2) *n* end *Warta-ityarlu Sunday pudnatha.* 'I will come at the end of Sunday.' ᴛᴍ (3) *adj* last, final ᴛᴍ

> **warta mankunthi** [warta manku-nthi] *v-tr* follow; go after; go behind ᴛᴍ
>
> **warta-ityatina** [warta-itya-tina] *n* weak-legged, thin person (insult) ᴛs,ᴛᴍ
>
> **warta-thurti** *n* upper arm ᴛs,ᴛᴍ,ᴡʏ
>
> **warta-warta** *n* private parts; genitals sᴛ
>
> **wartangka** [warta-ngka] (1) *loc* behind *Karra wartangka yuwarla.* 'They (two) are standing behind the redgum.' ᴛs,ᴛᴍ (2) *loc* after, following *wartangka padninthi* 'to follow along behind someone' ᴛs,ᴛᴍ (3) *adv* according to, in the manner of *Parnu tia wartangka taakarringa!* 'Sing along with him (you lot)!' ᴛs,ᴛᴍ
>
> **wartanthi** [warta-nthi] *v-tr* drag; pull (something) along (behind) ᴛs,ᴛᴍ
>
> **wartarrinthi** [warta-rri-nthi] *v-intr* drag, pull along ᴛs,ᴛᴍ
>
> **wartarninthi** [warta-rni-nthi] *v-intr* stay behind; hang around; loiter ᴛs,ᴛᴍ
>
> **wartarra** [warta-arra] *loc, temp* after; behind; following; later *Munarra padni! Yangadli'ai wartarra.* 'Go ahead! I will follow later.' ᴛs,ᴛᴍ
>
> **Wartiki** [wart(a)-(p)iki] *n* December ɴᴇᴡ

warta-pukarra *n* stormy weather (with north wind) ᴛs,ᴛᴍ

wartapurru [warta-purru] (var. **wartapurruna**) *n* all; whole *Witintu wartapurruna tinkyu!* 'Take all the branches away!' ᴛs,ᴛᴍ

warti₁ *n* (1) tail *wartiarra* '(to pull out) by the tail' ᴛs,ᴛᴍ (2) penis ᴛs,ᴛᴍ

> **warti-murtana** [warti-murtana] *adj* short-tailed; having a deformed tail ᴛs

warti₂ *n* (1) centre, middle *mamparlaku wartingka* 'between the knees' *Warti warltu-ana ngai payirrinthi.* 'I examine the difference.' *Naawi tirnturna wartingka ninkurna? – Wartingka ngai wanti kumarlukunti* 'How many days have you been on the road? – Between here and there I slept only once (i.e. two days)' ᴛs,ᴛᴍ (2) cause, origin, principle, root, source ᴛᴍ

> **warti nakunthi** [warti nhaku-nthi] know the cause, reason, origin ᴛᴍ
>
> **warti ngatpanthi** [warti ngatpa-nthi] instruct in knowledge ᴛᴍ
>
> **warti partana** [warti parta-na] *n* creator; maker *Ngaintyarlu miyu warti partana? ngaini warti ngatpantu!* 'How were people created? Instruct me in knowledge!' ᴛᴍ
>
> **warti tampinthi** [warti-tampi-nthi] understand or perceive the origin or cause of something ᴛᴍ
>
> **warti warltu** the centre point or the difference between two things ᴛᴍ
>
> **warti-ana** [warti-ana] *adj* middle-aged *wartiana miyu* 'a man of middle age' ᴛs,ᴛᴍ
>
> **warti-arra** *loc* down the centre; through the middle *warti-arra pakinthi* 'cut (something) through the middle' ᴛᴍ
>
> **warti-kurdana** *n* noon; midday *warti kurdanurlu* 'at noon' ᴛs,ᴛᴍ
>
> **warti-trruku** *n* centre; hub *warti trrukungka* 'in the centre, right in the middle' ᴛs,ᴛᴍ
>
> **warti-wartingka** [warti-warti-ngka] *adv* because of-; on account of-; sake of- (for the); about- *ngangki warti- wartingka tawarrinthi* 'to fight about a woman' ᴛs,ᴛᴍ

warti-warti *n* small flood ᴛᴍ

wartipardu [warti-pardu] *n* seal ɴᴇᴡ

wartpu => **warpu**

wartu *n* wombat ᴛs

warunthi [waru-nthi] (var. **waru-warunthi**) *v-tr* call; summon; fetch *Miyurna nintu waruthila ...* 'When you are going to call the men ...' ᴛs,ᴛᴍ,ᴡʏ,ᴡɪ

> **mara warunthi, mararlu warunthi** beckon to (someone) to come ᴛs,ᴛᴍ
>
> **warurrinthi** [waru-rri-nthi] *v-tr* call ᴛs

watharna [watha-rna] (var. **wathairna**) *inter* who?; which one?; what (of many)? ᴛs,ᴛᴍ

wati *n* name ᴡʏ,ʀᴏ

wati-wati *n* small burrowing animal ᴛs

watita *adj* hot or sultry; (weather) ᴛs,ᴛᴍ,ᴡɪ,sᴛ

watpa *n* cloak; animal skin cloak ᴛs,ᴛᴍ,ᴡʏ,sᴛ

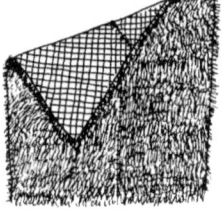

watpa

watpana *adj* soft; liquid; fluid *ngarrata-watpana* 'quick, swift, active' ᴛs,ᴛᴍ,ᴡʏ

watpanantinthi [watpana-nti-nthi] *v-intr* be/become soft or liquid ᴛᴍ

watparni-apinthi [watpa(na)-rni-(wa)pi-nthi] *v-tr* soften; moisten; liquify ᴛs, ᴛᴍ

watpanthi [watpa-nthi] *v-intr* run; gallop; jump; skip ᴛs, ᴛᴍ, ᴡʏ

watpapinthi [watpa-(wa)pi-nthi] *v-tr* make gallop, make jump ᴛᴍ

watu *n* branch (tree) ᴛs, ᴛᴍ

watuwardli [watu-wardli] *n* hut of branches ᴛs, ᴛᴍ

wauwa *n* beach; seashore ᴛs, ᴛᴍ

wauwi (see also: **nyaani**) *n* (1) grey kangaroo (female) ᴛs, ᴛᴍ, ᴡʏ, ᴘɪ (2) sheep ᴡʏ

wauwi-wityu (see also: **wityu**) ᴛs

wauwinthi => **wayinthi**

waya-wayanthi => **wayanthi**

wayaka *n* star name; constellation name ᴛs, ᴡʏ

wayangka [waya-ngka] *n* whisper; quiet, whispered speech ᴛs, ᴛᴍ

wayangkapina [waya-ngka-pina] *n* whisperer; someone who whispers ᴛs, ᴛᴍ

wayangkapinthi [waya-ngka-(w)api-nthi] *v-tr* whisper ᴛs

wayangkayinthi [waya-ngka-(wa)yi-nthi] (var. **wayangkinthi**) *v-intr* whisper ᴛs, ᴛᴍ

wayangkila [waya-ngk(a)-ila] *adj, adv* in a whisper, whispered ᴛᴍ

wayanthi [waya-nthi] (var. **waya-wayanthi**) *v-tr* inspect; examine ᴛs, ᴛᴍ

wayarnta (var. **wayangarnta**) *adv* well; ably; capably ᴛs, ᴛᴍ

wayi *n* fear *Wayintitya muri.* 'He has run away because of fear.' ᴛᴍ

wayikurtanthi [wayi-kurta-nthi] (1) *v-intr, v-tr* fear, dread ᴛs, ᴛᴍ (2) *v-tr* scare, intimidate (someone) *Padlu niina wayikurtanthi.* 'He intimidates you' *Nintu pa wayikurtanthi.* 'You scare him.' ᴛᴍ

wayikurtarrinthi [wayi-kurta-rri-nthi] *v-intr* be afraid *wayikurtarringkurti!* 'Don't be scared!' ᴛᴍ

wayirni-apinthi [wayi-rni-(w)api-nthi] (var. **wayinapinthi**) *v-tr* make afraid; intimidate; scare; frighten ᴛs, ᴛᴍ

wayirninthi [wayi-rni-nthi] *v-intr* fear, be afraid, scared; timid ᴛs, ᴛᴍ, ᴡʏ

wayiwayi *adj* afraid; scared; timid ᴛs, ᴛᴍ

wayiwilta *adj* brave; fearless; courageous ᴛs, ᴛᴍ

wayinthi [wayi-nthi] (var. **-kaiyinthi**; **-layi**; **wauwinthi**) (1) *v-intr* move, flow, turn, do *Kauwingka tikatina parna wayinthi.* 'The (birds) settle on the water.' ᴛs, ᴛᴍ, ᴋᴏ (2) *v-tr* cause, make *pirrki wayinthi* 'to break (something) into pieces' ᴛᴍ

wayirrinthi [wayi-rri-nthi] *v-intr* move, turn around, be shaken, tremble ᴛs, ᴡʏ, ᴡɪ

wayi-wayirrinthi [wayi-wayi-rri-nthi] *v-intr* move or shake violently ᴛᴍ

wayita *n* root (plant) ᴛs, ᴛᴍ

wayu *n* tree (like stringybark) ᴛs

widlanthi [widla-nthi] (var. **wilanthi**) *v-tr* gnaw; eat; tear off (with teeth) ᴛᴍ

widlu (var. **wilu**) *n* person whose sibling is dead ᴛᴍ

widni *n* (1) sinew ᴛs, ᴛᴍ, ᴡʏ (2) thread, cotton for sewing ᴛs, ᴡʏ

widnurru *adj* elastic; strong; tenacious ᴛᴍ

wiilta *n* pipe; tube ᴡʏ

wiini *n* snapper (fish) (*Chrysophrys auratus*) ᴡɪ

Wiiwilti *n* boy's name (uncertain) ᴡʏ

wika *n* (1) net *kuya wika* 'fishing net' ᴛs, ᴛᴍ (2) internet ɴᴇᴡ

wikaparntu [wika-parntu] *n* netball ɴᴇᴡ

wikapulthu [wika-pulthu] *n* website ɴᴇᴡ

wikatyi *n* men's net bag (men's) ᴛs, ᴛᴍ, ᴡɪ, ᴄᴀ, ᴋᴏ

wikarnti *n* man whose children are dead ᴛs, ᴛᴍ

wikinthi [wiki-nthi] (var. **wiki-wikinthi**) *v-tr* (1) throw down, put down (something) ᴛs, ᴛᴍ (2) shake the head ᴛs, ᴛᴍ (3) find fault with, despise, look down on (something) *Ninku warra pulthurna ngathu wikiwiki-utha. Wakinha pia witintya nintu pudlurri-apintu.* 'I will despise your empty words. Perhaps you speak evil (of them).' ᴛs, ᴛᴍ

wikirrinthi [wiki-rri-nthi] *v-intr* shake (oneself); throw (oneself) ᴛs, ᴛᴍ

wila *n* dust ᴡɪ

wilampa *n* yellow-tailed black cockatoo ᴛs, ᴛᴍ, ɢᴀ, ᴄᴀ

wilanthi => **widlanthi**

wili *n* chest (animal's) ᴛs, ᴛᴍ

wili kurntanthi [wili kurnta-nthi] *v-tr* divide a kangaroo ᴛs

wilpilpa *n* whistling ᴛs

wilpilpayinthi [wilp(a)-(w)ilpa-(w)ayi-nthi] *v-intr* whistle ᴛs

wilta *adj* (1) hard, firm, tenacious ᴛs, ᴛᴍ, ᴡʏ (2) tight *Wilta manmantu!* 'Tie it tighter!' ᴛs (3) correct *warra wilta* 'speaking properly, correct language' ᴛs, ᴛᴍ

wilta warra *n* terminology, jargon ɴᴇᴡ

wilta-itpurla [wilta-(pa)itpurla] *n* butter ɴᴇᴡ

wiltangaru [wilta-ngami-ngaru] *n* cheese ɴᴇᴡ

wiltarnapinthi [wilta-rni-(w)api-nthi] *v-tr* make firm; settle; cause to stay put *Yaku padlu wardli wiltarni- apinthi. Iyantu marnkuta.* 'He doesn't have a settled home. He likes to visit.' ₜₘ

   wiltarninthi [wilta-rni-nthi] *v-intr* be/become hard, firm, strong, determined *mii wiltarninthi* 'fix your eye on something, pay close attention' ₜₛ,ₜₘ

   wilta mankurrinthi [wilta manku-rri-nthi] stick close together, be packed tight ₜₘ

   wiltatinarrinthi [wilta-tina-rri-nthi] *v-intr* be/feel insecure ɴᴇᴡ

wilti-apinthi [wilti-(w)api-nthi] *v-tr* keep; lay aside; preserve; hide away ₜₘ

   wilti-tharralyi *n* cupboard ɴᴇᴡ

wiltirrkapinthi [wiltirrk(a)-(w)api-nthi] *v-tr* **(1)** surprise, shock, give a fright to (someone) *Wiltirrki-apirti ngu!* 'Don't frighten (the horse)!' ₜₛ,ₜₘ **(2)** (cause someone to) hide, conceal (themselves) ₜₘ

   wiltirrkarrinthi [wiltirrka-rri-nthi] *v-intr* be surprised ɴᴇᴡ

   wiltirrkayapinthi [wiltirrk(a)-(w)ay(i)-(w)api-nthi] *v-tr* frighten ₜₘ

   wiltirrkayinthi [wiltirrka-(wa)yi-nthi] *v-intr* **(1)** get a shock, take fright ₜₘ **(2)** hide, conceal (oneself) ₜₛ

wiltya-wiltyarrinthi [wiltya-wiltya-rri-nthi] *v-intr* be weak ₜₘ

   wiltya-iltyarri-purka [wiltya-(w)iltya-rri-purka] *n* weak person; someone who tires easily ₜₘ

wilu => **widlu**

wiluku *n* sound; percussion (in Kaurna music) ₜₘ

wiluti *n* gully ᴡɪ

wilya *n* foliage, leaves, young branches ₜₛ,ₜₘ,ɢᴀ

   wilya-kurntarti [wilya-kurnta-rti] *n, adj* beaten with branches (initiation stage) ₜₛ,ₜₘ,ᴇʏ

   wilyaru *n* young man (initiation stage) ₜₛ,ₜₘ,ᴇʏ

wilyu => **wityu**

wimari *n* bullroarer ₜₛ,ₜₘ,ᴄᴀ

winaityinaityi [winaity(i)-(w)inaityi] *n* birds; poultry ₜₛ

winana *n* native cockroach ᴡʏ,ᴋᴏ

wingku *n* breath, lungs *Wingku ngai tarta.* 'The breath stopped me.' ₜₛ,ₜₘ,ᴡʏ,ᴘɪ,ɢᴀ

   wingku kadlarninthi [wingku kadla-rni-nthi] *v-intr* experience interrupted breathing ₜₘ

   wingku marnirninthi [wingku marni-rni-nthi] *v-intr* **(1)** become content, calm, quiet *Nata ngai wingku marnini ngunukuntyanta ngathu wapithi; kuinyurnithama* 'Now I am content with what I have done, if I die.' ₜₘ **(2)** be pleased with, get a liking for, enjoy (something) ₜₘ

   wingku ngarnta-arntarrinthi [wingku ngarnta-(ng)arnta-rri-nthi] *v-intr* groan; moan ₜₘ

   wingku padminthi [wingku padmi-nthi] *v-intr* breathe quickly ₜₛ,ₜₘ

   wingku parlta-parltarrinthi [wingku parlta-parlta-rri-nthi] *v-intr* wish; long for; desire ₜₘ

   wingku parltarrinthi [wingku parlta-rri-nthi] *v-intr* die ʀᴏ

   wingku patirrinthi [wingku pati-rri-nthi] *v-intr* breathe; respire ₜₛ,ₜₘ,ᴡʏ

   wingku puntunthi [wingku puntu-nthi] *v-tr* blow into; inflate ₜₘ

   wingku tikanthi [wingku tika-nthi] *v-intr* **(1)** want, long for, desire *Parnukuntya ngai wingku tikanthi wirnta- ana. Paintya ngai yungkuntu!* 'I want his spear. Give me that one!' ₜₘ **(2)** be irritated, cross *Ngaityu wingkungka pirrku tikatha.* 'I will be really cross.' ₜₘ

   wingku warunthi [wingku waru-nthi] *v-intr* breathe heavily ₜₘ

   wingku yungkunthi [wingku yungku-nthi] *v-tr* stir up; irritate; aggravate; challenge *Turla wingkungka padlu wingku yungkutha.* 'He will make them really angry.' ₜₘ

   wingku-wingku *adj* irritable; sensitive; angry; grouchy; cross; cranky *Wingku-wingkurti!* 'Don't be cranky!' *Wingku-wingku tarrinthi pa.* 'He has gotten cross.' ₜₛ,ₜₘ

   wingku-wingkurlinthi [wingku-wingku-rli-nthi] *v-intr* groan; moan ₜₘ

   wingku-wingkurninthi [wingku-wingku-rni-nthi] *v-intr* become angry, irritated, violent ₜₘ

   wingku-wingkurru [wingku-wingku-rru] *adj, adv* angrily; violently *Wingku-wingkurru pa murinthi.* 'He has a bad temper.' ₜₛ,ₜₘ

   wingku-wingkurtarrinthi [wingku-wingku-rta-rri-nthi] *v-intr* stop breathing; die ₜₘ

   wingkungka [wingku-ngka] *n* place where someone dies ᴡʏ

   wingkura *n* wave *yarlu wingkura* 'surf of the sea' ᴡɪ

wininthi [wini-nthi] *v-intr* go; walk; travel (Rapid Bay dialect) ₜₛ,ₜₘ,ᴡʏ,ᴋᴏ,ᴄʜ

winpirra (var. **winpirri**) *n* whistle; flute; pipe (music) ₜₛ,ₜₘ

winta (var. **wintha**) *n* **(1)** owl ɴᴇᴡ **(2)** Eastern barn owl (*Tyto delicatula*) ₜₛ,ₜₘ,ᴡʏ,ᴄᴏ

wintunthi [wintu-nthi] *v-tr* make shaving motions;

smooth the surface of a spear ᴛᴍ

winturrinthi [wintu-rri-nthi] *v-tr* draw back; pull back ᴛs,ᴛᴍ

wirangka [wira-ngka] *loc* between; amongst; under *tutha wirangka* 'in, amongst the straw' *Wirangkadlu pamarriutha.* 'We will spear amongst each other' ᴛᴍ

wira-wirangka [wira-wira-ngka] *adv* because of; for the sake of; on account of; about ᴛs

wiranthi [wira-nthi] *v-tr* make yellow or yellowish-brownish ᴛᴍ

wiranirana [wira-n(a)-(w)ira-na] (1) *adj* yellow; yellowish-brownish ᴛs,ᴛᴍ (2) *n* yellow ochre ɴᴇᴡ

wiranirana kuya [wira-n(a)-(w)ira-na kuya] *n* goldfish *(Carassius auratus)* ɴᴇᴡ

wirarrinthi [wira-rri-nthi] *v-intr* turn yellow or brown (due to smoke, urine etc) ᴛᴍ

wirdupa *n* cockatiel ᴛs,ᴛᴍ,ᴡʏ,ᴄᴏ

wiri *n* shoulder blade, scapula *Wirirlaku wartingka pultha warta.* 'The 'pultha warta' is between the shoulder blades.' ᴛs,ᴛᴍ,ᴡʏ

wirila *adv* quickly; fast ᴛs,ᴛᴍ,ᴡʏ,ᴡɪ,ʀᴏ

wiri-wirila very quickly ᴛᴍ

wirka *n* dog ᴛᴍ

wirka wari a dog's tail ᴛᴍ

wirltu *n* (1) wedge-tailed eagle *(Aquila audax)* ᴛs,ᴛᴍ,ᴡʏ,ᴄᴏ,ʀᴏ (2) constellation indicating Spring ᴛs,ᴛᴍ,ᴋᴏ

Wirltu Tidna *n* Southern Cross constellation ɴᴇᴡ (inspired by Adnyamathanha *Wirldu Mantaawi* 'eagle's foot')

wirltu yarlu *n* sea eagle ɴᴇᴡ

wirltu-ngaru *n* tuft of eagle feathers (ceremony) ᴛs,ᴛᴍ

Wirltuthidnamiyu [wirltu-thidna-miyu] *n* Australian person; Southern Cross person ɴᴇᴡ

Wirltuthidnayarta [wirltu-thidna-yarta] *n* Australia (land of the Southern Cross) ɴᴇᴡ

wirltuti [wirltu-ti] (var. **wirluti**) *n* Spring (season) ᴛs,ᴛᴍ

wirnta *n* spear ᴛs,ᴡʏ,ᴄᴀ,ᴡɪ,ᴋᴏ

wirra₁ *n* forest; bush; grove ᴛs,ᴛᴍ

witawirra *n* a stand of Peppermint Gum trees ᴛs

wirra₂ *n* fight; battle *wirrana* 'to the fight' *wirrangka* 'because, on account of the fight' ᴛᴍ

wirraitya *n* dust; dust cloud; whirlwind (dust) ᴛs,ᴛᴍ,ᴡɪ

Wirramiyu [wirra-miyu] *n* person from 'Wirra' tribe (Ngadjuri person) ᴛs,ᴀɴ

Wirramu *n* Encounter Bay *Wirramukana* 'to Encounter Bay' *Wirramula* 'in or at Encounter Bay' ᴛᴍ (from Ramindjeri *Ramu*)

Wirramumiyu *n* person from Encounter Bay ᴛᴍ

wirrangku *n* borrowed object ᴛᴍ

wirrapi *n* sugar glider *(Petaurus breviceps)* ᴛs,ᴛᴍ,ᴡʏ,ᴡɪ

wirrarrinthi [wirra-rri-nthi] (var. **witharrinthi**) *v-intr* (1) be tired; lazy; fatigued ᴛᴍ,ᴛs,ᴡʏ (2) be withdrawn, concealed ᴛᴍ

wirrarri-purka [wirra-rri-purka] *n* lazy person; tired person ᴛs

wirri *n* (1) stick/club (for throwing) ᴛs,ᴛᴍ,ᴡʏ,ᴄᴀ,ᴡɪ,ᴘɪ (2) clapstick ᴘɪ (3) golf club ɴᴇᴡ

wirrilayinthi [wirri-(w)ayi-nthi] *v-intr* quiver; shake; tremble ᴛs

wirri (1)

wirringka [wirri-ngka] *adv* together; in common with ᴛs,ᴛᴍ

wirrka *n* liquid; moisture; fluid ᴛs

wirrkanthi [wirrka-nthi] *v-tr* (1) wash, clean, wipe, rub (something) ᴛs,ᴛᴍ,ᴡʏ (2) brush, scratch (something) ᴛs (3) prepare an animal skin by rubbing it and softening or breaking its fibres with a stone ᴛᴍ

wirrkarrinthi [wirrka-rri-nthi] *v-intr* wash (oneself); clean (oneself); brush (oneself) ᴛs,ᴛᴍ

wirrkarriti [wirrka-rri-ti] *n* brush ᴛs

wirrkati [wirrka-ti] (var. **wirrkiti**) *n* designs on animal skins ᴡʏ

wirrkuta *adj* active; diligent; lively *Ngai manti nguya, wirrkuta padni.* 'I am not sick, I am active/lively.' ᴛs,ᴛᴍ

wirrkutaiyinthi [wirrkuta-(wa)iyi-nthi] *v-intr* (1) be active, lively, brisk ᴛs,ᴛᴍ (2) be quick, industrious, diligent in your work ᴛᴍ

wirrkutarninthi [wirrkuta-rni-nthi] *v-intr* become active, diligent, lively ᴛᴍ

wirru-angkanthi [wirru-(k)angka-nthi] *v-tr* pass by ᴛᴍ

wirru-wirru padninthi [wirru-wirru padni-nthi] *v-intr* go around; take the long way around ᴛᴍ

wirru-wirrungka [wirru-wirru-ngka] *adv* in passing; nearby ᴛᴍ

wirrumanthi [wirru-ma-nthi] *v-tr* divide in two; part in two ᴛᴍ

wirrunthi [wirru-nthi] *v-tr* (1) saw ᴛs,ᴛᴍ,ᴋᴏ,ᴡʏ,ᴡɪ (2) shave, plane (something) (e.g. a piece of wood) ᴛs,ᴛᴍ (3) make long shaving or scraping movements as when smoothing a spear with a piece of glass ᴛᴍ (4) pull ᴛs

wirnta

wirru-arninthi [wirru-(alya)-rni-nthi] (var. **wirru-alyarninthi**) *v-intr* continue sawing, shaving or planing (e.g. wood) *tirntu karlangka wirru-alyarninthi* 'to continue sawing wood in the heat of the sun' ᴛᴍ

wirrupa *n* row; line ᴛꜱ

wirrupa murinthi go in a line, one after the other ᴛᴍ

wirti => **-rti**

wita *n* peppermint gum tree ᴛꜱ,ᴛᴍ,ᴡʏ,ᴡɪ

witharrinthi => **wirrarrinthi**

witi (1) *adj* large ᴛꜱ (2) *adv* very, much ᴛꜱ (3) *adv* quickly, ably, well ᴛꜱ

witi-witinthi [witi-witi-nthi] *v-tr* want; desire; demand; lust for *Padlu witi-witinthi ngaityu inha yangarra.* 'He lusts after this wife of mine.' ᴛᴍ

witkalya wear a cloak (so as to carry a baby) ᴄᴀ

witu *n* (1) rush, reed *Witungga* 'in the reeds, a placename' ᴛꜱ,ᴛᴍ,ᴡɪ,ʙʟ,ᴄᴀ (2) light spear made from a reed ᴄᴀ (3) straw ɴᴇᴡ

witu pamanthi [witu pama-nthi] sew ᴡʏ

witu-thurlu [witu-thurlu] (var. **witu-thurdlu**) *n* (1) anything cylindrical in shape ᴛꜱ (2) telescope ᴛꜱ (3) flute ᴛꜱ

witu

witu-witu *n* (1) head ornament (described in a variety of ways) ᴛꜱ,ᴡʏ,ᴄᴀ (2) bullroarer ᴀɴ

wityarninthi [witya-rni-nthi] *v-intr* (1) become thinner or smaller; wither away ᴛꜱ,ᴛᴍ (2) fade ᴛꜱ

wityu (var. **wilyu**) (see also: **wauwi-wityu**) *n* (1) bone ornament or tool (kangaroo); awl (bone) ᴛꜱ,ᴛᴍ,ᴡʏ,ᴄᴀ (2) needle ᴛꜱ (3) pin ᴛꜱ (4) nail ᴛꜱ

witu-witu (1)

wiwunthi [wiwu-nthi] *v-tr* annoy; tease; pinch ᴛꜱ,ᴛᴍ

wiwudla-wudla [wiwu-dla-(wi)wu-dla] (var. **wiwudli-wudla**) *adj* annoying; teasing ᴛꜱ,ᴛᴍ

wiwurra [wiwu-rra] *n* crowd ᴛꜱ,ᴛᴍ

wiwurrinthi [wiwu-rri-nthi] *v-tr* annoy, tease or pinch (each other) *Wiwurringurti!* 'Don't annoy me!' ᴛꜱ,ᴛᴍ

wityu(2)

wiwurriti [wiwu-rri-ti] *n* (1) annoyance; irritation ᴛꜱ,ᴛᴍ (2) quarrel; squabble ᴛꜱ,ᴛᴍ

wuingki *adj* weak *Pilta wuingki niina.* 'You are weak.' ᴛᴍ

wuinpanthi [wuinpa-nthi] (var. **wuingpanthi**) *v-tr* challenge; demand something *Wakinha'rna, ngathu wuinpanthi.* 'They are bad, I challenge (them).' *Ngathu parna ngaityu yungarna mankutha. Yaku pia parna pilyarniutha. Wuingpatha ngai parna, ngaityu yungarna.* 'I will help them, (they are) my brothers. Perhaps they will not be content. They (my brothers) will challenge or make demands of me.' ᴛᴍ

wuinpa-wuinpanthi [wuinpa-wuinpa-nthi] (var. **wuingpa-wuingparrinthi**) *v-intr* be enraged, very angry ᴛꜱ

wuinpa-wuinparri-purka [wuinpa-wuinpa-rri-purka] (var. **wuingpa-wuingparri-purka**) *n* angry person; furious person ᴛꜱ,ᴛᴍ

wuinparrinthi [wuinpa-rri-nthi] *v-intr* challenge (each other) ᴛᴍ

wuintyi *adv* perhaps; maybe *wuintyi'ai yangadli padnitha.* 'Perhaps I will go afterwards.' *Niina pa pia wuintyi pudna-utha? – Ngai pia pudnautha.* 'When will you perhaps come again? – I may perhaps come.' ᴛꜱ,ᴛᴍ

wuumi *n* worm ɴᴇᴡ (from English 'worm')

wuwuthiyadlu *n* kangaroo tooth (head ornament) ᴄᴀ

Y y

wuwuthiyadlu

yailtyanthi [yailtya-nthi] *v-tr* believe; think; suppose *Yailtyarringurti!* 'Don't believe it!' *Kurntanana purla yailtyarrithi.* 'They both thought that the other had been killed.' (var. **yailtyarrinthi**) ᴛꜱ,ᴛᴍ

yaintya *loc, dem* right here; this *Yaintya ngaityu nintu paki?* 'Is this one mine that you've cut?' *Yaintya tau-arra turlarninthi pulyurna miyurnalitya.* 'He is very angry with the black men.' *Yaintya tikanthi ngadlu, parnu iyaintya pa wangkathi pudnatitya.* 'We will sit here, he said he would come here.' *Yaintya!* 'Here I am!' *Yaintyanti wardli* 'Right here is the camping spot.' *Yaintya pudna-ina yalarra, ngadlu naki.* 'He has come just now, we have seen (him).' ᴛᴍ

yaintyanti just here, right here ᴛᴍ

yaintyarrinthi [yaintya-rri-nthi] *v-intr* be here, present (person) ᴛᴍ

yaitya (var. **iyaitya**) (see also: **irdi**) (1) *adj* indigenous, native, own *yaitya miyu* 'indigenous person' *yaitya warra* 'one's own language, vernacular' *yaityarna* 'native people' ᴛꜱ,ᴛᴍ (2) *adj* fresh, proper *yaitya kauwi* 'proper (fresh) water' ᴛꜱ (3) *adv* independently; without being forced; of one's own will *Yaitya parni.* '(He) came of his own accord.' *Yaitya yurlu ngathu yarltinthi.* 'On my own accord I forbid them.' *Yaitya* *yurluna pirrkapinana.* 'He has shot them of his own accord.' *Nintu piti yaitya yurlu warrapanthi.* 'You speak first on your own accord.' ᴛᴍ

Yaitya Wangirntu [(i)ya-itya wang(u)-(th)irntu] *n* NAIDOC Week ɴᴇᴡ

yaitya-kuinyu *adj* cheeky; rude ᴛs

Yaityirntu [(i)ya-ity(a)-(th)irntu] *n* National Aboriginal and Torres Strait Islanders Day ɴᴇᴡ

yaka! *intj* oh no! damn! (expression of aversion) *yaka manya* 'Be off rain!' *yaka manya* 'here is rain' ᴛs,ᴛᴍ,ʙʟ

yakalya! [yak(a)-alya] (var. **yaka-alya!**) *intj* sorry; oh dear!; alas!; oh no! ᴛs,ᴛᴍ

yakai! *intj* help!; hey! ɴᴇᴡ

yakaitya [yaka-itya] *intj* expression of anger or despair ᴛᴍ

yakaityayinthi [yaka-itya-(wa)yi-nthi] *v-intr* rage; lament; call out in anger or sadness ᴛᴍ

yakana (var. **yakanilya**) *n* older sister ᴛs,ᴛᴍ,ᴡʏ,ʙᴀ,ᴄʜ,ʀᴏ

yakanata [yakana-ta] *n* older sister relationship ᴛs,ᴛᴍ

yakanataurla [yakana-ta-(p)urla] two people in an older-younger sister relationship ᴛᴍ

yakanirna [yakana-rna] older sisters (plural) ᴛᴍ

yakanurla [yakan(a)-(p)urla] older sisters (dual) ᴛᴍ

yakanthi [yaka-nthi] (1) *v-intr* run ᴛs (2) *v-tr* chase, hunt, pursue (something) *yakaninyana* 'having been chased' ᴛs,ᴛᴍ

yakalakala [yaka-l(a)-(y)aka-la] *n* chaser ᴛᴍ

yakarninthi [yaka-rni-nthi] *v-intr* run around ᴛᴍ

yakarri-apinthi [yaka-rri-(w)api-nthi] *v-tr* make someone run *kadlirna niina yakarri-apituwayi ...* 'lest the dogs make you run ...' ᴛᴍ

yakarrinthi [yaka-rri-nthi] *v-intr* run; chase *turla yakarrinthi* 'run to fight' ᴛs,ᴛᴍ

yaki (1) *adj, adv* deep; low *yaki yapa* 'a deep hole' *Yaki kukantu!* 'Dig deeply!' ᴛᴍ,ᴛs (2) *n* valley; deep place *narnu yakingka* 'in the pine valley' ᴛs

yaki-arlti [yaki-(y)arlti] *adj* deeper *ninku wardli yaki-arlti* 'deeper than your house' ᴛᴍ

yaki-arra [yaki-arra] *adv* deeply *yaki-arra wanganthi* 'to speak to yourself silently, to meditate' ᴛᴍ

yaki-thukutya [yaki-thuku-tya] *n* soul; spirit ᴛs

yakingka [yaki-ngka] *loc* (1) under, below, behind *Wikatyi yakingka pa wantinthi.* 'It's under the net bag.' ᴛs,ᴛᴍ (2) in the depths ᴛᴍ

yakinhainguta [yaki-nhaingu-ta] *n* soft centre of bread ᴛs

yakintyarla [yaki-intyarla] (var. **yakinyarlu**) *adj* deeper; lower ᴛs,ᴛᴍ

yaku *adv* not; no *Yaku'athu naki.* 'I have not seen (it) / I do not know.' ᴛs,ᴛᴍ,ᴡɪ,ᴡʏ

yaku-alya! *intj* don't!; please don't! ᴛᴍ

yaku-anta! [yaku-anta] *intj* not at all! (emphatic) ᴛᴍ

yakuntyanthi [yaku-ntya-nthi] *v-intr* not do something anymore; stop doing something; quit ᴛᴍ

yakurni [yaku-rni] *adv* not at all ᴛᴍ

yaku *n* (1) gum (made from sap), resin *narnu yaku* 'gum from the native pine' ᴛs,ᴛᴍ (2) traditional knife (made using this gum) ᴛs

yala (1) *n* day ᴛᴍ (2) *temp* today ᴛᴍ

yala-tharrkarri [yala-tharrka-rri] (var. **yalarrkarri**; **yalta-tharrkarri**) *temp* tomorrow; day after tomorrow ᴛs,ᴛᴍ

yalaka (var. **yaltaka**) *temp* (1) now, today, at the moment, present (time) ᴛs,ᴛᴍ (2) yesterday ᴛᴍ,ᴡʏ,ʙʟ

yalakanta [yalaka-nta] *temp* just now ᴛs,ᴛᴍ

yalakarra [yalaka-(a)rra] *temp* lately; just now ᴛᴍ,ᴡʏ

yalakiana *adj* new; fresh ᴛs

yalakinyanta [yalak(a)-in(t)ya-nta] (var. **yaltakinyanta**) *temp* just now *Yalakinyanta ngai pudni.* 'I have come just now.' ᴛᴍ

yalarra [yala-(a)rra] *temp* a little while ago; earlier (today) ᴛs,ᴛᴍ,ᴡʏ,ᴡɪ

yala-yalarra [yala-yala-(a)rra] a short while ago ᴛᴍ

yalarraintyarlu [yala-(a)rra-intya-rlu] *temp* not long ago; a little while ago *Nala-alati ngurluntya yalarraintyarlu kumpathi?* 'When did he (just now?) go away?' ᴛᴍ

yalarrairdlu [yala-(a)rra-idlu] *temp* now; just now ᴛᴍ

yalartangka [yala-(na)rta-ngka] *temp* during the day; in the course of the day ᴛᴍ

yalatya [yala-itya] *temp* yesterday ᴡɪ

yala-wilya *n* fish scale ᴡɪ

yalampapatu *n* initiation stage ᴇʏ

yalka *n* onion ɴᴇᴡ (from Central Australian languages 'bush onion')

yaltanthi [yalta-nthi] *v-tr* mistake ᴡʏ

yaltinthi [yalta-nthi] *v-intr* be/become cool; cool down *Karla yaltingku.* 'The fire will cool down.' ᴛs,ᴛᴍ

yalta-yalta *adj* cool; fresh; airy ᴛs,ᴛᴍ

yaltana [yalta-na] *adj* fresh; airy; cool ᴛs,ᴛᴍ

yalti-apinthi [yalti-(w)api-nthi] *v-tr* cool (something) down ᴛs,ᴛᴍ

yaltu *n* pelican *(Pelecanus conspicillatus)* TS, CO

yalura *adj* perfect; whole; complete TM

yama (var. **yamayama**₁) *adj* (1) stupid, silly, foolish, ignorant, imprudent *Yama-yamarti!* 'Don't be silly!' TS, TM (2) disobedient, stubborn, rude *Yama-yamarti!* 'Don't be stubborn!' TM

    yama partana *n* stupid person; foolish person TM

    yama pintyanthi [yama pintya-nthi] *v-tr* persuade TM

    yama yungkunthi [yama yungku-nthi] *v-intr* lament TM

yamarninthi [yama-rni-nthi] (var. **yamarntinthi**) *v-intr* (1) become stupid, silly, foolish *Yamarnti-ntyana!* 'You have become quite silly!' TS, TM (2) become disobedient, rude, dissatisfied TS, TM

yamarrinthi [yama-rri-nthi] *v-intr* (1) be stupid, foolish, ignorant TS, TM (2) be disobedient, rude, stubborn, obstinate TS

yamayama [yama-yama] *n* doctor; teacher; sorcerer; traditional healer TS, TM, CA

yamaru (var. **yama-yama**) *n* bag (for supplies) TS, TM

yampina *n* widower TS, TM, WY, WI

yampu *n* dolphin TS, WI, WY

yangadli *temp* later; afterwards; in future *Yangadli niina warrapatha.* '(I) will speak with you later.' *yangadlituwayi* 'lest it be too late' TS, TM, BL, WY

    yangadlinti [yangadli-nti] *temp* not now; later TS, TM

    yangadlitya [yangadli-(i)tya] *adj* for the future TS, TM

yangarra *n* wife (wife) *yangarrila wantinthi* 'to lie with your wife' *ngaityu yangarra* 'my woman or wife' TS, TM, BA, BL, WY

    yangarra-tidli (var. **yangarra'idli**) *adj* married (man) TS, TM

    yangarranti-apinthi [yangarra-nti-(w)api-nthi] *v-tr* make someone your wife TM

    yangarrantinthi [yangarra-nti-nthi] *v-intr* become a wife TM

    yangarrataurla [yangarra-ta-(p)urla] *n* husband and wife; two wives (with the same husband) TM

    yangarru-tana [yangarra-tina] *adj* unmarried (man) TS, TM

yanta => **yarnta**₂

yantu *n* visit *yantu wayinthi* 'make a visit' TM, TS

yantu-apinthi [yantu-(w)api-nthi] *v-tr* visit (someone) TM

yantupina [yantu-pina] *n* a frequent visitor, parasite TM

yapa *n* hole; burrow; den *yapangka* 'in the hole' TS, TM, WY

    yapa-yaparri [yapa-yapa-rri] *n* burrowing animal TM

    yapangka yaparnapinthi [yapa-ngka yapa-rn(i)-(w)api-nthi] *v-tr* make a hole through TM

    yaparrinthi [yapa-rri-nthi] *v-tr* split wood WY

yaparra [yapa-rra] *adj* light (weight) TM

yara (1) *adj, adv* different, distinct, separate *yara warrarla* '(two) different words' *Yara wanti' adli* 'Let's sleep separately (i.e. Let's sleep apart)' *Yara yukungka ngadli pudni.* 'The two of us arrived in different ships.' *Yara ngangkidla purlaku.* 'Those two have different mothers.' TS, TM (2) *adj, adv* both, each other, reciprocally *Yara ngadli yungkurri.* 'We have exchanged (with each other).' *Yara pungkurri'adli!* 'Let's fight each other!' *yara marta- nungkurrinthi* 'to accuse each other' *Yara pamarri'ngadli* 'Let us two spear each other.' *Yara martanungkurrinthi puingurru-itya* 'They reproach each other on account of the puingurru' TS (3) *n* white of an egg WI, ST

    yara kati-katinthi [yara kati-kati-nthi] *v-tr* scatter; separate TM

    yara parltarrinthi [yara parlta-rri-nthi] (var. **yara parlta-parltarrinthi**) *v-intr* separate from each other TM

    yara-arta-artarninthi [yara (k)arta-(k)arta-rni-nthi] *v-intr* separate (oneself); scatter (oneself) TM

    yara-kartarta [yara-kart(a)-(k)arta] *adj* separate; scattered; disorderly; random (at) TS, TM

    yarakayinthi [yarak(a)-(w)ayi-nthi] *v-intr* separate into groups TM

    yaramanthi [yara-ma-nthi] *v-tr* divide; separate *Papilinungku warrarna yarama.* 'From Babel the languages were divided.' TM

    yaranta [yara-nta] *adj* not together; separately *yaranta pamanthi* 'bordering, meeting, touching (e.g. two countries)' *Yarantarla katitha purla.* 'They (two) will each fetch (something) separately.' TM

yararrinthi [yara-rri-nthi] *v-intr* be uncertain, undecided *Ngai wanti yararrinth'ai?* 'Where shall I go to? I'm undecided.' *Pia wanti pia? Purlaityi ngathu taparla muiyu mankunthi, yararrinth'ai.* 'Where shall I go? I like both roads. I am undecided.' *Pia ngaintya pia, yararrinth'ai* 'Whatever it is, I am uncertain' TS, TM

yamaru

Yaraitya [yara-itya] *n* birth-order name: second born (male) ₜₛ

yarapurla [yara-purla] *num* four ₜₛ,ₜₘ,ᵥᵧ

  yarapurla kuma [yara-purla kuma] *num* five ₜₛ

  yarapurla partirrka [yara-purla part(u)-irrka] *num* four hundred ₙₑᵥᵥ

  yarapurla purlaityi [yara-purla purlaityi] *num* six ₜₛ

  yarapurlarluku [yara-purla-rluku] *adv* four times ₜₛ,ₜₘ

  yarapurlawata [yara-purl(a)-(th)awata] *num* four thousand ₙₑᵥᵥ

  Yarapurliki [yara-purl(a)-(p)iki] *n* April ₙₑᵥᵥ

  Yarapurlirntu [yara-purl(a)-(th)irntu] *n* Thursday ₙₑᵥᵥ

  yarapurlirrka [yara-purl(a)-irrka] *num* forty ₙₑᵥᵥ

  yarapurliwurra [yara-purl(a)-(w)iwurra] *num* four million ₙₑᵥᵥ

Yarartu [yar(a)-(k)artu] *n* birth-order name: second born (female) ᵥᵧ

yariru => **yaru**

yarku *n* leg; shin; lower leg ₜₛ,ₜₘ,ᵥᵧ,ᵥᵢ,ₑₐ,ɢₐ,ₖₒ

  yarku kati-katinthi [yarku kati-kati-nthi] *v-intr* stretch your legs out (one on top of the other) ₜₘ

  yarku ngaitya *adj* weak-legged; not good at travelling on foot ₜₛ,ₜₘ

  yarku-ana [yarku-ana-(purla)] (var. **yarku-anaurla**) *n* pants; trousers ₜₛ,ₜₘ,ᵥᵧ

  yarku-paltha *n* stockings ₜₛ,ₜₘ

  yarkunta [yarku-nta] *n* (1) prop, pillar, support ₜₛ,ₜₘ (2) neck ₜₘ

yarla *n* calf (leg) ₜₘ

  yarla-marta *adv* coil ₜₛ

  yarla-marta tikanthi [yarla-marta tika-nthi] *v-intr* sit with your legs folded underneath you ₜₛ,ₜₘ

  yarla-muka *n* calf muscle (leg) ₜₛ,ᵥᵧ

  yarlata *n* legs (dual) ₜₘ

  yarlatitya [yarla-ta-itya] *adv* on the legs ₜₘ

yarli *n* man; male ₜₛ,ₜₘ,ᵥᵧ

  Yarli Tirntu [yarli-t(a)-(th)irntu] (var. **Yarlirntu**) *n* Father's Day *Ngunya Yarli Tirntu!* 'Happy Father's Day!' ₙₑᵥᵥ

  yarli-miyu *n* father ₜₛ,ₜₘ

  yarli-yarliwarta [yarli-yarli-warta] *n* people in a father relationship ₜₘ

  yarlina [yarli-na] *n* husband *yarlinukana* '(going) to the husband' *yarlinila wantinthi* 'to lie with your husband' ₜₛ,ₜₘ,ᵥᵧ,ʙₐ,ʙʟ,ᴘɪ

  yarlinidli [yarlin(a)-(t)idli] (var. **yarlina-tidli**) *adj* married (woman) ₜₘ

  yarlinu-tana [yarlina-tina] *adj* unmarried (woman) ₜₛ,ₜₘ

  yarlipurka [yarli-purka] *n* son; male child ₜₛ,ₜₘ

  yarlita [yarli-ta] *n* (1) father ₜₛ,ₜₘ (2) great-grandfather, ancestor ᵥᵧ

  yarlita-urla [yarli-ta-(p)urla] *n* father and child (dual) ₜₘ

  yarlitatila [yarli-ta-ila] father (with/at the) ₜₘ

yarltinthi [yarlti-nthi] (var. **yarltirrinthi**) *v-tr* (1) advise, persuade, command (someone) ₜₛ,ₜₘ (2) forbid, prohibit (someone) *Yarltirrintith'ai.* 'I will only continue to forbid them.' ₜₘ

  yarltirri-purka [yarlti-rri-purka] *n* counseller; adviser; commander ₜₛ

yarlu *n* sea; lake ₜₛ,ᵥᵧ

yarna *adj* naked; bald ₜₘ

yarna-yarna *n* undulating ground ᵥᵧ

yarnaki *n* owl species ₜₛ

yarnka *n* beard ₜₛ,ₜₘ

yarnkanthi [yarnka-nthi] *v-tr* (1) hang on to, join, depend on (someone) *Miyungka pa yarnki.* 'He's a hanger on.' *Miyu tarrangka pa yarnki.* 'He attached himself to someone.' *Miyu ngaringka pa yarnki* 'He forced himself upon the person.' ₜₛ,ₜₘ (2) infect (someone) *Naalityanungku parna yarnki.* 'They got it from you (plural).' *Tidla ngangki-ityanungku ngai yarnki.* 'I was infected from Tidla's mother.' ₜₛ,ₜₘ

  yarnka-yarnkanya [yarnka-yarnka-nya] *adj* (1) hanging *taa yarnka-yarnkanya* 'sulky' ₜₛ (2) infectious *yarnka- yarnkanya kuku* 'an infectious disease' ₜₛ,ₜₘ

  yarnkapinthi [yarnka-(wa)pi-nthi] *v-tr* (1) hang (something) up ₜₛ,ₜₘ (2) infect (someone) ₜₛ

yarnkurru *n* relative (uncertain – perhaps older sister) *Parni manmantu, pilyuniutha ninku yarnkurru.* 'Persuade your 'yarnkurru' to give it to me!' ₜₘ

yarnpana *n* (1) purple ochre ₜₛ,ₜₘ (2) purple ₙₑᵥᵥ

yarnta₁ *adj* large; wide *kuru yarnta* 'a large pot or container' ₜₛ

yarnta₂ (var. **yanta**) *loc* here; nearby *yarntangka* 'there below' ₜₛ,ₜₘ

  yarntaintya; yarntanya to here, to there *Yarntaintya parna wangkainama.* 'They have said (that they will come) towards here.' ₜₘ

  yarntarlu [yarnta-rlu] in this direction ₜₛ

  yarntarluntya? [yarnta-rlu-ntya] *inter* in this direction? ₜₛ

yarntarralika along upon this ᴛᴍ

yarnti *n* endive ᴡʏ

yarntuku *n* duck species ᴛꜱ

yarra [yarra-(yapa)] (var. **yarr'yapa**) *n* hollow at the back of knee; kneepit *(popliteal fossa)* ᴛꜱ,ᴛᴍ,ᴋᴏ

yarri (var. **yirri**) *n* pubic hair ᴛꜱ,ᴛᴍ

yarrkanthi [yarrka-nthi] *v-tr* stretch; level; spread out *yurinta ngaityu yarrka yarrkantu* 'Prepare me that skin.' ᴛᴍ

yarrki *n* animal (small, burrowing quadruped) ᴛꜱ,ᴛᴍ

    yarrki watpa cloak made from 'yarrki' skins ᴛꜱ,ᴛᴍ

yarru *adj* **(1)** wide ᴛꜱ,ᴛᴍ **(2)** torn up ᴛᴍ

    yarrunthi [yarru-nthi] *v-intr* talk too much; be a loudmouth ᴛᴍ

    yarrurri-apinthi [yarru-rri-(w)api-nthi] (var. **yirrurri-apinthi**) *v-tr* cause a breach, rupture or tear ᴛꜱ,ᴛᴍ

    yarrurrinthi [yarru-rri-nthi] *v-intr* **(1)** break apart, tear, separate violently, burst (something) ᴛꜱ,ᴛᴍ **(2)** expand, grow bigger ᴛᴍ

    yarrurriti [yarru-rri-ti] *n* tear; rupture ᴛꜱ,ᴛᴍ

yarta *n* land; earth; ground; soil; country *yartangka* 'on the ground' *yarta-ana* 'into or onto the ground' ᴛꜱ,ᴛᴍ,ᴡɪ,ᴡʏ,ʀᴏ,ᴋᴏ

    yarta ngatpanthi [yarta ngatpa-nthi] *v-tr* bury (in the ground) ᴡʏ

    yarta puku *n* bare ground ᴛꜱ,ᴛᴍ

    yarta turtu => **turtu**

    yarta-kungkurla *n* scorpion species (small) ᴛꜱ,ᴛᴍ

    Yarta-mitirntu [yarta-mit(i)-(th)irntu] *n* Proclamation Day ɴᴇᴡ

    yartala [yarta-la] *n* flood; overflowing river; inundation ᴛꜱ,ᴛᴍ

    yartamalyu [yarta-malyu] *n* slope; rise (hill); hillock ᴛꜱ

    yartamiyu *n* countryman; person from the same country as you ᴛꜱ,ᴡʏ

    yartanapinthi [yarta-n(a)-(w)api-nthi] *v-tr* press down; bend over; keep down ᴛᴍ

    yartangamaitya [yarta-ngama-itya] *n* countrywoman ᴡʏ

    yartapira [yarta-pira] *n* landform ɴᴇᴡ

    yartapirriti [yarta-pirri-ti] *n* **(1)** cricket (insect) ᴛꜱ,ᴛᴍ **(2)** cricket (sport) ɴᴇᴡ

    yartapurtu [yarta-purtu] *adj* dirty; full of dirt ᴛꜱ

    Yartapuulti [yarta-puulti] *n* land of the dead (Port Adelaide) ᴛᴍ

    yartanthi [yarta-nthi] *v-tr* bend; break; tear; lay down *Wirnta ngathu kurltu yarta.* 'I have broken the spear into pieces.' *Wirntarna yartanina. Nata padni'adlu.* 'The spears have been broken. Let's go now.' ᴛꜱ,ᴛᴍ,ᴋᴏ

    yartarninthi [yarta-rni-nthi] *v-intr* bend down; stoop *Yartarni, pardu nanga!* 'Stoop down and see the animal!' *Ngai nintaityangka kuntu yartarninthi.* 'I desire you.' ᴛᴍ

    yartarri-apinthi [yarta-rri-(w)api-nthi] *v-tr* break; break down (collapse) ᴛꜱ,ᴛᴍ

    yartarrinthi [yarta-rri-nthi] break, fracture, be broken ᴛᴍ,ᴛꜱ,ᴡʏ

yartati *n* knife ᴡʏ

yartpana [yart(a)-pa-na] *adj* flat; broad; smooth ᴛᴍ

    yartpanthi [yart(a)-pa-nthi] *v-tr* **(1)** smoothe, flatten (something) out *marlta yartpana* 'speaking incorrectly, not speaking fluently' ᴛᴍ **(2)** speak (Kaurna language) without the normal abbreviations and contractions that a fluent speaker would use. ᴛᴍ

yarta kurrurriti [yarta kurru-rri-ti] *n* year (uncertain) ᴛᴍ

yaru (var. **yariru**) *n* whirlwind ᴛꜱ,ᴡʏ,ᴛᴍ

yarukawu *n* painted snipe (wading bird) *(Rostratula australis)* ꜱᴛ

yathu *adj* big, stout, overweight ᴛᴍ

    yathu-apinthi [yathu-(w)api-nthi] *v-tr* raise; bring up; educate ᴛꜱ,ᴛᴍ

    yathu-yathungka [yathu-yathu-ngka] *adj* adult; grown up ᴛᴍ

    yathunthi [yathu-nthi] *v-intr* grow; grow up ᴛꜱ,ᴛᴍ

    yathuti [yathu-ti] *n* adult; grown-up *Ngai nata yathuti.* 'I am now an adult.' ᴛᴍ

yawu *n* seagull ᴛꜱ,ɢᴀ,ᴄᴏ

yayika *n* laughter (loud) ᴛꜱ,ᴛᴍ

yiira *n* cicada ᴡʏ

yiirrkurta *n* prickle; thorn ᴡʏ

Yiitya *n* Easter *Ngunya Yiitya!* 'Happy Easter!' ɴᴇᴡ (from English 'Easter')

Yiityu *n* Jesus ɴᴇᴡ (from English 'Jesus')

    Yiityuku Warnirntu [Yiityu-ku warn(i)-(th)irntu] *n* Christmas Day *Ngunya Yiityuku wardnirntu!* 'Happy Christmas!' ɴᴇᴡ

yinku *n* little button quail *(Turnix velox)* ᴡʏ,ʀᴏ

yipiti (var. **ipiti₂**) *n* orphan; motherless ᴛꜱ,ᴛᴍ,ᴡɪ,ᴡʏ,ꜱᴛ

yirra *n* mast ᴡʏ

yirri => **yarri**

yirrurri-apinthi => **yarrurri-apinthi**

yirtpinthi [yirtpi-nthi] (var. **yitpinthi**) *v-tr* turn inside out ₜₛ,ₜₘ
    yirtpirri-apinthi [yirtpi-rri-(w)api-nthi] *v-tr* make (something) turn inside-out ₜₘ
yirukawu *n* landrail (bird) *(Crex crex)* ₛₜ
yitpi *n* (1) seed ₜₛ (2) nut ₙₑw (3) soul, heart *Yangadli yitpi tukutya padlaitya pingkarri.* 'Later his soul had returned to him' ₜₘ,wy (4) will, inclination ₜₘ
    yitpi kaparrinthi [yitpi kapa-rri-nthi] *v-tr* hate; feel spite towards ₜₘ
    yitpi marnirninthi [yitpi marni-rni-nthi] *v-intr* reconcile; make up with ₜₘ
    yitpi ngarntanthi [yitpi ngarnta-nthi] *v-intr* dislike; feel antipathy towards ₜₘ **yitpi purti-purtinthi** [yitpi purti-purti-nthi] *v-intr* rejoice, be happy ₜₘ
    yitpi tukutya *n* (1) seed, pit, stone of a fruit ₜₘ (2) soul, spirit ₜₘ,ₑy
    yitpi-marni *adj* friendly towards ₜₘ
    yitpiwaadli [yitpi-waadli] *adj* hostile; hating ₜₘ
    yitpiwarra *n* meaning; semantics ₙₑw
yityangka => **ityangka**
yudlunthi [yudlu-nthi] *v-tr* (1) push, shove (something) ₜₛ,ₜₘ,wy,wɪ,ₛₜ (2) herd, drive sheep or livestock ₜₛ,ₜₘ (3) drive (a motor vehicle) ₙₑw
    yudlupiipa [yudlu-piipa] *n* driver's licence ₙₑw
    yudlurrinthi [yudlu-rri-nthi] *v-intr* push or shove (each other) ₜₘ
    yudlu-yudlurrinthi [yudlu-yudlu-rri-nthi] push and jostle each other (like when you're in a thick crowd) ₜₘ
yudna *n* covering for pubic area (men's) ₜₛ,ₜₘ,ₚɪ
yuka *n* hair (head) ₜₛ,wy,wɪ,ₑₐ,ɢₐ,ₚɪ,ₖₒ
    yuka mukartiana [yuka mukarta-iana] *n* cap (made of hair) ₜₛ
    yuka piltiti [yuka pilti-ti] (var. **yuka wiltiti**) *n* scissors (for cutting hair) ₜₛ
    yuka wilya cut or cropped hair wy
    yuka wirrkati [yuka wirrka-ti] *n* hairbrush, comb ₜₛ
yuku *n* (1) canoe, boat, ship, whaleboat ₜₛ,ₜₘ,wy,wɪ,ʀₒ,ɢₐ (2) large bark tray ₜₘ
    yuku katha *n* mast (of ship) wɪ
    yuku mathanya [yuku matha-nya] *n* (1) owner of a ship, captain ₜₛ (2) gentleman ₜₛ
    yukumularta [yuku-mularta] *n* oar ₙₑw
yukuna [yuku-na] *adj* (1) bent, curled, crooked ₜₛ,ₜₘ (2) crooked, bad, deformed *yukuna warra* 'untrue or false statement; offensive or suggestive (obscene) language' ₜₛ,ₜₘ

yukuna warra *n* false or untrue statement ₜₛ
yukurninthi [yuku-rni-nthi] *v-intr* (1) be/become crooked, bent, curled ₜₛ,ₜₘ (2) turn, wind, meander ₜₛ
yulta *n* noon; day *yultarlu* 'at noon or day' *yultarra* 'during the noon or day' ₜₛ,ₜₘ
    yultamai [yulta-mai] *n* midday meal, lunch ₜₛ
    yultamai-munthu [yulta-mai-munthu] *adj* having had lunch ₜₛ
yulthi *n* stringybark tree ₜₛ,wy,wɪ
    yulthiwirra [yulthi-wirra] *n* stringybark forest ₜₛ
yultu *n* frog ʀₒ
yumu *n* back *Nantu-yumungka tikanthi.* 'Riding on horse-back' ₜₛ
yunga *n* older brother ₜₛ,ₜₘ,wy,ʙₐ,cʜ
    yunga-yungawarta [yunga-yunga-warta] *n* (1) brother (in a general sense, not necessarily a blood relation) ₜₛ,ₜₘ (2) men from a friendly, neighbouring tribe; allies ₜₛ (3) brotherhood ₜₘ
    yungata [yunga-ta] *n* brother relationship (person in a) ₜₛ,ₜₘ,wy
    yungataurla [yunga-ta-(p)urla] (var. **yungatangkurla**) *n* two brothers (of the same father) ₜₛ,ₜₘ
yungkunthi [yungku-nthi] *v-tr* (1) give, hand over, impart (to someone) ₜₛ,ₜₘ,wy,wɪ,ɢₐ,cʜ (2) tell, communicate (to someone) ₜₛ
    yungki *adj* betrothed ʙₐ
    yungku-yungkunthi [yungku-yungku-nthi] *v-tr* offer (to someone), request or ask (of someone) ₜₘ
    yungkulungkula [yungku-l(a)-(y)ungku-la] *n* giver *mai yungkulungkula* 'generous with food' ₜₛ
    Yungkunthirntu [yungku-nth(i)-(th)irntu] *n* Boxing Day ₙₑw
    yungkurri-apinthi [yungku-rri-(w)api-nthi] *v-tr* (1) give away (something) ₜₛ,ₜₘ (2) receive (something) ₜₘ
    yungkurrinthi [yungku-rri-nthi] *v-tr* (1) give (each other) ₜₛ,ₜₘ (2) exchange, barter ɢₐ
    yungkuti *n* gift; present ₙₑw
yungura *n* crested pigeon; top knot pigeon wy,cₒ
yunta *n* eyebrow ɢₐ
yuparra *adj* heavy ₜₘ
yurda *n* Dreaming being, Rainbow Serpent ₜₛ,ₜₘ,cₐ
    yurda-kauwi *n* dark spots in the Milky Way ₜₛ
yurdi-ngari *n* noose; neck cord wy
yurdina (var. **yurdidna**) (1) *adj, n* left, left side ₜₛ,ₜₘ (2) *adj, adv* left-handed ₜₛ (3) *n* left hand ₜₛ,wy

yurdinukana towards the left ₜₘ

yurdinta *n* skin or hide (of an animal) *pirlta yurdinta* 'possum skin' ₜₛ,ₜₘ,ᵥᵥʸ

yurdlanthi => **yurlanthi**

yuri *n* ear *Yuridla* 'two ears (Mount Lofty & Mount Bonython)' ₜₛ,ₜₘ,ᵥᵥᵢ,ᵥᵥʸ,ₑₐ,ɢₐ,ₖₒ,ᴄʜ

  yuri kurrinthi [yuri kurri-nthi] (1) *v-intr* listen, be attentive ₜₛ (2) *v-intr, v-tr* pay attention to and obey (someone) ₜₛ

  yuri pamanthi [yuri pama-(rri)-nthi] (var. **yuri pamarrinthi**) *v-tr* hear; come into hearing, earshot *Yara padninga, yuri pamarringurti.* 'Go separately, so that you aren't heard.' ₜₘ

  yuri patinthi [yuri pati-nthi] *v-tr* be inattentive ₜₘ

  yuri payanthi [yuri paya-nthi] (var. **yuri paya-paiyanthi**) *v-tr* pay attention to; understand *Yuri paya-(p)ayantu'rna! Kurntatuwayi parna. Kurntatitya yungkunana yailtyarnana. Kudla parnaku niwaningkarna.* 'Pay attention to them (the goats)! Lest they kill them. They might think that they (the goats) have been provided for slaughter. (But) they are just for you (to breed with).' ₜₘ

  yuri tarrinthi [yuri tarri-nthi] *v-intr* be disobedient, stubborn, obstinate ₜₛ

  yuri-kaityanthi [yuri kaitya-nthi] *v-tr* listen to; obey *Padlu yurikaityarningki wangkanthi'adli.* 'He will listen while we (two) are speaking.' ₜₛ,ₜₘ,ᵥᵥʸ

  yuri-kaityarrinthi [yuri kaitya-rri-nthi] *v-tr* listen attentively to; pay attention to ₜₘ

  yuriapa [yuri-(y)apa] *n* inner ear ₖₒ

  yuringka [yuri-ngka] *adv* within hearing; in earshot ᵥᵥʸ,ᵥᵥᵢ,ₛₜ

  yuringka wangkanthi [yuri-ngka wangka-nthi] *v-intr* speak to (somebody) ₜₛ

  yuringkarninthi [yur(i)-ingkarni-nthi] *v-tr* listen to ₜₛ

  yurirka [yur(i)-(th)irka] *adj* attentive; obedient ₜₛ,ₜₘ

  yurirkantapinthi [yur(i)-(th)irka-nt(i)-(w)api-nthi] (var. **yurirkanti-apinthi**) *v-tr* obedient (make someone); attentive (make someone) ₜₛ,ₜₘ

  yurirkantinthi [yur(i)-(th)irka-nti-nthi] *v-intr* be/become obedient or attentive ₜₛ,ₜₘ

  yuritina [yuri-tina] *adj* (1) deaf ₜₛ,ₜₘ,ᵥᵥʸ (2) disobedient, stubborn, 'earless' ₜₛ,ₜₘ

yurirlu => **yurlu**

yurlanthi [yurla-nthi] (var. **yurdlanthi**) *v-intr* dribble; drip; fall in drops *miya yurlanthi* 'be sleepy, nodding off' ₜₛ,ₜₘ

yurlu (var. **yurirlu**) *n* (1) forehead ₜₛ,ₜₘ,ɢₐ,ᵥᵥᵢ,ᵥᵥʸ,ₖₒ (2) face, appearance ₜₘ

  yurlu inparrinthi [yurlu inpa-rri-nthi] *v-intr* see; know; recognise (someone's face) ₜₘ

  yurlu mintirninthi *v-intr* be impatient; wrinkle the forehead in impatience ₜₘ

  yurlu nakunthi [yurlu nhaku-nthi] *v-intr* see (someone's face) ₜₘ

  yurlu ngartinthi [yurlu ngarti-nthi] *v-tr* enquire after; ask about (someone) ₜₘ

  yurlu wiltarni-apinthi [yurlu wilta-rni-(w)api-nthi] *v-tr* make someone rude, cheeky ₜₘ

  yurlu-puyu-puyurri [yurlu-puyu-puyu-rri] *adj* serious; grave; earnest ₜₛ,ₜₘ

  yurlu-puyurringka [yurlu-puyu-rri-ngka] *adv* in earnest, seriously, gravely ₜₘ

  yurlu-thartarri [yurlu-tharta-rri] *adj* having a covered face ₜₘ

  yurlu-wiltana [yurlu-wilta-na] *adj* rude; cheeky; bold ₜₘ

yurlunthi [yurlu-nthi] *v-tr* reveal, make something appear visible *taa tarrki yurlunthi* 'to yawn, open the mouth wide' ₜₛ,ₜₘ,ᵥᵥʸ

yurlurrinthi [yurlu-rri-nthi] *v-intr* appear; become visible; spring up *Mudlha yapangka puiyu yurlurri.* 'Smoke appears in the nostril.' *tirntu yurlurrinthi* 'the sun rises' ₜₛ,ₜₘ

yurni *n* throat; front of neck *Kauwi ngarku'athu. Kurltirlu ngai yurni ngarntarrinthi.* 'I want to drink water. The cough makes my throat sore.' ₜₛ,ₜₘ,ᵥᵥʸ,ᵥᵥᵢ,ₖₒ

  yurni marngu *n* larynx ₖₒ

  yurni mintu-minturninthi [yurni mintu-mintu-rni-nthi] *v-intr* become angry or irritated ₜₘ

  yurni ngari *n* neck tie; scarf ₜₘ

  yurni ngarntanthi [yurni ngarnta-nthi] *v-intr* be/feel angry, discontent, dissatified, frustrated ₜₘ,ɴᴇᴡ

  yurni purnpunthi [yurni purnpu-nthi] *v-tr* take (someone) down by grabbing them around the neck ₜₘ

  yurni tarrinthi [yurni tarri-nthi] *v-intr* be disobedient, stubborn, careless, inattentive ₜₘ

  yurni turtpurninthi [yurni turtpu-rni-nthi] *v-intr* become weak and die of Tuberculosis ₜₘ

  yurni yartarrinthi [yurni yarta-rri-nthi] *v-tr* contradict ₜₘ

  yurni-ana *n* neckerchief; scarf ₜₛ,ᵥᵥʸ

  yurni-itya *adj* angry; provoked ₜₛ,ₜₘ

  yurningka turrkunthi [yurni-ngka turrku-nthi] *v-tr* contradict *Nganaitya nintu ngai* yurningka turrkunthi? Ngathu niina yaku yurningka turrkunthi. 'Why do you contradict me? I don't contradict you.' ᴛᴍ

yurningka wangkanthi [yurni-ngka wangka-nthi] *v-intr* speak to; tell ᴛᴍ

yurnti *adj* heavy; strong ᴛꜱ,ᴛᴍ

yurntu *n* small bag; pocket ᴛꜱ,ᴛᴍ

yurru *n* joke; prank; trick; act; jest ᴛꜱ,ᴛᴍ

  yurru warra joke, funny expression ᴛꜱ

  yurru-purka *n* sneaky person ᴛᴍ

  yurrungka wangkanthi [yurru-ngka wangka-nthi] (var. **yurru wangkanthi**) *v-intr* joke around; speak in a joking way ᴛꜱ,ᴛᴍ

  yurrunthi [yurru-(rri)-nthi] (var. **yurrurrinthi**) *v-intr* creep; sneak; sneak up on ᴛꜱ,ᴛᴍ,ᴡʏ,ʀᴏ

yuru *n* skink; lizard (small) ᴛꜱ,ɢᴀ

yutika *n* red-tailed black cockatoo (*Calyptorhynchus banksii*) ᴛꜱ,ᴛᴍ,ᴄᴏ

yutuki *n* sap of grass-tree ᴛꜱ

yuulti *n* shag or cormorant ᴡʏ,ᴄᴏ,ꜱᴛ

yuwanthi [yuwa-nthi] *v-intr* (1) stop, remain, be still ᴛꜱ,ᴡɪ,ꜱᴛ (2) stand, stand upright and still ᴛꜱ,ᴛᴍ,ᴡʏ,ᴋᴏ (3) stand watch or guard ᴡʏ

  yuwalayinthi [yuwa-(w)ayi-nthi] *v-intr* (1) post one's self (e.g. as a lookout) ᴛᴍ (2) take a stand, take a position ᴛᴍ

  yuwanyapinthi [yuwa-ny(a)-(w)api-nthi] (var. **yuwapinthi**) *v-tr* (1) make (someone) stand ᴛꜱ,ᴛᴍ (2) put (something) upright, raise (something) ᴛꜱ,ᴛᴍ

yuwati [yuwa-ti] *n* tap (water etc.) ɴᴇᴡ

ENGLISH – KAURNA WORD FINDER

Use this section to find an approximate Kaurna equivalent of the English word, then refer to the Kaurna word in the dictionary proper for a better understanding of the usage and sense of the Kaurna word.

A a

a lot nganta *adv*
abandon kupapinthi *v-tr*; kurta-kurtarrinthi *v-tr*; mukanta-wantanthi *v-tr*
abdomen munthu (var. murlu) *n*; tidli *n*
ably nganta *adv*; wayarnta (var. wayangarnta) *adv*; witi *adv*
about (because of) warti-wartingka *adv*; wira-wirangka *adv*
about that time? namutarla? *inter*
above karra$_2$ (var. karta$_2$) *loc*
abroad warru *n*
abscess irrkuta *n*
    develop an abscess irrkutantinthi *v-intr*
abscond wapayinthi *v-intr*
absence of (in the) -tila *suff (in nouns)*; -rtila *suff (in nouns)* (with pronouns)
    in my absence ngaityurtila *adv*
    in your absence ninkurtila *adv* (singular)
    in their absence parnakurtila *adv*
    in someone's absence kurlangka *loc, temp*
    in the absence of men miyutila *adv*
absolutely wantaka *adv*
abundance ngaraitya *n*
abuse verbally tawanthi *v-tr*
    abusive language tawarriti *n*
acacia tree mirnu *n (Acacia)*
    seedpod of acacia tree mingka$_1$ *n*
accept (as a fact) tiyati yailtyanthi *v-intr*
accidentally mardla (var. marla) *adv*; mardlaitirra (var. mardlatirra) *adv*
accompany kangkanthi *v-tr*; marangka padninthi *v-intr*; niipunthi *v-tr*; pirrku mankunthi *v-tr*
    accompany each other niipurrinthi *v-intr*
    accompanying taikurri *adv*
according to wartangka *adv*
accumulate irrkantinthi *v-intr*; irrkapanthi *v-tr*

accuse martanthi *v-tr*; turla minunthi *v-tr*; turla pintyanthi *v-tr*
    accuse of lying manta kurrurrinthi (var. manta kurrikurrinthi; manta kurrulyinthi; manta-urri-urrinthi) *v-tr*
    falsely accuse marta-martanthi *v-tr*
    accusation marta *n*
    accuser martalartala *n*
ache ngarntanthi *v-intr*; tiparrinthi (var. titparrinthi) *v-intr*
acknowledge tampinthi *v-tr*
acquainted tampinthi *v-tr*
across -arra (var. -tarra) *suff (on nouns)*; wara-wantaka *loc*
act wapinthi *v-tr*; yurru *n*
    act out ngayanthi (var. ngayarrinthi) *v-intr, v-tr*
active kalya (var. kailya) *adj*; kalyamarru *adj*; maityuka$_1$ *adj*; wirrkuta *adj*
    be active warpulayinthi *v-intr*; wirrkutaiyinthi *v-intr*
    become active wirrkutarninthi *v-intr*
Adam's apple piidna *n (laryngeal prominence)*
address (someone) warrapanthi *v-intr*
Adelaide Tarntanya *n*
    Adelaide Cup Day Paka-pakirntu *n*
    Adelaide rosella tudlyu (var. tulyu) *n*
adhere to midlimidlinthi *v-intr*; tarnparrinthi *v-intr*
adult pina *n*; taitpa *n*; yathuti *n*; yathu-yathungka *adj*; nanti-nhantina *adj*
    become an adult pinarninthi *v-intr*
advise yarltinthi (var. yarltirrinthi) *v-tr*
    adviser yarltirri-purka *n*
aeroplane karrikarriti *n*
affected by (be) kaintyirrinthi *v-tr*
affection muiyu *n*
afraid wayiwayi *adj*
    be afraid wayirninthi *v-intr*; wayikurtarrinthi *v-intr*; tangkarurninthi *v-intr*; mangkulayinthi *v-intr*

make afraid wayirni-apinthi (var. wayinapinthi) *v-tr*

after wartangka *loc*; wartarra *loc, temp*
    after you ninku pulthu (var. ninku pulthungka) *n, loc*
    afterwards kurla *adv*; yangadli *temp*

again kutini *adv*; muinmu (var. muyinmu) *adj, adv*; nintini *adv*

age (grow old) purkalainthi *v-intr*
    aged purtuna *adj*

aggravate wingku yungkunthi *v-tr*

agitate kutpanthi (var. kutpakutpanthi) *v-tr*; tunkunthi *v-tr*

aimless (be) warrarrinthi *v-intr*

air ngayirda *n*
    aircraft karrikarriti *n*
    airy yalta-yalta *adj*; yaltana *adj*

alarm clock kulurdu tirntu *n*

alas! yakalya! (var. yaka-alya!) *intj*

alcohol kupurlu *n*

alcove wangkurti *n*

alert tutu *adj*

alike (be) namutarnaintyanthi *v-intr*

alive purruna *adj*
    be alive purrunantinthi *v-intr*; purrutinthi *v-intr*
    make (someone) alive purrumanthi *v-tr*; purruti-apinthi *v-tr*

all purrutyi *adj, n*; purru *n*; tupa *n*; wartapurru (var. wartapurruna) *n*
    all together, all at once kumapurtu *adv*

ally yunga-yungawarta *n*

almost ningka *adv*

alone kudla *adv*; kurla *adv*; niipu-tina *adj*; turdi-thurdi *adv*
    be alone mukamukarninthi *v-intr*

along -arra (var. -tarra) *suff (on nouns) (perlative)*
    along here iyamu *loc*
    along there ngu-arra *loc*
    along with taikurri *adv*
    alongside of taikurra *loc*

alright! ku! *intj*

also kuma *adv*

always tuntarri *adv*

ambassador pirrku mankulankula *n*

ambitious munampi *adj*

ambush
    lie in ambush tutu tikanthi *v-intr*
    ambush prey wakanthi *v-tr*

Amen! wapirna *intj*

ammunition parntapurdi *n* (for a gun)

amongst wirangka *loc*

ancestors painingkiarna *n*; pukiana *n*

anchor tarnparriti (var. tanparriti) *n*

ancient munaintyarlu; munana *adj*; painingka-intyarla (var. painingka-intyardla) *temp*; puki *adj*; pukiana *adj*
    more ancient pukintyarlu (var. pukinyadlu) *temp*
    most ancient pukintyarlintya *temp*

angel pirrku mankulankula *n*

anger turla *n*; turla-parrku *n*; turlawingku *n*
    expression of anger yakaitya! *intj*

angry turla *adj*; wingku-wingku *adj*; yurni-itya *adj*
    angrily wingku-wingkurru *adj, adv*
    angry person marngupina *n*; wuinpa-wuinparri-purka (var. wuingpa-wuingparri-purka) *n*; pirra-pina *n*
    be angry turlalayinthi *v-intr*; tarrarrinthi *v-intr*; marngungkinthi *v-intr*; yurni ngarntanthi *v-intr*
    be angry with turla minunthi *v-tr*; turla pintyanthi *v-tr*
    be very angry wuinpa-wuinpanthi (var. wuingpa-wuingparrinthi) *v-intr*
    be/become angry turlarninthi *v-intr*
    become angry pirra-pirrarninthi *v-intr*; wingku-wingkurninthi *v-intr*; yurni mintu-minturninthi *v-intr*
    become very angry tangkarurninthi *v-intr*
    get over being angry turla mardlarrinthi *v-intr*

angle nurluta *n*

Anglo-Australian pinti miyu *n*

animal pardu *n*
    any large animal nantu *n* (e.g. kangaroo, horse, bullock)
    animal and its young ngangkitarla
    animal not fit for eating paitya *n*
    burrowing animal yapa-yaparri *n*
    turn into an animal pardurninthi *v-intr*
    animal droppings murta *n*
    animal skin kartantu *n* (of large animals); maikuntu *n*
    animal skin cloak watpa *n*
    animal track tainga *n*

ankle warru-marngu *n*

ankle bone tuntanta (var. tuntuntu) *n*; warrumarngu *n*
    back of the ankle tidnawarta *n*
annoy wiwunthi *v-tr*
    annoy each other wiwurrinthi *v-tr*
    be annoyed marngungkinthi *v-intr*
    annoyance wiwurriti *n*
    annoying warnutina *adj*; warpularra *adj*; wiwudla-wudla (var. wiwudli-wudla) *adj*
anoint marninthi *v-tr*
    anoint oneself marnirrinthi *v-intr*
another kuma *pro* (indefinite, ergative); kumanurlu *pro* (ergative); kutyu *n*
answer warra inpanthi *v-tr*; warra mankunthi *v-tr*
ant karltu *n*
    flying ant puruti *n*
    inch ant karltu *n*
    large black ant kumpulya *n*
    red ant maru *n*
    small ant species karltukarltunyi *n*
    white ant kadngi *n*
antagonistic irrapina (var. pirrapina) *adj, n*
anterior fontanelle miya *n*
anticipation marta *n*
antipathy towards (feel) yitpi ngarntanthi *v-intr*
anus murntu *n*
anxious (be/feel) kuntu pungkurrinthi *v-intr*; kuntu yartarrinthi *v-intr*; mukurrinthi *v-intr*
    anxious person kuntu pungkurripurka *n*
anyway mardlaitirra (var. mardlatirra) *intj*; turdi-thurdi *adv*
apart from kurlangka *loc, temp*
appear nakurri-apinthi *v-tr*; pudnanthi *v-intr*; tarnanthi (var. tarninthi) *v-intr*; wardninthi (var. warninthi) *v- intr*; yurlurrinthi *v-intr*
    appearance yurlu (var. yurirlu) *n*
    make something appear yurlunthi *v-tr*
appetite
    get an appetite for tangka marnirninthi *v-intr*
    lose your appetite tangka murrmarninthi *v-intr*
    regain your appetite tangka marnirninthi *v-intr*
apply (put on) paanthi *v-tr*
apply (use) marrkunthi *v-tr*
approach ityarrinthi *v-tr*; kurdanthi *v-intr, v-tr*; kurdarrinthi *v-intr*
approximate markanthi *v-tr*; markarrinthi *v-intr*

April Yarapurliki *n*
arable land putpa yarta *n*
arched mukurniti *adj*
    arch of foot tidnatangka *n*
argue with turla ngarkunthi *v-tr*
    argue with each other tawarrinthi *v-intr*
    argument nguyanguya *n*; tawarriti *n*; warltu (var. warti warltu) *n*
    argumentative irrapina (var. pirrapina) *adj, n*; paitpurtu *adj*; pulti-ulti *adj*; turlapina *n, adj*; turlawarpu *adj*; warpularra *adj*
    argumentative person marrkarripurka *n*; miyu-katha *n*; turlapina *n, adj*
arm turti *n*
    lower arm manarntu *n*
    upper arm narntu *n*; warta-thurti *n*
    armpit ngurdanya *n (axilla)*; wardliwitya (var. warliwitya) *n*
    arm string ornament ngunyakurla *n*
arrive pudnanthi *v-intr*
ascend tatinthi *v-intr*; wangkurrinthi *v-intr*
ashamed (be/feel) kurdukarrinthi *v-intr*
    make (someone) feel ashamed kurdukarriapinthi *v-tr*
ashes ngunkunya *n*; purta *n*
    cold ashes murdu *n*
    become ashes murdurninthi *v-intr*
ask ngartinthi (var. ngartirrinthi) *v-tr*; kaltinthi *v-tr*; marnkanthi *v-tr*; marnkarrinthi *v-intr*
    ask about (someone) ingkarrinthi *v-tr*; yurlu ngartinthi *v-tr*
    ask for oneself kaltirrinthi *v-intr*
    asking constantly kaltikaltinya *adj*
asleep puulti *adj*
assassin nukuna *n*
assemble kumangka malturri-apinthi *v-tr*; malturri-apinthi *v-tr*; manku-mankurrinthi *v-intr*; ngirrirrinthi *v- intr*; tultyunthi *v-tr*; tultyurrinthi *v-intr*
assist mankunthi *v-tr*
astray (be) wakarrinthi *v-intr*
at -ngka (var. -ngga) *suff (on nouns)* (locative); -ila (var. -illa) *suff (on nouns)* (locative); taikurra *loc*; -rlu (var. -dlu; -urlu) *suff (on nouns)* (temporal)
    at (someone/something) -ityangka (var. -lityangka) *suff (on nouns)* (comitative)
    at him/her/it padlaityangka *pro*

at what time? nalati (var. nadlati) *inter*
at the moment yalaka (var. yaltaka) *temp*
at night ngulthingka *temp*
atmosphere ngayirda *n*
attach nayanthi *v-tr*; tarnparriapinthi *v-tr*
   attach oneself tarnparriapinthi *v-intr*
   be attached to tarnparrinthi *v-intr*
attack turla yakarrinthi *v-intr*
   attacker turlapina *n* (in sport)
attentive maityuka$_1$ *adj*; yurirka *adj*
   be attentive yuri kurrinthi *v-intr*
   be/become attentive yurirkantinthi *v-intr*
   make someone attentive yurirkantapinthi (var. yurirkanti-apinthi) *v-tr*
   attentively sit up tutu tikanthi *v-intr*
August Ngarliki *n*
aunt ngarrpadla *n*
Australia Wirltuthidnayarta *n*
   Australia Day Ngadluku Tirntu *n*
   Australian person Wirltuthidnamiyu *n*
autumn parnati$_2$ *n*
   autumn star parna$_2$ (var. padna$_2$) *n* (undefined)
   mid-autumn waadlawarnkati *n*
awake nakarra *adj*
   be awake nakurrinthi *v-intr*
aware (be) nakunthi *v-intr, v-tr*
away nurnti *adv*
   away from -nungku (var. -anangku; -nangku; -unungku) *suff (on nouns)* (ablative)
   away from me ngathaityanungku *pro* (ablative)
   away from you nintaityanungku *pro* (singular ablative)
awkwardly waadli *adv*
awl (bone) wityu (var. wilyu) *n*
axe tamiaku *n*

B b

baby wakwaku *n*; ngartu *n*; tukutya *n*
   newborn baby muinyi munthu *n*
   baby wati-wati pirrkirna *n*
bachelor ngarilta *n*
back ngurru *n*; yumu *n*
   backbone ngarrata *n*; parntala (var. parntadla) *n*
   backpack yamaru (var. yama-yama) *n*
   backside turrku *n*
bad waadli *adj*; wakinha *adj*; yukuna *adj*
   be/become bad waadlirninthi *v-intr*
   become bad wakinharninthi (var. wakinhantinthi) *v-intr*
   make bad wakinhanti-apinthi (var. wakinhantapinthi) *v-tr*
   bad language murntu warra *n*
   bad smell puwa *n*
   bad-tempered turlawarpu *adj*; tiyarrka *adj*
   badly waadli *adv*
bag tantu *n*
   bag for magic objects pingki$_1$ *n*
   bag for supplies yamaru (var. yama-yama) *n*
   bag made of string or net purnu *n*, wikatyi *n* (men's)
   bag made of woven rushes tainkyadli *n*
   leather bag tantu *n*
   shopping bag yamaru (var. yama-yama) *n*
   sleeping bag ngudli wantiti *n*
   small bag yurntu *n*
bait mai pudnapiti *n*
bake kampanthi *v-tr*
   baked purtarti *adj*
   baker kampalampala *n*
   bakery kamparriti *n*
   bake in an earth oven kanyanthi *v-tr*
bald pintapinta *adj*; pukupuku *adj*; yarna *adj*
   become bald pintarninthi *v-intr*
   go bald murrmarninthi *v-intr*
   make someone bald pintarni-apinthi (var. pintapintarni-apinthi) *v-tr*
   bald coot kawana *n*
ball parntu *n*
   basketball tantyalu-parntu *n*
   football tidnaparntu *n*
   netball wikaparntu *n*
   ball of the foot tidnakuntu *n*
banana nurlimai *n*
band pirku *n* (of people)
bandaid pakapaltha *n*
bandicoot marti *n*
bank (financial institution) kanyawardli *n*
banksia tarnma *n* (*Banksia marginata*)
barber marlta pirralirrala *n*; pirra-pirrala *n*
bare puku *adj*
   bare ground yarta puku *n*
   barefoot tidnapalthatina *adj*

bark (dog) warru-warrukanthi *v-intr*; warrukayinthi *v-intr*
  bark at warrukapinthi *v-tr*
  barking warru-warruka (var. warrarruka) *n*
  barking owl warrukiti *n (Ninox connivens)*

bark (tree)
  dry bark paka *n*
  green bark tidli *n*
  bark of gum tree tarrkarta *n*
  bark canoe pakayuku *n*
  bark shield wakalti *n*
  large bark tray yuku *n*

barn owl winta (var. wintha) *n (Tyto delicatula)*

barren (childless) tukupitina *adj*

barrier ngangka *n*; tirra *n*

barter tanta *n*; tita *n*; titangka yungkunthi *v-tr*; wakuinya *n*; wakuinyapinthi *v-tr*; yungkurrinthi *v-tr*

basket tantyalu *n*
  basket for carrying a baby kantarra *n*
  basketball tantyalu-parntu *n*

bat species maityumaityu *n (undefined)*

bath kudlikuru *n*
  bathroom kudli kuu *n*
  bathtime kudlithirntu *n*
  bathe kunturrinthi *v-intr*; pukanthi *v-intr*

battle irra *n*; wirra₂ *n*

beach wauwa *n*

beak taamanti *n*

beard marlta *n*; ngarrkiarru *n*; yarnka *n*
  bearded dragon kadnu (var. kanu) *n*

beat kurntanthi *v-tr*; parltanthi *v-tr*; pungkunthi *v-tr*; pirrki parltanthi *v-tr (into pieces)*; midli kurntanthi *v-tr (into bits)*
  beat down parltanthi *v-intr, v-tr*
  beat each other pungkurrinthi *v-intr*
  beat one's self kurntarrinthi *v-intr*
  beat out fire padlu-parltanthi *v-tr*
  beat to death padlu-kurntanthi *v-tr*
  beat upon parltanthi *v-intr, v-tr*
  beating kurntarriti (var. kurnta₂) *n*
  beaten with branches (initiation stage) wilya-kurntarti *n, adj*

beat (rhythm) ipila *n*
  beat time markarrinthi *v-intr*; parltanthi *v-intr, v-tr*

because of -pira *suff (on nouns)*; martungka; warti-wartingka *adv*; wira-wirangka *adv*

beckon with the hand mara warunthi, mararlu warunthi; turti waru-warunthi *v-tr*

become (inchoative) -rni (var. -ni; -rnti) *suff (on verbs)*

bed itharti *n*
  bedroom miitu kuu *n*
  bedding kupiti *n*
  bedsheet miituthurnki *n*
  bedstead karrapiri *n*
  bedtime miituthirntu *n*
  bedtime song miituthirntu palti *n*
  bedtime story miituthirntu pirrku *n*

bee (native) kardlaparti *n*
  bee-eater (rainbow – bird) tinta-inta *n (Merops ornatus)*

beetle
  lamellicorn beetle turla-yiira *n*
  longicorn beetle karriparti *n*
  water beetle turluntyaru *n (Gyrinus)*

before munarra *adv*; piti (var. 'iti) *adv*; puru-iti (var. puru-piti) *adv*
  beforehand muna *adv*; munangka *adv*; pulthupuru *adv*

beg marnkanthi *v-tr*; kaltinthi *v-tr*; marnkarrinthi *v-intr*
  beggar marnkalarnkala *n*; marnkarri-purka *n*

beget parltanthi *v-tr*

beginning munaintya *n*
  in the beginning munaintyarlu

begrudge tatarrinthi *v-intr*

behind nguntarta *loc*; nurnti-nhurnti (var. nurnti-urnti) *loc*; warta *n*; wartangka *loc*; wartarra *loc, temp*; yakingka *loc*
  coming behind wartangka *loc*

belch ngungulurdu *n*; tangkalurdu (var. tangka kulurdu) *n*

believe yailtyanthi (var. yailtyarrinthi) *v-tr*
  believe to be true tiyati yailtyanthi *v-intr*

belligerent irrapina (var. pirrapina) *adj, n*

belly munthu (var. murlu) *n*
  having a full belly maimunthu *adj (after eating)*
  belly button mintawarta (var. mintuwarta) *n*; murluwarta *n*

belong
  belonging (somewhere) yaitya (var. iyaitya) *adj*
  belonging to everyone taikurringka *adj*

belongings kurrpu *n*
below yakingka *loc*
bench tarralyi *n*
bend parruntayinthi *v-intr*; yartanthi *v-tr*
   bend down warkanthi *v-intr*; yartarninthi *v-intr*
   bend over yartanapinthi *v-tr*
   bend the neck forwards manuwartarninthi *v-intr*
   bend (in a river) nurlu *n*
   bent mukurniti *adj*; nurru-nhurru *adj*; yukuna *adj*
   be/become bent yukurninthi *v-intr*
   bent over warka *adj*
betrothed yungki *adj*
between wirangka *loc*
beyond nguntarta *loc*; nurnti-nhurnti (var. nurnti-urnti) *loc*
bicycle maityuwampi *n*
bier tirkati *n* (for corpse)
big partu *adj*; tawarra *adj*; yathu *adj*
   big toe tidnangangki *n*; tidnayarli *n*
   big-headed gudgeon parntu mukarta waitku *n* (Philypnodon grandiceps)
bike maityuwampi *n*
bilby pingku *n*
bile tangka-umpu *n*
bin mapakuru *n*
binge on tarnkunthi *v-tr*
birds winaityinaityi *n*
   Adelaide rosella tudlyu (var. tulyu) *n*; warltu-arri *n*
   barking owl warrukiti *n* (Ninox connivens)
   barn owl winta (var. wintha) *n* (Tyto delicatula)
   black honeyeater warntu *n* (Sugomel niger)
   black swan kudlyu *n* (Cygnus atratus)
   blue mountain parrot ngarri *n*
   blue-winged shoveler duck tawanta *n* (Spatula rhynchotis)
   bronzewing pigeon marnpi *n*
   brown-breasted honeyeater karrawintha *n* (Meliphaga)
   budgerigar tirkura *n*
   bush turkey waltha *n* (Ardeotis australis)
   bustard waltha *n* (Ardeotis australis)
   butcherbird paku-paku *n*
   Cape Barren goose pita *n* (Cereopsis novaehollandiae)
   cockatiel wirdupa *n*
   cockatoo (white) kurdaki *n*
   coot or swamp hen kawana *n*
   cormorant yuulti *n*
   crested or topknot pigeon yungura *n*
   crow kuwa *n*
   duck tawanta *n*
   European goose pinti pita *n*
   grey butcherbird kurrka *n* (Cracticus torquatus)
   grey currawong kuyurra *n* (Strepera versicolor)
   hawk karrkanya *n*; munkaka *n*
   kestrel hawk manimani *n* (Falco cenchroides)
   kingfisher tiintinti *n*
   landrail yirukawu *n* (Crex crex)
   large shrike katungki *n*
   lark tirritpa *n* (Grallina cyanoleuca)
   little button quail yinku *n* (Turnix velox)
   malleefowl pudni *n* (Leipoa ocellata)
   nightjar narni *n*
   owl winta (var. wintha) *n*
   painted snipe yarukawu *n* (wading bird) (Rostratula australis)
   parrot palti-palti *n*
   quail tinkyadla *n* (Coturnix pectoralis) yinku *n*
   rainbow bee-eater tinta-inta *n* (Merops ornatus)
   rainbow lorikeet ngakala *n*
   red-tailed black cockatoo yutika *n* (Calyptorhynchus banksii)
   red-tipped pardalote karltu-arltuku *n*
   river birds paripardu *n*
   robin red breast tutha-ipiti *n* (Petroica)
   shag yuulti *n*
   shrikethrush turngu *n* (large, slate-coloured)
   sparrow hawk purpurta *n*
   star finch tiitha *n*
   stubble quail tinkyadla *n* (Coturnix pectoralis)
   swift turlu *n*
   wattlebird katpamartu *n*
   wedge-tailed eagle wirltu *n* (Aquila audax)
   welcome swallow manimaninya *n*
   white cockatoo kurdaki *n*
   yellow-tailed black cockatoo tiwu *n*; wilampa *n*
birth (give) kangkarrinthi *v-intr* munthu wayirrinthi *v-intr*
   birthday warnirntu *n*
   Happy Birthday! mingki warnirntu! *intj*
birth-order name warninhari *n*
   1st born Kartamiru *n* (male); Kuyata *n* (male);

Kartanya (var. Kartani) *n* (female); Kartiartu *n* (female)

2nd born Warritya *n* (male); Yaraitya *n* (male); Warruyu *n* (female); Warri-artu *n* (female); Yarartu *n* (female)

3rd born Kudnuitya *n* (male); Kudnartu *n* (female)

4th born Munaitya *n* (male); Munartu *n* (female)

5th born Midlaitya *n* (male); Midlartu *n* (female)

6th born Marrutya *n* (male); Marruartu (var. Marruyu) *n* (female)

7th born Wangutya *n* (male); Wanguartu *n* (female)

8th born Ngadlaitya *n* (male); Ngadlartu *n* (female)

9th born Pauwani *n* (male or female)

biscuit pirrkiti *n*

bit (piece) pirrki *n*; ika *n*; kalya (var. kailya) *n*

bite payanthi *v-tr*; payarrinthi *v-tr*

biting animal or insect paitya *n*

bitter kitya *adj*

black pulyuna *adj*
    be black pulyurrinthi *v-intr*
    cause to become black pulyu-ulyapinthi *v-tr*
    black cockatoo (red-tailed) yutika *n* (*Calyptorhynchus banksii*)
    black cockatoo (yellow-tailed) tiwu *n*; wilampa *n*
    blackfish (river) pari pulyuna kuya *n* (*Gadopsis marmoratus*)
    black fly (common) tapu *n*
    black swan kudlyu *n* (*Cygnus atratus*)
    blackboard markapulyuna *n*

bladder tidli-umpu (var. tidli-kumpu) *n*

blanket palangkita *n*

blaze purtanthi *v-intr*

bleed kaaru-wayinthi *v-intr*

blind paityutina *adj*
    blind person paityuti *n*
    go blind paityuti-antinthi *v-intr*

blister punturrpa *n*

block (an attack) karnkanthi *v-tr*

block of wood waadla *n*

blood kaaru *n*
    human blood karti *n*
    blood used in ceremony paityakudna *n*
    blood vessel kaaruwardli *n*

blossom ngurika *n*

blow kurrunthi (var. kurrurrinthi) *v-intr*
    blow into wingku puntunthi *v-tr*
    blow (with the mouth) puntunthi *v-tr*
    blowfly tupurra *n*

blubber (from a whale) kuntuli *n*

blue/green kardalta *adj*
    blue mountain parrot ngarri *n*

blunt tiya-tina *adj*

blush kurdukarrinthi *v-intr*
    make someone blush kurdukarri-apinthi *v-tr*; nganparri-apinthi *v-tr*
    blushing kurdukarri *n*

board (made of wood etc) tarralyi *n*

boastful (be) nangkarrinthi *v-intr*

boat yuku *n*

body nudnu (var. nunu) *n*

boil (heat in liquid) kampanthi *v-tr*; ngardlinthi *v-intr*
    boil over marrarrinthi *v-intr*
    boiled purtarti *adj*

boil (pustule/sore) nguya (var. nguiya) *n*

bold pulthawilta *adj*; yurlu-wiltana *adj*

bombyx kupi *n*

bone warpu (var. wartpu) *n*
    ankle bone warrumarngu *n*
    bone for ceremony puingurru *n*
    kangaroo bone ornament or tool wityu (var. wilyu) *n*
    boneless warputina *adj*
    bone marrow kapa *n* (bodypart)

book piipa *n*

boomerang wadna *n* (as found in all other Thura-Yura languages)

boot tidnapaltha *n*

border inpanthi *v-tr*
    border on pamanthi *v-tr*
    border on each other pamarrinthi *v-intr*

born (be) wardninthi (var. warninthi) *v-intr*

borrowed object wirrangku *n*

both yara *adj, adv*

bottle (glass) maki kuru *n*

bottom (bodypart) murntu *n*; warnu *n*

bounded by inpanthi *v-tr*

boutique mutyarta wardli *n*

bow the head manuwartarninthi *v-intr*
bowels kudna *n*; piti *n*
    bowels and excrement of kangaroo multyumultyu *n*
bowl kuru *n*; tamikuru (var. tamuru) *n*
boxer marapina *n*
Boxing Day Yungkunthirntu *n*
boy kurrkurra *n*
    boy aged 8 to 20 tinyarra *n*
bra ngamipaltha *n*
brain mukamuka *n*; ngarumuka *n*
branch parra *n*; turti *n*
    big branch parrarra *n*
    tree branch watu *n*
    branches tinkyuwatu *n*
    young branches wilya *n*
brandish karra nuunthi (var. karra nununthi) *v-tr*
brave pulthawilta *adj*; tangkaru wilta *adj*; warpu-wilta (var. warpu-wiltu) *adj*; wayiwilta *adj*
    become brave warpuwiltarninthi *v-intr*
brawler marapina *adj, n*
breach (cause a) yarrurri-apinthi (var. yirrurri-apinthi) *v-tr*
bread murdumurdu *n*
    soft centre of bread yakinhainguta *n*
break yartanthi *v-tr*; yartarri-apinthi *v-tr*; pirrki wayinthi *v-intr*; piltilinthi *v-intr*; parltanthi *v-tr*
    break apart yarrurrinthi *v-intr*
    break down (collapse) yartarri-apinthi *v-tr*
    break down (car) ngirlinthi (var. ngirtinthi) *v-intr*
    break free tiltyalayinthi (var. tiltyalinthi) *v-intr*
    break into bits pirrki-apinthi$_1$ *v-tr*
    break off parltarri-apinthi *v-tr*
    break through tapalayinthi *v-intr*
    break up kalya-pungkunthi *v-tr* (to powder); kalyarni-apinthi *v-tr*
    breakable pirrkiparltaparltanya *adj*
    breakers (waves) kungkurra *n*; tarni *n*
    breakfast panyimai *n*
bream karrka$_2$ *n (Acanthopagrus butcheri)*
breast (female) ngami *n*
    breastfeed nuinpinthi *v-tr*
breath wingku *n*
    breath in cold weather taawu *n*
    breathe wingku patirrinthi *v-intr*

breathe heavily kathinthi *v-intr*; wingku warunthi *v-intr*
breathe quickly wingku padminthi *v-intr*
stop breathing wingku-wingkurtarrinthi *v-intr*
breeze kurruti *n*; maikurru *n*
    evening breeze karrkawarri *n*
briar pitpa *n*
bridge waadlakatha *n*; waadlatarra *n*
bright parkana *adj*; walara *adj*
bring pudnapinthi (var. pudnanyapinthi) *v-tr*; katinthi *v-tr*; kurda-kurdanthi *v-tr*
    bring about mankunthi *v-tr*
    bring close together maltunthi *v-tr*
    bring near kurdanthi *v-intr, v-tr*
    bring together tultyunthi *v-tr*
    bring up (child) pinanapinthi *v-tr*; yathu-apinthi *v-tr*
brittle pirrkiparltaparltanya *adj*
broad takana$_2$ *adj*; yartpana *adj*
broccoli purakali *n*
broken mingkamingka *adj*; murtana *adj*; ngirla *adj*; waadli yarrurrina *adj*
    become broken murta-wardninthi *v-intr*
bronzewing pigeon marnpi *n*
brood kuntu pungkurrinthi *v-intr*
broth kauwirrka (var. kawirrka) *n*
brother
    older brother yunga *n*
    two brothers with the same father yungataurla (var. yungatangkurla) *n*
    brother (figurative) yunga-yungawarta *n*
    person in a brother relationship yungata *n*
    brother-in-law taru *n* (man's); taruta *n* (man's)
    brothers-in-law (dual) tarutangkurla (var. tarutaurla) *adj*
    brother of a hanged person ngari wilu *n*
    brotherhood yunga-yungawarta *n*
    younger brother (or sister) panya *n*; panyapi *n*
    person whose younger brother has died karraki *n*
brownish-coloured purnkipurnki *adj*
    brown snake paitya *n*
    brown trout purnkipurnki mipurli *n (Salmo trutta)*
brush kurliti *n*; wirrkanthi *v-tr*; wirrkarriti *n*
    hairbrush yuka wirrkati *n*
    brush tailed possum pirlta *n* (brush-tailed)

brush oneself wirrkarrinthi *v-intr*

brussels sprout tinkyuyuri *n*

budgerigar tirkura *n*

buggy pudniwarta *n*

build tayinthi (var. tayirrinthi) *v-tr*; pintyanthi (var. pingkanthi; pingyanthi; pinkanthi) *v-tr*; minunthi *v-tr*

    building wardli (var. warli) *n*

    builder tayilayila *n*

bulky ngama *adj*

bullet parntapurdi *n* (for a gun)

bullfrog kantu *n*

bullroarer kadnumarnguta (var. kanumarnguta) *n*; wimari *n*; witu-witu *n*

bullrush root warnpa *n* (*Typha*)

bullshit (full of) kudnapurtu *adj* (nonsense)

bum warnu *n*; murntu *n*

bumpy marngu-marngu *adj*

burn ngardlinthi *v-intr*; purtanthi *v-intr*; kampanthi *v-tr*

    burn holes through tapa ngardlinthi *v-tr*

    burning (still) kardlapurruna *adj*

    burnt nuinpa *adj*

    burning embers purta *n*

    burnt stick ngarra *n*

    burnt tree stump ngarra *n*; purtultu *n*

burp ngungulurdu *n*; tangkalurdu (var. tangka kulurdu) *n*; warntalinthi *v-intr*

burrow yapa *n*

    burrows waarki *n* (animal burrows)

burst yarrurrinthi *v-intr*

    bury wanganthi (var. wangarrinthi) *v-tr*

    bury in the ground yarta ngatpanthi *v-tr*

    bury a corpse nudnu wanganthi *v-intr*

bus paatya *n*

bush karrawadlu *n*; karta$_3$ *n*; wirra$_1$ *n*

bush turkey waltha *n* (*Ardeotis australis*)

bustard waltha *n* (*Ardeotis australis*)

busy (be) warpulayinthi *v-intr*

but pirdi (var. pirdina) *adv*

butcherbird paku-paku *n*

    grey butcherbird kurrka *n* (*Cracticus torquatus*)

butcher's shop parduwardli *n*

butter wilta-itpurla *n*

    butterfly pilyapilya *n*

buttocks kardlu-ardlu *n*; murntu *n*; pilta-muka *n*; warnu *n*

button marngu$_2$ *n*; tita *n*; turnki marngu *n*; turnkithita *n*

buy titangka mankunthi *v-tr*

by means of him/her/it padluntya *pro*

bye! nakutha! *intj*

C c

cabbage pirira *n*

calf (leg) yarla *n*

    calf muscle yarla-muka *n*

call karlta *n*; karltanthi *v-tr*; wanpanapinthi *v-tr*; warunthi (var. waru-warunthi) *v-tr*; warurrinthi *v-tr*

    call (someone) taakanthi *v-tr*; taakarrinthi *v-intr*

    calling karlta-karltanya *n*

calm turlatina *adj*

    be calm kuntu yartarninthi *v-intr*

    become calm pilyurninthi *v-intr*; wingku marnirninthi *v-intr*

    calm down tangka wiltarninthi *v-intr*

candy pinyata *n*

cannibal miyu maimaingka *n*; miyu paityarri *n*; miyu trruku-ana *n*

canoe yuku *n*

canteen maiwardli *n*

cap (hat) mukarti-ana *n*

    cap made of hair yuka mukartiana *n*

capably wayarnta (var. wayangarnta) *adv*

Cape Barren goose pita *n* (*Cereopsis novaehollandiae*)

capsicum katpikama *n*

captain (of ship) yuku mathanya *n*

car padnipadniti *n*

carcass nudnu (var. nunu) *n*

care for kangkanthi *v-tr*; warpulayinthi *v-intr*

    carer kangkalangkala *n*

    careless (be) yurni tarrinthi *v-intr*

    carelessly itirra *adv*

caress pitunthi *v-tr*

carnal person ngangki-pardu *n*

carp (European) tukapina *n* (*Cyprinus carpio*)

carrot tidla *n*

carry katinthi *v-tr* namarrinthi *v-tr*

    carry (a child on your back) mamanthi *v-tr*

    carry (hanging on shoulder) tarranthi *v-tr*

carry on your back namanthi *v-tr*
carry (somewhere) katinthi *v-tr*
carry lots wadlunthi₁ (var. wadlu-wadlunthi) *v-intr*
cart pudniwarta *n*
cascade warkanta *n*
cask kuru *n*
cast
  cast a line ngari patinthi *v-tr* (fishing)
  cast a shadow turalayinthi *v-tr*
  cast a spell on kurrkunthi *v-tr*
  cast out kapanthi *v-tr*
casuarina karku *n* kurlwi *n*
catch
  catch (in your hand) karrampu mankunthi *v-tr*
  catch fire ngardlinthi *v-intr*
  catch fish pirri-wirrkinthi *v-tr*
  catch yabbies ngaltaityapinthi *v-tr*
catfish (eel-tailed) ngalta yawitya *n* (*Tandanus tandanus*)
cauliflower partu-yuri *n*
cause -api (var. -kapi; -pi) *suff (on verbs)* (causative); mankunthi *v-tr*; warti₂ *n*; wayinthi (var. -kaiyinthi; -layi; wauwinthi) *v-intr*
  cause damage nuinyarrinthi *v-intr*
celebrate mukamukarrinthi *v-intr*
celibate murntuwaadli *adj*
cemetery wangayarta *n*
centipede species ngaruta (var. ngarruta) *n* (undefined)
centre trruku *n*; warti-trruku *n*; warti₂ *n*
  down the centre warti-arra *loc*
ceremony palti *n*; kurdi *n*; ngunyawayiti *n*
  perform ceremony mukanthi (var. mukarrinthi) *v-intr*; ngunya-wayinthi *v-intr*; tuki-apinthi *v-intr* (undefined)
  ceremony of the Karnu Miyurna palti₁ *n*
  ceremony of the Murray people kurru-angku *n*
  ceremonial scar(s) manka *n*; pakurta *n*
  ceremonial cut(s) ngulta *n*; ngurra *n*
certainly tiyati *intj, adv*
chain titapinthi *v-tr*
chair tikathikati *n*
chalk ngaru *n*
challenge karra nuunthi (var. karra nunanthi) *v-tr*; pardu-apinthi (var. pardu-pardu-apinthi) *v-tr*; wingku yungkunthi *v-tr*; wuinpanthi (var. wuingpanthi) *v-tr*
  challenge each other wuinparrinthi *v-intr*
change
  change (coins) pirrkirna *n*
  change direction mikarrinthi (var. mikamikarrinthi) *v-intr*
  change shape nadla-nhadlarrinthi (var. nala-nhalarrinthi) *v-intr*; nadlarrinthi *v-tr*
characterised by -purtu *suff (on nouns)*
  gain a characteristic warrirninthi (var. warrirntinthi) *v-intr*
charcoal pidna *n*
  become charcoal pidnarninthi *v-intr*
charm (magic) nurruti *n*
chase nurrunthi *v-tr*; yakanthi *v-tr*; yakarrinthi *v-intr*
  chaser yakalakala *n*
chaste murntuwaadli *adj*
chat wangkanthi *v-intr*
  chat with warrapanthi *v-intr*
  chatter minyangkayinthi (var. minyarrangkinthi) *v-intr*
  chattering pilyapilya *n*
  chatterbox warrapina *n*
cheek marlta warta *n*; marltaitya *n*
  cheeky kurduwilta *adj*; yaitya-kuinyu *adj*; yurlu-wiltana *adj*
  be cheeky nurnpurrinthi *v-intr*
  become cheeky kurdu-wiltarninthi *v-intr*
  make someone cheeky yurlu wiltarni-apinthi *v-tr*
cheer up purti-apinthi *v-tr*
  cheerful kalyamarru *adj*
cheese wiltangaru *n*
cherry tilti *n*
  native cherry tilti *n* (*Exocarpos cupressiformis*)
chest (bodypart) kuntu₁ *n*
  animal's chest wili *n*
  chest bone kuntu warpu *n* (*sternum*)
chew payanthi *v-tr*; parranthi *v-tr*; kuinpinthi *v-tr*
  chew on payarrinthi *v-tr*
  chewed (fibre of pityarra mallow) tiyapi *n*
chicken murta-ana-itya *n*
child ngartu *n*; wakwaku *n*; tukutya *n*
  male child yarlipurka *n*
  favourite child kurlakurlana (var.

kurlakurlanta) *n*
motherless child yipiti (var. ipiti₂) *n*
childless tukupitina *adj*
having two children tuku-purlaitya *adj*
have many children tuku-angkirninthi *v-intr*
child generation kurlana *n*
child-bearing age (past) pirdipirdi *adj*
chilly manyapayana *adj*
chin ngurtuwarta *n*
Chinese or Asian person Kunthi *n*
chip of wood tarralyi *n*
chirp tititayinthi *v-intr*
choke midlinthi (var. milinthi) *v-tr*
Christmas Day Yiityuku Warnirntu *n*
    Happy Christmas! Ngunya Yiityuku Warnirntu! *intj*
church Sunday warli *n*
cicada yiira *n*
cicatrix manka *n*
cigar/cigarette puyu (var. puiyu) *n*
cinema turawardli *n*
circle tuturtu *n*; kurruru *n*; kurdi *n*
    sit in/form a circle kurdingkainthi *v-intr*
circumcised person wariparti *n*
    undergo circumcision paapa yuwanthi *v-intr*
    person who performs circumcision turlu *n*
    person directing circumcision ceremony paapa-mathanya *n*
    person in circumcision ceremony tapu *n*
clan pirku *n* (of people)
clapstick wirri *n*
clasp mankurrinthi *v-tr*; martinthi *v-tr*
clasp with talons warkinthi *v-tr*
claw pirri *n*
clay tuka *n*
    pipe clay ngaru *n*
clean kudlinthi *v-tr*; kurlinthi *v-tr*; muyinthi *v-tr*; wirrkanthi *v-tr*
    clean oneself wirrkarrinthi *v-intr*
clear walara *adj*; warlta *adj* (weather); makutina *adj* (sky)
    clear-headed mukarta tawutawu *adj*; mukarta walara *adj*
    clear a passage warlturri-apinthi *v-tr*
clench the teeth tiyarla-tharnparrinthi *v-intr*

clever walara *adj*
cliff
    cliff edge kauwamarlta *n*
    cliff face kauwa *n*
climb tatinthi *v-intr*; wangkurrinthi *v-intr*
    climbing galaxias tati mipurli *n* (*Galaxias brevipinnis*)
cloak watpa *n*; turnki *n*
clock tirntu *n*
clod turtu (var. yarta turtu) *n*
close (near) kurda *loc*
    bring close together maltunthi *v-tr*
    close by ityangka (var. yityangka) *loc*; kurdanta *loc*; parnidlu *loc*
    come close kurdantarninthi *v-intr*
    come closer tirdi-apinthi *v-tr*
    closeness kurta *n*
close over tartanthi *v-tr*
    close the eyes pitpayinthi *v-intr*
cloth watpa *n*; turnki *n*
    clothing mutyarta *n*; turnki *n*
    clothes basket mutyarta tainkyadli *n*
    clothes container mutyarta kuru *n*
    clothes dryer murlapiti *n*
    clothes peg mutyarta tita *n*
    clothes shop mutyarta wardli *n*
cloud maku *n*
club (weapon) wirri *n* (for throwing); katha *n*; katha wirri *n* (decorated with streaks like the wirri); parnga *n*; tatarta *n*; pangkawirri *n* (Ngarrindjeri)
    long and heavy club ngarlawirri *n*
coal (red hot) ngauwaka *n*
coat turti-ana *n*; turti-anurla *n*
cockatiel wirdupa *n*
cockatoo
    red-tailed black cockatoo yutika *n* (*Calyptorhynchus banksii*)
    yellow-tailed black cockatoo tiwu *n*; wilampa *n*
    white cockatoo kurdaki *n*
cockroach (native) winana *n*
cod (Murray) parntu *n* (*Maccullochella peelii*)
coffee kuupi *n*
coil yarla-marta *adv*
cold (illness) kurlti *n*
    have a cold nuki ngarntanthi *v-intr*

cold (not hot) manya *n*
  be cold manyarrinthi *v-intr*; martarninthi *v-intr*
  be very cold pakirrinthi *v-intr*
  become very cold payanantinthi *v-intr*
  feel cold manyarrinthi *v-intr*
  get cold manya payarnantinthi *v-intr*
  very cold (weather) manyapayana *adj*
collapse piltilinthi *v-intr*
  collapse (faint) tungki warturrinthi *v-intr*
collarbone ngukurda *n*
  indentation above the collarbone kauwiyapa *n*
collect kumangka malturri-apinthi *v-tr*; malturri-apinthi *v-tr*; ngirrinthi *v-tr*; tultyurri-apinthi *v-tr*; tuyunthi (var. tuiyunthi) *v-tr*
comb yuka wirrkati *n*
come pudnanthi *v-intr*
  come! kawai! *intj*
  come back again nungku-nhungkurninthi *v-intr*
  come close kurdantarninthi *v-intr*
  come closer tirdi-apinthi *v-tr*
  come forth tarnanthi (var. tarninthi) *v-intr*
  come here (you all) kawainga! *v-imp*
  come near kurdarrinthi *v-intr*
  come near to ityarrinthi *v-tr*
  come of age (females) ngama-ngamaityarntinthi *v-intr*
  come out tapalayinthi *v-intr*
  coming from -nungku (var. -anangku; -nangku; -unungku) *suff (on nouns)* (ablative)
comfortable (be) kuntu yartarninthi *v-intr*
command kalti-apinthi *v-tr*; kaltinthi *v-tr*; yarltinthi (var. yarltirrinthi) *v-tr*
  commander yarltirri-purka *n*
common
  in common with wirringka *adv*
  common grey mouse purkupurku *n*
  common jollytail (fish) mipurli *n (Galaxias maculatus)*
communal (shared) taikurringka *adj*
communicate mailtyarrinthi *v-intr*
  communicate a message mailtyarri-apinthi *v-intr*
  communicate to warra yungkunthi *v-tr*; yungkunthi *v-tr*
  communicate with marrkarriapinthi *v-tr*

compact kadlunthi *v-tr*
companion niipu *n*
company (of soldiers) pirku *n*
compare mailtyamailtyarrina
compass tuturtu *n*
compassion (have) tangka wayinthi (var. tangka wayirrinthi) *v-intr*
  compassion for (have) tangka mankurrinthi$_1$ *v-intr*
compatriot miyuwarta *n*
complain marrkarri-apinthi *v-intr*; tatarrinthi *v-intr*
  complaining person marrkarripurka *n*
complete mardlarri-apinthi (var. marlarri-apinthi) *v-tr*; murla parltanthi *v-tr*; purruna *adj*; yalura *adj*
  completely -anta$_1$ (var. -nta$_1$; -nti) *suff (on nouns)*
complex sentence wapiwarrarla karrpa *n*
compose oneself manyinthi *v-intr*; pilyurninthi *v-intr*
compressed kartaityarri *adj*
computer mukarntu *n*
conceal ngaranthi (var. ngara-ngaranthi) *v-intr*; tirra-apinthi *v-tr*
  concealed tirrangka *adj*
  conceal oneself tirranthi *v-intr*; wiltirrkayinthi *v-intr*
concerned (be) kuntu yartarrinthi *v-intr*
condole tangka wayinthi (var. tangka wayirrinthi) *v-intr*
conference panpa-panpalya *n*
congolli warapina *n (Pseudaphritis urvilli)*
connect tarraitpayinthi *v-tr*
connoisseur ngaingku *n*
consider kuinpinthi *v-tr*; nakurninthi *v-intr*; payinthi (var. payirrinthi) *v-tr*
  consider sacred or forbidden kuinyuntapinthi *v-tr*
  make someone consider payirri-apinthi *v-tr*
console (oneself) pilyurninthi *v-intr*
constantly nurntirdlu-arra (var. nurntirluarra) *adv*
constellation
  Orion Tininyarrarna *n*
  Seven Sisters Mankamankarrarna *n (Pleiades)*
  Southern Cross Wirltu Tidna *n*
construct pintyanthi (var. pingkanthi; pingyanthi; pinkanthi) *v-tr*
consume kurrkinthi *v-tr*; ngarkunthi *v-tr*
contagious yarnka-yarnkanya *adj*

container kuru *n*
contemplate mukarta karra-yarnkanthi *v-intr*
contemporary kurlana *adj*
content (be) kuntu yartarninthi *v-intr*
    content (become) wingku marnirninthi *v-intr*
continue -alya *suff (on verbs)*; muinmurninthi *v-intr*; turtpanthi *v-intr*
    continuing nurntina *adv*
    continually tiwi *adv*; nurntiki *adv*; nurntirdluarra (var. nurntirluarra) *adv*; tudnu₁ *adv*
contract minturninthi (var. mintuminturninthi) *v-intr*
contradict manta kurrurrinthi (var. manta kurrikurrinthi; manta kurrulyinthi; manta-urri-urrinthi) *v-tr*; manta-urri-urrinthi *v-tr*; yurni yartarrinthi *v-tr*; yurningka turrkunthi *v-tr*
converse with warrapanthi *v-intr*
cook kampalampala *n*; kampanthi *v-tr*
    cooked mutarta (var. murtata; mutata) *adj*
    cooking bench kampa-tharralyi *n*
    cooking pit kanyayapa *n*
cool yalta-yalta *adj*; yaltana *adj*
    be/become cool yaltinthi *v-intr*
    become cool ngapurlantinthi *v-intr*
    cool (something) down yalti-apinthi *v-tr*
coot kawana *n*
copy mailtyanthi *v-tr*
cord ngari *n*
cordial kuntanyi *n*
cormorant yuulti *n*
corn kuuni *n*
corner nurlu *n*; nurluta *n*; wangkurti *n*
    corner of mouth taa-nhurlu *n*
corpse kadli-adli (var. kadli-kadli) *n*; karltathakarra *n*; nudnu (var. nunu) *n*; tuwarri *n*
correct tiyati *intj, adv*; numa *adj*; wilta *adj*
    be/become correct wiltarninthi *v-intr*
    correctly numa *adv*
corrupt waadli-apinthi *v-tr*
cotton for sewing widni *n*
cough kurlti *n*; kurltinthi *v-intr*
counseller yarltirri-purka *n*
count wanpa-wanpanthi *v-tr*; marka-markanthi *v-tr*
country yarta *n*; pangkarra *n* (inherited land)
    countryman miyuwarta *n*; yartamiyu *n*
couple partatangkurla *n*
    married couple kartutarla *n*
courageous pulthawilta *adj*; tangkaru wilta *adj*; wayiwilta *adj*
cousin kauwawa *n* (mother's brother's/father's sister's child)
cover kuu (var. kuukuu) *n*; taa tartati *n*; tartanthi *v-tr*; tirra tartanthi *v-tr*
    cover over tartarrinthi *v-tr*
    cover over (hole) taa tartanthi *v-tr*
    cover with wadlu pumanthi *v-tr*
    get covered in purturninthi *v-intr*
    having a covered face yurlu-thartarri *adj*
    covered house tarta wardli *n*
    covering (for body) turnki *n*
    covering for pubic area yudna *n* (men's)
covertly ngararaka *adv*
covet padlurninthi *v-tr*
crab tarnipaitya *n*
crackle ngintirrinthi *v-intr*; tarntinthi *v-intr, v-tr*
    crackle (fire) parntinthi *v-intr*; piltilainthi *v-intr*
cranky wingku-wingku *adj*
crave padlurninthi *v-tr*
crawl maranthi *v-intr*; maturrinthi *v-intr*; tirdinthi *v-intr*
crayfish (freshwater) kungkurla *n* (*Cherax destructor*); ngaltaitya *n* (*Cheerax destructor*)
creased nipa-nhipa *adj*
create pintyanthi (var. pingkanthi; pingyanthi; pinkanthi) *v-tr*
    creation munaintya *n*
    creator pintyalintyala (var. pingkya-lingkyala) *n*; warti partana *n*
    Creation being Munaintyarlu *n*; Nadnu (var. Nanu) *n*
creek pari *n*
creep yurrunthi (var. yurrurrinthi) *v-intr*
    creep back nguimpayinthi *v-intr*
    creeping muri-murinya *adj*
crested pigeon yungura *n*
cricket (sport or insect) yartapirriti *n*
crippled tidna murtana *n*
criticise nunyanthi (var. nunya-nhunyanthi) *v-tr*; pilyunthi *v-tr*; tawanthi *v-tr*
cross (angry) wingku-wingku *adj*
    be cross waadli kudnanthi (var. wadli kudna-kudnanthi) *v-intr*; wingku tikanthi *v-intr*

cross (Christian) tatayaingki *n*

cross (wooden) tarralyi *n*

crosscut saw maana *n*; tiya wirruti (var. tiya wirruta) *n*

cross-wise sticks (ceremony) palyathata *n*

crow kuwa *n*

    crow's nest manara *n*

crowd kanyanya *n*; wiwurra *n*

crown of the head kurdu *n*

cruel tangkawilta *adj*

    become cruel tangka wiltarninthi *v-intr*

    cruel person tangka pardu *n*

crush midli mankunthi *v-tr*; midlinthi (var. milinthi) *v-tr*

cry (call) karlta *n*

    cry out karltanthi *v-tr*

    cryer karlta-karltanya *n*

    crying karlta-karltanya *n*

cry (with emotion) murrkanthi *v-intr*; kukarrinthi *v-intr*; ngarrinthi (var. ngarri-ngarrinthi) *v-intr*; ngartarrinthi *v-intr*

    crying miimurrka *n*; murrka *n*

    cry over murrka yungkunthi *v-intr*

    make someone cry murrkamanthi *v-tr*

crystal maki *n*

cup tukuru (var. tukukuru) *n*

    cup the hands marawakanthi *v-tr* (to drink or catch something)

cupboard wilti-tharralyi *n*

curious (be/feel) yurlu wayanthi *v-intr*

curled yukuna *adj*

    be/become curled yukurninthi *v-intr*

currawong (grey) kuyurra *n* (*Strepera versicolor*)

curry pardu-wirrka *n*

curse (magic) warrarra (var. warra-warra) *n*

curve nurlu *n*

cut mingka$_2$ *n*; pakinthi *v-tr*; kurntanthi *v-tr*

    get cut mingkarninthi *v-intr*

    cut into pieces pirrki pakinthi *v-tr*

    cut it out! tiwirti! *intj*

    cut off piltinthi *v-tr*; purtunthi *v-tr*

    cut off (someone's) hair pintarni-apinthi (var. pintapintarni-apinthi) *v-tr*

    cut open taapa pakinthi *v-tr*

    cut through piltinthi *v-tr*

    cut up midli kurntanthi *v-tr* (into bits)

cutting board paki-tharralyi *n*

ceremonial cut(s) ngulta *n*; ngurra *n*

cut oneself kurntarrinthi *v-intr*; pakirrinthi *v-intr*; pungkurrinthi *v-intr*

cylinder witu-thurlu (var. witu-thurdlu) *n*

cyprus pine narnu *n* (*Callitris*)

D d

dad ngaityarli *n*

dagger (made of wood or bone) warpu (var. wartpu) *n*

daggy (sheep) kudnapurtu *adj*

damaged mingkamingka *adj*

damn! yaka! *intj* (expression of aversion)

damp nungurru (var. nungnurru) *adj*

    become damp ngapurlantinthi *v-intr*; nungurru-antinthi (var. nungnurru-antinthi) *v-intr*

dance mukanthi (var. mukarrinthi) *v-intr*; ngunya-wayinthi *v-intr*; ngunyawayiti *n*; palti$_1$ *n*

dangerous (spiritually) kuinyunta *adj*

dark (coloured) pulyuna *adj*

    be/become dark coloured pulyurrinthi *v-intr*

    cause to become dark pulyu-ulyapinthi *v-tr*

dark (weather) madlumadlu (var. madluadlu) *adj*

    be/become dark and cloudy pulyurrinthi *v-intr*

    get dark madlu-adlurninthi (var. madlumadlurninthi) *v-intr*

    darkness madlu *n* (weather)

darkness (night) ngulthi *n*

    be dark ngulthinthi *v-intr*

    get dark ngulthirninthi *v-intr*

    still dark ngulthi-puru *temp*

data projector turapati *n*

date (go out with) kaka-papanthi *v-tr*

daughter tukuparka *n*

dawdle pidnarrinthi (var. pidna-pidnarrinthi) *v-intr*

dawn tirntu-umpu *n*

day tirntu *n*; yala *n*; yulta *n*

    during the day yalartangka *temp*

    day after tomorrow yala-tharrkarri (var. yalarrkarri; yalta-tharrkarri) *temp*

    daylight (become) walarantinthi *v-intr*

    Monday Kumirntu *n*

    Tuesday Purlirntu *n*

    Wednesday Marnku-irntu *n*

    Thursday Yarapurlirntu *n*

Friday Milirntu *n*
Saturday Padnipadninyirntu *n*
Sunday Minkirntu *n*

dead padli *adj*; miitu puulti *adj* (euphemistic); tuwarri *adj*
   dead body tuwarri *n*
   dead person kuinyu *n*; kadli-adli (var. kadli-kadli) *n*; karltathakarra *n*; padluntyila *n*
   be dead and drying out murlanthi *v-intr*
   avoid mentioning the dead kurdinthi (var. kuyinthi) *v-tr*
   deadly! paitya! *intj*
deaf yuritina *adj*
dear alya *cli, intj*
decay parltarrinthi (var. parlta-parltarrinthi) *v-intr*; tungkirninthi *v-intr*
deceased relatives
   deceased father pukilya *n*
   deceased mother arratina *n*
   deceased older sister kutarri *n*
   deceased younger siblings panyarla *n*
   deceased brother-in-law tanturlatina *n*
deceive manta wangkanthi *v-intr*; manta warrawarrarninthi *v-intr*
December Wartiki *n*
decrease murrmarninthi *v-intr*
   decrease (number) tukutyarninthi (var. tukutyarntinthi) *v-intr*
deep yaki *adj, adv*
   deep place yaki *n*
   deeper yaki-arlti *adj*; yakintyarla (var. yakinyarlu) *adj*
   deeply yaki-arra *adv*
defecate kudnatinthi *v-intr*; murtatinthi *v-tr*
defective murtana *adj*
defender (sport) tirrapina *n*
defiance nangkarra
   be defiant nangkarrinthi *v-intr*
definitely wantaka *adv*
deformed murtana *adj*; yukuna *adj*
   deformed foot tidna murtana *n*
dejected (be) kurturrinthi *v-intr*
   be/look dejected katpinthi *v-intr*
delay pidnanthi *v-intr*; turdi-thurdirninthi *v-intr*
delicate mananya *adj*
demand kaltinthi *v-tr*; witi-witinthi *v-tr*
   be demanding nurnpurrinthi *v-intr*
   demanding person kaltikaltinya *adj*
   demand something wuinpanthi (var. wuingpanthi) *v-tr*
den pinti *n*; yapa *n*
dense fog putyi *n*
dental floss tiyangari *n*
depend on yarnkanthi *v-tr*
depend upon nangkarrinthi *v-intr*
deposit kurda-kurdanthi *v-tr*
depression below the sternum muiyuminti *n* (scrobiculus cordis/epigastric fossa)
depths (in the) yakingka *loc*
descend trrukanthi (var. turrukanthi) *v-intr, v-tr*; trrukarrinthi *v-intr*
designs on animal skins wirrkati (var. wirrkiti) *n*
desire kuntu warpurninthi *v-tr*; padlurninthi *v-tr*; wingku parlta-parltarrinthi *v-intr*; wingku tikanthi *v-intr*; witi-witinthi *v-tr*; muiyu *n*
   desire women murntu padlunthi *v-intr*
   desiring -marnguta *suff* (on nouns); padlurnintyarla *adj*
despise kurta-kurtarrinthi *v-tr*; wikinthi (var. wiki-wikinthi) *v-tr*
destitute maitina *adj*
destroy nuinyanthi *v-tr*
   be destructive nuinyarrinthi *v-intr*
   destructive person nuinyarri-purka *n*
deter parnpanthi *v-tr*
   deterring parnpa-parnpanya *n*
deteriorate (cause to) wakinhanti-apinthi (var. wakinhantapinthi) *v-tr*
determined (be or become) wiltarninthi *v-intr*
detest waadli nakunthi *v-tr*
devil kuinyu *n*
devour ika-payanthi *v-tr*; kurrkinthi *v-tr*; tarnkunthi *v-tr*
dew kudmu *n*; purrku *n*
diaphragm tangka-artarta *n*
dictionary warrapiipa *n*
die padlunthi *v-intr*; mardlinthi *v-intr*; kuinyurninthi *v-intr*; wingku parltarrinthi *v-intr*; tuwarrinthi *v-intr*; maitkanthi *v-intr*; miiturninthi *v-intr*; wingku-wingkurtarrinthi *v-intr*
   die from a disease warrangkurninthi *v-intr*
difference warltu (var. warti warltu) *n*

different kumarta *adj*; yara *adj, adv*
dig kukanthi *v-tr* (not deeply)
    dig out karnkanthi *v-tr*
    dig up pakanthi *v-tr*
    digger (person) kukalukala *n*
    digging stick katha *n*
diligent maityuka₁ *adj*; wirrkuta *adj*
    be diligent wirrkutaiyinthi *v-intr*
    become diligent wirrkutarninthi *v-intr*
diminish tukutyarninthi (var. tukutyarntinthi) *v-intr*
dingo kadli *n*
    untamed dingo warru-kadli *n*
    dingo hide maikuntu *n*
dining room muta-mutanya kuu *n*
dinner
    midday meal kurdana mai *n*; yultamai *n*
    evening meal tawu-mai *n*
dip into ngatpanthi *v-intr* (e.g. water)
direct mikarri-apinthi *v-tr*; patinthi (var. pati-patinthi) *v-tr*
    direct a horse kurtarri-apinthi *v-tr*
directly tutu *adj*; tutumpurri *adv*
dirt yarta *n*; mapa *n*
    dirty yartapurtu *adj*; kudnapurtu *adj*; maparra *adj*; trrunga (var. trrunga-trrunga) *adj*
    be/become dirty pulyurrinthi *v-intr*
    cause to become dirty pulyu-ulyapinthi *v-tr*
    lump of dirt turtu (var. yarta turtu) *n*
disagreement nguyanguya *n*; warltu (var. warti warltu) *n*
    disagreeable warpularra *adj*
disappear kumpanthi *v-intr*; pulthurninthi *v-intr*
disappointed tangka marnitina
discontent (be) yurni ngarntanthi *v-intr*
    discontented person taa pidlarri-purka *n*
disease kuku *n*; warrangku *n*
    infectious or contagious disease yarnka-yarnkanya *adj*
    be/become diseased kukurninthi *v-intr*
disembowel kudnanthi *v-tr*
disengage tiltyalayinthi (var. tiltyalinthi) *v-intr*
disentangle tiltyalayinthi (var. tiltyalinthi) *v-intr*
dish mai wantawantati *n*
    dish containing both meat and vegetable foods nantarti *n*

dishonest person mantapartana *n*
dislike kuntu pamanthi *v-tr*; kuntu pungkunthi *v-tr*; waadlirrinthi *v-intr*; yitpi ngarntanthi *v-intr*
    disliking- -waadli *suff* (on nouns)
disobedient yama (var. yamayama₁) *adj*; yuritina *adj*
    be disobedient nuinyarrinthi *v-intr*; yamarrinthi *v-intr*; yuri tarrinthi *v-intr*; yurni tarrinthi *v-intr*
    become disobedient yamarninthi (var. yamarntinthi) *v-intr*
disorderly yara-kartarta *adj*
disorientated (on waking up) miituthungki *adj*
disperse piarri-apinthi *v-tr*
    dispersed paintya-yaintya *adj*
disprove manta kururrinthi (var. manta kurrikurrinthi; manta kurrulyinthi; manta-urri-urrinthi) *v-tr*; manta- urri-urrinthi *v-tr*
dissatisfied (be) marrkarri-apinthi *v-intr*; nuinyanthi *v-intr*; waadli kudnanthi (var. wadli kudna-kudnanthi) *v- intr*; yurni ngarntanthi *v-intr*
    become dissatisfied yamarninthi (var. yamarntinthi) *v-intr*
dissolve kalyarninthi *v-intr*
dissuading parnpa-parnpanya *n*
distant karradla (var. karradlu; karraidla) *loc*; nurnti *adv*
distinct kumarta *adj*; yara *adj, adv*
distort nadla-nhadlarrinthi (var. nala-nhalarrinthi) *v-intr*
distribute pirrki-apinthi₁ *v-tr*
district pangkarra *n* (inherited land)
ditch pinti *n*
dive panminthi *v-intr*
    dive into ngatpanthi *v-intr* (the water, a room, an item of clothing)
    dive (into or under) kaka-ngatpanthi *v-intr*
divide kumartapinthi *v-tr*; pirrki-apinthi₁ *v-tr*; yaramanthi *v-tr*
    divide in two wirrumanthi *v-tr*
    divide a kangaroo wili kurntanthi *v-tr*
division (group) pirku *n* (of people)
do wapinthi *v-tr*; wayinthi (var. -kaiyinthi; -layi; wauwinthi) *v-intr*
    do together (with someone else) taikurri-apinthi *v-tr*
    do not -rti (var. -ngkurti; -ngurti; -urti; wirti) *suff* (on verbs) (prohibitive)
dob on mangki-mangki-apinthi *v-tr*

doctor warrarra (var. warra-warra) *n*; yamayama *n*
dog kadli *n*; putyita *n*; wirka *n*
    wild dog warru-kadli *n*
    dog owner kadli mathanya *n*
    dog-ear kadliyuri *n*
dolphin yampu *n*
domineering person kaltikaltinya *adj*
donor yungkulungkula *n*
don't -rti (var. -ngkurti; -ngurti; -urti; wirti) *suff (on verbs) (prohibitive)*
    don't! yaku-alya! *intj*
    don't fight! turlarti! *intj*
door narna *n*
dorsal vertebrae pulthawarta *n*
dots pakurta *n*
doubled over purla pilta-pilturru *adj*
doubt someone manta kurrurrinthi (var. manta kurrikurrinthi; manta kurrulyinthi; manta-urri-urrinthi) *v-tr*
down (feel) kadlurrinthi *v-intr*
down (of feather) ngaru *n*
draft (into the army) tantapinthi *v-tr*
drag (something) wartanthi *v-tr* (behind)
    drag your feet warka-warkarrinthi *v-intr*
dragonfly species puntu-untu *n* (large)
draw (following pre-marked lines) pulthu-arrapinthi *v-intr*
draw (pull)
    draw back winturrinthi *v-tr*
    draw back legs taturrinthi *v-intr*
    draw out (extract) karnkanthi *v-tr*; manthi *v-tr*
    draw out or up namarrinthi *v-tr*
    draw near kurdantarnthi *v-intr*
dread wayikurtanthi *v-intr, v-tr*
    be full of dread mangkulayinthi *v-intr*
dream tangkuinya *n*; tangkuinyinthi *v-intr*
    cause to dream tangkuinyapinthi *v-tr*
    Dreamtime munaintya *n*
    Dreaming story munaintya pirrku
dressed (get) tarrinthi *v-tr*
dribble trrukanthi (var. turrukanthi) *v-tr*; yurlanthi (var. yurdlanthi) *v-intr*
drink mutanthi *v-tr*; ngarkunthi *v-tr*
    be drunk (intoxicated) wakarrinthi *v-intr*
drip yurlanthi (var. yurdlanthi) *v-intr*

drive yudlunthi *v-tr*
    driver's licence yudlupiipa *n*
drizzling rain kauwimiila *n*; putyi *n*
drool tadlirrkantinthi *v-intr*
drop trrukanthi (var. turrukanthi) *v-tr*; wardni-apinthi *v-tr*; wardninthi (var. warninthi) *v-intr*
    droppings madlara *n* (of herbivore)
drown mudlharrangkinthi *v-intr*
    drowned mudlharrangki *adj*
drum (possum skin) tapurru *n*
    drumming on cloaks in ceremony munti *n*
drunk (be) wakarrinthi *v-intr*
dry murla *adj*; pulturru *adj*
    be/become dry warpurninthi *v-intr*
    dry (something) murla-ityarri-apinthi *v-tr*
    dry out murlanthi *v-intr*; murlarninthi *v-intr*
    dry air pulturru *n*
    dry leaf tinkyu *n*
    dry riverbed purtu pari *n*
    dry a skin papanthi *v-tr*
    dryer murlapiti *n*
duck
    blue-winged shoveler tawanta *n* (Spatula rhynchotis)
dull mantinguya *adj*
dumb (speechless) warratina *adj*
dung kudna *n*; murta *n*
dunny kudnawardli *n*
during the day yalartangka *temp*
during the night ngulthingka *temp*
dusk karrka₁ *n*; tawu *n*
dust murdu *n*; wirraitya *n*
    turn to dust murdurninthi *v-intr*
    dust cloud wirraitya *n*
dwell tikanthi *v-intr*
    dwelling wardli (var. warli) *n*
dying padlunyana *adj*

E e

each other -nungkurrinthi *suff (on verbs)*; -rri *suff (on verbs) (reflexive/reciprocal)*; yara *adj, adv*
eagle (wedge-tailed) wirltu *n* (Aquila audax)
    eagle species pila *n* (undefined)
ear yuri *n*
    inner ear yuriapa *n*

earshot (come into) yuri pamanthi (var. yuri pamarrinthi) *v-tr*

early
    early morning ngulthi-puru *temp*
    earlier yalarra *temp* (today)

earnest yurlu-puyu-puyurri *adj*
    in earnest turla *adv*; yurlu-puyurringka *adv*

earth yarta *n*
    earth oven kanyayapa *n*

easily minkuminku *adv*

east marri *n*
    easterly marriku (var. marrika) *dir*

Easter Yiitya *n*
    Easter Sunday Tarnirntu *n*
    Happy Easter! Ngunya Yiitya! *intj*

eat ngarkunthi *v-tr*; mainthi *v-tr*; mutanthi *v-tr*; payanthi *v-tr*; widlanthi (var. wilanthi) *v-tr*
    eat greedily tarnkunthi *v-tr*
    eat hungrily turla ngarkunthi *v-tr*
    eat meat and vegetables together nantanthi *v-tr*
    eat quickly mutanthi *v-tr*
    eat while you walk along karrampu ngarkunthi *v-tr*
    eater ngarkularkula *n*

edge marlta *n*

edible mutarta (var. murtata; mutata) *adj*
    edible foods ngarku-ngarkunya *n*
    edible root (undefined) ngampa *n*; tidla *n*; walyu *n*
    edible root of marshmallow plant pityarra *n*

educate nakurni-apinthi (var. nakulyarni-apinthi) *v-tr*; yathu-apinthi *v-tr*

eel-tailed catfish ngalta yawitya *n* (*Tandanus tandanus*)

egg muka *n*
    eggshell tarrka *n*
    egg white ngayirda *n*
    egg yolk mininta *n*

eight ngarla *num*
    eighteen kumirrka ngarla *num*
    eighty ngarlirrka *num*
    eight hundred ngarla partirrka *num*
    eight thousand ngarlawata *num*
    eight million ngarliwurra *num*
    eighth-born child Ngadlaitya *n* (male); Ngadlartu *n* (female)

elastic nainguta *adj*; widnurru *adj*

elbow tidngi *n*
    inside of the elbow karltapinti *n*

Elder purka *n*

eldest child in family marna *n* (male or female)

electricity karntu *n*
    electric wire/cord karntungari *n*
    electric heater karntu nguyuti *n*

eleven kumirrka kuma *num*
    eleven million kumirrka kumiwurra *num*

eloquent marltawilta *adj*
    not eloquent marltangaitya *adj*

email karntiipa *n*

embarrass (someone) kurdukarri-apinthi *v-tr*
    embarrassment kurdukarri *n*
    be/feel embarrassed kurdukarrinthi *v-intr*

ember (glowing) ngauwaka *n*
    embers of fire kardla (var. karla) *n*

embrace martinthi *v-tr*; martirrinthi *v-intr*

emerge tapalayinthi (var. tapa-thapalayinthi) *v-intr*

employ (use) marrkurri-apinthi *v-tr*
    employ (hire) tantapinthi *v-tr*

empty kurla *adv*
    emptiness kurlapulthu *n*

emu kardi *n*
    female emu murltarra *n*; taitya *n*
    young emu kuri-kuri *n*
    emu feathers in a tuft kardiwapa *n*

enchant kurrkunthi *v-tr*; nurrunthi *v-tr*
    enchantment nurruti *n*

encircle kurdinthi (var. kuyinthi) *v-tr*

enclose kurdirri-apinthi *v-tr*; purnpunthi *v-tr*

Encounter Bay Wirramu *n*

encourage marka wayinthi *v-tr* (someone to do something)

end warta *n*
    end (of object) wari *n*; munu *n*; mudlha-iku *n*

endive yarnti *n*

engage (hire) tantapinthi *v-tr*

enjoy ngarkunthi *v-tr*; ngunya mankunthi *v-tr*; wingku marnirninthi *v-intr*; mutanthi *v-tr*

enlarge yarrurrinthi *v-intr*

enough pirdi (var. pirdina) *adj*; pirdina *adj*; ngaraitya *n*
    enough! natapirdi! *intj*

enquire ingkarninthi *v-tr*
   enquire after ngartinthi (var. ngartirrinthi) *v-tr*; yurlu ngartinthi *v-tr*

enraged turla *adj*
   be enraged wuinpa-wuinpanthi (var. wuingpa-wuingparrinthi) *v-intr*
   become enraged tangkarurninthi *v-intr*

enter ngatpanthi *v-intr* (the water, a room, an item of clothing); ngatparrinthi *v-intr*; tidnatidnanthi *v-intr*

entirely -anta$_1$ (var. -nta$_1$; -nti) *suff (on nouns)*; partana (var. -partana) *adj*; tudnu$_1$ *adv*
   entirety tupa *n*

entrails piti *n*

entreat marnkanthi *v-tr*

envy marngu$_1$ *n*; marngutanthi *v-intr*
   be envious marngungkinthi *v-intr*

epigastric fossa muiyuminti *n* (*scrobiculus cordis*)

equal to turathurana *adj*
   equinox turathurana ngulthi *n*

equip (oneself) with tarranthi *v-tr*

erase kurlinthi *v-tr*
   eraser kumpapiti *n*

erect pintyanthi (var. pingkanthi; pingyanthi; pinkanthi) *v-tr*; tayinthi (var. tayirrinthi) *v-tr*
   erection (sexual) nita *n*

err wakarrinthi *v-intr*

escape pulthurninthi *v-intr*; taltapinthi *v-intr*
   allow to escape pulthurniapinthi *v-tr*

escort pirrku mankunthi *v-tr*

essence martu *n*; martu *n*

euro tarka *n*

European pinti *adj*; pintinungku *adj*
   European carp tukapina *n* (*Cyprinus carpio*)
   European goose pinti pita *n*
   European person kuinyu *n*; pinti miyu *n*

evacuate the bowels kudnatinthi *v-intr*

even (smooth) maturta *adj*

evening ngulthi-warta *n*; tawu *n*
   evening breeze karrkawarri *n*; tawurri *n*
   evening meal ngulthi-mai *n*
   redness of the evening sky tawurri *n*

every
   every time partarluku *adv*
   everyday tirntu-irntu *temp*
   everything tupa *n*

evidence pulthu *n*

evil wakinha *adj*
   evil spirit nukuna *n*

eviscerate kudnanthi *v-tr*

examine payinthi (var. payirrinthi) *v-tr*; naku-nhakunthi *v-tr*; wayanthi (var. waya-wayanthi) *v-tr*; nguntiapinthi *v-tr*

exchange tanta *n*; tita *n*; wakuinya *n*; wakuinyapinthi *v-tr*; yungkurrinthi *v-tr*
   in exchange titangka

excited (be) purtinthi *v-intr*

excrement kudna *n*; madlara *n* (of herbivore)
   animal excrement murta *n*
   excrement and bowels of kangaroo multyumultyu *n*

exert oneself warpulayinthi *v-intr*; warpuwiltarrinthi *v-intr*

exhaustion kathi *n*

exist wantinthi *v-intr*

expand yarrurrinthi *v-intr*

expect martarrinthi *v-tr*

experience mailtyanthi *v-tr*

expert ngaingku *n*
   be/become an expert ngaingkurni-apinthi *v-intr*

expire tuwarrinthi *v-intr*

explain mailtyarri-apinthi *v-intr*

extend pudnanthi *v-intr*; turtpanthi *v-intr*; tuwinarntinthi *v-intr*
   extensive takana$_2$ *adj*

exterior warru *n* (of something)

extinguish padlu-parltanthi *v-tr*

extremity wari *n*

extricate tiltyalayinthi (var. tiltyalinthi) *v-intr*

eye mii *n*; miina *n*
   eyeball miimunthu *n*
   eyebrow piku (var. piku-puthi) *n*
   eyelashes miipadlu *n*
   eyelid miipaltha *n*; miiwardli *n*
   white of the eye miiparkana *n* (*sclera*)
   have eyes wide open miipudnanthi *v-intr*

F f

face murki *n*; yurlu (var. yurirlu) *n*; mika *n*
   face mask murkipaltha *n*

fade wityarninthi *v-intr*
faeces kudna *n*
faint ngaityana *adj*
    faint- -ngaitya *suff (on nouns)*
    faint (pass out) tungki warturrinthi *v-intr*
fall wardninthi (var. warninthi) *v-intr*
    fall apart pirrki wayinthi *v-intr*; parltarrinthi (var. parlta-parltarrinthi) *v-intr*
    fall asleep miiturninthi *v-intr*
    falling asleep miitu-itya *adj*
    be falling asleep miitu kadlunthi (var. miitu kadlurrinthi) *v-intr*
    fall down wardninthi (var. warninthi) *v-intr*; kaka-wardninthi (var. kaka-warninthi) *v-intr*; trrukanthi (var. turrukanthi) *v-intr*
    falling wardni-wardninya *adj*
    cause to/let fall wardni-apinthi *v-tr*
    fall heavily parltanthi *v-intr*, *v-tr*
    fall in drops yurlanthi (var. yurdlanthi) *v-intr*
    fall in love with muiyu mankunthi *v-tr*
    fallen log waadla *n*
    fallen tree waadlawarnka *n*
    fallen tree across a river waadlakatha *n*
false waadli *adj*
    false statement manta warrawarra *n*; yukuna warra *n*
    falsely accuse marta-martanthi *v-tr*
family taikurtirna *n*
fan (air) wampi (var. wampiti) *n*; wampinthi *v-intr*, *v-tr*
far away karradla (var. karradlu; karraidla) *loc*; nurnti-anta *loc*
    far away from nurntidlu (var. nurntirlu) *loc*
    far off nurnti *adv*
farmland putpa yarta *n*
    farmhouse putpayartawardli *n*
farther nurntiki *loc*
    farther away nurntiki *loc*
    farther away on the other side nguntartinyarlangka *loc*
fast (quickly) nganta *adv*; wirila *adv*; kumatpi *adv*; kurla-ityu *adv*
    fast food muta-mutarru *n*
fasten nayanthi *v-tr*; tarnpanthi *v-tr*; tarnparri-apinthi *v-tr*; titapinthi *v-tr*
    fastener tita *n*
fat marni *n*; kurrkurla *n*; paitpurla *n*

be fat marninthi *v-intr*
get fat marnirninthi *v-intr*
fat person ngurrunturru *n*
father yarli-miyu *n*; yarlita *n*
    my father ngaityarli *n*
    your father ninkarli *n*
    father's father madlala (var. marlala) *n*
    father's mother ngapapi *n*
    father's sister ngarrpadla *n*
    father's older brother ngangaitya (var. ngangaityi) *n*
    man's father-in-law kauwani *n*; ngarrparrpu *n*
    man's father-in-law relationship kauwanata *n*
    people in a father relationship yarli-yarliwarta *n*
    father and child yarlita-urla *n*
    at/with the father yarlitatila
    father of -purka *suff (on nouns)*
    father of hanged person ngari wikarnti *n*
    deceased father pukilya *n*
    fatherless person warnpi *n*; warrinya *n*
    Father's Day Yarli Tirntu (var. Yarlirntu) *n*
    Happy Father's Day! Ngunya Yarli Tirntu! *intj*
fatigue kathi *n*
    be fatigued ngarrampulanthi *v-intr*; wirrarrinthi (var. witharrinthi) *v-intr*
fault (find) wikinthi (var. wiki-wikinthi) *v-tr*
favourite martu-alya
    favourite child kurlakurlana (var. kurlakurlanta) *n*
    get into favour with (someone) tangka mankunthi *v-tr*
fear wayi *n*; tangkaru *n*; wayikurtanthi *v-intr*, *v-tr*; wayirninthi *v-intr*
    be fearful mangkulayinthi *v-intr*
    fearless pulthawilta *adj*; tangkaru wilta *adj*; wayiwilta *adj*
feather tarlti *n*; wapa *n*
    feathers pardlu *n*
    feather headdress witu-witu *n*
    ceremonial feathers wirltu-ngaru *n*
    featherfoot (kadaitja) nukuna *n*
February Purliki *n*
feeble ngaityana *adj*; parltarta (var. parltarti) *adj* (object)
feel kurdanthi *v-intr*, *v-tr*
    feelings muiyu *n*

feel attached to tangka mankurrinthi₁ *v-intr*
feel pain ngarntanthi *v-intr*; tiparrinthi (var. titparrinthi) *v-intr*
cause to feel (touch) pantyapinthi *v-tr*
make someone feel sorry (for you) tangka mankurrinthi₂ *v-tr*
not feel like (doing something) waadli ngarntanthi (var. waadli-arntanthi) *v-intr*

feet tidnarla *n*
feign turtanthi₁ (var. turtarrinthi) *v-intr*
feisty turlapina *n, adj*
female ngangki *n*
    adult female ngamaitya (var. ngama-ngamaitya) *n*
    young female mankarra *n*
    female parent ngangki-miyu *n*
    female relative ngarna *n* **female genitals** minhi *n*
    female pubic area ngarta *n*

fence tarralyi *n*
    fence in kurdirri-apinthi *v-tr*
fend off (an attack) kapanthi *v-tr*
    fend off a spear karnkanthi *v-tr*
fertile putpa *adj*
    fertile land putpa yarta *n*
    become fertile (female) tuku-angkirninthi *v-intr*

fester kaikurninthi *v-intr*
fetch pudnapinthi (var. pudnanyapinthi) *v-tr*; katinthi *v-tr*; katirrinthi *v-intr*; pirrku mankunthi *v-tr*; tultyunthi *v-tr*; warunthi (var. waru-warunthi) *v-tr*
few kutyu *adj*; tukutya *adj*
    just a few kutyunti *adj*
fib manta *n*
fibrous titparra *adj*
fifteen kumirrka mila *num*
fifth-born child Midlaitya *n* (male); Midlartu *n* (female)
fifty milirrka *num*
fight irra *n*; wirra₂ *n*; turla *n*; pungkunthi *v-tr*; kurntanthi *v-tr*
    fighter irrapina (var. pirrapina) *n*; marapina *n*; miyu-katha *n*
    fight with turla ngarkunthi *v-tr*
    fight with each other tawarrinthi *v-intr*
    fight each other pungkurrinthi *v-intr*
    feel like fighting pirra-pirrarninthi *v-intr*
    pretend to fight tarntinthi *v-intr, v-tr*
    start a fight turla yakarrinthi *v-intr*
    hold someone back to stop them fighting purnpunthi *v-tr*
    not good in a fight wardni-wardninya *adj*
    fighting stick parnga *n*; tantanaku *n*
    two-edged fighting stick katha *n*; katha wirri *n* (decorated with streaks like the wirri)

filthy trrunga (var. trrunga-trrunga) *adj*
final warta *n*
finch pimpina *n*
    star finch tiitha *n*
find warri-apinthi (var. warri-warri-apinthi) *v-tr*
    find fault with wikinthi (var. wiki-wikinthi) *v-tr*
finger mangkiti *n*; mara *n*
    index finger marayarli *n*; nuuti *n*; wama₂ *n*
    little finger kurta-unyu *n*; marakurta-unyu *n*
    fingernail marapirri *n*; pirri *n*
    fingertip marawari *n*
finish murla parltanthi *v-tr*
    finish mourning tangka wiltarninthi *v-intr*
fire kardla (var. karla) *n*
    firewood kardla (var. karla) *n*; ngauwa (var. ngawaka) *n*
    feed the fire pawunthi *v-tr*
    stoke the fire purtamanthi *v-tr*
    beat out fire padlu-parltanthi *v-tr*
    firestick kardla purtultu *n*
    ceremonial firesticks purtultu kuinyu *n*
    firearm parntapurdi *n*
    firemaking apparatus kuru *n*
firm tarnpa-tharnparni *adj*; titparra *adj*; wilta *adj*
    be/become firm wiltarninthi *v-intr*
    make firm wiltarnapinthi *v-tr*
first muna *adv*; munangka *adv*; munarra *adv*; piti (var. 'iti) *adv*; pulthupuru *adv*; puru-iti (var. puru-piti) *adv*
    be/come first marka wayinthi *v-intr*
    in first place (in sport) piti (var. 'iti) *adv*
    first-born child marna *n* (male or female); Kartamiru *n* (male); Kuyata *n* (male); Kartanya (var. Kartani) *n* (female); Kartiartu *n* (female)
fish kuya *n* (in general)
    big-headed/flat-headed gudgeon parntu mukarta waitku *n* (*Philypnodon grandiceps*)
    bream karrka₂ *n* (*Acanthopagrus butcheri*)

brown trout purnkipurnki mipurli *n* (*Salmo trutta*)

climbing galaxias tati mipurli *n* (*Galaxias brevipinnis*) common

common jollytail mipurli *n* (*Galaxias maculatus*)

congolli warapina *n* (*Pseudaphritis urvilli*)

eel-tailed catfish ngalta yawitya *n* (*Tandanus tandanus*)

European carp tukapina *n* (*Cyprinus carpio*)

goldfish wiranirana kuya *n* (*Carassius auratus*)

mosquitofish kuntipaitya kuya *n* (*Gambusia affinis/holbrooki*)

mountain galaxias karnu mipurli *n* (*Galaxias olidus*)

mullet kuraitya *n* (*Aldrichetta forsteri*); marilana *n* (*Aldrichetta forsteri*)

Murray cod parntu *n* (*Maccullochella peelii*)

Murray rainbowfish kurdanyi kuya *n* (*Melanotaenia fluviatilis*)

pouched lamprey ngudlitidli nuinpi *n* (*Geotria australis*)

purple-spotted gudgeon marngu-marngu waitku *n* (*Mogurnda adspersa*)

rainbow trout kurdanyi mipurli *n* (*Oncorhynchus mykiss*)

redfin taltharni parra *n* (*Perca fluviatilis*)

river blackfish pari pulyuna kuya *n* (*Gadopsis marmoratus*)

short-headed lamprey warltutina nuinpi *n* (*Mordacia mordax*)

small-mouthed hardyhead tukuthaa kuya *n* (*Atherinosoma microstoma*)

snapper wiini *n* (*Chrysophrys auratus*)

Swan River goby patpa kupi *n* (*Pseudogobius olorum*)

tench tintyi *n* (*Tinca tinca*)

trout mipurli *n*

tupong warapina *n* (*Pseudaphritis urvilli*)

western carp gudgeon tukapina waitku *n* (*Hypseleotris klunzingeri*)

fishing (go) kuya pirriwirrkinthi *v-tr*; kuyarnapinthi *v-intr*

  fishing rod mularta *n*

  fishing line kuyangari *n*

  fishing net kuyawika *n*

  fishing spot kuya ngani *n*

  fish hook kuyapirri *n*

  fish scales kuyaparra *n*

five $mila_2$ *num*; yarapurla kuma *num*

fifteen kumirrka mila *num*

fifty milirrka *num*

five hundred mila partirrka *num*

five thousand milawata *num*

five million miliwurra *num*

flame miita *n*; kardla tadlanyi *n*; ngauwa (var. ngawaka) *n*; purta *n*

flap wampinthi *v-intr, v-tr*

flash $pinkyarrinthi_1$ (var. $pintyarrinthi_2$) *v-intr, v-tr*

flat tami *adj*; yartpana *adj*

  flatten yartpanthi *v-tr*

  flat land $wama_1$ *n*; tampa *n*; matu *n*

  flat-headed gudgeon parntu mukarta waitku *n* (*Philypnodon grandiceps*)

flavour martu *n*

flee paitya-marrinthi *v-intr*

flesh itya *n*; nudnu (var. nunu) *n*; pardu *n*

flexible pika *adj*; pika-pika *adj*

  become flexible pika-pikarninthi *v-intr*

flint maki *n*; minpi (var. mingpi) *n*

flirt with kaka-papanthi *v-tr*

flood yartala *n*

  small flood warti-warti *n*

floss tiyangari *n*

flour murdumurdu *n*

flow wayinthi (var. -kaiyinthi; -layi; wauwinthi) *v-intr*

  flow into ngatpanthi *v-intr*

flower mitika *n*; ngurika *n*; purrumpa *n*

  banksia flower kuntanyi *n*

fluent marltawilta *adj*

fluid wirrka *n*; watpana *adj*

flute winpirra (var. winpirri) *n*; witu-thurlu (var. witu-thurdlu) *n*

flutter tuki-thukinthi *v-intr*

fly karrinthi *v-intr*; wampinthi *v-intr, v-tr*

  flying karrikarrinya *adj*

  black fly tapu *n*

  blowfly tupurra *n*

  flying ant puruti *n*

  gadfly tumpula *n*

foam tadli *n*

  foam of the ocean kungkurra *n*

fog kudmu *n*; madlu *n* (weather)

  dense fog putyi *n*

  foggy madlumadlu (var. madluadlu) *adj*

fold nipa (var. niparra) *n*
   fold back on itself (e.g. clothes) pintyanthi (var. pingkanthi; pingyanthi; pinkanthi) *v-tr*
   fold together turtparninthi *v-intr*
foliage wilya *n*
follow warta mankunthi *v-tr*
   following wartangka *loc*; wartarra *loc, temp*
fondle pitunthi *v-tr*
food mai *n*
   meat food pardu *n*
   fast food muta-mutarru *n*
   having food maitidli (var. mai'dli) *adj*
   without food maitina *adj*
fool wakarripurka *n*
   fool (trick someone) manta-apinthi (var. mantapinthi) *v-tr*
   foolish yama (var. yamayama$_1$) *adj*
   be foolish wakarrinthi *v-intr*; yamarrinthi *v-intr*
   become foolish yamarninthi (var. yamarntinthi) *v-intr*
   foolish person yama partana *n*
foot tidna *n*
   football tidnaparntu *n*
   footprint tainga *n*; tidna *n*
   arch of foot tidnatangka *n*
   ball of foot tidnakuntu *n*
   instep of foot tidnapultha *n*
   deformed foot tidna murtana *n*
for -pira *suff* (on nouns)
   for (instead of) someone martungka
   for (the sake of) martu-itya
   for how much? nganangka? *inter*
   for what reason? nganapurtu-itya? *inter*
   for whom? nganalalitya? *inter*
   for (someone/something) -itya (var. -litya; -titya) *suff* (purposive)
   for me ngathaitya *pro* (purposive)
   for you nintaitya *pro* (singular purposive)
   for him/her/it padlaitya *pro* (purposive)
   for us two ngadlilitya *pro* (dual purposive)
   for us ngadlulitya *pro* (plural purposive)
   for you two niwadlitya *pro* (dual purposive)
   for you mob naalitya *pro* (purposive)
   for them parnalitya *pro* (plural purposive)
   for them two purlalitya *pro* (dual purposive)
forbid yarltinthi (var. yarltirrinthi) *v-tr*
   forbidden kuinyunta *adj*

force midla (var. mila$_1$) *n*
   without being forced yaitya (var. iyaitya) *adv*
fore
   forearm manarntu *n*
   forefinger marayarli *n*; nuuti *n*; wama$_2$ *n*
   forehead murki *n*; yurlu (var. yurirlu) *n*
   foreskin parrpa *n*
foreign pinti *adj*
forest wirra$_1$ *n*
   red gum forest karrawirra *n*
forever tudnu$_1$ *adv*
forget mukanta-wantanthi *v-tr*; mukantarri-apinthi *v-tr*; mukantarrinthi *v-tr*; wakarrinthi *v-intr*
   forget and leave behind wakarri-apinthi *v-tr*
   forgetful mukarta wangkiwangki *adj*
fork pardu-pamamati *n*
form (make) pintyanthi (var. pingkanthi; pingyanthi; pinkanthi) *v-tr*
   form a circle kurdingkainthi *v-intr*
   form a group ngirrirrinthi *v-intr*
   form a hole pintirninthi *v-intr*
former munana *adj*; painingkiana *adj*; puki *adj*
   formerly puki *temp*
forsake kupapinthi *v-tr*; nurnti kurtarrinthi; wantarrinthi *v-tr*
forty yarapurlirrka *num*
forward nurntina *adv*
foul (in sport) waadli *n*
foul smell puwa *n*
four yarapurla *num*
   fourteen kumirrka yarapurla *num*
   forty yarapurlirrka *num*
   four hundred yarapurla partirrka *num*
   four thousand yarapurlawata *num*
   four million yarapurliwurra *num*
   four times yarapurlarluku *adv*
   fourth-born child Munaitya *n* (male); Munartu *n* (female)
fragile pilta-wuingki *adj*; pirrkiparltaparltanya *adj*
fragment kalya (var. kailya) *n*; pirrki *n*
frail (become) murta-wardninthi *v-intr*
free titatina *adj*
   break free tiltyalayinthi (var. tiltyalinthi) *v-intr*
freeze makirninthi *v-intr*; manya payarnantinthi *v-intr*
   freezer maki kuu *n*

frequently tawarluku *adv*

fresh irdi *adj*; yaitya (var. iyaitya) *adj*; yalakiana *adj*; yalta-yalta *adj*; yaltana *adj*

Friday Milirntu *n*

fridge manya kuu *n*

friend niipu *n*
   friends yunga-yungawarta *n*
   friendly towards yitpi-marni *adj*
   make friends with tangka mankurrinthi₁ *v-intr*

fright tangkaru *n*
   frighten wayirni-apinthi (var. wayinapinthi) *v-tr*; wiltirrkapinthi *v-tr*; wiltirrkayapinthi *v-tr*
   frighten (with stories) ngutanthi *v-tr*
   be frightened tangkarurninthi *v-intr*
   take fright wiltirrkayinthi *v-intr*

frillneck lizard kadnu (var. kanu) *n*

fringe worn around the waist kuntyi *n*

frog (bullfrog) kantu *n*
   frog species (undefined) ngurtu *n*

from -nungku (var. -anangku; -nangku; -unungku) *suff (on nouns)* (ablative)
   from whom? nganangku? *inter*
   from where? waathangku? *inter*
   away from me ngathaityanungku *pro* (ablative)
   away from you nintaityanungku *pro* (singular ablative)
   away from him/her/it padlaityanungku *pro* (ablative)

front warnka₁ (var. warnkata) *n, loc*
   along the front warnkarlu *loc*
   towards the front warnkarlu *loc*

frost pakadla *n*; purka *n*

froth tadli *n*

fruit pinyamai *n*
   fruit stone warpu (var. wartpu) *n*
   fruit of the pigface plant multyu *n*

frustrated (be/feel) yurni ngarntanthi *v-intr*

frying pan tadli-thadli *n*

fuel kardla (var. karla) *n*

full taa purti-purti *adj*
   full up taa purti-purti *adj*
   be full up taa purta-purtanthi *v-intr*
   full of -purtu *suff (on nouns)*; partana (var. -partana) *adj*
   full of dirt yartapurtu *adj*
   full of holes mingkamingka *adj*
   become full of purturninthi *v-intr*
   be full purlinthi *v-intr* (after eating)
   full (of food) maimunthu *adj* (after eating); munthu partu *adj*; munthu tauata *adj*
   half full ngarawaadli *adj*
   not full ngarawaadli *adj*; taarrka *adj*

funeral palti wanga *n*
   funeral movements wana-wana *n* (ceremony)

fungus species (undefined) kumaranki *n*; pilki *n*; tangkairda *n*; taulta *n*; warnka-warnka *n*

funny malyupartana *adj*

fur pardlu *n*

furious (be/become) tangkarurninthi *v-intr*
   furious person wuinpa-wuinparri-purka (var. wuingpa-wuingparri-purka) *n*

furniture kurrpu *n*; mudli (var. murli) *n*

further nurntiki *adv*

fury turlawingku *n*

future
   in the future yangadli *temp*
   further in the future tarrkarrintyarlu (var. tarrkarrintyarla; tarrkarrinyadlu) *temp*
   in the distant future tarrkarri *temp*
   for the future yangadlitya *adj*

G g

gadfly tumpula *n*

galaxias (climbing) tati mipurli *n* (*Galaxias brevipinnis*)

galaxias (mountain) karnu mipurli *n* (*Galaxias olidus*)

galaxy – Magellanic Cloud ngakalamurdu *n*

gall tangka-umpu *n*
   gall bladder tangka-umpu *n*

gallop watpanthi *v-intr*
   make gallop watpapinthi *v-tr*

game (animal) pardu *n*

game (sport/fun) mukati *n*

gap kadla *n*; warltu (var. warti warltu) *n*
   gape taa tarrkinthi *v-intr*

garbage mapa *n*
   garbage bin mapakuru *n*

gas
   gas lighter tipu *n*
   gas oven miitayapa *n*
   gas heater miita nguyuti *n*

gather kumangka malturri-apinthi *v-tr*; malturri-apinthi *v-tr*; ngirrinthi *v-tr*; tuyunthi (var. tuiyunthi) *v-tr*
    gathering place ngani *n*
generation in the middle warti-ana *adj*
generous (with food) maiwaadli *adj*
genitals warta-warta *n*
    female genitals minhi *n*
    male genitals mirrka *n*
gently minkuminku *adv*; naingu *adv*; pintya (var. pinkya) *adv*
germinate tarnanthi (var. tarninthi) *v-intr*
get
    mankunthi *v-tr*
    get away (from someone) tiltyalayinthi (var. tiltyalinthi) *v-intr*
    get out! nurnti-nhurnti (var. nurnti-urnti) *intj*
    get out of the way karrinthi *v-intr*
    get out of the way! nurnti-nhurnti (var. nurnti-urnti) *intj*
    get over (recover) kaarurninthi *v-intr*; mardlarrinthi *v-intr*
    get up! karrikarri! *intj*
    get dressed tarrinthi *v-tr*
    get sympathy tangka mankurrinthi$_2$ *v-tr*
ghost kuinyu *n*; tuwila *n*
    ghostly warputina *adj*
giddy wakarrinthi *v-intr*
gig (cart/carriage) pudniwarta *n*
gingerly tarka-arka *adv*
girdle waikurta *n*
    girdle for waist tidli-kurriti *n*
    girdle made of hair or fur kardluti *n*
girl mankarra *n*
    girlfriend turlta *n*
    girl whose father has died maityuka$_2$ *n*
give yungkunthi *v-tr*; parni mankunthi (var. pardni-mankunthi) *v-tr*; parni-apinthi (var. padni-apinthi) *v-tr*
    give (each other) yungkurrinthi *v-tr*
    give away yungkurri-apinthi *v-tr*
    give in exchange titangka yungkunthi *v-tr*
    give birth kangkanthi *v-tr*; kangkarrinthi *v-intr*; munthu wayirrinthi *v-intr*
    give one's word tantapinthi *v-tr*
    give way piltilinthi *v-intr*
    cause to be given up on wantarni-apinthi *v-tr*
given yungki *adj*
giver yungkulungkula *n*
gift yungkuti *n*
glad (be) kaaru-marrarninthi *v-intr*; ngunyinthi *v-intr*; purtinthi *v-intr*
glare at wadlunthi$_2$ *v-tr*
glass maki *n*
    glass bottle maki kuru *n*
    glasses (for eyes) miimaki *n*
glenoid cavity pilta-yurlu *n*
glitter mirnurrinthi *v-intr*
    glittering mirnunirnuna *adj*
globular mukumukurru *adj*
glow manngimanngirrinthi *v-intr*; mirdilyayinthi (var. mirdimirdilyayinthi) *v-intr*
    glowing talthaityai *adj*
    glowing coals talthu (var. tarltu) *n*
glue nayati *n*; tarnpanthi *v-tr*
glutton munthu padlunintyarla *n*; ngarkularkula *n*
    gluttonous maimarnguta *adj*; maiminma *adj*
gnaw widlanthi (var. wilanthi) *v-tr*
go padninthi *v-intr*; murinthi (var. muyinthi) *v-intr*; wininthi *v-intr* (Rapid Bay dialect)
    go (somewhere) quickly muringkayinthi *v-intr*
    going quickly padni-padninya *n*
    going to (future) -ngutha (var. -ngkutha; -tha; -utha) *suff (on verbs)* (immediate future)
    go after/behind warta mankunthi *v-tr*
    go ahead! kupirdi! *intj*
    go along with marangka padninthi *v-intr*
    go around wirru-wirru padninthi *v-intr*
    go around something kurdirrinthi (var. kuyirrinthi) *v-intr*
    go between two things warlturninthi *v-intr*
    go down ngatpanthi *v-intr* (e.g. the sun)
    go downwards pintirninthi *v-intr*; trrukarrinthi *v-intr*
    go into ngatpanthi *v-intr* (the water, a room, an item of clothing)
    go off (leave) karrinthi *v-intr*
    go off alone marrinthi *v-intr, v-tr*
    go off somewhere taltapinthi *v-intr*
    go on (continue) muinmurninthi *v-intr*
    go on ahead tapa warunthi *v-intr*
    go on the road tapangkanthi *v-intr*; taparninthi *v-intr*
    go straight on pulthurni-apinthi *v-tr*

go through taunthi *v-tr*
go up tatinthi *v-intr*; wangkurrinthi *v-intr*
go with (each other) niipurrinthi *v-intr*
go bald murrmarninthi *v-intr*
go blind paityutiantinthi *v-intr*
go off (rot) tungkirninthi *v-intr*
goal! (sport) ngatpa! *n, intj*
    goal posts ngatpa murlarta *n*
goanna kaityita *n*
    goanna species (undefined) puntunya *n*
goat munthuthakana *n*
    goatsucker (bird) narni *n*
God (creator) pintyalintyala (var. pingkya-lingkyala) *n*
goldfish wiranirana kuya *n (Carassius auratus)*
golf club wirri *n*
good marni *n*; numa *adj*
    good at learning mukarta marni *adj*
    good at remembering mukarta warpu *adj*
    Good Friday Titapirntu *n*
    goodbye! nakutha! *intj*
goose
    Cape Barren goose pita *n (Cereopsis novaehollandiae)*
    European goose pinti pita *n*
gormandize tarnkunthi *v-tr*
gossip mangki-mangkinthi *v-intr*
    gossip about mangki-mangki-apinthi *v-tr*
grab mankunthi *v-tr*; mankurrinthi *v-tr*
gradually kuma mamaityarri *adv*
grand tawarra *adj*
    grandmother kamami *n* (mother's mother); ngapapi *n* (father's mother)
    grandfather madlala (var. marlala) *n* (father's father); tamamu *n* (mother's father)
    grandchild kamilya *n* (of mother's mother); madlanta *n* (of father's father); ngapitya *n* (of father's mother); tamu *n* (of mother's father)
    granddaughter kamilya *n* (of mother's mother); madlanta *n* (of father's father); ngapitya *n* (of father's mother); tamu *n* (of mother's father)
    grandson kamilya *n* (of mother's mother); madlanta *n* (of father's father); ngapitya *n* (of father's mother); tamu *n* (of mother's father)
    grandfather relationship tamamuta *n* (to daughter's child)
    grandson relationship tamuta *n* (to mother's father)
grape kaaru *n*
    grape juice kaaru *n*
grass tutha *n*
    tuft of grass ngurrku *n*
    grass shirt pingki$_2$ *n*
    grasshopper kanuitya *n* (undefined); nukuna *n* (small wingless); pirriwarta *n* (short-winged)
    grasshoppers paitya *n*
    grass tree kuru *n (Xanthorrhoea)*
    grass tree sap yutuki *n*
grateful (be/feel) muiyu yungkunthi *v-intr*
grave (burial) pinti *n*; pinti-wanga; wanga *n*
    from the grave pintinungku *adj*
    graveyard wangayarta *n*
grave (serious) yurlu-puyu-puyurri *adj*
    gravely yurlu-puyurringka *adv*
gravy kauwirrka (var. kawirrka) *n*
graze (animal) mainthi *v-tr*; warkanthi *v-intr*
    grazier shiipi kangkalangkala *n*
grease kurrkurla *n*; marni *n*; marniti *n*; paitpurla *n*
    grease up marninthi *v-tr*
    grease (oneself) up marnirrinthi *v-intr*
great tawarra *adj*
    great-grandfather yarlita *n*
greedy for -marnguta *suff* (on nouns)
    be greedy for marngutanthi *v-intr*
    greedy (for food) maimarnguta *adj*; maiminma *adj*
green kardalta *adj*; timana *adj* (unripe)
    green/blue kardalta *adj*
    green bark tidli *n*
    greengrocer's maiwardli *n*
grey
    grey butcherbird kurrka *n (Cracticus torquatus)*
    grey currawong kuyurra *n (Strepera versicolor)*
    grey kangaroo nantu *n* (male); tarka *n* (male); wauwi *n* (female)
grieve over tangka mampinthi *v-intr*
grind tawinthi *v-tr*; midlinthi (var. milinthi) *v-tr*; turrunthi *v-tr*
    grinding stone tawiti *n*
groan ngarrinthi (var. ngarri-ngarrinthi) *v-intr*; wingku ngarnta-arntarrinthi *v-intr*; wingku-wingkurlinthi *v-intr*
grog kupurlu *n*

groin palti₂ (var. paltiwalti; paltiwarltu) *n*
grouchy wingku-wingku *adj*
ground yarta *n*
    bare ground yarta puku *n*
    fertile ground putpa yarta *n*
group pirku *n* (of people); kanyanya *n*
    form a group ngirrirrinthi *v-intr*
    remain in a group malturrinthi *v-intr*
grove wirra₁ *n*
grow yathunthi *v-intr*
    grow bigger yarrurrinthi *v-intr*
    grow up yathunthi *v-intr*; pinarninthi *v-intr*; tawarrantinthi *v-intr*
    grown up nanti-nhantina *adj*; yathu-yathungka *adj*; purtuna *adj*
    grown-up yathuti *n*
    grown-up female tukuparka *n*
grub parti *n*
    grub hook palya *n*
    grub in redgum kupi *n*
    large, edible grub species (undefined) taingila *n*; turluka *n*
grudge tatarrinthi *v-intr*
grumble marrkarri-apinthi *v-intr*; nuinyanthi *v-intr*; tatarrinthi *v-intr*
    grumbling person marrkarripurka *n*
grumpy paitpurtu *adj*; pulti-ulti *adj*; tiyarrka *adj*
    be grumpy tararrinthi *v-intr*
    grumpy person marngupina *n*
gudgeon
    big-headed/flat-headed gudgeon parntu mukarta waitku *n* (*Philypnodon grandiceps*)
    purple-spotted gudgeon marngu-marngu waitku *n* (*Mogurnda adspersa*)
    western carp gudgeon tukapina waitku *n* (*Hypseleotris klunzingeri*)
guess markanthi *v-tr*; markarrinthi *v-intr*
guide mikarri-apinthi *v-tr*
guilty (be/feel) muiyu wakinharninthi *v-intr*
gull yawu *n*
gullet wangki *n*
gully (with creek bed) pari *n*
gum (edible) kungkurri *n*; yaku *n*; mirnu *n* (wattle gum)
gum tree
    peppermint gum wita *n*
    red gum karra₁ *n*
    stringybark yulthi *n*
    swamp gum patha *n*
    white gum kuraka *n*; tamingka *n*; tarma *n* (*Eucalyptus viminalis*)
    gum tree species (undefined) marltarra *n* (similar to stringy bark)
gun parntapurdi *n*
    gunpowder tipukardla *n*
gut maipadniti *n*; munthu (var. murlu) *n*; kudnanthi *v-tr*
    guts kudna *n*

H h

hail stones miri *n*; tarlta (var. tadlta) *n* (large)
hair yuka *n*; pardlu *n*
    facial hair katpa *n*
    pubic hair titinta *n*
    men's hairstyle mamparta *n*
    hairbrush yuka wirrkati *n*
    hairless pukupuku *adj*
    hairy puthi *adj*
half kuma purlaityila *num*
    half full ngarawaadli *adj*
hand mara *n*
    right hand turturntu *n*
    hand (something to someone) parni mankunthi (var. pardni-mankunthi) *v-tr*; parni-apinthi (var. padni-apinthi) *v-tr*
    hand over karra manthi *v-tr*; tarraitpapinthi (var. tarra-arraitpapinthi; tarra-tharraitpapinthi) *v-tr*; yungkunthi *v-tr*
    hand up karra mankunthi *v-tr*
    put your hand into a gap tinkunthi *v-intr*
    hand saw tiya turruti (var. tiya turruta) *n*
handkerchief nukiana *n*; nuki wirrkiti *n*
handle mantharra *n*; tarra *n*; tita *n*; karnkati *n*
hang titapinthi *v-tr*; tukinthi *v-intr* (to the side); warntapinthi *v-tr*
    hang down kadlurrinthi *v-intr*
    hang on to yarnkanthi *v-tr*
    hang around wartarninthi *v-intr*
    hang (something) up yarnkapinthi *v-tr*
    hanged person ngaritya *n*
    hanging yarnka-yarnkanya *adj*
happy (be) mingkinthi *v-intr*; mingkilayinthi *v-intr*; mukamukarninthi *v-intr*; ngunyinthi *v-intr*; purtinthi *v-intr*; yitpi purti-purtinthi *v-intr*

make someone happy purti-apinthi *v-tr*
happy person mingkipina *adj, n*
happiness mingki (var. maingki) *n*
Happy Birthday! mingki warnirntu! *intj*
Happy Christmas! Ngunya Yiityuku Warnirntu! *intj*
Happy Easter! Ngunya Yiitya! *intj*
Happy Mother's Day! Ngunya Ngaityairntu! *intj*
Happy Father's Day! Ngunya Yarli Tirntu! *intj*
hard wilta *adj*; tarnpa-tharnparni *adj*
  be/become hard warpurninthi *v-intr*; wiltarninthi *v-intr*
  hard-hearted tangkawilta *adj*
  hard centre of something warpu (var. wartpu) *n*
hardyhead (small-mouthed) tukuthaa kuya *n* (Atherinosoma microstoma)
harsh to (be) kapakapanthi *v-tr*
hastily warpu-warpurru *adv*
hat mukarti-ana *n*
  straw hat tainkyadli mukartiana *n*
hate muiyu kapanthi; waadli nakunthi *v-tr*; kuntu pamanthi *v-tr*; kuntu pungkunthi *v-tr*; yitpi kaparrinthi *v-tr*; waadlirrinthi *v-intr*
  hating yitpiwaadli *adj*
haughty person kararri-purka *n*
having -tidli (var. -idli) *suff* (on nouns)
  having had (something) done to you -nana *suff* (on verbs) (past perfect)
hawk karrkanya *n*; munkaka *n*
  kestrel hawk manimani *n* (Falco cenchroides)
hay tutha *n*
he pa *pro* (nominative/accusative); padlu *pro* (ergative)
  him pa *pro* (nominative/accusative)
  his parnu (var. parnuku) *pro*; inhaku *dem*
head mukarta *n*; kaka *n*
  back of the head manuwarta *n*
  have a headache miya yurlanthi *v-intr*
  shake the head wikinthi (var. wiki-wikinthi) *v-tr*
  head hair yuka *n*
  headdress witu-witu *n*; tiyarrku *n*
  headband manga *n* (worn in ceremony)
heal mintirninthi *v-intr*; ngurratinthi *v-intr* (cut); purruti-apinthi *v-tr*
  healer warrarra (var. warra-warra) *n*; yamayama *n*

healthy purruna *adj*
  not healthy mananya *adj*
heap irrka *n*
  heap up irrkapanthi *v-tr*; ngirrinthi *v-tr*
hear yuri pamanthi (var. yuri pamarrinthi) *v-tr*
heart pultha *n*; karltu *n*
  heart (figurative) tangka *n*; yitpi *n*
heat kardla (var. karla) *n*; miita *n*; ngauwa (var. ngawaka) *n*
  heat up nguyunthi (var. nguiyunthi) *v-tr*
  heated miita *adj*
  heatwave warltawingkura *n*
  heater nguyuti *n*
  electric heater karntu nguyuti *n*
  gas heater miita nguyuti *n*
  water heater kauwi nguyuti *n*
heaven karralika *n*
heavy ngama *adj*; purku *adj*; yuparra *adj*; yurnti *adj*
  be heavy kadlurrinthi *v-intr*
  become heavy purkurninthi *v-intr*
heel tuntanta (var. tuntuntu) *n*; tidnawarta *n*
helicopter puntuntu *n*
hell kardlapinti *n*; kardlayapa *n*
  (what the) hell! alya *cli, intj*
help mankunthi *v-tr*
  help! yakai! *intj*
hen murta-ana-itya *n*
her pa *pro* (nominative/accusative)
  her(s) parnu (var. parnuku) *pro*; inhaku *dem*
herd yudlunthi *v-tr*
here inha *loc*; inhaintya *loc*; iya *loc*; paintya *loc, dem*
  to here parni *dir* (allative)
  right here yaintya *loc, dem*
  be here yaintyarrinthi *v-intr* (person)
hesitate pidnanthi *v-intr*; warrarrinthi *v-intr*
hey! iya! *intj*; wai! *intj*; yakai! *intj*
hiccup ngungulurdu *n*; tangkalurdu (var. tangka kulurdu) *n*
  have hiccups kathinthi *v-intr*; warntalinthi *v-intr*
hidden tirrangka *adj*
hide (conceal) ngaranthi (var. ngara-ngaranthi) *v-intr*; tirra tartanthi *v-tr*; tirra-apinthi *v-tr*
  hide away wilti-apinthi *v-tr*
  hide (oneself) ngarrarrinthi *v-intr*; tirranthi *v-intr*; wiltirrkayinthi *v-intr*
  cause to hide wiltirrkapinthi *v-tr*

hidden ngararaka *adv*
hide (skin) kartantu *n* (of large animals); mantinta *n*; yurdinta *n*
   dingo hide maikuntu *n*
high karra₂ (var. karta₂) *loc*
   higher/highest karra-intyarla *adj*
   on high karralika *loc*
hill karnu *n*; mukurta *n*
   hillock yartamalyu *n*
him pa *pro* (nominative/accusative)
hindrance ngangka *n*; tirra *n*
hip miti *n*; pilta *n*; pilta-yurlu *n*
   hip bone miti warpu *n*; pilta-mukurta *n*; pilta-warpu *n*; pilta-yurlu *n*
hire tantapinthi *v-tr*
his parnu *pro* (var. parnuku); inhaku *dem*
hit kurntanthi *v-tr*; parltanthi *v-tr*; patinthi (var. pati-patinthi) *v-tr*
hither parni *dir* (allative)
hoar frost pakadla *n*
hockey mularta parntu *n*
hold on to mankurrinthi *v-tr*; martinthi *v-tr*; tarnparriapinthi *v-intr*
   hold on to (each other) purnpurrinthi *v-tr*
   hold together nayinmanthi *v-tr*
   hold with claws warkinthi *v-tr*
   hold with tongs warkinthi *v-tr*
   hold (someone) back parnpanthi *v-tr*
   holding (someone) back parnpa-parnpanya *n*
hole yapa *n*; tau *n*; taa *n*
   hole in clothing mingka₂ *n*
   hole in the ground pinti *n*; waarki *n* (animal burrows)
   cut a hole taapa pakinthi *v-tr*
   make a hole taapa ngurinthi *v-tr* (by throwing something)
   make a hole through yapangka yaparnapinthi *v-tr*
   form a hole pintirninthi *v-intr*
   full of holes mingkamingka *adj*; turnta *adj*
holiday ngunyirntu *n*
home wardli (var. warli) *n*
   staying at home warru-mpi *adj*
honey (native) tiwa *n*
   black honeyeater warntu *n* (bird) *(Sugomel niger)*
   brown-breasted honeyeater karrawintha *n* (bird) *(Meliphaga)*
   native honeysuckle tarnma *n* *(Banksia marginata)*
hook pirri *n*
   hook made from myrtle palya *n*
hop murtpanthi *v-intr*
hopeful (be/feel) tangkarninthi (var. tangka-angkarninthi) *v-intr*
horny (be) murntu padlunthi *v-intr*
horror struck tangkarurninthi *v-intr*
horse nantu *n*; pinti nantu *n*
hospitable maiwaadli *adj*
hospital kukuwardli *n*
hostile turla *adj*; turlapurtu *adj*; yitpiwaadli *adj*
   hostility turla *n*
hot kardla (var. karla) *n*; warlta *adj* (weather); miita *adj*; watita *adj* (weather)
   very hot kardla-kardlantu *adj*
   red hot talthaityai *adj*
   red hot embers talthu (var. tarltu) *n*
   be hot kamparrinthi *v-intr*; tirntu kamparrinthi *v-intr* (weather)
   get hot miitarninthi *v-intr*
   hot season warltati *n*
hotel kupurluwardli *n*
hour tukirntu *n*
house wardli (var. warli) *n*
   householder wardlipurka *n*
   house key wardli nurliti
   interior of a house wardliyapa *n*
   abandoned house wardli pulthu *n*
hover warntanthi *v-intr*
   cause to hover warntapinthi *v-tr*
how? ngaintya? *inter*; ngaintyarlu? *inter*; nganarlu? *inter*
   how long? ngaintyatana? *inter*
   how many? naawi? *inter*; ngaintya? *inter*
   how many times? naawirluku? *adv*
   how often? naawirluku? *adv*
however pirdi (var. pirdina) *adv*
hub warti-trruku *n*
hungry taityu₁ *adj*; tidli *adj*; maimpi *adj*
   be hungry martarninthi *v-intr*
hunt yakanthi *v-tr*; nurrunthi *v-tr*
   hunter ngarrka *n*
hurry nganta padninthi *v-intr*; warpu-warpulayinthi *v-intr*; mukurrinthi *v-intr*

in a hurry natampi *adv*

hurry up! pintya-pintyarti! (var. pinkyapinkyarti!) *intj*

hurt mingkamingka *adj*; kuku *adj*; murtana *adj*

  hurt (someone/something) titpanthi *v-tr*

  be/feel hurt mintamintarrinthi *v-intr*; ngarntanthi *v-intr*; tiparrinthi (var. titparrinthi) *v-intr*

  get hurt mingkarninthi *v-intr*; murta-wardninthi *v-intr*

  hurt (each other's) feelings tiparrinthi (var. titparrinthi) *v-intr*

  hurt oneself murtarrinthi *v-intr*

husband ngupa *n* (husband); yarlina *n*

  husband and wife partatangkurla *n*; yangarrataurla *n*

husk paka *n*

hut wardli (var. warli) *n*

  mud hut parntawardli *n*

  hut of branches watuwardli *n*

I i

I ngai (var. 'ai) *pro* (nominative/accusative); ngathu (var. 'athu) *pro* (ergative)

ice maki *n*

idea marta *n*

idle wadlu warta *adj*

  be idle ngarrampulanthi *v-intr*

if -ma (var. -ama) *suff*

ignite parranthi *v-tr*

ignorant kudnuna *adj*; yama (var. yamayama$_1$) *adj*

  be ignorant yamarrinthi *v-intr*; wakarrinthi *v-intr*; mukantarrinthi *v-tr* (of something)

  ignorant person wakarripurka *n*

ill kuku *adj*; kuiyu *adj*

  be/become ill kukurninthi *v-intr*

  illness kuiyu *n*; kuku *n*; warrangku *n*

illuminate pinkyarrinthi$_1$ (var. pintyarrinthi$_2$) *v-intr, v-tr*

image tura *n*

imitate mailtyanthi *v-tr*; marka-apinthi *v-tr*; markanthi *v-tr*

  imitate someone's speech warra mailtyanthi *v-tr*

immature (girl) ngarnta warnga *adj*

immediately taityu$_2$ *adv*; wantaka *adv*

immoral wakinha *adj*

  become immoral wakinharninthi (var. wakinhantinthi) *v-intr*

  cause to act immorally wakinhanti-apinthi (var. wakinhantapinthi) *v-tr*

immovable (be) tintanthi *v-intr*

impart yungkunthi *v-tr*

imperfect waadli *adj*

  imperfectly waadli *adv*

impersonate marka-apinthi *v-tr*

  impersonator mailtyarripurka *n*

impregnate parltanthi *v-tr*

imprudent yama (var. yamayama$_1$) *adj*

in -ila (var. -illa) *suff (on nouns)* (locative); -ngka (var. -ngga) *suff (on nouns)* (locative); -rlu (var. -dlu; -urlu) *suff (on nouns)* (temporal)

  in what? nganangka? *inter*; waangka? *inter*

  in where? waangka? *inter*

  in front of mikangka (var. mikamikangka) *loc*; minkarra (var. minkaminkarra) *loc*; warnkangka *loc*

  be in front marka wayinthi *v-intr*

  in spite of turdi-thurdi *adv*

  in that case ngurluntya *pro*

  in the beginning munaintyarlu

  inner part tangka *n*

  inner ear yuriapa *n*

inattentive mukarta wangkiwangki *adj*

  be inattentive yuri patinthi *v-tr*; yurni tarrinthi *v-intr*

incapable (be) mantimantirrinthi *v-intr*

incense tumpu *n*

inch ant karltu *n*

incite tunkunthi *v-tr*

incorporeal ityatina warputina *adj*

incorrect waadli *adj*

incubate (eggs) kadlunthi *v-tr*

independently kurdantana *adv*; yaitya (var. iyaitya) *adj*

index finger marayarli *n*; wama$_2$ *n*

indicate (by pointing) nuunthi (var. nununthi) *v-tr*

indifferent mardlaitirra (var. mardlatirra) *adj*

  indifferently mardla (var. marla) *adv*

indigenous yaitya (var. iyaitya) *adj*; irdi *adj*

individually kumarru *adv*

industrious (be) wirrkutaiyinthi *v-intr*

infect yarnkapinthi *v-tr*

infect (someone) yarnkanthi *v-tr*
get infected by kaintyirrinthi *v-tr*
infectious yarnka-yarnkanya *adj*
inflate wingku puntunthi *v-tr*
inform pudlunthi *v-intr, v-tr*; turrkunthi *v-tr*; mailtyarrinthi *v-intr*; warra katinthi *v-tr*; warra yungkunthi *v-tr*; warra parltanthi *v-tr*; marrkarriapinthi *v-tr*
    inform (each other) pudlurrinthi *v-intr, v-tr*; turrkurrinthi *v-tr*
    inform on mangki-mangki-apinthi *v-tr*
ingratiate tangka mankunthi *v-tr*; tangka mankurrinthi₁ *v-intr*
initiate wilyaru *n*; marniti *n*; partamu *n*
    initiated man ngulta *n*
    initiated young man wilyaru *n*
    initiation stage wilyaru *n*; yalampapatu *n*
injured murtana *adj*
innocent kudnu *adj*; kudnuna *adj*
inquest (into death) wadna-wadna *n*
inquire ngartinthi (var. ngartirrinthi) *v-tr*
    inquire of the dead kadlunthi *v-tr* (during an inquest)
    inquirer ngartilartila *n*
insect (generic) parti *n*
    black fly tapu *n*
    butterfly/moth pilyapilya *n*
    centipede species ngaruta (var. ngarruta) *n* (undefined)
    cicada yiira *n*
    cockroach winana *n*
    cricket yartapirriti *n*
    dragonfly species puntu-untu *n* (large)
    flying ant puruti *n*
    gadfly tumpula *n*
    grasshopper/locust parraitpa (var. parraipa) *n*
    leaf insect kunyu *n*
    longicorn beetle karriparti *n*
    mosquito kuntipaitya *n*
    preying mantis pukuli *n*
    scorpion karntuwarti *n*
    spider waku *n*
    termite/white ant kadngi *n*
    water beetle turluntyaru *n* (Gyrinus)
insecure (be/feel) wiltatinarrinthi *v-intr*
inside trruku *n*
    turn inside out pilta-pilunthi (var. pila-pilunthi) *v-intr*

insinuate tangka mankunthi *v-tr*
insist upon nangkarrinthi *v-intr*
inspect naku-nhakunthi *v-tr*; nguntiapinthi *v-tr*; wayanthi (var. waya-wayanthi) *v-tr*
instantly taityu₂ *adv*
instead of -tila *suff (on nouns)*; martungka
    instead of you ninku pulthu (var. ninku pulthungka) *n, loc*
instep tidnapultha *n* **instruct** nakurni-apinthi (var. nakulyarni-apinthi) *v-tr*; ngutu-atpanthi *v-tr*
insufficient (be) mantimantirrinthi *v-intr*
intelligent walara *adj*; mukarta walara *adj*; mukarta marni *adj*; mukarta warpu *adj*
    intelligent person tirkalirkala *n*
intend (to) wapinthi *v-tr*
inter (bury) wanganthi (var. wangarrinthi) *v-tr*
interfere in a fight tirra mankunthi *v-tr*
interior trruku *n*
    interior of a house wardliyapa *n*
internet wika *n*
interpret warra tarra-tharra-itpapinthi
intervene ngangka mankunthi
intestines (small) kudna *n*
intimidate ngutanthi *v-tr*; wayikurtanthi *v-intr, v-tr*; wayirni-apinthi (var. wayinapinthi) *v-tr*
intoxicated (be) wakarrinthi *v-intr*
    intoxicating spirits kupurlu *n*
intrepid wayiwilta *adj*
introduce (groups of people) panpa-panpalyarninthi *v-intr*
inundation yartala *n*
investigate (make someone) payirri-apinthi *v-tr*
invite tantapinthi *v-tr*; wanpanapinthi *v-tr*
iris (eye) miimaintya (var. miimuntya) *n*
iron (clothing etc) pithapitharni-apinthi *v-tr*
iron (metal) tininya *n*
ironstore tininyawardli
irritate wingku yungkunthi (var. karra nununthi) *v-tr*; karra nuunthi *v-tr*
    be irritated wingku tikanthi *v-intr*
    become irritated wingku-wingkurninthi *v-intr*; yurni mintu-minturninthi *v-intr*
    irritable paitpurtu *adj*; wingku-wingku *adj*; pulti-ulti *adj*; warpularra *adj*
    irritation wiwurriti *n*
-ish -rli *suff (on nouns)*

island karta₄ *n*
    Kangaroo Island Karta₄ *n*; Pintingka *n*
isolated (be) mukamukarninthi *v-intr*
it pa *pro* (nominative/accusative); padlu *pro* (ergative)
    its parnu (var. parnuku) *pro* (possessive); inhaku *dem* (possessive)
    it is said ... warra wardninthi *v-intr*
itch kukarriti *n*

J j

jacket turti-ana *n*; turti-anurla *n*
jammed (be) tintanthi *v-intr*
January Kumiki *n*
jargon wilta warra *n*
jealous (be) marngutanthi *v-intr*
    jealous person marngupina *n*
    jealousy marngu₁ *n*
Jehova Yiuwa *n*
jest yurru *n*
Jesus Yiityu *n*
Jew lizard kadnu (var. kanu) *n*
job warpulayi *n*
jocularity mingki (var. maingki) *n*
joey idla *n*; kurtaka *n*
join taikunthi *v-tr*; yarnkanthi *v-tr*
    join in taikamanthi *v-intr*
    join together nantanthi *v-tr*; tarraitpayinthi *v-tr*
    something joined together with something else nantarti *n*
    joint kadla *n*
joke niku *n*; yurru *n*; nikurninthi *v-intr*; nikurrinthi *v-intr*
    joker nikupina *n*
    jokingly nikunikungka *adv*
    speak in a joking way yurrungka wangkanthi (var. yurru wangkanthi) *v-intr*
jollytail (common) mipurli *n* (*Galaxias maculatus*)
joy mingki (var. maingki) *n*; ngunya (var. ngunyi) *n*
    be joyful ngunyinthi *v-intr*; purtinthi *v-intr*
judge ngaingku *n*
July Wanguiki *n*
jump padminthi *v-intr*; murtpanthi *v-intr*; watpanthi *v-intr*; purtpurrinthi *v-intr* (like a kangaroo)
    make jump watpapinthi *v-tr*
    jumping padmi-padminya *n*
June Marruiki *n*

just -anta₁ (var. -nta₁; -nti) *suff (on nouns)*; mardla (var. marla) *adv*; pirdi (var. pirdina) *adv*
    just a few kutyunti *adj*
    just a little kutyunti *adj*
    just like this namuntya *adv*
    just about to -ngutha (var. -ngkutha; -tha; -utha) *suff (on verbs)* (immediate future)
juvenile emu kuri-kuri *n*

K k

kadaitja nukuna *n*
kangaroo
    grey kangaroo nantu *n* (male); wauwi *n* (female)
    euro tarka *n*
    red kangaroo tarnta *n* (male); kurlu (var. kurlyu) *n* (female)
    be/become a male red kangaroo tarntarninthi *v-intr*
    young kangaroo kurtaka *n*
    kangaroo pouch ngudli *n*
    kangaroo skin mantinta *n*
    kangaroo tooth puntulti *n* (in spear thrower); wuwuthiyadlu *n* (head ornament)
    kangaroo rat kurka *n*; muka muka *n*
    Kangaroo Island Karta₄ *n*; Pintingka *n*
kebab pardu mulartila *n*
keep wilti-apinthi *v-tr*
    keep aside kudlaityapinthi *v-tr*; kumartapinthi *v-tr*
    keep down yartanapinthi *v-tr*
    keep on -alya *suff (on verbs)*; muinmurninthi *v-intr*
    keep together nayinmanthi *v-tr*
kestrel hawk manimani *n* (*Falco cenchroides*)
kettle kuru *n*
key nurliti (var. taa nurliti; wilta nurliti) *n*
    house key wardli nurliti
kick tatunthi *v-tr*; taturrinthi *v-intr*
    kick with the heels tunta-untarlayinthi *v-intr*
kidneys purdita *n*
kill padlu-apinthi *v-tr*; marrpurrinthi *v-tr*; kurntanthi *v-tr*; pungkunthi *v-tr*
    killed pungki *adj*
    continue killing pungku-arninthi *v-tr*
    kill (by throwing) padlu-parltanthi *v-tr*
    kill (oneself/each other) kurntarrinthi *v-intr*; pungkurrinthi *v-intr*
kind (be) numarninthi *v-intr*

kindle (fire) parranthi *v-tr*
  kindling kardla (var. karla) *n*; ngauwa (var. ngawaka) *n*

king purka *n*
  kingfisher tiintinti *n*

kiss taapa *n*; taapaanthi *v-tr*; taaparrinthi₂ *v-intr*

kitchen kamparriti *n*

knapsack yamaru (var. yama-yama) *n*

knee mampa *n*; matha *n*
  kneecap karlta-thukutya *n*; purdilya *n*
  kneepit yarra (var. yarr'yapa) *n* *(popliteal fossa)*
  kneel matha tararta tikanthi; tulturlu tikananthi *v-intr*

knife pakipakiti *n*; yaku *n*

knob marngu₂ *n*
  knobbly marngu-marngu *adj*

knock parltanthi *v-tr*
  knock down patinthi (var. pati-patinthi) *v-tr*
  knock over tawanthi *v-tr*
  knocking parlta-parlta *n*

knot marngu₂ *n*; tita *n*

know nakunthi *v-intr, v-tr*; tampinthi *v-tr*; tirkanthi *v-intr*; mukapanthi *v-tr*; yurlu inparrinthi *v-intr* (someone's face); yailtyanthi *v-tr* (believe)
  know (a language) payanthi *v-tr*
  knowledge ngutu *n*
  be/become knowledgeable ngaingkurni-apinthi *v-intr*

koala kuula *n*

kookaburra ngungana *n*; kukatka *n*; mingkipina *adj, n*

L l

labour warpulayi *n*; warpulayinthi *v-intr*
  labourer kukalukala *n*
  Labour Day Warpulayi-layila Tirntu *n*
  be in labour munthu wayirrinthi *v-intr*

lacking -mpi *suff (on nouns)*; -tina (var. -tana₁) *suff (on nouns) (privative)*; -pulyu *suff (on nouns)*; marraka *adj*

lacrosse mularta wikatidli parntu *n*

lad tinyarra *n*; kurrkurra *n*

lagoon pangka *n*

lake pangka *n*; yarlu *n*
  Lake Alexandrina Pangka *n*

lame (be) ngunirrinthi *v-intr*
  lamely tarka-arka *adv*

lamellicorn beetle turla-yiira *n*

lament murrka yungkunthi *v-intr*; murrkanthi *v-intr*; yakaityayinthi *v-intr*
  lament for a dead person kuinyu murrkanthi *v-intr*

lamp kardlayirdi (var. kardlayiri; karlayiri) *n*
  oil lamp kuntuli kardlayirdi *n*

lamprey (pouched) ngudlitidli nuinpi *n* *(Geotria australis)*

lamprey (short-headed) warltutina nuinpi *n* *(Mordacia mordax)*

land yarta *n*; pangkarra *n* (inherited land)
  landform yartapira *n*
  land of the dead Yartapuulti *n* (Port Adelaide)
  landrail (bird) yirukawu *n* *(Crex crex)*

language warra *n*

lap karta₁ *n*

large partu *adj*; tawarra *adj*; yarnta₁ *adj*
  large shrike (bird) katungki *n*

lark species tirritpa *n* *(Grallina cyanoleuca)*

last kurla *adv*; warta *n*
  last night ngulthingka *temp*

later kurla-intyarlu *adj*; kurlana *adj*; wartarra *loc, temp*; yangadli *temp*; yangadlinti *temp*
  lately yalakarra *temp*

laugh karnkinthi *v-intr*; maingki; mingkilayinthi *v-intr*; mingkinthi *v-intr*; ngunyinthi *v-intr*
  laughter mingki (var. maingki) *n*; yayika *n* (loud)

laundry kudlirriti *n*

lavatory kudnawardli *n*

lay (something) down yartanthi *v-tr*
  lay aside wilti-apinthi *v-tr*
  lay an egg kaityanthi *v-tr*

lazy mantikatpa *adj*; mantinguya *adj*; wadlu warta *adj*
  be lazy ngarrampulanthi *v-intr*; nitatinthi *v-intr*; turtanthi₁ (var. turtarrinthi) *v-intr*; wirrarrinthi (var. witharrinthi) *v-intr*
  become lazy nguntarninthi *v-intr*
  lazy person nitati-purka *n*; pidnarri-purka *n*; turtarri-purka *n*; wirrarri-purka *n*
  laziness nita *n*

lead (direct) kangkanthi *v-tr*
  leader yarltirri-purka *n*

leaf tinkyu *n*
  leaves wilya *n*
  dry leaves and sticks tinkyu *n*

leaf insect kunyu *n*
   leafy vegetable pirira *n*
   leaves of 'kantara' wailyu *n*
leak nuinpirrinthi *v-intr*
   leaky turnta *adj*
lean (thin) ityatina *adj*; putyurra *adj*
   lean meat itya *n*
   be/become lean warpurninthi *v-intr*
lean (to the side) tukinthi *v-intr* (to the side)
   lean on kadlurrinthi *v-intr*
leap murtpanthi *v-intr*; padminthi *v-intr*
learn tirkanthi *v-intr*
leather bag tantu *n*
leave kumpanthi *v-intr*; kurta-kurtarrinthi *v-tr*; wantanthi *v-tr*
   leave home kurtanthi *v-tr*
   make someone leave kumpapinthi *v-tr*
   leave secretly kupayinthi *v-intr*; wapayinthi *v-intr*
   leave for later wantanthi *v-tr*
   cause to leave for later wantapinthi *v-tr*
   leave behind mukanta-wantanthi *v-tr*; mukantarri-apinthi *v-tr*; wantanthi *v-tr*; wantarrinthi *v-tr*
   leave (someone) behind kurtanthi *v-tr*; tapa warunthi *v-intr*
   leave (something) behind wakarri-apinthi *v-tr*
   cause to be left behind wantarni-apinthi *v-tr*
leech species mirdilta (var. mirdinta) *n*
left yurdina (var. yurdidna) *adj, n*
   left hand yurdina (var. yurdidna) *n*
   left-handed yurdina (var. yurdidna) *adj, adv*
   left side yurdina (var. yurdidna) *adj, n*
leg yarku *n*
   legs yarlata *n* (dual)
   upper leg kanthi *n*; miti *n*
   on the legs yarlatitya *adv*
   leg of lamb kanthi *n*
   legless lizard kurrayi *n*
lest -tuwayi *suff (on verbs)* (aversive)
let go pati-apinthi *v-tr*
lethal kuinyunta *adj*
letter piipa *n*
lettuce pirirarli *n*
level maturta *adj*; yarrkanthi *v-tr*
liberated titatina *adj*

lice eggs nirrkinya *n*
licence (driver's) yudlupiipa *n*
lid taa tartati *n*
lie (untruth) manta *n*; manta warrawarra *n*; manta wangkanthi *v-intr*; manta warrawarrarninthi *v-intr*
   lying mantapartana *adj*
   liar mantapartana *n*
lie down wantinthi *v-intr*
   lie down together waaturlayinthi *v-intr* (dual)
   make each other lie down wanti-apirrinthi *v-tr*
   make or allow to lie down wanti-apinthi *v-tr*
   lie on the side pantyinthi (var. paintyanthi) *v-intr*
   lie on your side kurtanthi *v-intr*
   cause to lie on the side pantyapinthi *v-tr*
life purruna *n*
   lifestyle tapa *n*
   lifeless tuwarri *adj*; purrunatina *adj*
lift karnkanthi *v-tr*
   lift up pintyanthi (var. pingkanthi; pingyanthi; pinkanthi) *v-tr*; pintyarri-apinthi (var. pingyarri-apinthi) *v-tr*
   be lifted up pintyarninthi (var. pingkarninthi) *v-intr*
light (bright) walara *adj*
   light-coloured parkana *adj*
light (source) kardlayirdi (var. kardlayiri; karlayiri) *n*
   give light walarantinthi *v-intr*
   light a fire parranthi *v-tr*
   lightning karntu *n*; piturru *n*
   thunder and lightning karntu *n*
light (weight) parltarta (var. parltarti) *adj*; yaparra *adj*
like (love) numa-nhakunthi *v-tr*
   get a liking for wingku marnirninthi *v-intr*
-like (similar to) -purtu *suff (on nouns)*; -rli *suff (on nouns)*; -rrka *suff (on nouns)*; -rta *suff (on nouns)*
   be like namutarnaintyanthi *v-intr*
   like this namu (var. -amu) *adj, adv*; namurli (var. namudli) *adv*; turathurana *adv*
   like this one namu (var. -amu) *adj, adv*
   like these (ones) namutarna (plural)
   become like these ones namudlinyarnanthi (var. namudliarnanthi) *v-intr*
   likeness tura *n*

likely pirdi (var. pirdina) *adv*
lilac (native) tantutiti *n (Hardenbergia violacae)*
lime (mineral) ngaru *n*
   limestone parnta *n*
limp ngirlinthi (var. ngirtinthi) *v-intr*; ngunirrinthi *v-intr*
line (e.g. boundary) warltu (var. warti warltu) *n*
line (fishing, clothes etc.) ngari *n*
line (row) wirrupa *n*
   railway line tininya tapa *n*
link tarra *n*; tarraitpayinthi *v-tr*
lip taamanti *n* (lower); taaminu *n* (upper)
   stick one's lip out taa pidlanthi (var. taa pidlarrinthi) *v-intr*
liquid wirrka *n*; watpana *adj*
   be liquid puikurrinthi *v-intr*
   be/become liquid watpanantinthi *v-intr*
   liquify watparniapinthi *v-tr*
liquor kupurlu *n*
listen (to) yuringkarninthi *v-tr*; yuri-kaityanthi *v-tr*; warra ingkarninthi *v-tr* (someone's words)
   be listening yuri kurrinthi *v-intr*
   listen attentively to yuri-kaityarrinthi *v-tr*
little tuku$_1$ *adj*; tukutya *adj*
   little one ngartu *n*; wakwaku *n*
   little finger kurta-unyu *n*; marakurta-unyu *n*
   little toe ngaikinta *n*
   a little kutyu *adj*
   a little while ago yalarra *temp* (today); yalarraintyarlu *temp*
   little button quail yinku *n (Turnix velox)*
live purrutinthi *v-intr*; tikanthi *v-intr*; wantinthi *v-intr*
   live on (something) mainthi *v-tr*
   live with wanti-apinthi *v-tr*
   alive/living purruna *adj*
   lifeless tuwarri *adj*; purrunatina *adj*
   lively kalya (var. kailya) *adj*; kalyamarru *adj*; maityuka$_1$ *adj*; wirrkuta *adj*
   be lively mukamukarninthi *v-intr*; wirrkutaiyinthi *v-intr*
   become lively wirrkutarninthi *v-intr*
liver tangka *n*
lizard yuru *n* (small); tuparra *n* (small, black bands); taru-tharu *n* (small); wakurri *n* (undefined)
   bearded dragon kadnu (var. kanu) *n*
   blue-tongued/stumpy-tailed lizard kalta *n*

   goanna puntunya *n*
   legless lizard kurrayi *n*
loaded down (be) wadlunthi$_1$ (var. wadlu-wadlunthi) *v-intr*
locust parraitpa (var. parraipa) *n*; nukuna *n* (small wingless)
   locusts paitya *n*
loins purdita *n*
   loin covering tudna$_1$ *n* (men's)
loiter pidnarrinthi (var. pidna-pidnarrinthi) *v-intr*; wartarninthi *v-intr*
   loiterer pidnarri-purka *n*
lollies pinyata *n*
lonely (be) mukamukarninthi *v-intr*
long tuwina *adj*
   longer nurntiki *adv*
   become long tuwinarntinthi *v-intr*
   long ago munaintyarlu; painingka-intyarla (var. painingka-intyardla) *temp*
   very long ago paini-painingka *temp*; pukipuki *temp*
   from very long ago pukintyarlintya *temp*
   not long ago yalarraintyarlu *temp*
long for kuntu warpurninthi *v-tr*; ngudli wayirrinthi (var. ngudli wayarrinthi) *v-intr*; padlurninthi *v-tr*; tangka martulayinthi *v-intr*; wingku parlta-parltarrinthi *v-intr*
loo kudnawardli *n*
look nakunthi *v-intr, v-tr*; nanganthi *v-tr*; miinantinthi *v-intr* (in a certain direction)
   look at naku-nhakunthi *v-tr*; miiwartarninthi *v-intr* (sideways)
   look for miipayinthi *v-tr*; nguntinthi *v-tr*; payinthi (var. payirrinthi) *v-tr*; tadnunthi *v-tr*; warrinthi *v-tr*
   make someone look for payirri-apinthi *v-tr*
   look after kangkanthi *v-tr*
   look down on kurta-kurtarrinthi *v-tr*; wikinthi (var. wiki-wikinthi) *v-tr*
   look into nguntiapinthi *v-tr*
   look out for ingkarninthi *v-tr*
loose kidlala *adj*
   be loose ngunirrinthi *v-intr*
lorikeet (rainbow) ngakala *n*
lose mukantarri-apinthi *v-tr*; wakarri-apinthi *v-tr*; wardni-apinthi *v-tr*
   lose your appetite tangka murrmarninthi *v-intr*
   be lost wakarrinthi *v-intr*

lots partana (var. -partana) *adj*

loud
    make a loud noise pirrkurninthi *v-intr*
    be a loudmouth yarrunthi *v-intr*

louse (native) kudlu *n*

love muiyu *n*; numa-nhakunthi *v-tr*; muiyu mankunthi *v-tr*
    lover kaka-aka (var. kaka kaka) *n*; turlta *n*
    be lovers turltata tikanthi *v-intr*
    make love with kaka-papanthi *v-tr*

low yaki *adj, adv*
    lower yakintyarla (var. yakinyarlu) *adj*
    lower (something) trrukanthi (var. turrukanthi) *v-tr*
    lower arm manarntu *n*
    lower leg yarku *n*
    lower lip taamanti *n* (lower)
    lower oneself trrukarrinthi *v-intr*

lumbar region parntala (var. parntadla) *n*

lump (of earth) turtu (var. yarta turtu) *n*

lunch kurdana mai *n*; yultamai *n*
    having had lunch yultamai-munthu *adj*

lungs pirra *n*; wingku *n*; karltu *n*

lust nita *n*
    lust after witi-witinthi *v-tr*

lying (untruthful) mantapartana *adj*

M m

mad (angry) (be) turlalayinthi *v-intr*

Magellanic Cloud (galaxy) ngakalamurdu *n*

maggot pardi *n*; ngarrakultu *n* (large)

magic nurruti *n*
    do magic nurrunthi *v-tr*; pinyanthi *v-tr*

magpie kurraka *n*
    magpie lark tirritpa *n* (*Grallina cyanoleuca*)

make minunthi *v-tr*; pintyanthi (var. pingkanthi; pingyanthi; pinkanthi) *v-tr*; wapinthi *v-tr*; wayinthi (var. -kaiyinthi; -layi; wauwinthi) *v-intr*
    make (someone/something do something) -api (var. -kapi; -pi) *suff (on verbs)* (causative)
    make friends with tangka mankurrinthi₁ *v-intr*
    make up with (someone) mankurrinthi *v-tr*; yitpi marnirninthi *v-intr*
    make love with kaka-papanthi *v-tr*
    maker partana (var. -partana) *adj* (e.g. rain-); pintyalintyala (var. pingkya-lingkyala) *n*; warti partana *n*

male yarli *n*
    male genitals mirrka *n*

mall tita trruku *n*; trruku *n*

malleefowl pudni *n* (*Leipoa ocellata*)

mallow plant kanunta *n*

malnourished putyurra *adj*

man miyu *n*; yarli *n*; pina *n*; tarrkanyi *n* (at initiation stage)
    fully initiated man purka *n*
    old man purka *n*
    man who -purka *suff (on nouns)*
    man from -purka *suff (on nouns)*
    men miyurna *n*

mango purditarli *n*

manure murta *n*

many ngaraitya *n*; partana (var. -partana) *adj*; tawata *adj*
    many times ngararluku *adv*; tawarluku *adv*
    not many kutyunti *adj*

March Marnkuiki *n*

mark marka *n*; pulthu *n*; murtpamanku *n* (in football)

market tanta *n*
    market place tita trruku *n*

marrow (bone) kapa *n* (bodypart)

marry parranthi *v-tr*
    married kartu-tidli *adj* (man); yangarra-tidli (var. yangarra'idli) *adj* (man); yarlinidli (var. yarlina-tidli) *adj* (woman)

marshmallow plant nguna *n*

mast katha *n*; yirra *n*; yuku katha *n* (of ship)

master mathanya *n*

mat tainkyadli *n*

matches tipukardla *n*

mate (friend) niipu *n*

maternal grandfather tamamu *n* (mother's father)

maternal grandmother kamami *n* (mother's mother)

mattress itharti *n*; kakapiti *n*; kupiti *n*

mature nanti-nhantina *adj*
    mature woman ngamaitya (var. ngama-ngamaitya) *n*

May Miliki *n*
    May Day Milikirntu *n*

may not -rti (var. -ngkurti; -ngurti; -urti; wirti) *suff (on verbs)* (prohibitive)

maybe -ma (var. -ama) *suff*; pia *aux*; wuintyi *adv*
me ngai (var. 'ai) *pro* (nominative/accusative)
    for me ngathaitya *pro* (purposive)
    from me ngathaityanungku *pro* (ablative)
    to me ngathaitya *pro* (allative)
    with me ngathaityangka *pro* (comitative)
meal
    breakfast panyimai *n*
    lunch kurdana mai *n*; yultamai *n*
    evening meal ngulthi-mai *n*
mean (unkind) tangkawilta *adj*
    become mean tangka wiltarninthi *v-intr*
    mean person tangka pardu *n*
meander yukurninthi *v-intr*
meaning yitpiwarra *n*
measure marka-markanthi *v-tr*
meat pardu *n*
mecca ngani *n*
mediate ngangka mankunthi; tirra mankunthi *v-tr*
    mediator tirra mankulankula *n*
meditate katpirrinthi (var. katpi-katpirrinthi) *v-intr*; kurturrinthi *v-intr*; muka wangkawangkanthi *v-intr*; mukapapanthi *v-intr*
meet inpanthi *v-tr*
    meet (someone) nakunthi *v-intr, v-tr*
    meet (each other) inparrinthi *v-intr*
    meeting panpa-panpalya *n*
melt kalyarninthi *v-intr*; multinthi *v-intr*; puikurrinthi *v-intr*
membrane nipa (var. niparra) *n*
mend nantarri-apinthi *v-tr*
menstruation kartinya *n*
mention (someone) taakanthi *v-tr*; taakarrinthi *v-intr*
mesembryanthemum karrkala *n*
mess around nikurninthi *v-intr*; nikurrinthi *v-intr*
message pirrku *n*; warra *n*
    send a message pudlurri-apinthi *v-tr*
    bring a message warra katinthi *v-tr*
    give a message pirrkunthi *v-intr*
    message stick warra tatarta *n*
    messenger pirrku mankulankula *n*
    person who accompanies a messenger pirrkuwarta *n*
microwave tukuwingkura *n*
midday kurdana *n*; warti-kurdana *n*; yulta *n*

midday meal kurdana mai *n*; yultamai *n*
middle warti$_2$ *n*
    through the middle warti-arra *loc*
    middle-aged warti-ana *adj*
milk ngamingaru *n*; ngaru *n*
    Milky Way Wardlipari *n*
milt matumidla *n*
mine (pit) pinti *n*
mine (possession) ngaityu *pro* (singular); ngaityu'rla *adj* (dual); ngaityu'rna *adj* (plural)
minute (unit of time) purirntu *n*
mirror makithura *n*; tura nakunhakurriti *n*
misbehave nuinyanthi *v-intr*; nuinyarrinthi *v-intr*
miscarry munthungka padlunthi *v-intr*
misrepresent manta-apinthi (var. mantapinthi) *v-tr*
miss (emotion) ngudli wayirrinthi (var. ngudli wayarrinthi) *v-intr*; tangka martulayinthi *v-intr*
miss (throw) waadli parltanthi *v-tr*
mist madlu *n* (weather)
    misty madlumadlu (var. madluadlu) *adj*
mistake yaltanthi *v-tr*
mistletoe tainmunta *n*
mix together taikurri-apinthi *v-tr*
    be mixed together taikurrinthi *v-intr*
moan wingku ngarnta-arntarrinthi *v-intr*; wingku-wingkurlinthi *v-intr*
mob kanyanya *n*; wiwurra *n*
mobile phone warraityati *n*
modern kurlana *adj*
moiety names Kararru *n*; Mathari *n*
moist nungurru (var. nungnurru) *adj*
    become moist ngapurlantinthi *v-intr*; nungurru-antinthi (var. nungnurru-antinthi) *v-intr*
    moisture wirrka *n*
Monday Kumirntu *n*
money kanya *n*; parnta *n*; mani *n*
monster kuinyu *n*; paitya *n*
month piki *n*; kakirra$_1$ *n*; marriru *n*
    January Kumiki *n*
    February Purliki *n*
    March Marnkuiki *n*
    April Yarapurliki *n*
    May Miliki *n*
    June Marruiki *n*
    July Wanguiki *n*
    August Ngarliki *n*

September Pauwiki *n*
October Kumirrkaiki *n*
November Tutha-piki *n*
December Wartiki *n*
mood
    get in the mood for tangka marnirninthi *v-intr*
moon kakirra$_1$ *n*; piki *n*; marriru *n*
    moonlit night manmarra (var. marmarra) *n*
mope kuntu pungkurrinthi *v-intr*; kurturrinthi *v-intr*
    moping kudlayurlu *adj*
more (comparative/superlative) -intyarla (var. -nyarla) *suff*; -ntya *suff*
more (continue) muinmu (var. muyinmu) *adj*, *adv*; nurntiki *adv*
morning (early) panyi *n*
    morning (after sunrise) panyiwarta *n*
morose (look/be) katpinthi *v-intr*
mortar (building) tuka *n*
mosquito kuntipaitya *n*
mosquito fish kuntipaitya kuya *n* (*Gambusia affinis/holbrooki*)
most ngaraityintyarla
    most likely pirdi (var. pirdina) *adv*
moth pilyapilya *n*
mother ngangkita *n*
    my mother ngaityai *n*
    your mother ninkai *n*
    mother's ngangkiku *n* (possessive)
    Mother's Day Ngaityairntu *n*
    Happy Mother's Day! Ngunya Ngaityairntu! *intj*
    mother and child ngangkitarla
    mother of -ngangki *suff* (on nouns)
    mother of many children kangkarri-purka *n*; tuku-angki *n*
    mother relationship ngaityaingkula *adj*
    mother whose child has died murdanyi *n*
    deceased mother arratina *n*
    motherless child yipiti (var. ipiti$_2$) *n*
    mother-in-law ngangaitya (var. ngangaityi) *n*; ngauwalyu *n* (man's); wapu *n*
    maternal grandmother kamami *n* (mother's mother)
    paternal grandmother ngapapi *n* (father's mother)
motor waipiti *n*
    outboard motor warrulyi *n*
    motor vehicle padnipadniti *n*
moulder puikurrinthi *v-intr*
mountain karnu *n*
    mountain galaxias karnu mipurli *n* (*Galaxias olidus*)
    mountain parrot kawapupa *n*
mourn tangka mampinthi *v-intr*
mouse species ngarrpa *n* (large, brown); pilta-pilta *n* (undefined)
    common grey mouse purkupurku *n*
moustache taamiti *n*
mouth taa *n*; naparta *n*
    inside of the mouth taayapa *n*
move wayinthi (var. -kaiyinthi; -layi; wauwinthi) *v-intr*; mukurrinthi *v-intr*; wayirrinthi *v-intr*; kutpanthi (var. kutpakutpanthi) *v-tr*
    move to and fro parruntayinthi *v-intr*
    move away! ngarra-ngarra tika! *intj*
    movements during funeral wana-wana *n* (ceremony)
    move along in a squat tirdinthi *v-intr*
movies turarna *n*
    movie theatre turawardli *n*
much nganta *adv*; partana (var. -partana) *adj*; witi *adv*
mucus nuki *n*
mud tuka *n*
    mudlark tirritpa *n* (*Grallina cyanoleuca*)
mullet (fish) kuraitya *n* (*Aldrichetta forsteri*); marilana *n* (*Aldrichetta forsteri*)
multiply tawatantinthi *v-intr*
    multitude kanyanya *n*; wiwurra *n*
mum ngaityai *n*
    your mum ninkai *n*
muntrie berry mantirri *n* (*Kunzea pomifera*)
murder marrpu (var. murtpu) *n*; marrpurrinthi *v-tr*
    murderer marrpuna *n*
Murray River Ngalta *n*
    Murray River people Pita Miyurna *n*
    Murray cod parntu *n* (*Maccullochella peelii*)
    Murray magpie tirritpa *n* (*Grallina cyanoleuca*)
    Murray rainbowfish kurdanyi kuya *n* (*Melanotaenia fluviatilis*)
muscle (bodypart) itya *n*; taingi *n*
    muscular taingipartana *adj*; tiltyapartana *adj*
    buttock muscle madliarri *n* (*gluteous*)
mushroom (species) parnapi *n*

music ipila *n*

musket makiti *n*; parntapurdi *n*

mussel (shellfish) kakirra₂ *n*

my ngaityu *pro* (singular); ngaityu'rla *adj* (dual); ngaityu'rna *adj* (plural)
    my mum ngaityai *n*
    my dad ngaityarli *n*

myrtle kalyu (var. kailyu) *n*

N n

NAIDOC Week Yaitya Wangirntu *n*

nail (finger) marapirri *n*

nail (for hammering) wityu (var. wilyu) *n*

naked puku *adj*; turnki marraka *adj*; yarna *adj*

name nari *n*; mityi *n*; wati *n*
    name (someone) taakarrinthi *v-intr*
    surname kangkarlta *n*
    birth-order name warninhari *n*
    moiety name Kararru *n*; Mathari *n*
    totemic name kangkarlta *n*
    no-name naritina *n* (person whose regular name can't be used)

nankeen kestrel manimani *n* (*Falco cenchroides*)

nape (of neck) warltu (var. warti warltu) *n*

nappy warnupaltha *n*

narrow (be) tintanthi *v-intr*
    narrow and long turtpa (var. turtpu) *adj* (space)
    be/become narrow and long turtparninthi *v-intr*

nasal bone kuingkukuingkula *n*

nasal discharge nuki *n*

National Aboriginal and Islanders Day Yaityirntu *n*

native irdi *adj*; yaitya (var. iyaitya) *adj*
    native bee kardlaparti *n*
    native cherry tilti *n* (*Exocarpos cupressiformis*)
    native cockroach winana *n*
    native flax kurdaki yuri *n*
    native fruit (red or green) wadni *n* (undefined)
    native honey tiwa *n*
    native honeysuckle tarnma *n* (*Banksia marginata*)
    native lilac tantutiti *n* (*Hardenbergia violacae*)
    native louse kudlu *n*
    native pine narnu *n* (*Callitris*)
    native robin tutha-ipiti *n* (*Petroica*)

naughty wakinha *adj*; taltaitpi *adj*
    be naughty nuinyanthi *v-intr*; taltanthi *v-intr*
    naughty person nuinyarri-purka *n*

navel mintawarta (var. mintuwarta) *n*; murluwarta *n*

near kurdanta *loc*; taikurra *loc*
    nearby ityangka (var. yityangka) *loc*; kurda *loc*; parnidlu *loc*; wirru-wirrungka *adv*; yarnta₂ (var. yanta) *loc*
    draw nearer tirdi-apinthi *v-tr*
    nearly ningka *adv*
    nearness kurta *n*

neck yarkunta *n*
    back of neck warltu (var. warti warltu) *n*
    front of the neck yurni *n*
    nape of the neck manuwarta *n*; warltu (var. warti warltu) *n*
    necktie yurni ngari *n*
    neck cord yurdi-ngari *n*
    neckerchief yurni-ana *n*

nectar from banksia tree pitpauwi *n*

nectar from grass tree pinyata *n*

needle wityu (var. wilyu) *n*

neighbour niipu *n*; taikurtiata *n*
    be a neighbour to someone niipunthi *v-tr*

nephew ngarrputya *n* (man's younger sister's son); nirdiana *n*; wangardi *n* (older sister's child)

nest (crow's) manara *n*

net wika *n*; minthi *n*; munta *n* (for large game)
    net bag purnu *n*; wikatyi *n* (men's)
    make net bags pungkunthi *v-tr*
    net worn by men taara *n* (in battle)
    netball wikaparntu *n*

never mind mardlaitirra (var. mardlatirra) *intj*

new kurlana *adj*; yalakiana *adj*
    newborn baby muinyi munthu *n*

news pirrku *n*
    newsagent piipathitawardli *n*; pirrkupiipawardli *n*
    newspaper pirrku-piipa *n*

next day (the) tirnturlu *temp*

Ngayawang person pita miyu *n*

ngumunta grub ngumunta parti *n*

niche wangkurti *n*

niece ngauwadli *n* (man's brother's daughter); wangardi *n* (older sister's child)

night ngulthi *n*
  at night ngulthingka *temp*; ngulthirlu *temp*
  during the night ngulthirlu *temp*
  nightjar (bird) narni *n*
nine pauwa *num*
  nineteen kumirrka pauwa *num*
  ninety pauwirrka *num*
  nine hundred pauwa partirrka *num*
  nine thousand pauwata *num*
  nine million pauwiwurra *num*
  ninth-born child Pauwani *n* (male or female)
nipple nuinpiti *n*
nits nirrkinya *n*
no mardlana *adj, adv*; yaku *adv*
  no more! natapirdi! *intj*; tiwirti! *intj*
  no-name naritina *n* (person whose regular name can't be used due to death taboo)
nod off kaka-wardninthi (var. kaka-warninthi) *v-intr*
noise kulurdu *n*; parrku *n*; waatu *n*
  make a noise parrku-manthi *v-tr*; parrkulayinthi *v-intr*
  make a loud noise pirrkurninthi *v-intr*
  noise (of talking) pilyapilya *n*
non-Aboriginal person pinti miyu *n*
none mardlana *adj, adv*
nook wangkurti *n*
noon kurdana *n*; warti-kurdana *n*; yulta *n*
noose yurdi-ngari *n*
north kawanta *n*
  north-westerly wind pukarra *n*
  northerly kawarta *dir*
nose mudlha *n*
  septum of nose mudlhayala *n*
  side of the nose mudlhakanthi *n*
  nose piercing mudlharta *n*
nostrils mudlhayapa *n*
not mardlana *adj, adv*; yaku *adv*
  not at all yakurni *adv*
  not many kutyunti *adj*
  not do (something) anymore yakuntyanthi *v-intr*
  not feel like waadli ngarntanthi (var. waadli-arntanthi) *v-intr*
  not want to waadli ngarntanthi (var. waadli-arntanthi) *v-intr*
  not full taarrka *adj*
  not now yangadlinti *temp*
  not long ago yalarraintyarlu *temp*
  not yet kutpuru *adv*; purupuru *adv*
  not yet! puru-iti (var. puru-piti) *intj*; purumpi *adv, intj*
  not at all! yaku-anta! *intj* (emphatic)
noun mudliwarra *n*
November Tutha-piki *n*
now nata *temp*; pirdi (var. pirdina) *adv*; yala *temp*; yalaka (var. yaltaka) *temp*; yalarrairdlu *temp*
  just now yalakanta *temp*; yalakarra *temp*; yalakinyanta (var. yaltakinyanta) *temp*; yalarrairdlu *temp*
  a very long time from now tarrkarrintyarlu (var. tarrkarrintyarla; tarrkarrinyadrlu) *temp*
  not now yangadlinti *temp*
number wanpa *n*; wanpa-wanpanthi *v-tr*
nut yitpi *n*

O o

oar yukumularta *n*
obey yuri-kaityanthi *v-tr*
  pay attention to and obey yuri kurrinthi *v-intr*
  obedient yurirka *adj*
  be/become obedient yurirkantinthi *v-intr*
  make someone obedient yurirkantapinthi (var. yurirkanti-apinthi) *v-tr*
oblivious (be) itirrantinthi *v-intr*
obscene language murntu warra *n*
obscure tirra tartanthi *v-tr*
obstacle ngangka *n*; tirra *n*
obstinate (be) yamarrinthi *v-intr*; yuri tarrinthi *v-intr*
ocean yarlu *n*; tarni *n*
ochre
  purple ochre yarnpana *n*
  red ochre karrku *n*; milthi *n*
  white ochre ngaru *n*
  yellow ochre wiranirana *n*
October Kumirrkaiki *n*
octopus marawiti *n*
oesophagus maipadniti *n*
offend (someone) kurta-kurtarrinthi *v-tr*
  offend (each other) tiparrinthi (var. titparrinthi) *v-intr*
  be offended marngungkinthi *v-intr*
  offensive tungki *adj*

office piipawarpulayi kuu (var. piipawarpulayi-wardli) *n*

offspring wakwaku *n*

often ngararluku *adv*; partarluku *adv*; tawarluku *adv*; tiwi *adv*; tiwita *adv*

oh dear! tamurti! *intj*; yakalya! (var. yaka-alya!) *intj*

oh no! tamurti! *intj*; yaka! *intj* (expression of aversion); yakalya! (var. yaka-alya!) *intj*

oil paitpurla *n*
- **oil lamp** kuntuli kardlayirdi *n*

okay! ku! *intj*; kupirdi! *intj*

old pirdipirdi *adj*; pukiana *adj*; purka *adj*; purtuna *adj*
- **old man** purka *n*
- **old woman** pintiwaadli *n*
- **be/become old** purkarninthi *v-intr*
- **become old** purkalainthi *v-intr*; purtunantinthi (var. purtunarntinthi) *v-intr*
- **become an old woman** pintiwaadlirninthi *v-intr*
- **old, dying person** padlu-padlunya *n*
- **older brother** yunga *n*
- **older sister** yakana (var. yakanilya) *n*; kutarri *n* (deceased)

omentum warnka$_1$ (var. warnkata) *n*

on -ngka (var. -ngga) *suff (on nouns)* (locative); -ila (var. -illa) *suff (on nouns)* (locative); -rlu (var. -dlu; -urlu) *suff (on nouns)* (temporal)
- **on top** karra$_2$ (var. karta$_2$) *loc*
- **on the side of** wara-wantaka *loc*
- **on this side** parnata (var. parnati$_1$) *loc*
- **on the other side** kuma paintya *loc*; nguntarta *loc*; nurnti-nhurnti (var. nurnti-urnti) *loc*
- **on account of** warti-wartingka *adv*; wira-wirangka *adv*
- **on account of you mob** naalitya *pro* (purposive)
- **on behalf of** martu-itya
- **on guard** tutu *adj*
- **onward** nurntina *adv*

one kuma *num*
- **one hundred** kuma partirrka *num*
- **one hundred and one** kuma partirrka kuma *num*
- **one thousand** kumawata *num*
- **one million** kumiwurra *num*
- **one after another** karta-arta *adj*; kuma mamaityarri *adv*
- **once** kumarluku *adv*

onion yalka *n*

Onkaparinga Ngangkiparingga *n*

only -anta$_1$ (var. -nta$_1$; -nti) *suff (on nouns)*; mardla (var. marla) *adv*; pirdi (var. pirdina) *adv*

onward nurntina *adv*

open taaparrinthi$_1$ *v-intr*
- **be open** taa tarrkinthi *v-intr*; tarrkinthi *v-intr*; taaparrinthi$_1$ *v-intr*
- **open-minded** mukarta tawutawu *adj*
- **opening** kadla *n*; tau *n*; taa *n*

opposite kuma paintya *loc*
- **opposed to** -waadli *suff (on nouns)*
- **opponent** nguyanguya *n* (sport)

oppressive (be) kamparrinthi *v-intr*

oral cavity taayapa *n*

orange (fruit) kuntanyimai *n*

order (command) kalti-apinthi *v-tr*

origin warti$_2$ *n*

Orion (constellation) Tininyarrarna *n*; kurrkukurrkurra *n*

orphan yipiti (var. ipiti$_2$) *n* maityuka$_2$ *n*; warnpi *n*; warrinya *n*

other side (on the) kuma paintya *loc*; nguntarta *loc*; nurnti-nhurnti (var. nurnti-urnti) *loc*

our(s) ngadliku *pro* (dual possessive); ngadluku *pro* (plural possessive)

out
- **outside** warru *n* (of something)
- **outer space** ngayirda *n*
- **outboard motor** warrulyi *n*
- **out of the way!** karrikarri! *intj*; nurnti-nhurnti (var. nurnti-urnti) *intj*

oval muka *n* (thing)

oven kardlayapa *n* (wood-fired)
- **electric oven** karntuyapa *n*
- **gas oven** miitayapa *n*
- **earth oven** kanyayapa *n*

over karra$_2$ (var. karta$_2$) *loc*
- **over there** ngununtya *loc*
- **over there somewhere** ngunta *loc, dem*
- **overseas** warru *n*
- **overweight** munthu partu *adj*; yathu *adj*

owl winta (var. wintha) *n*
- **barn owl** winta (var. wintha) *n* (*Tyto delicatula*)
- **barking owl** warrukiti *n* (*Ninox connivens*)
- **owl species (undefined)** nguku *n*; yarnaki *n*

own kumarta *adj*; yaitya (var. iyaitya) *adj*

owner mathanya *n*
owner (of a ship) yuku mathanya *n*
of one's own will yaitya (var. iyaitya) *adv*

P p

pacify pilyurni-apinthi *v-tr*
pain ngarnta *n*; kuiyu *n*; ngarnta-ngarntanya *n*
    painful kuiyu *adj*; ngarntana *adj*
    be in pain mintamintarrinthi *v-intr*; ngarntanthi *v-intr*; tiparrinthi (var. titparrinthi) *v-intr*
painted snipe yarukawu *n* (wading bird) *(Rostratula australis)*
pair
    pair of siblings ngarnataurla *n* (same mother)
palm (of hand) marawardli *n*; marathangka *n*; maratha *n*
pan (frying) tadli-thadli *n*
pant (like a dog) munyarrinthi *v-intr*
pants kanthi-ana (var. kanthi-anurla) *n*; yarku-ana (var. yarku-anaurla) *n*
    underpants kanthi-apa *n*
paper piipa *n*
parakeet katpa-atpa *n* (small)
parasite yantupina *n*
parasol kurduthura *n*
parched (become) murlarninthi *v-intr*
pardalote (red-tipped) karltu-arltuku *n*
parent kangkalangkala *n*
    parent-in-law relation ngauwalyata *n*
parrot palti-palti *n*
    Adelaide rosella warltu-arri *n*
    blue mountain parrot ngarri *n*
    mountain parrot kawapupa *n*
    parrot species (undefined) katpa-atpa *n* (small); ngauwaka *n* (blue head and red breast); titititya *n*
part in two wirrumanthi *v-tr*
participate taikamanthi *v-intr*
partner kartu *n* (wife); yangarra *n* (wife); ngupa *n* (husband); taikunthi *v-tr*
    in partnership waatu *adv*
pass parni-apinthi (var. padni-apinthi) *v-tr*; parni mankunthi (var. pardni-mankunthi) *v-tr*
    pass between warlturrinthi *v-intr*
    pass by ngauwinthi *v-intr*; wirru-angkanthi *v-tr*
    pass from hand to hand tarraitpapinthi (var. tarra-arraitpapinthi; tarra-tharraitpapinthi) *v-tr*
    pass over kararrinthi *v-intr*
    in passing wirru-wirrungka *adv*
    passing from hand to hand marrku *n*
    passage through tau *n*
past (in the) painingka *temp*; puki *temp*
pat matunthi *v-tr*
patella karlta-thukutya *n*
paternal grandfather madlala (var. marlala) *n* (father's father)
paternal grandmother ngapapi *n* (father's mother)
path tapa *n*
    make a path between things warlturri-apinthi *v-tr*
patronage kurta *n*
pause (in a song) karrpa *n*
paw mara *n*
pay attention to yuri payanthi (var. yuri paya-paiyanthi) *v-tr*; yuri-kaityarrinthi *v-tr*; warra ingkarninthi *v-tr* (someone's words)
    pay attention to and obey yuri kurrinthi *v-intr*
peace pilyu *n*
    peaceful turlatina *adj*
    peaceable kudlayurlu *adj*
    pacify pilyurni-apinthi *v-tr*
peas pirrkipirrki *n*
pee kumpu (var. kumpurra) *n*; kumputinthi *v-intr*
peel paka *n*; pakamanthi *v-tr*
    peeler pakamati *n*
    peeled pakapuruti *adj*
peewee tirritpa *n* (*Grallina cyanoleuca*)
pelican yaltu *n* (*Pelecanus conspicillatus*)
pen (for writing) tarlti *n*
penalty wakinha *n* (in sports)
penetrate taunthi *v-tr*; taapa nakunthi *v-tr*
penis mirrka *n*; warti$_1$ *n*
people miyurna *n*
    people who lived long ago painingkiarna *n*
peppermint gum wita *n*
Peramangk people Marri Miyurna
perceive nakurninthi *v-intr*; tampinthi *v-tr*; tirkanthi *v-intr*
percussion wiluku *n* (in Kaurna music)
perfect yalura *adj*
perform wapinthi *v-tr*
    performance ngunyawayiti *n*; palti$_1$ *n*

perhaps -ma (var. -ama) *suff*; wuintyi *adv*; pia *aux*; wakurti (var. 'akurti) *adv*

perimeter fence kurditi *n*

periwinkle kurlutumi *n*

permanently tudnu₁ *adv*

perpendicular tutu *adj*

person miyu *n*
    person who -pina *suff (on nouns)*
    European person pinti miyu *n*; kuinyu *n*
    people miyurna *n*

personal effects kurrpu *n*

perspire kantarlantinthi *v-intr*
    perspiration kantarla *n*

persuade yarltinthi (var. yarltirrinthi) *v-tr*; pilyurni-apinthi *v-tr*

petition marnkanthi *v-tr*

phlegm kurlti *n*

phone warraityati *n*

photo tura *n*
    photocopier tura-thurarni-apiti *n*

phyllium kunyu *n*

pick up karra manthi *v-tr*; karra mankunthi *v-tr*; tuyunthi (var. tuiyunthi) *v-tr*; warri-apinthi (var. warri-warri-apinthi) *v-tr*
    pick up (a date) ngirrinthi *v-tr*
    pick up and carry mamanthi *v-tr*; namanthi *v-tr*

picket fence tarralyi *n*

picture tura *n*
    pictures turarna *n*
    picture theatre turawardli *n*

piece pirrki *n*; ika *n*; kalya (var. kailya) *n*
    pierce pamanthi *v-tr*; pungkunthi *v-tr*
    pierce each other pamarrinthi *v-intr*
    pierced pungki *adj*
    continue piercing pungku-arninthi *v-tr*
    piercing in the septum of the nose mudlhayala *n*

pig piiki *n*
    pigface (plant) karrkala *n*; ngangki *n*
    fruit of the pigface multyu *n*

pigeon (bronzewing) marnpi *n*
    topknot pigeon kawu *n*

pile irrka *n*
    put into a pile irrkapanthi *v-tr*; nantarri-apinthi *v-tr*; ngirrinthi *v-tr*

pillar karrpa *n*; yarkunta *n*

pillow katparti *n*; kakapiti *n*

pin wityu (var. wilyu) *n*

pincers nayinmayinmati *n*; warki (var. warkiti) *n*

pinch (squeeze) midlinthi (var. milinthi) *v-tr*; warkinthi *v-tr*; wiwunthi *v-tr*
    pinch each other wiwurrinthi *v-tr*
    pinch off piltinthi *v-tr*

pinch (steal) mitinthi (var. mitimitinthi) *v-tr*

pine (native) narnu *n (Callitris)*
    pine resin narnu yaku *n*

pipe (tube) wiilta *n*
    pipe (for smoking) puyu (var. puiyu) *n*
    pipe (music) winpirra (var. winpirri) *n*
    pipe clay ngaru *n*

piss kumpu (var. kumpurra) *n*; kumputinthi *v-intr*

pit pinti *n*
    pit of the stomach muiyupinti *n*

pizza kurdimai *n*

place -ngka (var. -ngga) *suff (on nouns) (locative)*; –ila (var. –illa) *suff (on nouns) (locative)*; tikanyapinthi *v-tr*
    place where something used to be pulthu *n*

placid turlatina *adj*

plain (flat land) wama₁ *n*; tampa *n*; matu *n*
    plains parpunta *n*

plane (aircraft) karrikarriti *n*

plane (something) wirrunthi *v-tr* (e.g. a piece of wood)
    continue planing wirru-arninthi (var. wirru-alyarninthi) *v-intr* (e.g. wood)

plank tarralyi *n*

plate mai wantawantati *n*; tamiami *n*
    plate-like tami *adj*
    platter mai wantawantati *n*

platypus kauwirlta *n*

play mukanthi (var. mukarrinthi) *v-intr*; ngunya-wayinthi *v-intr*
    play around mukamukarrinthi *v-intr*
    play at ngayanthi (var. ngayarrinthi) *v-intr*, *v-tr*
    playing card tamianta *n*

plaza tita trruku *n*

pleat nipa (var. niparra) *n*

Pleiades (constellation) Mankamankarrarna *n*

plenty ngaraitya *n*
    have plenty maimunthu tikanthi *v-intr*

pliable nainguta *adj*; pika *adj*; pika-pika *adj*; pituka *adj*

pluck parltarri-apinthi *v-tr*; pirranthi *v-tr* (hair)
  pluck off ngarrurrinthi *v-intr*; parltanthi *v-tr*
plumage pardlu *n*
pocket yurntu *n*
point wari *n*; munu *n*; mudlha-iku *n*
  spearpoint kayawari *n*
  point (football) ningkatpa *n*
  point at nuunthi (var. nununthi) *v-tr*
  point out mikangkanthi *v-tr*; mukapanthi *v-tr*
  point upwards karra nuunthi (var. karra nununthi) *v-tr*
  point with your nose mudlharninthi *v-intr*
  pointer finger marayarli *n*
  pointing nuuti *n*
  pointedly tutu *adj*
  pointlessly kudla *adv*
poison dust (ceremony) paityamurdu *n*
poke out in front warnkarrinthi *v-intr*
pole mularta *n*
police officer tulya *n*
  police station tulyawardli *n*
polka-dot marngu-marngu *adj*
pond tarnanta *n*
pony nantu *n*
poo kudna *n*; kudnatinthi *v-intr*; murtatinthi *v-tr*
  animal poo madlara *n* (of herbivore); murta *n*
pool tarnanta *n*
poorly waadli *adv*
porpoise yampu *n*
position (oneself) somewhere ipilayinthi *v-intr*
positively wantaka *adv*
possum pirlta *n* (brush-tailed); madlurta (var. malurta) *n* (ring-tailed)
  sugar glider wirrapi *n* (*Petaurus breviceps*)
  young possum puinyu *n*
  possum skin drum tapurru *n*
  pygmy possum wangku *n* (small)
post (oneself) as lookout yuwalayinthi *v-intr*
post office piipakaityawardli *n*
posterior tudna$_2$ *n*; turrku *n*
pot (container) kuru *n*
potato parnguta *n*
pouch (marsupial) ngudli *n*
  pouched lamprey (fish) ngudlitidli nuinpi *n* (*Geotria australis*)

poultry winaityinaityi *n*
pound kalya-pungkunthi *v-tr* (to powder); pirrki parltanthi *v-tr* (into pieces)
pour marranthi *v-tr*; ipinthi *v-tr*
  pourer ipidlipidla *n* (person)
powder murdu *n*
power midla (var. mila$_1$) *n*; taingi *n*; tiltya *n*
  powerful taingiwilta *adj*; tiltyapartana *adj*; warpu-wilta (var. warpu-wiltu) *adj*
  become powerful warpuwiltarninthi *v-intr*
prank yurru *n*
prawn tarni-kungkurla *n*; tuku-kungkurla *n*
pray marnkanthi *v-tr*
  prayer marnka *n*
  praying mantis pukuli *n*
precipice kauwa *n*
pregnant munthurntu *adj*
  be pregnant malyurninthi *v-intr*
  get pregnant munthurntu-antinthi *v-intr*
prepare a corpse nudnu-nhudnu-apinthi (var. nunu-nhunu-apinthi) *v-intr*
prepare animal skins kantapinthi *v-tr*; wirrkanthi *v-tr*
present (be) yaintyarrinthi *v-intr* (person); tarrkarrinthi (var. tarrkarrantinthi) *v-intr*
  presence mika *n*
present (gift) yungkuti *n*
present (time) yala *temp*; yalaka (var. yaltaka) *temp*
preserve wilti-apinthi *v-tr*
press kadlunthi *v-tr*; kapanthi *v-tr*; pitunthi *v-tr*
  press down yartanapinthi *v-tr*
  press heavily kadlurrinthi *v-intr*
  press together nayinmanthi *v-tr*
  press tightly together maltu mankunthi *v-tr*
  be pressed together nayinmarrinthi *v-intr*
pretend martarrinthi *v-tr*; manta warrawarrarninthi *v-intr*; turtanthi$_1$ (var. turtarrinthi) *v-intr*
pretzel ngarimurdu *n*
prevent kuukuu yarltirrinthi *v-tr*; tirra-apinthi *v-tr*
  prevent from doing something parnpanthi *v-tr*
  preventing from doing something parnpa-parnpanya *n*
previous painingkiana *adj*
  previously painingka *temp*
price (what)? nganangka? *inter*

prick nunanthi *v-tr*; pungkunthi *v-tr*
   prickle pitpa *n*; yiirrkurta *n*
principle warti$_2$ *n*
print-based resources piipamudlirna *n*
prior to pulthupuru *adv*
private parts warta-warta *n*
probably pirdi (var. pirdina) *adv*; wakurti (var. 'akurti) *adv*
proclaim warra katinthi *v-tr*
   Proclamation Day Yarta-mitirntu *n*
produce pintyanthi (var. pingkanthi; pingyanthi; pinkanthi) *v-tr*
progeny kurlana *n*
prohibit kuukuu yarltirrinthi *v-tr*; yarltinthi (var. yarltirrinthi) *v-tr*
prolific woman tuku-angki *n*
promise tantapinthi *v-tr*
prop karrpa *n*; yarkunta *n*; kukanyi *n*
proper irdi *adj*; yaitya (var. iyaitya) *adj*
   proper marriage ngantara *n*
protect tirra-apinthi *v-tr*
   protector tirra mankulankula *n*
   protection kurta *n*
protrude warnkarrinthi *v-intr*
   protrusion kuntu$_1$ *n*
proud (be) kararrinthi *v-intr*; kunturrkinthi *v-intr*; tarra-tarrarrinthi *v-intr*
   proud person kararri-purka *n*; tarrarri-purka *n*
provide with tidlirni-apinthi *v-tr*
provoke tunkunthi *v-tr*
   provoked turla *adj*; yurni-itya *adj*
   be provoked turlalayinthi *v-intr*
   be/become provoked turlarninthi *v-intr*
proximity kurta *n*
pubic area idla *n* (male); ngarta *n* (female)
   pubic bone kumpurru *n*
   pubic hair ngarta yarri *n*; yarri (var. yirri) *n*
   pubic covering tudna$_1$ *n* (men's)
pugnacious marapina *adj, n*; turlapina *n, adj*; irrapina (var. pirrapina) *adj, n*; pirra-pina *adj*
pull manthi *v-tr*; namarrinthi *v-tr*; wirrunthi *v-tr*
   pull (something) along wartanthi *v-tr* (behind)
   pull back winturrinthi *v-tr*
   pull off parltarri-apinthi *v-tr*
   pull out parltanthi *v-tr*; pirranthi *v-tr* (hair)
pulse kaaru *n*

pupil (learner) tirkalirkala *n*
pupil (of eye) miipulyuna *n*
puppy idla *n*
purchase titangka mankunthi *v-tr*
purple yarnpana *n*
   purple ochre yarnpana *n*
   purple-spotted gudgeon marngu-marngu waitku *n* (*Mogurnda adspersa*)
purpose marrku *n*
pursue yakanthi *v-tr*
pus kaiku *n*
push yudlunthi *v-tr*; parltanthi *v-tr*; tawanthi *v-tr*
   push (each other) yudlurrinthi *v-intr*
   push in front marka wayinthi *v-intr*; nurnpurrinthi *v-intr*
   push over patinthi (var. pati-patinthi) *v-tr*
   be pushy nurnpurrinthi *v-intr*
put wantanthi *v-tr*; tikanyapinthi *v-tr*
   put down wantanthi *v-tr*; wantarrinthi *v-tr*; tikanyapinthi *v-tr*; kaityanthi *v-tr*; wikinthi (var. wiki-wikinthi) *v-tr*
   cause to put down wantapinthi *v-tr*
   cause to be put down wantarni-apinthi *v-tr*
   put on (apply) paanthi *v-tr*
   put on (clothes/equipment) tarrinthi *v-tr*; tarranthi *v-tr*
   put (oneself) somewhere ipilayinthi *v-intr*
   put oneself into ngatparrinthi *v-intr*
   put (something) into ngatpanthi *v-tr*
   put together nantarri-apinthi *v-tr*
   put up (erect) tayinthi *v-tr*
   put upright yuwanyapinthi (var. yuwapinthi) *v-tr*
   cause to stay put wiltarnapinthi *v-tr*
   put a spell on nurrunthi *v-tr*
   put under foot kaka-mankunthi *v-tr*
putrid tungki *adj*
   putrify multinthi *v-intr*
pygmy possum wangku *n* (small)
pyjamas miitu mutyarta *n*

Q q

quail
   little button quail yinku *n* (*Turnix velox*)
   stubble quail tinkyadla *n* (*Coturnix pectoralis*)
   quail species (undefined) kapa-apata *n*; kurrkintya *n*

quake wayi-wayirrinthi *v-intr*; wirrilayinthi *v-intr*

quandong kurti *n*

quarrel tawarriti *n*; wiwurriti *n*
  quarrelsome irrapina (var. pirrapina) *adj, n*; paitpurtu *adj*; pulti-ulti *adj*; turla *adj*; warpularra *adj*
  quarrelsome person marrkarripurka *n*; miyu-katha *n*; turlapina *n, adj*

quarter kuma yarapurlangka *num*

queen ngangkipurka *n*
  Queen's Birthday Paityapuulti Warnirntu *n*

question ngartiti *n*

quick maityuka₁ *adj*
  be quick wirrkutaiyinthi *v-intr*
  quickly wirila *adv*; nganta *adv*; kumatpi *adv*; kurla-ityu *adv*; natampi *adv*; warpu-warpurru *adv*
  breathe quickly wingku padminthi *v-intr*
  eat quickly mutanthi *v-tr*
  go somewhere quickly muringkayinthi *v-intr*
  walk quickly nganta padninthi *v-intr*

quiet kudlayurlu *adj*; warrapulyu *adj*
  become quiet wingku marnirninthi *v-intr*
  be quiet! warrarti! *intj*
  quiet, whispered speech wayangka *n*

quit yakuntyanthi *v-intr*

quiver wirrilayinthi *v-intr*

quoll mapu *n*

R r

radiate (light and heat) paanthi *v-intr*; paarrinthi *v-intr*

radish kantarda *n*
  white radish walyu *n*

rage tangkaru *n*; turlawingku *n*; yakaityayinthi *v-intr*
  get into a rage tangkarurninthi *v-intr*
  rage (storm) purtanthi *v-intr*

railway line tininya tapa *n*

rain manya *n*; kunturu *n*; manya parltarrinthi *v-intr*
  drizzling rain kauwimiila *n*
  rainy manya *n*
  rain-maker manyapartana *n*

rainbow kurdanyi *n*
  inner rainbow ngamaitya kumpu *n*
  outer rainbow miyu kumpu *n*
  rainbow bee-eater tinta-inta *n* (*Merops ornatus*)
  rainbow lorikeet ngakala *n*
  rainbow trout kurdanyi mipurli *n* (*Oncorhynchus mykiss*)
  Murray rainbow fish kurdanyi kuya *n* (*Melanotaenia fluviatilis*)

raise karnkanthi *v-tr*; pintyanthi (var. pingkanthi; pingyanthi; pinkanthi) *v-tr*; tayinthi (var. tayirrinthi) *v-tr*; yuwanyapinthi (var. yuwapinthi) *v-tr*
  raise (a child) yathu-apinthi *v-tr*; pinanapinthi *v-tr*
  raise from death purrumanthi *v-tr*; purruti-apinthi *v-tr*

ram (something down) kadlunthi *v-tr*
  ramrod tipu-ngatpa-ngatpati *n* (for a musket)

rambler mukurripurka *n*

random (at) yara-kartarta *adj*

rat nungata *n*
  kangaroo rat kurka *n*; muka muka *n*
  rat species (undefined) narrpa *n*

raw timana *adj*; tintyu-thintyu *adj*
  be raw tintyurninthi *v-intr*

razor marlta pirrati *n*

reach turtpanthi *v-intr*
  reach with your hand turtirninthi *v-intr*
  reach the ear yuri pamanthi (var. yuri pamarrinthi) *v-tr*

read tampithirkanthi *v-intr*

rear (back) ngurru *n*

rear (bring up) yathu-apinthi *v-tr*

reason (for no) kudnu *adj*

receive yungkurri-apinthi *v-tr*

recent kurlana *adj*
  more recent kurla-intyarlu *adj*

reciprocally yara *adj, adv*

recognise tampinthi *v-tr*; yurlu inparrinthi *v-intr* (someone's face)

recollect mukapanthi *v-tr*

reconcile mankurri-apinthi *v-tr*; mankurrinthi *v-tr*; yitpi marnirninthi *v-intr*
  reconciliation nguyanguya muri *n*

recover purrutinthi *v-intr*; kaarurninthi *v-intr*

red kaaru-kaaru *n, adj*; karrku *adj*; milthi *adj*; taltharni *adj*
  reddish brown purnkipurnki *adj*
  red hot talthaityai *adj*
  red hot embers talthu (var. tarltu) *n*

red object taltharni *n*
red ochre karrku *n*; milthi *n*
red kangaroo tarnta *n* (male); kurlu (var. kurlyu) *n* (female)
red shirt taltharnirla *n*
red-bearded marlta purnkipurnki *adj* (used as an insult)
red-bellied black snake ilya *n*
redfin (fish) taltharni parra *n* (*Perca fluviatilis*)
red-tailed black cockatoo yutika *n* (*Calyptorhynchus banksii*)
red-tipped pardalote karltu-arltuku *n*
red gum tree karra$_1$ *n*
red gum forest karrawirra *n*
red gum sap karrakaaru *n*
red gum seed pod kangkulya *n*
redness of evening sky tawurri *n*
reduce tukutyarninthi (var. tukutyarntinthi) *v-intr*
reed witu *n*
    roots of reeds minukura *n*
reflection tura *n*; punga *n*
    reflect turalayinthi *v-intr*
    look at your reflection turalayinthi *v-intr*
refrigerator manya kuu *n*
regain your appetite tangka marnirninthi *v-intr*
regardless turdi-thurdi *adv*
rejoice kaaru-marrarninthi *v-intr*; mingkilayinthi *v-intr*; purtinthi *v-intr*; yitpi purti-purtinthi *v-intr*
relationship (be in a) turltata tikanthi *v-intr*
relative taikurti *n*; taikurtiata *n*
    relatives taikurtirna *n*
relax tangka wiltarninthi *v-intr*
release pati-apinthi *v-tr*; patinthi (var. pati-patinthi) *v-tr*
    released person mamanana *n*
remain pidnanthi *v-intr*; yuwanthi *v-intr*
    remain still partarrinthi *v-intr*
    remain in a group kumangka malturrinthi *v-intr*
    remain (somewhere) nidlanthi *v-intr*
    (the) remainder kutyu *n*
remember mukapanthi *v-tr*; mukaparrinthi *v-intr*; nakunthi *v-intr, v-tr*; kuinpi kangkanthi *v-tr* (after trying to recall something)
    in remembrance of martungka
remove murinthi (var. muyinthi) *v-tr*; kumpapinthi *v-tr*

repeat kutinthi *v-tr*
    repeat (someone's words) warra mankunthi *v-tr*
    repeatedly tiwi *adv*; tiwita *adv*; tuntarri *adv*
repel kapanthi *v-tr*
reply warra inpanthi *v-tr*; warra mankunthi *v-tr*
report pudlunthi *v-intr, v-tr*; warra katinthi *v-tr*
    give a report pirrkunthi *v-intr*
represent miipudlunthi *v-tr*; mukapanthi *v-tr*
reptile paitya *n*
request marnkanthi *v-tr*; marnkarrinthi *v-intr*; kaltinthi *v-tr*
resemble -rli *suff (on nouns)*; namutarnaintyanthi *v-intr*
reserve kudlaityapinthi *v-tr*; kumartapinthi *v-tr*
    reserved (quiet) warrapulyu *adj*
reside tikanthi *v-intr*
    residence wardli (var. warli) *n*
    resident wardlipurka *n*
resin kirrki *n*; yaku *n*; mirnu *n* (wattle gum)
    pine resin narnu yaku *n*
resistance nangkarra
    be resistant nangkarrinthi *v-intr*
resources (written) piipamudlirna *n*
respire wingku patirrinthi *v-intr*
respond warra inpanthi *v-tr*
rest (the) kutyu *n*
restless warnutina *adj*
restrain purnpunthi *v-tr*
resurrect purrumanthi *v-tr*; purruti-apinthi *v-tr*
resuscitate purruti-apinthi *v-tr*
retain kumartapinthi *v-tr*
retract nguimpayinthi *v-intr*
return nungku-nhungkurninthi *v-intr*; pudnanthi *v-intr*
    return (something) pudnapinthi (var. pudnanyapinthi) *v-tr*
    returning nungku (var. nangku) *adv*
reveal miipudlunthi *v-tr*; yurlunthi *v-tr*
    reveal oneself nakurri-apinthi *v-tr*
revenge martu *n*
revere kuinyuntapinthi *v-tr*
    revered kuinyunta *adj*
revive purrumanthi *v-tr*; purruti-apinthi *v-tr*; purrutinthi *v-intr*

rhythm ipila *n*
rib tininya *n*
   ribs region tiki *n*
rice pardi *n*
ridge top turru *n*
rifle parntakarla *n*; parntapurdi *n*
right (correct) numa *adj*
right here inhaintyanta *loc*
righthand side turturntu *n*
ring (circle) kurruru *n*
   ring (jewellery) tukurruru *n*
   ring-tailed possum madlurta (var. malurta) *n*
rip parltanthi *v-tr*; parrarratangkurla *n* (into two large pieces)
ripple mampinthi *v-intr*
rise malyu *n*; tarnanthi (var. tarninthi) *v-intr*
   rise (hill) yartamalyu *n*
   rise over kararrinthi *v-intr*
river pari *n*
   overflowing river yartala *n*
   dry riverbed purtu pari *n*
   river blackfish pari pulyuna kuya *n* (*Gadopsis marmoratus*)
road tapa *n*
   be on the road tapangkanthi *v-intr*; taparninthi *v-intr*
roast kampanthi *v-tr*; wardunthi *v-tr* (in the ashes)
   roasted purtarti *adj*
robber mitilitila *n*; mitirripurka *n*
robin tutha-ipiti *n* (*Petroica*)
robust taingipartana *adj*
rock kanya *n*
rod mularta *n*
roll (something) turdlunthi (var. turlunthi) *v-tr*
   roll (something) over pilunthi *v-tr*
   roll around to scratch an itch nunarrinthi (var. nuna-nhunarrinthi) *v-intr*
roof of the mouth naparta *n*
room kuu (var. kuukuu) *n*
   make room karrinthi *v-intr*
root (origin) warti$_2$ *n*
root (plant) wayita *n*
   bullrush root warnpa *n* (*Typha*)
   root of marshmallow plant nguna *n*; pityarra *n*
   roots of reeds minukura *n*

   edible root (undefined) kunti *n* (red); parnguta *n* (bulbous)
rope ngari *n*
rosella (Adelaide) tudlyu (var. tulyu) *n*; warltu-arri *n*
rot multinthi *v-intr*; tungkirninthi *v-intr*
   rotten tungki *adj*
round muka *n* (thing); mukumukurru *adj*
rover mukurripurka *n*
row (line) tararta *n*; wirrupa *n*; warltu (var. warti warltu) *n*
   row of teeth tiya *n*
rub kurlinthi *v-tr*; wirrkanthi *v-tr*; turrunthi *v-tr*
   rub an itch nunarrinthi (var. nuna-nhunarrinthi) *v-intr*
rubbish mapa *n*; mudli (var. murli) *n*
   rubbish bin mapakuru *n*
   full of rubbish mapapurtu *adj*
rude kurduwilta *adj*; yaitya-kuinyu *adj*; yurlu-wiltana *adj*; yama (var. yamayama$_1$) *adj*; tarnangka *adj*
   be rude tararrinthi *v-intr*; yamarrinthi *v-intr*
   become rude kurdu-wiltarninthi *v-intr*; yamarninthi (var. yamarntinthi) *v-intr*
   make someone rude yurlu wiltarni-apinthi *v-tr*
ruin wardli pulthu *n*
rumour is ... (the) warra wardninthi *v-intr*
run yakanthi *v-intr*; yakarrinthi *v-intr*; watpanthi *v-intr*; padninthi *v-intr*
   run around yakarninthi *v-intr*
   run away taltapinthi *v-intr*
   run fast paitya-marrinthi *v-intr*
   run through a gap warlturrinthi *v-intr*
   run to muringkayinthi *v-intr*
   make someone run yakarri-apinthi *v-tr*
   running padni-padninya *n*
rupture yarrurriti *n*
   cause a rupture yarrurri-apinthi (var. yirrurri-apinthi) *v-tr*
rush (hurry) nganta padninthi *v-intr*
   rush of water wadlala *n*
rush (plant) witu *n*
   rush bag tainkyadli *n*
   rush basket tantyalu *n*
   bullrush root warnpa *n* (*Typha*)
   rush species (undefined) nilti *n*

S s

sacred kuinyunta *adj*
  hold sacred kuinyuntapinthi *v-tr*
sad (be/look) katpinthi *v-intr*; kurturrinthi *v-intr*
  call out in sadness yakaityayinthi *v-intr*
sails (ship) turnki *n*
sake of (for the) warti-wartingka *adv*; wira-wirangka *adv*
salivate tadlirrkantinthi *v-intr*
salt pakadla *n*
  salty kitya *adj*
  salt crystals miri *n*
  salt water kupurlu *n*; tarni *n*
  salt water lakes (placename) Pinta kurltu-kurltu *n* (placename – undefined)
salute purti-apinthi *v-tr*
same turathurana *adj*
  in the same way as wartangka *adv*
sand wara *n*
  sandstone purdi *n* (used for scoring animal skins)
sandwich murdu-murdurla *n*
sap (tree) kirrki *n*
  edible sap kungkurri *n*
  red gum sap karrakaaru *n*
  sap of grass-tree yutuki *n*
satisfied maimunthu *adj* (after eating)
be satisfied purlinthi *v-intr* (after eating)
Saturday Padnipadninyirntu *n*
saucepan kampakuru *n*
saucer tukami *n*
saviour tirra mankulankula *n*
savoury pinyatutana *adj*
saw turrunthi *v-tr*; wirrunthi *v-tr*
  crosscut saw maana *n*; tiya wirruti (var. tiya wirruta) *n*
  hand saw tiya turruti (var. tiya turruta) *n*
say wangkanthi *v-intr*; warranthi *v-intr*; pudlunthi *v-intr, v-tr*
  say someone's name taakanthi *v-tr*; taakarrinthi *v-intr*
scab paka *n*
scaffold piri *n*
scale(s) (fish) kuyaparra *n*; yala-wilya *n*
scalp kurdu *n*
scapula wiri *n*

scar minti *n*
  ceremonial scar(s) manka *n*; ngulta *n*; ngurra *n*; pakurta *n*
  scarred one mankitya *n*
scare wayikurtanthi *v-intr, v-tr*; wayirni-apinthi (var. wayinapinthi) *v-tr*
  scared wayiwayi *adj*
  be scared wayirninthi *v-intr*; mangkulayinthi *v-intr*
  scare with stories ngutanthi *v-tr*
scarf yurni ngari *n*; yurni-ana *n*
scatter karta-artarninthi *v-intr*; marranthi *v-tr*; piarri-apinthi *v-tr*; yara kati-katinthi *v-tr*
  scattered karta-arta *adj*; paintya-yaintya *adj*; yara-kartarta *adj*
  be scattered piarrinthi *v-intr*
  scatter (oneself) yara-arta-artarninthi *v-intr*
school piipawardli *n*
scissors piltiti *n*
  hair cutting scissors yuka piltiti (var. yuka wiltiti) *n*
scold nuinyanthi *v-tr*; nunyanthi (var. nunya-nhunyanthi) *v-tr*; pilyunthi *v-tr*; tawanthi *v-tr*
scoop karku *n*
scorpion karntuwarti *n*
  scorpion species (small) yarta-kungkurla *n*
  scorpion species (undefined) turtu-artu *n*
scowl at wadlunthi$_2$ *v-tr*
scrape kukanthi *v-tr*
  scrape animal skins kantapinthi *v-tr*; tawinthi *v-tr*
scratch pirranthi *v-tr*; nunanthi *v-tr*; kukanthi *v-tr*; wirrkanthi *v-tr*
  scratch an itch nunarrinthi (var. nuna-nhunarrinthi) *v-intr*
  scratching kukarriti *n*
scream kukarrinthi *v-intr*; ngartarrinthi *v-intr*
screen tirra *n*; tirra-apinthi *v-tr*
scrub (vegetation) karrawadlu *n*; karta$_3$ *n*
sea yarlu *n*; tarni *n*
  seawater kupurlu *n*; tarni *n*
  sea eagle wirltu yarlu *n*
  seagull yawu *n*
  seashore wauwa *n*
  seaweed parraitya *n*
  sea monster Nganu *n*
seal wartipardu *n*

search for miipayinthi *v-tr*; payinthi (var. payirrinthi) *v-tr*; tadnunthi *v-tr*

seat tikathikati *n*
   seat of emotions tangka *n*

second (unit of time) taityirntu *n*

second-born child Warritya *n* (male); Yaraitya *n* (male); Warruyu *n* (female); Warri-artu *n* (female); Yarartu *n* (female)

secretly ngararaka *adv*

see nakunthi *v-intr, v-tr*; nakurrinthi *v-intr*; nanganthi *v-tr*
   see (someone's face) yurlu nakunthi *v-intr*
   make someone see (something) nakurni-apinthi (var. nakulyarnapinthi) *v-tr*
   let oneself be seen nakurri-apinthi *v-tr*

seed yitpi *n*
   seedpod of pittosporum kurti *n*
   seedpod of red gum kangkulya *n*
   seedpod of sheoak tree karku-marngu *n*
   seedpod of wattle mingka₁ *n*

seek warrinthi *v-tr*

selfish pidlingka (var. -pidlingka) *adj*

sell titangka yungkunthi *v-tr*

semantics yitpiwarra *n*

send kaityanthi *v-tr* (e.g. on an errand); patinthi (var. pati-patinthi) *v-tr*
   send a message pudlurri-apinthi *v-tr*
   send (someone) away kapakapanthi *v-tr*; kapanthi *v-tr*

sensible (be) mukarta partarninthi *v-intr*

sensitive wingku-wingku *adj*

sentence karrpa *n*

separate karta-arta *adj*; kudla *adv*; kumarta *adj*; yara *adj, adv*; yara-kartarta *adj*; kurla *adv*; kumartapinthi *v-tr*; yaramanthi *v-tr*; piarrinthi *v-intr*; karta-artarninthi *v-intr*; yara kati-katinthi *v-tr*
   separate from each other yara parltarrinthi (var. yara parlta-parltarrinthi) *v-intr*
   separate (oneself) marrinthi *v-intr, v-tr*; yara-arta-artarninthi *v-intr*
   separate into groups yarakayinthi *v-intr*
   separate into small groups pirrki wayinthi *v-intr*
   separate violently yarrurrinthi *v-intr*
   separate pieces kurltu *adj*
   separately turdi-thurdi *adv*; yaranta *adj*

September Pauwiki *n*

septum of nose mudlhayala *n*

sepulchre wanga *n*

series tararta *n*

serious yurlu-puyu-puyurri *adj*
   very serious turlawarpu *adj*
   seriously turla *adv*; yurlu-puyurringka *adv*
   be serious katpirrinthi (var. katpi-katpirrinthi) *v-intr*
   be/become serious turla warpurninthi *v-intr*

serve warpulayinthi *v-intr*

set ngatpanthi *v-intr* (e.g. the sun)
   set in place kaityanthi *v-tr*

settle wiltarnapinthi *v-tr*
   settle down! paitpurturti! *intj*

seven wangu *num*
   seventeen kumirrka wangu *num*
   seventy wangirrka *num*
   seven hundred wangu partirrka *num*
   seven thousand wangawata *num*
   seven million wangiwurra *num*
   seven days wangu tirnturna *n*
   Seven Sisters (constellation) Mankamankarrarna *n* (Pleiades)
   seventh-born child Wangutya *n* (male); Wanguartu *n* (female)

sew nayanthi *v-tr*; nayarrinthi *v-intr*
   sew together nantarri-apinthi *v-tr*

sex parta *n*
   have sex nurtunthi *v-tr* (man); nurturrinthi *v-intr* (with each other); parta mankunthi *v-intr* (woman); parta yungkunthi *v-intr* (man)

shackle titapinthi *v-tr*

shade punga *n*; tura *n*

shadow punga *n*; tura *n*
   cast a shadow turalayinthi *v-tr*

shaft (of spear) kayamunthu *n*

shag (bird) yuulti *n*

shake kutpanthi (var. kutpakutpanthi) *v-tr*; ngunirrinthi *v-intr*; wirrilayinthi *v-intr*
   be shaken wayirrinthi *v-intr*
   shake (oneself) wikirrinthi *v-intr*
   shake violently wayi-wayirrinthi *v-intr*
   shake the head wikinthi (var. wiki-wikinthi) *v-tr*
   shake (the legs) whilst dancing makanthi *v-tr*
   shaky kidlala *adj*

shallow karrapaka *adj*; ngarnta warnga *adj*

shame kurdukarri *n*
   shame (someone) kurdukarri-apinthi *v-tr*;

nganparriapinthi *v-tr*
shampoo tadlaitpurla *n*
shared taikurringka *adj*
shark nakudla *n*
sharp tiyarrka *adj*
   sharpen manku-mankunthi *v-tr* (a spear); tawinthi *v-tr*; turrunthi *v-tr*
shave marlta pirranthi *v-tr*; pirranthi *v-tr*; turrunthi *v-tr*; wirrunthi *v-tr* (e.g. a piece of wood)
   shaver (razor) marlta pirrati *n*
   make shaving motions wintunthi *v-tr*
   continue shaving wirru-arninthi (var. wirru-alyarninthi) *v-intr* (e.g. wood)
she pa *pro* (nominative/accusative); padlu *pro* (ergative)
sheep nyaani *n*; wauwi *n*
sheet miituthurnki *n*
shelf tarralyi *n*
shell (small, freshwater univalve) tirntu-mata *n*
shelter kuu (var. kuukuu) *n*; tirra tartanthi *v-tr*; tirra-apinthi *v-tr*
sheoak karku *n (Casuarina)*; kurlwi *n (Casuarina)*
shepherd shiipi kangkalangkala *n*; kangkanthi *v-tr*
shield murlapaka *n*
shin (leg) yarku *n*
shine paanthi *v-intr*; mirdilyayinthi (var. mirdimirdilyayinthi) *v-intr*; mirnurrinthi *v-intr*; paarrinthi *v-intr*; parkarninthi (var. parkanthi) *v-intr*; walarantinthi *v-intr*
   shining mirnunirnuna *adj*
ship yuku *n*
   ship's captain/owner yuku mathanya *n*
shirt mutyarta *n*; turti-ana *n*; turti-anurla *n*
   shirt made of grass pingki$_2$ *n*
shit kudna *n*; kudnatinthi *v-intr*
   shit of animals murta *n*
   shitty (dirty) kudnapurtu *adj*
   full of shit kudnapurtu *adj* (nonsense)
shock wiltirrkapinthi *v-tr*
   get a shock wiltirrkayinthi *v-intr*
shoe tidnapaltha *n*
shoot pirrki-apinthi$_2$ *v-tr*
   be shot pirrki-apirninthi *v-intr*
shop tita-wardli *n*
   butcher's shop parduwardli *n*
   clothing shop mutyarta wardli *n*
   greengrocer's maiwardli *n*
   newsagent piipathitawardli *n*; pirrkupiipawardli *n*
   take-away shop mutarru wardli *n*
   toy shop ngunyawayiti wardli *n*
   shopping centre tita trruku *n*; trruku *n*
shore wauwa *n*
short kurltu *adj*
   very short kurlturru *adj*
   short, compact person/thing nadli *n*
   short pass parni-api kurda *n* (football)
   short-tempered (person) turlapina *n, adj*
   short-winged grasshopper pirriwarta *n* (short-winged)
   short-headed lamprey warltutina nuinpi *n (Mordacia mordax)*
   short-tailed warti-murtana *adj*
   a short while ago yala-yalarra
   shorten (it/oneself) ngarrurrinthi *v-intr*
shot parntapurdi *n* (for a gun)
   be shot pirrki-apirninthi *v-intr*
shoulder kartaka *n*
   shoulder blade wiri *n*
   shoulder joint ngukurda *n*
shout karlta *n*; karlta pathinthi *v-intr*; karltanthi *v-tr*
   shout for joy purtinthi *v-intr*
   shout (during song) waatu *n*
shove yudlunthi *v-tr*
   shove (each other) yudlurrinthi *v-intr*
shovel tuku$_2$ *n* (wooden)
   shoveler duck tawanta *n (Spatula rhynchotis)*
show miipudlunthi *v-tr*; mikangkanthi *v-tr*; mukapanthi *v-tr*
   showing nuuti *n*
   Show Day Nakupirntu *n*
shower ipiti$_1$ *n*
shred parltanthi *v-tr*
shrike (large) katungki *n*
   shrikethrush turngu *n* (large, slate-coloured)
shrink nadlarrinthi *v-tr*; nadla-nhadlarrinthi (var. nala-nhalarrinthi) *v-intr*; murrmarninthi *v-intr*; tukutyarninthi (var. tukutyarntinthi) *v-intr*; minturninthi (var. mintuminturninthi) *v-intr*
shrivel up minturninthi (var. mintuminturninthi) *v-intr*
   shrivelled up mintuna *adj*
shrubs (undefined) ngumunta *n* (with yellow

flowers); palya *n* (similar to myrtle); tiyarra (var. tiyangarra) *n*

Swainsona tunkurta *n*

shut nayanthi *v-tr*; nayarrinthi *v-intr*; taa tartanthi *v-tr*

    shut the door taa nayanthi *v-tr*

    shut up (something) tartanthi *v-tr*

    shut up! warrarti! *intj*

sibling (younger) panyapi *n*

    pair of siblings ngarnataurla *n* (same mother)

sick kuku *adj*; kuiyu *adj*; ngarntana *adj*; warrangku *adj*

    be/become sick warrangkurninthi *v-intr*

    sickness kuku *n*; kuiyu *n*; ngarnta *n*

    be sick (unwell) ngarntanthi *v-intr*; ngarntarrinthi *v-intr*

    be sick (vomit) kapinthi *v-intr*

    get sick kuiyuninthi *v-intr*

    having become sick ngarnta-ngarntayana *adj*

    sick person ngarnta-ngarntanya *n*

side kurta *n*; pantyi (var. paintyi; pantya) *n*; pilta *n*

    on the side of wara-wantaka *loc*

    on this side parnata (var. parnati$_1$) *loc*

    side-on to wara-wantaka *loc*

    side of taikurti *n* (someone/something)

    side (of the body) tiki *n*

    side of the ribs wardliwitya (var. warliwitya) *n*

    side (of something/someone) taikurti *n*

silent warrapulyu *adj*

    be silent warra kumpanthi *v-intr*

silly mukatina *adj*; yama (var. yamayama$_1$) *adj*

    be silly yamarrinthi *v-intr*

    become silly yamarninthi (var. yamarntinthi) *v-intr*

similar to -rli *suff (on nouns)*; -rrka *suff (on nouns)*; -rta *suff (on nouns)*; turathurana *adj*

    be similar to namutarnaintyanthi *v-intr*

    become similar to these ones namudlinyarnanthi (var. namudliarnanthi) *v-intr*

simple sentence kumanti wapiwarra karrpa *n*

simultaneously kumapurtu *adv*

sin wakinha *n*

sincerely turla *adv*

sinew taingi *n*; tiltya *n*; widni *n*

sing taakarrinthi *v-intr*; mukanthi (var. mukarrinthi) *v-intr*

    sing comfortingly ngarrinthi (var. ngarri-ngarrinthi) *v-intr*

    sing like Europeans do karlta-manthi *v-tr*

single kartu-tina *adj* (man); miyuti *adj* (woman); yangarru-tana *adj* (man)

    single woman takana$_1$ *n*

sink kudlikuru *n*; ngatparrinthi *v-intr*

    sink inwards pintirninthi *v-intr*

    sinker ngatparriti *n* (fishing)

sister yakana *n* (older); ngarna *n*

    younger sister (or brother) panya *n*; panyapi *n*

    older sister yakana (var. yakanilya) *n*; kutarri *n* (deceased)

    older sister relationship yakanata *n*

    person whose older sister has died parrka (var. parrka-widlu; parrka-wilu) *n*

sit tikanthi *v-intr*

    sit down tikapirrinthi *v-intr*

    sit up straight tutu tikanthi *v-intr*

    sit in a circle kurdingkainthi *v-intr*

    make someone sit tikapinthi *v-tr*

    sit (someone) down tikapinthi *v-tr*

    sit with legs folded underneath yarla-marta tikanthi *v-intr*

    sit with legs outstretched (like a corpse) tuwa-thuwarrinthi *v-intr*

six marru *num*; yarapurla purlaityi *num*

    sixteen kumirrka marru *num*

    sixty marrirrka *num*

    six hundred marru partirrka *num*

    six thousand marrawata *num*

    six million marriwurra *num*

    sixth-born child Marrutya *n* (male); Marruartu (var. Marruyu) *n* (female)

skeleton kuinyu *n*

skilful numa *adj*

skin paka *n*; maikuntu *n*

    skinless pakapuruti *adj*

    animal skin kartantu *n* (of large animals); mantinta *n*; yurdinta *n*

    human skin parrpa *n*

    foreskin parrpa *n*

    dry out animal skins papanthi *v-tr*

skink yuru *n* (small)

skinny ityatina *adj*; putyurra *adj*

skip padminthi *v-intr*; watpanthi *v-intr*

    skipping padmi-padminya *n*

skull mukarta *n*

sky ngayirda *n*
   bright, clear, evening sky takana *n*

slander marta *n*; martanthi *v-tr*; mangki-mangki-apinthi *v-tr*
   slanderer martalartala *n*

slate (writing) marka *n*

sleek pintapinta *adj*

sleep miitu *n*
   asleep puulti *adj*
   sound asleep miituthungki *adj*
   sleepy mii-thurtpu *adj*; miitu-itya *adj*; miitumpi *adj*
   be sleepy matpinthi *v-intr*; miitu padlunthi *v-intr*; miitu payirrinthi *v-intr*; miya yurlanthi *v-intr*
   fall asleep miiturninthi *v-intr*
   be falling asleep miitu kadlunthi (var. miitu kadlurrinthi) *v-intr*
   lie down asleep miitu wantinthi *v-intr*
   not sleepy miitutina *adj*
   sleeping bag ngudli wantiti *n*
   sleepy lizard kalta *n*

sleeves turti-anurla *n*

slender kayarrka *adj*; putyurra *adj*

slip off marrinthi *v-intr, v-tr*
   slippery mirnunirnuna *adj*

slope yartamalyu *n*

slow mantikatpa *adj*; mantinguya *adj*; wadlu warta *adj*
   slowly minkuminku *adv*; pintya (var. pinkya) *adv*
   slow-moving muri-murinya *adj*
   slow-witted mukartatana *adj*
   slow down! pinkya-pinkya! (var. pintya-pintya!) *intj*

sluggish ngarrampulanthi *v-intr*
   be sluggish turtanthi$_1$ (var. turtarrinthi) *v-intr*
   sluggish person turtarri-purka *n*

small tuku$_1$ *adj*; tukutya *adj*; kurltu *adj*
   smaller ngartu-arla *adj* (child)
   become smaller tukutyarninthi (var. tukutyarntinthi) *v-intr*; wityarninthi *v-intr*
   small intestines kudna *n*
   small-mouthed hardyhead (fish) tukuthaa kuya *n* (*Atherinosoma microstoma*)
   smallpox nguya (var. nguiya) *n*
   smallpox song (ceremony) nguyapalti *n*

smart (clever) walara *adj*; mukarta marni *adj*

smear paanthi *v-tr*
   smear with faeces kudnapanthi *v-tr*

smell martu *n*; kungarrinthi *v-intr*; martulayinthi *v-intr*
   smell (something) mailtyanthi *v-tr*; martu mailtyanthi *v-tr*; mudlhanthi *v-tr*
   bad smell puwa *n*
   smelly tungki *adj*

smiling mingki (var. maingki) *n*

smoke puyu (var. puiyu) *n*; tumpu *n*; puyurrinthi *v-intr*; manyurrinthi *v-intr*
   smoke out (animal) tumpunthi *v-tr*
   smoke possums out of trees wadlunthi *v-tr*
   smoking incense paapa tumpu *n* (ceremony)

smooth maturta *adj*; pintapinta *adj*; pithapitha *adj*; yartpana *adj*
   smoothe yartpanthi *v-tr*
   smoothe the surface of a spear wintunthi *v-tr*; wirrunthi *v-tr*

smoulder manyurrinthi *v-intr*

snack muta-mutarru *n*
   snack on something mutanthi *v-tr*

snake paitya *n*
   brown snake paitya *n*
   red-bellied black snake ilya *n*
   species of snake (grey) turdnu (var. tudnu$_2$; turnu) *n*
   snake species (undefined) mititya *n*; tangaka *n*; tangku *n*; tudnu-ununya *n* (small)

snap ngintirrinthi *v-intr*
   snapper wiini *n* (*Chrysophrys auratus*)

sneak yurrunthi (var. yurrurrinthi) *v-intr*
   sneak away pulthurninthi *v-intr*
   sneak off kupayinthi *v-intr*; wapayinthi *v-intr*
   allow to sneak off pulthurniapinthi *v-tr*
   sneak up on yurrunthi (var. yurrurrinthi) *v-intr*
   sneakily ngararaka *adv*
   sneaky person yurru-purka *n*

sneeze kurrutinthi (var. kurrutunthi) *v-intr*
   sneezing kurruta *n*

sniff mucus back up your nose nuki winturrinthi *v-intr*

snipe (painted) yarukawu *n* (wading bird) (*Rostratula australis*)

snoring kulturnta *n*

snort mucus back up your nose nuki winturrinthi *v-intr*

snot nuki *n*

snow maadlhu *n*
    snow peas maadlhupirrki *n*

so namu (var. -amu) *adj, adv*

soak pudna *n*
    soaked kauwirrka (var. kawirrka) *adj*

soap tadlipurdi *n*

soar (like a bird) warntanthi *v-intr*
    cause to soar like a bird warntapinthi *v-tr*

socks tidna-ana *n*

soft mutarta (var. murtata; mutata) *adj*; nainguta *adj*; pika *adj*; pituka *adj*; watpana *adj*
    very soft pika-pika *adj*
    softly minkuminku *adv*; naingu *adv*; pintya (var. pinkya) *adv*; tarka-arka *adv*
    become soft pika-pikarninthi *v-intr*
    be/become soft watpanantinthi *v-intr*
    soften something manyinthi *v-tr*; watparni-apinthi *v-tr*
    soft drink kuntanyi *n*
    soft centre of bread yakinhainguta *n*

soil yarta *n*
    soiled trrunga (var. trrunga-trrunga) *adj*

soldier tulya *n*

sole (of foot) tidnakuntu *n*

solemn (very) turlawarpu *adj*
    be/become solemn turla warpurninthi *v-intr*

solitary niipu-tina *adj*

solstice tuwinirntu *n* (summer); kurltirntu *n* (winter)

some kutyu *adj*
    someone ngurluntya *pro* (ergative); ngapidlu *pro* (indefinite); kumanurlu *pro* (ergative)
    somebody kumanurlu *pro* (ergative)
    something ngapidlu *pro* (indefinite)
    somewhere (over there) ngunta *loc, dem*
    somewhere in that direction nguntarlu *loc*

son kunga *n*; yarlipurka *n*
    son-in-law ngarrputya *n* (of man)
    son-in-law relation ngarrputyata *n*
    son of hanged person ngari warrinya *n*

song palti$_1$ *n*
    bedtime song miituthirntu palti *n*
    songs (at a ceremony) kurdi *n*

soon purupuru *adv*
    sooner piti (var. 'iti) *adv*

sorcerer warrarra (var. warra-warra) *n*; yamayama *n*; nurrulurrula *n*

sore irrkuta *n*; nguya (var. nguiya) *n*; kuku *adj*; mingkamingka *adj*
    become sore irrkutantinthi *v-intr*; kukurninthi *v-intr*

sorry! yakalya! (var. yaka-alya!) *intj*
    be/feel sorry for someone kuntu pungkurrinthi *v-intr*
    make someone feel sorry for you tangka mankurrinthi$_2$ *v-tr*

soul tuwila *n*; yitpi *n*; yitpi tukutya *n*; yaki-thukutya *n*

sound kulurdu *n*; parrku *n*; wiluku *n* (in Kaurna music)
    make a sound parrkunthi *v-intr*
    sound out (letters) parrkulayinthi *v-intr*
    sounds made during ceremonies ipila *n*
    sound asleep miituthungki *adj*

sour pinyatutana *adj*

source warti$_2$ *n*

south patpa *n*
    Southern Cross Wirltu Tidna *n*

space (gap) kadla *n*; warltu (var. warti warltu) *n*
    space in front of something warnka$_1$ (var. warnkata) *n, loc*
    spacious takana$_2$ *adj*
    outer space ngayirda *n*

spade tuku$_2$ *n* (wooden); karku *n*; karnkati *n*

spaghetti ngarimai *n*

spark parntinthi *v-intr*; tipu *n* (fire)
    sparkle parntinthi *v-intr*; piltilainthi *v-intr*

sparrow hawk purpurta *n*

speak wangkanthi *v-intr*; warranthi *v-intr*
    speak to warrapanthi *v-intr*; yuringka wangkanthi *v-intr*; yurningka wangkanthi *v-intr*
    speak of the dead kuinyu purtpurrinthi *v-tr*
    speaking incorrectly marltangaitya *adj*; marltayartpana *adj*
    speaking poorly ngarrparrpa *adj*
    not speaking fluently marltayartpana *adj*
    speak like a beginner yartpanthi *v-tr*
    not speak well ngarrparrinthi (var. ngarrparrparrinthi) *v-intr*
    stop speaking warra kumpanthi *v-intr*

spear kaya *n*; wirnta *n*; kuntaru *n* (ceremonial); pamanthi *v-tr*

spear each other pamarrinthi *v-intr*
spearpoint kayawari *n*
spear-thrower midla (var. mila₁) *n*; parnta-midla *n*; tarralyi *n*
  toy spear kutpi *n*; matamudlu *n*
  light reed spear witu *n*
specialist ngaingku *n*
speckled marngu-marngu *adj*
speech warra *n*
  speechless warratina *adj*
spell (magic) nurruti *n*; warrarra (var. warra-warra) *n*
  put a spell on nurrunthi *v-tr*
spider waku *n*
  spider web waku ngari (var. waku-ari) *n*
spill marranthi *v-tr*; marrarrinthi *v-intr*
spin nurlinthi *v-tr*
  spindle mangathata *n* (long vertical piece); mangayaingki (var. mangayaintya) *n* (horizontal cross piece)
spine ngarrata *n*; parntala (var. parntadla) *n*
spinster takana₁ *n*
spirit tuwila *n*; yaki-thukutya *n*; yitpi tukutya *n*
  spirits (alcohol) kupurlu *n*
  evil spirit nukuna *n*
  spirit world karralika *n*
  spirited wirrkuta *adj*
spit tadli *n*; tadli-patinthi *v-intr*
  spit at/on tadlipanthi *v-tr*
  spit out tadli-patinthi *v-intr*
spite muiyu kapanthi
  feel spite towards yitpi kaparrinthi *v-tr*
splash kuntunthi *v-tr*
spleen matumidla *n*
splinter tarralyi *n*
split parltanthi *v-tr*
  split wood yaparrinthi *v-tr*
spoil nuinyanthi *v-tr*; waadli-apinthi *v-tr*; wakarri-apinthi *v-tr*
sponge (animal) putaputa *n* (bottle-shaped)
sponsor yungkulungkula *n*
spoon karnkati *n*; mai karnkarnkati *n*
sport
  basketball tantyalu-parntu *n*
  football tidnaparntu *n*
  hockey mularta parntu *n*
  lacrosse mularta wikatidli parntu *n*
  netball wikaparntu *n*
  running padni-padninya *n*
  swimming pariparinya *n*
spotty marngu-marngu *adj*
spouse kaka-aka (var. kaka kaka) *n*; kartu *n* (wife); yangarra *n* (wife); ngupa *n* (husband)
spread (something) paanthi *v-tr*
  spread out yarrkanthi *v-tr*
  spread around marranthi *v-tr*
sprightly kalya (var. kailya) *adj*
spring wirltuti (var. wirluti) *n* (season); pudna *n*
  spring up tarnanthi (var. tarninthi) *v-intr*; yurlurrinthi *v-intr*
sprinkle ipinthi *v-tr*
  sprinkler ipidlipidla *n* (person); ipiti₁ *n*
  sprinkle with water purninthi *v-tr*
sprout tarnanthi (var. tarninthi) *v-intr*
sputum kurlti *n*
squabble wiwurriti *n*
squat down tirdinthi *v-intr*
squeeze parntanthi *v-tr*
squid kiwiti *n*
squint miiwartarninthi *v-intr* (sideways)
St Valentine's Day Turlta Tirntu *n*
stab pamanthi *v-tr*; pungkunthi *v-tr*
  stab (oneself/each other) pamarrinthi *v-intr*; pungkurrinthi *v-intr*
  continue stabbing pungku-arninthi *v-tr*
  stabbed pungki *adj*
stagger mampinthi *v-intr*
stammer ngarrparrinthi (var. ngarrparrparrinthi) *v-intr*
  stammering ngarrparrpa *adj*
stand yuwanthi *v-intr*
  stand up karrinthi *v-intr*
  stand up! karrikarri! *intj*
  stand still yuwanthi *v-intr*
  make (someone/something) stand upright yuwanyapinthi (var. yuwapinthi) *v-tr*
  stand guard yuwanthi *v-intr*
star purli *n*
  Southern Cross Wirltu Tidna *n*
  autumn star parna₂ (var. padna₂) *n* (undefined)
  star names (undefined) Parnakuyarli *n*; wayaka *n*

star finch tiitha *n*
stare miipudnanthi *v-intr*
   stare at wadlunthi₂ *v-tr*
starving (be) martarninthi *v-intr*
stay pidnanthi *v-intr*; tikanthi *v-intr*
   stay behind wartarninthi *v-intr*
   stay together kumangka malturrinthi *v-intr*
   stay at home nidlanthi *v-intr*
   staying at home warru-mpi *adj*
   staying still nurnti-anta *adv*
   cause to stay put wiltarnapinthi *v-tr*
steal mitinthi (var. mitimitinthi) *v-tr*; mitirrinthi (var. mitimitirrinthi) *v-tr*
stealthily ngararaka *adv*
steam kauwiku *n*; ku *n*; kurrinthi (var. ku(k)arrinthi) *v-intr*
   steam in an earth oven kanyanthi *v-tr*
steel tininya *n*
steep kauwa *adj*
steer mikarri-apinthi *v-tr*
stem (of yakka) kayamunthu *n*
step tidnatidnanthi *v-intr*
   step on kadlunthi *v-tr*
   step into the way wakanthi *v-tr*
   stepfather kurlantu *n*; ngadla *n*
sternum kuntu warpu *n* (*sternum*)
   sternum tip pilupiluna *n* (*ensiform cartilage*)
stew (in an earth oven) kanyanthi *v-tr*
stick (wood) mularta *n*; ngarra *n*; tatarta *n*
   burnt stick ngarra *n*
   digging stick katha *n*
   dry leaves and sticks tinkyu *n*
   fighting stick tantanaku *n*
   stick for tree climbing wadna *n*
stick (attach) tarnpanthi *v-tr*
   stick to tarnparrinthi *v-intr*; tarnparri-apinthi *v-tr*; midlimidlinthi *v-intr*
   stick together nayinmarrinthi *v-intr*; tarnparri-apinthi *v-tr*; nantanthi *v-tr*
   stick close together maltu mankurrinthi *v-intr*
stick out
   stick one's chest out kunturrkinthi *v-intr*
   stick one's head out mukartantinthi *v-intr*
   stick one's lip out taa pidlanthi (var. taa pidlarrinthi) *v-intr*; taa pirrikayinthi *v-intr*
stiffness (sexual) nita *n*

still puru *adv*; tiwi *adv*; pirdi (var. pirdina) *adv*
   be still yuwanthi *v-intr*
   staying still nurnti-anta *adv*
   be still-born munthungka padlunthi *v-intr*
stinging animal or insect paitya *n*
stingy maikudna *adj*; pidlingka (var. -pidlingka) *adj*
   stingy with -kudna *suff* (*on nouns*)
stink puwa *n*; kungarrinthi *v-intr*
stinky tungki *adj*
stir nuunthi (var. nununthi) *v-tr*
   stir up karra nuunthi *v-tr*; tunkunthi *v-tr*; wingku yungkunthi *v-tr*
   stir the fire pawunthi *v-tr*
stockings yarku-paltha *n*
stoke pawunthi *v-tr*
   stoke the fire purtamanthi *v-tr*; turdlunthi (var. turlunthi) *v-tr*
stomach munthu (var. murlu) *n*; ngangki-munthu *n*; tidli *n*
   pit of the stomach karltu *n*
stone kanya *n*; purdi *n*
   stone in fruit warpu (var. wartpu) *n*; yitpi tukutya *n*
stool ngarra-papaltu *n*
stoop warkanthi *v-intr*; yartarninthi *v-intr*
   stooping nurru-nhurru *adj*
stop yuwanthi *v-intr*; mardlarrinthi *v-intr*
   stop doing something yakuntyanthi *v-intr*
   make (something) stop mardlarri-apinthi (var. marlarri-apinthi) *v-tr*
   stop (somewhere) nidlanthi *v-intr*
   stop being angry turla mardlarrinthi *v-intr*
   stop breathing wingku-wingkurtarrinthi *v-intr*
   stop speaking warra kumpanthi *v-intr*
   stop working on wantanthi *v-tr*
   cause to stop working on wantapinthi *v-tr*
stormy weather (with north wind) warta-pukarra *n*
story pirrku *n*
   bedtime story miituthirntu pirrku *n*
   storytime pirrku tirntu *n*
stout ngama *adj*; yathu *adj*
   stout person ngurrunturru *n*
stove kampati *n*
straight maturta *adj*; tutu *adj*; tutumpurri *adj*; tutuwari *adv*

straight away taityu₂ *adv*; wantaka *adv*
straight on tutumpurri *adv*
   go straight on pulthurni-apinthi *v-tr*
stranger kuma miyu
strangle midlinthi (var. milinthi) *v-tr*
strap on tarranthi *v-tr*
straw tutha *n*; witu *n*
   straw hat tainkyadli mukartiana *n*
   strawberry tuthilti *n*
stray piarrinthi *v-intr*
stream pari *n*
strength midla (var. mila₁) *n*; taingi *n*; tiltya *n*
stretch turtpa-thurtpanthi *v-intr*; turtpanthi *v-intr*; yarrkanthi *v-tr*
   stretch out tuwimanthi (var. tuwirunthi) *v-tr*; tuwinarntinthi *v-intr*
   stretch out your hand turtirninthi *v-intr*
   stretch your legs taturrinthi *v-intr*
   stretch your legs out yarku kati-katinthi *v-intr* (one on top of the other)
   stretch the legs straight turtpanthi *v-intr*
   stretched tuwiruti *adj*
   stretched out tuwina *adj*
   stretching (oneself) parlta-parltarriti *n*
   stretch oneself nadla-nhadlarrinthi (var. nala-nhalarrinthi) *v-intr*; parltarrinthi (var. parlta-parltarrinthi) *v-intr*
stride kadlunthi *v-tr*
strife tawarriti *n*
strike (hit) kurntanthi *v-tr*; parltanthi *v-tr*
   strike with terror tangkaru parltanthi *v-tr*
string ngari *n*; manga *n*
   string bag purnu *n*; wikatyi *n* (men's)
   string girdle tarra *n* (women's); waikurta *n*
   string handle mantharra *n*
   string for carrying 'tantu' tantuthita *n*
   stringybark tree yulthi *n*
   stringybark forest yulthiwirra *n*
stripe warltu (var. warti warltu) *n*
   striped mankamanka *adj*
strive to be first marka wayinthi *v-intr*
stroke matunthi *v-tr*
strong taingiwilta *adj*; taingipartana *adj*; tiltyapartana *adj*; warpu-wilta (var. warpu-wiltu) *adj*; widnurru *adj*; yurnti *adj*
   be/become strong wiltarninthi *v-intr*
   become strong warpuwiltarninthi *v-intr*

strongly nganta *adv*
stubble quail tinkyadla *n* (*Coturnix pectoralis*)
stubborn taltaitpi *adj*; yama (var. yamayama₁) *adj*; yuritina *adj*
   be stubborn taltanthi *v-intr*; turdi-thurdirninthi *v-intr*; yamarrinthi *v-intr*; yuri tarrinthi *v-intr*; yurni tarrinthi *v-intr*
stuck (be) tintanthi *v-intr*
student tirkalirkala *n*
stuff kurrpu *n*
   stuffed (with food) munthu tauata *adj*
   stuff oneself with tarnkunthi *v-tr*
stumble ngirlinthi (var. ngirtinthi) *v-intr*
   stumbling wardni-wardninya *adj*
stump ngarra-papaltu *n*; papaltu *n*
   burnt tree stump ngarra *n*; purtultu *n*
   stumpy-tailed lizard kalta *n*
stupid yama (var. yamayama₁) *adj*; mukartatana *adj*; mukatina *adj*
   be stupid wakarrinthi *v-intr*; yamarrinthi *v-intr*
   become stupid yamarninthi (var. yamarntinthi) *v-intr*
   stupid person wakarripurka *n*; yama partana *n*
stutter ngarrparrinthi (var. ngarrparrparrinthi) *v-intr*
   stuttering ngarrparrpa *adj*
subsist on mainthi *v-tr*
suck nuinpinthi (var. nuingpinthi) *v-tr*
   suckle nuinpinthi *v-tr*
suet warnka₁ (var. warnkata) *n*
suffer mintamintarrinthi *v-intr*
   suffer from kaintyirrinthi *v-tr*
   suffering ngarnta *n*; ngarnta-ngarntanya *n*
sufficient pirdi (var. pirdina) *adj*
suffocate midlinthi (var. milinthi) *v-tr*
   suffocate with smoke tumpunthi *v-tr*
sugar pinyata *n*
   sugar glider wirrapi *n* (*Petaurus breviceps*)
   sugarbag tiwa *n*
   without sugar pinyatutana *adj*
sulky (be) kadlurrinthi *v-intr*; taa pidlanthi (var. taa pidlarrinthi) *v-intr*; taa pirrikayinthi *v-intr*
   sulky person taa pidlarri-purka *n*
sullen (be/look) katpinthi *v-intr*
sultry watita *adj* (weather)
   be sultry tirntu kamparrinthi *v-intr* (weather)

summer warltati *n*
  summer solstice tuwinirntu *n*
summon warunthi (var. waru-warunthi) *v-tr*; wanpanapinthi *v-tr*
sun tirntu *n*
  sunrise tirntu parka-parka *n*
  sunset karrka$_1$ *n*
  sunshine tirntu-karla *n*
  sunscreen tirntuthirra *n*
  Sunday Minkirntu *n*
superficial karrapaka *adj*
supplicate marnkanthi *v-tr*
supply tidlirni-apinthi *v-tr*
support karrpa *n*; yarkunta *n*; kukanyi *n*; tipanthi *v-tr*
suppose martanthi *v-tr*; yailtyanthi (var. yailtyarrinthi) *v-tr*
surely pirdi (var. pirdina) *adv*; wantaka *adv*
surf ilyala (var. kilyala) *n*; kungkurra *n*; tarni *n*
surname kangkarlta *n*
surprise wiltirrkapinthi *v-tr*
  be surprised wiltirrkarrinthi *v-intr*
surround kurdinthi (var. kuyinthi) *v-tr*; mankurri-apinthi *v-tr*; purnpunthi *v-tr*
survive purrutinthi *v-intr*
suspect martanthi *v-tr*
  suspicion marta *n*
swallow kurrkinthi *v-tr*
  swallow (bird) manimaninya *n*
swamp tartu *n*
  swampy pituka *adj*
  swampy land tukayarta *n*
  swamp gum patha *n*
  swamp hen kawana *n*
swan (black) kudlyu *n* (*Cygnus atratus*)
  Swan River goby (fish) patpa kupi *n* (*Pseudogobius olorum*)
swap tita *n*
swear (promise) tantapinthi *v-tr*
swearing (bad language) murntu warra *n*
sweat kantarla *n*; kantarlantinthi *v-intr*
  sweaty kantarlangkanthi *v-intr*
  sweat of a dying person ngulya-ngulya *n*
sweet pinyata *adj*
  sweets pinyata *n*
  sweetened water kuntanyi *n*; pitpauwi *n*

swell irrkutantinthi *v-intr*
  swell up malyurninthi *v-intr*
  swelling irrkuta *n*; malyu *n*
swift (bird) turlu *n*
swim parinthi (var. pathinthi) *v-intr*; pukanthi *v-intr*
  swim underwater ngurrumpayinthi *v-intr*
  swimmer madli *n*; puka-pukanya *n*
  swimming pariparinya *n*
swing wampinthi *v-intr, v-tr*
switch tipumarngu *n* (electric)
swollen malyu *adj* (landscape)
sympathise tangka wayinthi (var. tangka wayirrinthi) *v-intr*
  seek or gain sympathy tangka mankurrinthi$_1$ *v-intr*

T t

table tarralyi *n*
taboo kuinyunta *adj*
tadpole warati *n*
tail warti$_1$ *n*
take mankunthi *v-tr*; karra manthi *v-tr*
  take off (remove) manthi *v-tr*
  take away mitinthi (var. mitimitinthi) *v-tr*; mitirrinthi *v-tr*; murinthi (var. muyinthi) *v-tr*
  take-away food muta-mutarru *n*
  take-away shop mutarru wardli *n*
  take back again nungkumanthi *v-tr*
  take in exchange titangka mankunthi *v-tr*
  take fright wiltirrkayinthi *v-intr*
  take turns tarraitpapinthi (var. tarra-arraitpapinthi; tarra-tharraitpapinthi) *v-tr*
  take up a position yuwalayinthi *v-intr*
  take with tongs warkinthi *v-tr*
talk wangkanthi *v-intr*; warranthi *v-intr*; minyangkayinthi (var. minyarrangkinthi) *v-intr*
  talk about (someone behind their back) mangki-mangkinthi *v-intr*
  talk too much yarrunthi *v-intr*
  talkative person warrapina *n*
  talking rubbish kudnapurtu *adj* (nonsense)
  noise of talking pilyapilya *n*
tall tawarra *adj*
  tall and thin kayarrka *adj*
tallow paitpurla *n*
talon pirri *n*
tap marra yuwati *n* (water etc); yuwati *n*

target for spearing practice mukarta *n*

tarry warrarrinthi *v-intr*

taste martu *n*; tamartu *n*; mailtyanthi *v-tr*; martu mailtyanthi *v-tr*

tea tii *n*

teach ngutu-atpanthi *v-tr*; nakurni-apinthi (var. nakulyarni-apinthi) *v-tr*

   teacher yamayama *n*

tear (rip) mingka₂ *n*; yarrurriti *n*; parrarratangkurla *n* (into two large pieces); parltanthi *v-tr*; yartanthi *v-tr*

   tear apart yarrurrinthi *v-intr*; pirrki-apinthi₁ *v-tr*

   cause a tear yarrurri-apinthi (var. yirrurri-apinthi) *v-tr*

   tear off (with teeth) widlanthi (var. wilanthi) *v-tr*

tears (crying) miikauwi *n*; miimurrka *n*

tease ngayanthi (var. ngayarrinthi) *v-intr*, *v-tr*; wiwunthi *v-tr*; mailtyarripurka *n*

   tease each other wiwurrinthi *v-tr*

   teasing mingki (var. maingki) *n*; wiwudla-wudla (var. wiwudli-wudla) *adj*

teenager (male) tinyarra *n*; kurrkurra *n*; paapa *n*

telephone warraityati *n*

telescope witu-thurlu (var. witu-thurdlu) *n*

television turaityati *n*

tell pudlunthi *v-intr*, *v-tr*; warra yungkunthi *v-tr*; turrkunthi *v-tr*; mailtyarri-apinthi *v-intr*; marrkarriapinthi *v-tr*; yurningka wangkanthi *v-intr*

   tell (each other) pudlurrinthi *v-intr*, *v-tr*; turrkurrinthi *v-tr*

   tell off nuinyanthi *v-tr*; nunyanthi (var. nunya-nhunyanthi) *v-tr*; pilyunthi *v-tr*

   tell on mangki-mangki-apinthi *v-tr*

   tell tales mangki-mangki-apinthi *v-tr*

   tell the truth tiyati wangkanthi *v-intr*

temples (bodypart) katparntu (var. katparnta) *n*

ten kumirrka *num*

   ten thousand kumirrkawata *num*

   ten million kumirrkiwurra *num*

tenacious widnurru *adj*; wilta *adj*

tench (fish) tintyi *n* (*Tinca tinca*)

tent turnkiwardli *n*

terminology wilta warra *n*

termite kadngi *n*

terrify tangkaru parltanthi *v-tr*

be terrified tangkarurninthi *v-intr*

territory pangkarra *n* (inherited land)

test mailtyanthi *v-tr*

testicles kardlumuka *n*

thanks ngaityalya *intj*

that (person/thing) ngu *dem*; ngurlu *dem* (ergative)

   that one paintya *dem*

   that way ngurlu *dir*

   in that direction ngurlu *dir*

   somewhere in that direction nguntarlu *loc*

their(s) parnaku *pro* (plural possessive); purlaku *pro* (dual possessive)

   their father purlakarli *n* (dual)

them parna₁ (var. 'rna; padna₁) *pro* (plural nominative/accusative)

   them (two) purla (var. 'rla) *pro* (dual nominative/accusative)

   for them (two) purlalitya *pro* (dual purposive)

   for them parnalitya *pro* (plural purposive)

   to them (two) purlalitya *pro* (dual allative)

   to them parnalitya *pro* (plural allative)

then nguntya *loc, temp*

   then? namutarla? *inter*

   then (in that case) ngurluntya *pro*

there ngu *dem*; nguntya *loc, temp*; pa *loc*; paintya *loc, dem*

these itu *dem*

   these two idlu-urla *dem* (dual)

they parna₁ (var. 'rna; padna₁) *pro* (plural nominative/accusative); parnarlu *pro* (plural ergative)

   they (two) purla (var. 'rla) *pro* (dual nominative/accusative); purlarlu *pro* (dual ergative)

   they say ... warra wardninthi *v-intr*

thick partu *adj*

   thick lipped taa-partu *adj*

thief mitilitila *n*; mitirripurka *n*

   thieve mitinthi (var. mitimitinthi) *v-tr*

thigh kanthi *n*; miti *n*

   upper thighs kardlu-ardlu *n*

thin ityatina *adj*; putyurra *adj*

   tall and thin kayarrka *adj*

   thin, weak-legged person warta-ityatina *n* (insult)

   become thinner tukutyarninthi (var. tukutyarntinthi) *v-intr*; wityarninthi *v-intr*

thing mudli (var. murli) *n*; kurrpu *n*

think yailtyanthi (var. yailtyarrinthi) *v-tr*; mukarta karra-yarnkanthi *v-intr*
    think about payinthi (var. payirrinthi) *v-tr*
    think deeply katpirrinthi (var. katpi-katpirrinthi) *v-intr*; muka wangkawangkanthi *v-intr*; mukapapanthi *v-intr*
    think of mukapanthi *v-tr*
    think over kuinpinthi *v-tr*
    think to oneself mukaparrinthi *v-intr*
third kuma marnkutyila *num* (fraction)
    third-born child Kudnuitya *n* (male); Kudnartu *n* (female)
thirsty kuntu warpu *adj*; kuntu warpurninthi *v-tr*
thirteen kumirrka marnkutyi *num*
thirty marnkuirrka *num*
this iya *dem*; yaintya *loc, dem*
    this one idlu (var. irdlu) *dem* (ergative); idluntya *dem* (ergative, emphatic); inha *dem*; paintya *dem*
    like this namurli (var. namudli) *adv*
    on this side parnata (var. parnati₁) *loc*
    this time idlu *temp*
thorn pitpa *n*; yiirrkurta *n*
those ngurna *dem*
    those two ngurlu-urla *pro*; purla (var. 'rla) *pro* (dual nominative/accusative)
    those there parnaintya (var. padnaintya) *pro*
    those over there nguntartinyarna *dem*; ngurna *dem*; ngurnaintya (var. ngurnintya) *pro* (plural)
    those on this side parnatinya'rna
thought mukamuka *n*
thousand (one) kumauwata *num*
    two thousand purlauwata *num*
    three thousand marnkauwata *num*
    four thousand yarapurlauwata *num*
    five thousand milauwata *num*
    six thousand marrauwata *num*
    seven thousand wangauwata *num*
    eight thousand ngarlauwata *num*
    nine thousand pauwata *num*
    ten thousand kumirrkauwata *num*
thread manga *n*; widni *n*
    thread through pungkunthi *v-tr*
threaten karra nuunthi (var. karra nununthi) *v-tr*; ngutanthi *v-tr*; pardu-apinthi (var. pardu-pardu-apinthi) *v-tr*
three marnkutyi *num*
    thirteen kumirrka marnkutyi *num*
thirty marnkuirrka *num*
    three hundred marnkutyi partirrka *num*
    three thousand marnkuawata *num*
    three million marnkuiwurra *num*
    three times marnkurluku *adv*
    a third kuma marnkutyila *num* (fraction)
throat maipadniti *n*; wangki *n*; warra *n*; yurni *n*
through -arra (var. -tarra) *suff (on nouns)*
throw patinthi (var. pati-patinthi) *v-tr*; parltanthi *v-tr*; ngurinthi *v-tr* (with a spear thrower)
    throw down wardni-apinthi *v-tr*; wikinthi (var. wiki-wikinthi) *v-tr*
    throw (oneself) patirrinthi *v-intr*; wikirrinthi *v-intr*
    throwing stick wirri *n*
thrust into the ground patinthi (var. pati-patinthi) *v-tr*
thumb mara-angki *n*
thunder piturru *n*
    thunder and lightning karntu *n*
Thursday Yarapurlirntu *n*
thus namu (var. -amu) *adj, adv*; turathurana *adv*
tickle kitikitinthi *v-tr*
    tickler kitilitila *n*
tie mankunthi *v-tr*; tita *n*; titapinthi *v-tr*
    tie up kurdinthi (var. kuyinthi) *v-tr*; mamanthi *v-tr*; titapinthi *v-tr*
tie (necktie) yurni ngari *n*
tight turtpa (var. turtpu) *adj* (space); wilta *adj*
    be tight tintanthi *v-intr*
    be/become tight turtparninthi *v-intr*
timber tarralyi *n*
time tirntu *n*
    time out warru-thirntu *n*
    time piece tirntu *n*
    times -rluku *suff (on nouns)*
    waste time turdi-thurdirninthi *v-intr*
timid wayiwayi *adj*
    be timid wayirninthi *v-intr*
tip wari *n*; mudlha-iku *n*; munu *n*
tipsy (be) wakarrinthi *v-intr*
tired mii-thurtpu *adj*; narntu ngaitya *adj* (person); ngaityana *adj*
    be tired ngarrampulanthi *v-intr*; kurturrinthi *v-intr*; matpinthi *v-intr*; mintamintarrinthi *v-intr*; turturninthi *v-intr*; wirrarrinthi (var. witharrinthi) *v-intr*

become tired ngaityarninthi *v-intr*;
  nguntarninthi *v-intr*; purkurninthi *v-intr*
make (someone) tired ngaityarni-apinthi *v-tr*
be tired of waadlirrinthi *v-intr*
tired person wirrarri-purka *n*
tiring purku *adj*
not tired miitutina *adj*

tissue nuki wirrkiti *n*; nukiana *n*

to (someone) -itya (var. -litya; -titya) *suff (on nouns)* (allative)
  to whom? nganalalitya? *inter*
  to me ngathaitya *pro* (allative)
  to you nintaitya *pro* (singular allative)
  to him/her/it padlaitya *pro* (allative)
  to us two ngadlilitya *pro* (dual allative)
  to us ngadlulitya *pro* (plural allative)
  to you two niwadlitya *pro* (dual allative)
  to you mob naalitya *pro* (allative)
  to them (two) purlalitya *pro* (dual allative)
  to them parnalitya *pro* (plural allative)

to (somewhere) -ana (var. -kana; -tana₂) *suff (on nouns)* (allative)

toaster murdumurdu kampati *n*

tobacco kapi *n*
  tobacco pipe puyu (var. puiyu) *n*

today yala *temp*; yalaka (var. yaltaka) *temp*

toe
  big toe tidnangangki *n*; tidnayarli *n*
  little toe ngaikinta *n*
  toenail pirri *n*

together kumangka *adj*; piltangka; taikurra *loc*; waatu *adv*; wirringka *adv*
  be together taikurrinthi *v-intr*
  bring together mankurri-apinthi *v-tr*
  come together tultyurrinthi *v-intr*
  stay together malturrinthi *v-intr*; manku-mankurrinthi *v-intr*
  two together nantarla *n*
  not together yaranta *adj*

toilet kudnawardli *n*

tomahawk tamiaku *n*

tomato tumatu *n*

tomb pinti-wanga

tomorrow panyingkurlu *n*; tarrkalyarlu (var. tarrkarrilyarlu) *temp*; tirnturlu *temp*; yala-tharrkarri (var. yalarrkarri; yalta-tharrkarri) *temp*

tongs warki (var. warkiti) *n*
  hold with tongs warkinthi *v-tr*

tongue tadlanya (var. tadlanyi) *n*

tonight ngulthingka *temp*
  early tonight karrkarlu *temp*

too kuma *adv*

tool mudli (var. murli) *n*
  tools kurrpu *n*
  tool for lifting things karnkati *n*
  tool for preparing skins kantapi *n*

tooth tiya *n*
  toothbrush tiya-wirrkarriti (var. tiyawirrkati) *n*
  toothpaste tiyangaru *n*
  toothless tiya-tina *adj*
  teeth tiyarla

top knot pigeon yungura *n*

torch kardlayirdi (var. kardlayiri; karlayiri) *n*

torn up yarru *adj*

tortoise marungayu *n*

totem kangkarlta *n*

tottering kidlala *adj*

touch pitunthi *v-tr*; mankunthi *v-tr*; kurdanthi *v-intr, v-tr*; pamanthi *v-tr*; nunanthi *v-tr*
  touch each other pamarrinthi *v-intr*
  cause to touch pantyapinthi *v-tr*

tough titparra *adj*

towards (go) tatinthi *v-intr*
  towards (someone) -itya (var. -litya; -titya) *suff (on nouns)* (allative)
  towards (somewhere/something) -ana (var. -kana; -tana₂) *suff (on nouns)* (allative)
  towards the front warnkarlu *loc*

towel murlamurla *n*

town/township wardliwardli *n*

toy ngunyawayiti *n*
  toy shop ngunyawayiti wardli *n*
  toy spear matamudlu *n*

trace marka-markanthi *v-tr*; markanthi *v-tr*; markarrinthi *v-intr*; pulthu *n*
  trace an outline pulthu-arrapinthi *v-intr*

trachea warra padniti *n*; warrawiilta *n*

track marka *n*; marka-markanthi *v-tr*; pulthu *n*; tainga *n*
  tracks tidna *n*

trade tita *n*; tanta *n*; wakuinya *n*; wakuinyapinthi *v-tr*
  trader titapina *n*

trading place tanta *n*
traditional healer warrarra (var. warra-warra) *n*; yamayama *n*
train (railway) tininya ngaruta *n*
tram tininya parti *n*
translate warra tarra-tharra-itpapinthi
trash mapa *n*
   trash can mapakuru *n*
travel padninthi *v-intr*; murinthi (var. muyinthi) *v-intr*; wininthi *v-intr* (Rapid Bay dialect)
   not good at travelling on foot yarku ngaitya *adj*
treacherously ngararaka *adv*
tread on kadlunthi *v-tr*
   tread to pieces kalya-kadlunthi *v-tr*
treat unkindly kapakapanthi *v-tr*
tree
   tree branch watu *n*
   tree stump papaltu *n*
   tree lying on the ground waadla *n*
   fallen tree waadlawarnka *n*
trees
   golden wattle mirnu *n (Acacia)*
   grass tree kuru *n (Xanthorrhoea)*
   gum tree (manna, white, ribbon) tarma *n (Eucalyptus viminalis)*
   native pine narnu *n (Callitris)*
   peppermint gum wita *n*
   red gum karra$_1$ *n*
   sheoak karku *n (Casuarina)*
   stringybark yulthi *n*
   swamp gum patha *n*
   white gum kuraka *n*; tamingka *n*
   yakka kuru *n (Xanthorrhoea)*
tremble wayirrinthi *v-intr*; wirrilayinthi *v-intr*
trick yurru *n*
troop pirku *n* (of people)
trot paka-pakanthi *v-intr*
troublesome warnutina *adj*
trousers kanthi-ana (var. kanthi-anurla) *n*; yarku-ana (var. yarku-anaurla) *n*
trout (fish) mipurli *n*
   brown trout purnkipurnki mipurli *n (Salmo trutta)*
true tiyati *intj, adv*
   truth tiyati warra *n*
   tell the truth tiyati wangkanthi *v-intr*

trust (win someone's) tangka mankunthi *v-tr*
try mailtyamailtyarrina; mailtyanthi *v-tr*
   try hard warpuwiltarrinthi *v-intr*
tube wiilta *n*
Tuesday Purlirntu *n*
tuft of eagle feathers (ceremony) wirltu-ngaru *n*
tuft of grass ngurrku *n*
tune ipila *n*
tupong warapina *n (Pseudaphritis urvilli)*
turkey (wild) waltha *n (Ardeotis australis)*
turn nurlinthi *v-tr*; mikarrinthi (var. mikamikarrinthi) *v-intr*; yukurninthi *v-intr*
   turn around pintyanthi$_1$ (var. pingkanthi; pingyanthi; pinkanthi) *v-tr*; pintyarninthi (var. pingkarninthi) *v-intr*; pintyarri-apinthi (var. pingyarri-apinthi) *v-tr*; pintyarrinthi$_1$ (var. pinkyarrinthi$_2$) *v-intr*; wayirrinthi *v-intr*
   turn back pintyarrinthi$_1$ (var. pinkyarrinthi$_2$) *v-intr*; warrarrinthi *v-intr*
   turn inside out pilta-pilunthi (var. pila-pilunthi) *v-intr*; yirtpinthi (var. yitpinthi) *v-tr*
   make something turn inside out yirtpirri-apinthi *v-tr*
   turn over pilta-pilunthi (var. pila-pilunthi) *v-intr*; pilunthi *v-tr*
   take turns tarraitpapinthi (var. tarra-arraitpapinthi; tarra-tharraitpapinthi) *v-tr*
   turn the head mukartantinthi *v-intr*
turtle (freshwater) marungayu *n*
twelve kumirrka purlaityi *num*
   twelve thousand kumirrka purlawata *num*
   twelve million kumirrka purliwurra *num*
twenty purlirrka *num*
twice purlarluku *adv*
twilight karrka$_1$ *n*
twinkle the eyes pitpayinthi *v-intr*
twins nantarla *n*
twist nurlinthi *v-tr*
twitter tititayinthi *v-intr*
two purlaityi *num*
   two hundred purlaityi partirrka *num*
   two thousand purlawata *num*
   two million purliwurra *num*
   two ply purla pilta-pilturru *adj*
   two times purlarluku *adv*

U u

ulcer irrkuta *n*
   develop an ulcer irrkutantinthi *v-intr*
umbrella kunturu katiti *n*
unable manti *adj, adv*
   be unable to manti-apinthi *v-intr*; mantimantirrinthi *v-intr*
   be unable to go out nganparrinthi *v-intr*
unaware (be) itirrantinthi *v-intr*
unborn pintiti *adj*
uncertain (be) yararrinthi *v-intr*
uncircumcised person mudnu *n*; pardurdu *n*
   uncircumcised boy marntu (var. marnu) *n*
uncle (maternal) kauwanu *n*
uncomfortable (be/feel) mukurrinthi *v-intr*
uncooked timana *adj*
uncooperative (be) turdi-thurdirninthi *v-intr*
uncovered turnki marraka *adj*
undecided (be) yararrinthi *v-intr*
under yakingka *loc*; wirangka *loc*
   underneath yakingka *loc*
   undergrowth karta$_3$ *n*
   undies/underpants kanthi-apa *n*
understand payanthi *v-tr*; yuri payanthi (var. yuri paya-paiyanthi) *v-tr*; tirkanthi *v-intr*; tampinthi *v-tr*; nakunthi *v-intr, v-tr*
   understand (what was said) warra nakunthi *v-intr*; warra payanthi *v-tr*
   understand a language warra payanthi *v-tr*
   not understand wakarrinthi *v-intr*
undulate mampinthi *v-intr*
   undulating malyu *adj* (landscape)
   undulating ground yarna-yarna *n*
uneasy (be) kuntu pungkurrinthi *v-intr*
unemployed warpulayitina *adj*
uneven marngu-marngu *adj*; malyu *adj* (landscape)
   become uneven malyurninthi *v-intr*
ungenerous tangkawilta *adj*
   become ungenerous tangka wiltarninthi *v-intr*
unhelpful taltaitpi *adj*
   be unhelpful taltanthi *v-intr*
unintended mardla (var. marla) *adv*
   unintentionally itirra *adv*; mardlaitirra (var. mardlatirra) *adv*
unite mankurri-apinthi *v-tr*; taikunthi *v-tr*
   be united taikurrinthi *v-intr*
unkind taltaitpi *adj*
   be unkind taltanthi *v-intr*
   be unkind to kapakapanthi *v-tr*
unmarried yangarru-tana *adj* (man); yarlinu-tana *adj* (woman)
   unmarried young man ngarilta *n*
   unmarried woman takana$_1$ *n*
unnoticed itirra *adv*
unpeeled pakapuru *adj*
unpleasant warpularra *adj*
unripe tintyu-thintyu *adj*; timana *adj*
unstable kidlala *adj*
untamed dingo warru-kadli *n*
untie pati-apinthi *v-tr*; patinthi (var. pati-patinthi) *v-tr*
untruth manta *n*
   untrue statement yukuna warra *n*
unwell warrangku *adj*
   be/become unwell warrangkurninthi *v-intr*
up karra$_2$ (var. karta$_2$) *loc*
   upright tutu *adj*; tutumpurri *adj*
   upper arm narntu *n*; warta-thurti *n*
   upper leg kanthi *n*
   upper lip taaminu *n*
urge marka wayinthi *v-tr* (someone to do something)
urine kumpu (var. kumpurra) *n*
   urinate kumputinthi *v-intr*
us
   us (two) ngadli (var. 'adli; 'dli) *pro* (dual nominative/accusative)
   us mob ngadlu (var. 'adlu; 'dlu) *pro* (plural nominative/accusative)
   for us two ngadlilitya *pro* (dual purposive)
   for us ngadlulitya *pro* (plural purposive)
   to us two ngadlilitya *pro* (dual allative)
   to us ngadlulitya *pro* (plural allative)
use marrku *n*; marrkunthi *v-tr*
   cause to be used marrkurri-apinthi *v-tr*
   using what? waardlu? (var. waarlu) *inter*
   use a 'kantapi' kantapinthi *v-tr*

V v

vagabond mukurripurka *n*
vagina minhi *n*
valley warltu (var. warti warltu) *n*; yaki *n*

go through a valley warlturninthi *v-intr*

vegetable mai *n*
   vegetable peeler pakamati *n*
   broccoli purakali *n*
   brussels sprout tinkyuyuri *n*
   cabbage pirira *n*
   carrot tidla *n*
   cauliflower partu-yuri *n*
   endive yarnti *n*
   potato parnguta *n*
   radish kantarda *n*
   yam parnguta *n*
   zucchini tukini *n*

vehicle padnipadniti *n*

vein tiltya *n*

venereal disease matpu *n*; wamanyu *n*; warnka$_2$ *n*
   get venereal disease warkarninthi *v-intr*

verb wapiwarra *n*
   verbally abuse tawanthi *v-tr*

vermin paitya *n*

very paityarri *adj* (comparative affix); witi *adv*
   very many wiwurra *n*

vessel (boat) yuku *n*

vessel (container) kuru *n*

vest tikiana *n*

vigilant tutu *adj*

vigorously nganta *adv*

vineyard kaaruyarta *n*

violence midla (var. mila$_1$) *n*
   become violent wingku-wingkurninthi *v-intr*
   violently wingku-wingkurru *adj, adv*

virgin kuntimarntu *n*
   female virgin takana$_1$ *n*

visible (become) yurlurrinthi *v-intr*
   make visible yurlunthi *v-tr*

visit yantu *n*
   visit (someone) yantu-apinthi *v-tr*
   frequent visitor yantupina *n*

voice warra *n*
   voice recorder warramankuti *n*

voluntarily irdi *adj*; kurdantana *adv*

vomit kapi *n*; kapinthi *v-intr*

vulnerable mananya *adj*

W w

waist kurtapiku *n*; tidli *n*; tiki *n*
   waistcoat tikiana *n*

wait pidnanthi *v-intr*; ngaranthi (var. ngara-ngaranthi) *v-intr*
   wait for katpirrinthi (var. katpi-katpirrinthi) *v-intr*; warra ingkarninthi *v-tr* (someone's words)
   wait! puru-iti (var. puru-piti) *intj*; purumpi *adv, intj*

wake up miipudnanthi *v-intr*; miitu parltanthi *v-intr*; miitu patinthi *v-intr*; nakarrantinthi *v-intr*

walk padninthi *v-intr*; murinthi (var. muyinthi) *v-intr*; wininthi *v-intr* (Rapid Bay dialect)
   walk quickly nganta padninthi *v-intr*
   walk slowly pidnarrinthi *v-intr*; warka-warkarrinthi *v-intr*
   walk unsteadily ngunirrinthi *v-intr*
   walk right up to someone tutuangkanthi *v-intr*

wallaby kurnta$_1$ *n*; wadlha *n*
   female wallaby kunadna *n*

want padlurninthi *v-tr*; kuntu warpurninthi *v-tr*; tangkarninthi (var. tangka-angkarninthi) *v-intr*; wingku tikanthi *v-intr*; witi-witinthi *v-tr*
   wanting -marnguta *suff (on nouns)*; -mpi *suff (on nouns)*; padlurnintyarla *adj*
   wanting food maimpi *adj*
   not want to waadli ngarntanthi (var. waadli-arntanthi) *v-intr*

ward off karnkanthi *v-tr*

warm warlta *adj*; miita *adj*; wardu *adj*
   warm (oneself) up kardla parrinthi *v-intr*; nguyurrinthi *v-intr*
   warm (something) kardlapanthi (var. karlapanthi) *v-tr*; kardlarlu parrinthi *v-tr*; nguyunthi (var. nguiyunthi) *v-tr*
   become warm miitarninthi *v-intr*
   warm (weather) warlta *adj* (weather)

warning wapituwayi *n*

warp nadla-nhadlarrinthi (var. nala-nhalarrinthi) *v-intr*; nadlarrinthi *v-tr*

warrior irrapina (var. pirrapina) *n*

wart karditpi *n*

wash (something) kudlinthi *v-tr*; kuntunthi *v-tr*; wirrkanthi *v-tr*
   wash (oneself) kudlirrinthi *v-intr*; kunturrinthi *v-intr*; wirrkarrinthi *v-intr*
   wash basin kudlikuru *n*
   washing machine kudliti *n*

washing liquid tadliwirrka *n*
washing powder tadlimurdu *n*
wasp pamaparti *n*
waste time turdi-thurdirninthi *v-intr*
watch tirntu *n*
   be on watch tutu tikanthi *v-intr*
water kauwi *n*
   spray of water kauwimiila *n*
   water beetle turluntyaru *n (Gyrinus)*
   watercourse pari *n*
   waterfall warkanta *n*
   waterfowl paripardu *n*
   waterhole pudna *n*
   water heater kauwi nguyuti *n*
wattle mirnu *n (Acacia)*; tililya *n (Acacia saligna)*
   wattle flower purrumpa *n*
   wattle gum mirnu *n*
   wattlebird katpamartu *n*
wave wingkura *n*; wampinthi *v-intr, v-tr*
   waves at the shore ilyala (var. kilyala) *n*
   waver mampinthi *v-intr*
   wavering kidlala *adj*
way (route) tapa *n*
we ngadlu (var. 'adlu; 'dlu) *pro (plural nominative/accusative)*
   we (two) ngadli (var. 'adli; 'dli) *pro (dual nominative/accusative)*
weak -ngaitya *suff (on nouns)*; ngaityana *adj*; narntu ngaitya *adj (person)*; wuingki *adj*; pilta-wuingki *adj*; mananya *adj*; parltarta (var. parltarti) *adj (object)*
   weakness kathi *n*
   be weak ngaityarninthi *v-intr*
   weaken (something) ngaityarni-apinthi *v-tr*
   weak-armed narntu ngaitya *adj (person)*; turti-murla *adj*
   weak-legged yarku ngaitya *adj*
   weak person ngaityarni-purka *n*; wiltya-iltyarri-purka *n*
   weak-legged, thin person warta-ityatina *n (insult)*
wear out parltarrinthi (var. parlta-parltarrinthi) *v-intr*
weary ngaityana *adj*
web waku ngari (var. waku-ari) *n*
   website wikapulthu *n*
wedged (be) tintanthi *v-intr*
   wedge-tailed eagle wirltu *n (Aquila audax)*

Wednesday Marnku-irntu *n*
week wangirntu (var. wanguirntu) *n*; wangu tirnturna *n*
   weekend milirntu warta *n*
weep kukarrinthi *v-intr*
weigh down kadlurrinthi *v-intr*
well (ably) nganta *adv*; numa *adv*; wayarnta (var. wayangarnta) *adv*; witi *adv*
   be well-stocked maimunthu tikanthi *v-intr*
well (healthy) purruna *adj*
well (waterhole) pudna *n*
west wangka *n*
   western carp gudgeon tukapina waitku *n (Hypseleotris klunzingeri)*
wet nungurru (var. nungnurru) *adj*; kauwirrka (var. kawirrka) *adj*
   be wet puikurrinthi *v-intr*
   get wet kauwirninthi *v-intr*; nungurru-antinthi (var. nungnurru-antinthi) *v-intr*
   wet (something) purninthi *v-tr*
whale kuntuli *n*
   whaleboat yuku *n*
   whale blubber paitpurla *n*
what? nga? *inter*; ngaintya? *inter*; ngana? *inter*
   what (is it)? wamina? *intj*
   what for? nganaitya? *inter*; nganapira? *inter*
   what kind? ngaintyatana? *inter*
   in what way? ngaintyarlu? *inter*
   what time? nganarlu? *inter*
   what's wrong? nganapurtu? *inter*; waapurti? *intj*
   what (of many)? watharna? (var. wathairna?) *inter*
wheel tuturtu *n*
when? nalati? (var. nadlati) *inter*; nganarlu? *inter*
where? waa? *inter*; waatha? (var. waatha-waatha) *inter*; waatha-intyarla *inter*
   where to? wanti? *inter*
   where from? waathangku? *inter*
   whereabouts? waamu? *inter*
which? ngana? *inter*
   which one? watharna? (var. wathairna) *inter*
   which ones? waa'rna? *inter*; waatha-intyarna *inter*
   which place? waatha? (var. waatha-waatha) *inter*
whine ngarrinthi (var. ngarri-ngarrinthi) *v-intr*
whirl wayirrinthi *v-intr*
   whirlwind yaru (var. yariru) *n*

whirlwind (dust) wirraitya *n*

whiskers marlta *n*

whisper wayangka *n*; wayangkapinthi *v-tr*; wayangkayinthi (var. wayangkinthi) *v-intr*

    whisperer wayangkapina *n*

whistle nguitkurrinthi (var. nguiku-ikurrinthi) *v-intr*; titayinthi *v-intr*; wilpilpayinthi *v-intr*; winpirra (var. winpirri) *n*

    whistling nguitkurra *n*; titita *n*; wilpilpa *n*

    whistle (like birds) tititayinthi *v-intr*

white parkana *adj*

    be white parkarninthi (var. parkanthi) *v-intr*

    turn white parkanarntinthi *v-intr*

    whiten parka-ityinthi (var. parka-ityayinthi) *v-tr*; parkanantiapinthi *v-tr*

    white-wash parka-ityinthi (var. parka-ityayinthi) *v-tr*

    white substance ngaru *n*

    white person pinti miyu *n*; kuinyu *n*

    white of the eye miiparkana *n (sclera)*

    white of an egg ngayirda *n*

    white ant kadngi *n*

    whiteboard markaparkana *n*

    white cockatoo kurdaki *n*

    white gum kuraka *n*; tamingka *n*; tarma *n* (*Eucalyptus viminalis*)

    white ochre ngaru *n*

    white radish walyu *n*

who? nga? *inter*; ngantu? *inter* (ergative singular); watharna? (var. wathairna) *inter*

    whose? ngangku? *inter*

whole purru *n*; purruna *adj*; wartapurru (var. wartapurruna) *n*; yalura *adj*

    whole amount purrutyi *adj, n*

why? nganaitya? *inter*; nganapira? *inter*; nganapurtu-itya? *inter*

wicked wakinha *adj*

wide takana₂ *adj*; yarnta₁ *adj*; yarru *adj*

widow tuinya *n*

    widower yampina *n*

wife kartu *n*; yangarra *n*

    become a wife yangarrantinthi *v-intr*

    make someone your wife yangarranti-apinthi *v-tr*

    husband and wife partatangkurla *n*; yangarrataurla *n*

    two wives (same husband) yangarrataurla *n*

wild warru *adj*; tulya (angry)

    wild dog warru-kadli *n*

    wild turkey waltha *n* (*Ardeotis australis*)

will (figurative) yitpi *n*

win marka wayinthi *v-intr*

    winner marka wayipina *n*

wind (that blows) warri *n*; maikurru *n*; kurruti *n*

    cold wind waitpi *n*

    dry wind pulturru *n*

    north-westerly wind pukarra *n*

    windpipe warra padniti *n*; warrawiilta *n*

wind (twist) yukurninthi *v-intr*

window makithau *n*

wine kaaru *n*

wing tarlti *n*; turti *n*

    wing of a large bird wampi (var. wampiti) *n*

    get wings tarltirninthi *v-intr*

winter kudlila *n*

    solstice kurltirntu *n* (winter)

wipe wirrkanthi *v-tr*

    wipe away muyinthi *v-tr*

wise person tirkalirkala *n*

wish wingku parlta-parltarrinthi *v-intr*

    wish for kuntu warpurninthi *v-tr*

witch (old) paityapuulti *n*

with -rlu (var. -dlu; -urlu) *suff (on nouns)* (instrumental); taikurra *loc*; taikurri *adv*

    with what? waardlu? (var. waarlu) *inter*

    with whom? nganalalityangka? *inter*

    with (someone) -ityangka (var. -lityangka) *suff (on nouns)* (comitative)

    with me ngathaityangka *pro* (comitative)

    with you nintaityangka *pro* (singular comitative)

    with him/her/it padlaityangka *pro*; padluntya *pro*

    with my mum ngaityaita *n*

withdraw nguimpayinthi *v-intr*; nurnti kurtarrinthi

wither away wityarninthi *v-intr*

    withered arm turti-murla *n*

withhold ngaranthi (var. ngara-ngaranthi) *v-intr*

without -tina (var. -tana₁) *suff (on nouns)* (privative); -pulyu *suff (on nouns)*; -tidla (var. -idla) *suff (on nouns)*; marraka *adj*

    without me ngaityurtila *adv*

    without food mai-idla (var. maitidla)

witty (be) mukarta partarninthi *v-intr*
wobble ngunirrinthi *v-intr*
wok kunthikuru *n*
woman ngangki *n*; ngamaitya (var. ngama-ngamaitya) *n*
    become a woman ngama-ngamaityarntinthi *v-intr*
    old woman paityapuulti *n*; pintiwaadli *n*
    become an old woman pintiwaadlirninthi *v-intr*
    woman not yet having children kuntimarntu *n*
    woman with many children kangkarri-purka *n*
    woman in funeral ceremony tutha-kuinyu *n*
    Women's Day Ngangkirntu *n*
wombat wartu *n*
wood tarralyi *n*
    piece of wood ngarra *n*
    woodchip tarralyi *n*
    wooden dagger warpu (var. wartpu) *n*
    put wood on the fire pawunthi *v-tr*
woomera midla (var. mila$_1$) *n*; tarralyi *n*
word warra *n*
work warpulayi *n*; warpulayinthi *v-intr*
    workbench warpulayi tarralyi *n*
worm wuumi *n*
worn out purtuna *adj*
    be worn out ngaityarninthi *v-intr*
    become worn out looking purtunantinthi (var. purtunarntinthi) *v-intr*
worry (about someone) kuntu pungkurrinthi *v-intr*; ngudli wayirrinthi (var. ngudli wayarrinthi) *v-intr*
    be worried kuntu yartarrinthi *v-intr*
    worry incessantly pungkurrinthi *v-intr*
wound (injury) mingka$_2$ *n*; kuku *n*
    wounded mingkamingka *adj*
wow! paitya! *intj*; paya! *intj*
wrap in wadlu pumanthi *v-tr*
wrath turla-parrku *n*; turlawingku *n*
    wrathful turlapurtu *adj*
wrestle purnpunthi *v-tr*
    wrestle with purnpurrinthi *v-tr*
wring out parntanthi *v-tr*
wrinkle nipa (var. niparra) *n*
    wrinkly nipa-nhipa *adj*
    wrinkled mintuna *adj*
wrist ngantamanu *n*
write pintyanthi (var. pingkanthi; pingyanthi; pinkanthi) *v-tr*
wrong waadli *adj*; wakinha *adj*
    wrong marriage nyurrkarda *n*

Y y

yabby kungkurla *n*; ngaltaitya *n* (*Cheerax destructor*)
yakka kuru *n* (*Xanthorrhoea*)
    yakka sap yutuki *n*
    yakka stem kayamunthu *n*
yam parnguta *n*
yawn taa tarrkinthi *v-intr*
year warltati *n*
yellow wiranirana *adj*
    make yellow wiranthi *v-tr*
    yellowish-brownish wiranirana *adj*
    make yellowish-brownish wiranthi *v-tr*
    yellowish-red taltharni *adj*
    yellowish-red object taltharni *n*
    yellow ochre wiranirana *n*
    yellow-tailed black cockatoo tiwu *n*; wilampa *n*
yes nii *intj*; tiyati *intj*, *adv*
yesterday pukilyarlu *temp*; yalaka (var. yaltaka) *temp*; yalatya *temp*
yet pirdi (var. pirdina) *adv*; puru *adv*
    not yet kutpuru *adv*; purupuru *adv*
    not yet! puru-iti! (var. puru-piti) *intj*; purumpi! *intj*
yolk (egg) mininta *n*
you niina (var. 'ina) *pro* (singular nominative/accusative); nintu (var. 'ntu) *pro* (singular ergative)
    you two niwa *pro* (dual nominative/accusative)
    you mob naa (var. -nhaa) *pro* (plural nominative/accusative)
    your(s) ninku *pro* (singular, possessive); niwadluku *pro* (dual possessive); naaku *pro* (plural possessive)
    for you nintaitya *pro* (singular purposive)
    for you two niwadlitya *pro* (dual purposive)
    to you all naalitya *pro* (plural allative)
    with you nintaityangka *pro* (singular comitative)
    with you two niwadlityangka *pro* (dual comitative)
    with you all naalityangka *pro* (plural comitative)
    to you nintaitya *pro* (singular allative)
    to you two niwadlitya *pro* (dual allative)
young

young woman (unmarried) mankarra *n*
young woman (before childbearing)
  puyumara *n*
young man kurrkurra *n*; tinyarra *n*
young man (initiation stage) wilyaru *n*
younger sibling (brother or sister) panya *n*;
  panyapi *n*
youngest (in the family) kurlakurlana (var.
  kurlakurlanta) *n*
youngest generation kurlana *n*

young emu kuri-kuri *n*
young possum puinyu *n*
young (unripe) tintyu-thintyu *adj*
  become young tintyurninthi *v-intr*
youth (male) tinyarra *n*; kurrkurra *n*; paapa *n*

Z z

zero mardla (var. marla) *n*
zucchini tukini *n*

Other Kaurna Learning Resources

A Kaurna Learner's Guide

A Kaurna Learner's Guide is available from Wakefield Press
www.wakefieldpress.com.au

Other Kaurna Learning Resources

Resources available from KWK/KWP: www.kaurnawarra.org.au

Your notes ...

Your notes ...

Wakefield Press is an independent publishing and
distribution company based in Adelaide, South Australia.
We love good stories and publish beautiful books.
To see our full range of books, please visit our website at
www.wakefieldpress.com.au
where all titles are available for purchase.
To keep up with our latest releases, news and events,
subscribe to our monthly newsletter.

Find us!

Facebook: www.facebook.com/wakefield.press
Twitter: www.twitter.com/wakefieldpress
Instagram: www.instagram.com/wakefieldpress

www.ingramcontent.com/pod-product-compliance
Lightning Source LLC
Chambersburg PA
CBHW061748290426
44108CB00028B/2926